SUNDAY MISSAL

2017-2018

Compliments of Deacon Tony

Living with Christ
1 Montauk Avenue, Suite 200
New London, CT 06320
1-800-321-0411
www.livingwithchrist.us

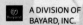 A DIVISION OF
BAYARD, INC.

Design and Layout: Jessica Llewellyn

Illustrations and photo credits: page 8, Michael Connors

ISBN 978-1-62785-282-1

Printed in Canada

To order more copies:
Tel: 1-800-321-0411
Website: www.livingwithchrist.us

CONTENTS

How to Use This Missal

YOUR COMPANION FOR PRAYING AND LIVING THE EUCHARIST

Over the years, the use of personal missals has changed. Before Vatican Council II (1962-65), when the Mass was said in Latin, most people needed a missal during the Mass to understand the priest's words.

Vatican II made important changes in the Mass because it recognized that the celebration of Mass was lacking several important things. First, it needed to be in language the people could understand. Second, the people were to be truly involved as "full, conscious, and active" participants in the many prayers, songs, and ritual actions of the celebration.

The Mass is not to be something that just the priest does, but something that the whole community or assembly does together—singing, listening to God's word, praying for the needs of the Church and world, thanking God, sharing the consecrated bread and wine, and finally being sent back to their homes, schools, and workplaces to live what they celebrated: God present with us to change our lives and gather us into God's own community of justice, love, and peace.

As a result, after Vatican II many parishes encouraged more participation and discouraged using missals during Mass, except perhaps by those who could not hear the readings. The focus was on listening when the Scriptures were proclaimed aloud—a reminder that God was present and speaking to us in that word.

USING THE MISSAL TO PREPARE FOR SUNDAY

So, if we are not encouraged to use our missal at Mass, is there still a use for a Sunday missal? The answer is yes. But we should now use our missal at home to help us prepare to celebrate the Sunday Eucharist more fully.

The Mass celebrates God's presence with us in word and sacrament. Through Scripture we learn how God has been present with us and what we must do to live rightly in relation to God and others. But making Scripture's message our own is not always easy. In order to get more out of our Sunday listening, we should preview the readings at home during the week.

This Sunday Missal offers resources for you, your family, and your friends to prepare for a richer celebration each Sunday. Different from other Sunday missals, this missal includes not only all the prayers and Scripture readings for the Sunday Masses, but also a variety of other helps to use at home so you can participate at Mass more "fully, consciously, actively, and as befits a community," as Vatican II desired.

WEEKLY RESOURCES FOR PREPARING FOR SUNDAY

This Sunday Missal helps you to pray and live the Eucharist by preparing each week for a richer celebration of Mass. For each Sunday throughout the year, you will find:

- **A brief reflection** inspired by the readings to consider how God's message might resonate with everyday life
- **The complete text of all of the Mass prayers and Scripture readings** chosen by the Church. Also included are these other major feast days: Mary's Immaculate Conception (December 8), Ash Wednesday (February 14), the sacred three days of Holy Week, i.e., the Triduum—Holy Thursday, Good Friday, and Holy Saturday (March 29-31)—Mary's Assumption into Heaven (August 15), and All Saints (November 1)
- At the end of each Sunday, there are helps for deepening your appreciation of both the Scripture readings and the Mass prayers from the Roman Missal:

- **Responding to the word**: questions that help you pray about and discuss the meaning and application of the Scripture readings
- **Taking a closer look**: information and reflections on biblical words and themes from the Scripture texts (indicated in bold and followed by a ✝ in the text)

GENERAL HELPS FOR PRAYING AND LIVING THE EUCHARIST

In addition to the weekly helps, this missal contains several features that you will find helpful for deepening both your understanding of the Church's liturgical year and your prayer, including:

- **Seasonal backgrounds** at the start of each liturgical season, together with suggestions for praying and living each liturgical season (e.g., pages 65-66)
- **Basic questions for exploring Scripture** (see page 578) that you can use to discover the meaning and application to your life of any Scripture reading
- **Explanations of the Church's liturgical year,** including the Church's liturgical calendar (see page 581) and the lectionary (see page 583)
- **A brief overview of Mark's gospel** (see page 585), the primary gospel proclaimed on Sundays this year
- **The differences between liturgical and devotional prayer** (see page 589), both of which help us grow in our life as disciples
- **A treasury of prayers** (see page 592) taken from Scripture, the saints, and the Christian tradition; and also a simple ritual for receiving Communion outside of Mass
- **A pronunciation guide for biblical words** (see page 616) for words indicated by an asterisk (*) in the Scripture readings

Our Eucharistic

Liturgy *The Order of Mass*

WE ARE A EUCHARISTIC PEOPLE

The celebration of the Eucharist or Mass is the central action that defines us as Catholics and directs our efforts to realize God's kingdom community today.

Our celebration is a ritual action that is repeated over and over so that by participating in it we can bring to consciousness, through word and sacrament, the deepest meaning of our lives.

Our celebration is *eucharist*, Greek for "thanksgiving," to remind us that our basic human relationship to God is a response to God's gifts. Everything that we have is God's gift. In our ritual, we celebrate the gift of God's own presence in the assembly that gathers, in God's word that we hear, in the consecrated bread and wine that are Christ's body and blood, and in the person of the priest who presides during the celebration.

Our celebration is also Mass, from the final Latin words of sending, *Ite missa est*, meaning "Go, you are sent." As we finish our prayer, we are reminded that we are sent to discover and proclaim God's presence in all the situations of our daily lives.

As Christians, we not only *pray* the Eucharist, but we are also called upon to *live* "eucharistic" lives. Just as Jesus took the bread, his body, and blessed and broke it to share with others, so we ask God to *take* us, *bless* us, *break* us, and *share* us with others so that "through him, and with him, and in him" we may also become sources of God's new life for the world.

INTRODUCTORY RITES

ENTRANCE ANTIPHON (Turn to the appropriate day)

GREETING

In the name of the Father, and of the Son,
  and of the Holy Spirit. *Amen.*

❶ The grace of our Lord Jesus Christ,
  and the love of God,
  and the communion of the Holy Spirit
  be with you all.
  And with your spirit.

❷ Grace to you and peace from God our Father
  and the Lord Jesus Christ.
  And with your spirit.

❸ The Lord be with you.
  And with your spirit.

PENITENTIAL ACT

Brethren (brothers and sisters), let us acknowledge our sins,
and so prepare ourselves to celebrate the sacred mysteries.

After a brief pause for silence, one of the following forms is used:

❶ *I confess to almighty God*
  and to you, my brothers and sisters,
  that I have greatly sinned,
  in my thoughts and in my words,
  in what I have done and in what I have failed to do,
    (And, striking their breast, they say:)

through my fault, through my fault,
through my most grievous fault;
therefore I ask blessed Mary ever-Virgin,
all the Angels and Saints,
and you, my brothers and sisters,
to pray for me to the Lord our God.

May almighty God have mercy on us,
forgive us our sins,
and bring us to everlasting life.
Amen.

2 Have mercy on us, O Lord.
For we have sinned against you.

Show us, O Lord, your mercy.
And grant us your salvation.

May almighty God have mercy on us,
forgive us our sins,
and bring us to everlasting life.
Amen.

3 The celebrant makes the following or other invocations:

You were sent to heal the contrite of heart:
Lord, have mercy. Or Kyrie, eleison.
Lord, have mercy. Or *Kyrie, eleison.*

You came to call sinners:
Christ, have mercy. Or Christe, eleison.
Christ, have mercy. Or *Christe, eleison.*

You are seated at the right hand of the Father
    to intercede for us:

Lord, have mercy. Or Kyrie, eleison.
Lord, have mercy. Or *Kyrie, eleison.*

May almighty God have mercy on us,
forgive us our sins,
and bring us to everlasting life.
Amen.

The following invocations in either English or the ancient Greek
are said, unless they have just occurred in a formula of the
Penitential Act:

Lord, have mercy.   Or   Kyrie, eleison.
  Lord, have mercy.   *Kyrie, eleison.*
Chriŝt, have mercy.   Christe, eleison.
  Christ, have mercy.   *Christe, eleison.*
Lord, have mercy.   Kyrie, eleison.
  Lord, have mercy.   *Kyrie, eleison.*

GLORY TO GOD
Glory to God in the highest,
and on earth peace to people of good will.

We praise you,
we bless you,
we adore you,
we glorify you,
we give you thanks for your great glory,
Lord God, heavenly King,
O God, almighty Father.

Lord Jesus Christ, Only Begotten Son,
Lord God, Lamb of God, Son of the Father,
you take away the sins of the world,
    have mercy on us;
you take away the sins of the world,
    receive our prayer;
you are seated at the right hand of the Father:
    have mercy on us.

For you alone are the Holy One,
you alone are the Lord,
you alone are the Most High,
Jesus Christ,
with the Holy Spirit,
in the glory of God the Father. Amen.

COLLECT (Turn to the appropriate day)

LITURGY OF THE WORD

READINGS (Turn to the appropriate day)

PROFESSION OF FAITH: NICENE CREED
I believe in one God,
the Father almighty,
maker of heaven and earth,
of all things visible and invisible.
I believe in one Lord Jesus Christ,
the Only Begotten Son of God,

born of the Father before all ages.
God from God, Light from Light,
true God from true God,
begotten, not made, consubstantial with the Father;
through him all things were made.
For us men and for our salvation
he came down from heaven,
> (At the words that follow, up to and including
> and became man, all bow.)

and by the Holy Spirit was incarnate of the Virgin Mary,
and became man.

For our sake he was crucified under Pontius Pilate,
he suffered death and was buried,
and rose again on the third day
in accordance with the Scriptures.
He ascended into heaven
and is seated at the right hand of the Father.
He will come again in glory
to judge the living and the dead
and his kingdom will have no end.

I believe in the Holy Spirit, the Lord, the giver of life,
who proceeds from the Father and the Son,
who with the Father and the Son is adored and glorified,
who has spoken through the prophets.

I believe in one, holy, catholic and apostolic Church.
I confess one Baptism for the forgiveness of sins
and I look forward to the resurrection of the dead
and the life of the world to come. Amen.

OR

APOSTLES' CREED

The baptismal Symbol of the Roman Church, known as the
Apostles' Creed, may be used instead of the Nicene Creed,
especially during Lent and Easter Time:

I believe in God,
the Father almighty,
Creator of heaven and earth,
and in Jesus Christ, his only Son, our Lord,
> (At the words that follow, up to and including
> the Virgin Mary, all bow.)
who was conceived by the Holy Spirit,
born of the Virgin Mary,
suffered under Pontius Pilate,
was crucified, died and was buried;
he descended into hell;
on the third day he rose again from the dead;
he ascended into heaven,
and is seated at the right hand of God the Father almighty;
from there he will come to judge the living and the dead.

I believe in the Holy Spirit,
the holy catholic Church,
the communion of saints,
the forgiveness of sins,
the resurrection of the body,
and life everlasting. Amen.

PRAYER OF THE FAITHFUL

Liturgy of the Eucharist

PREPARATION OF GIFTS

Blessed are you, Lord God of all creation,
for through your goodness we have received
the bread we offer you:
fruit of the earth and work of human hands,
it will become for us the bread of life.
Blessed be God for ever.

By the mystery of this water and wine
may we come to share in the divinity of Christ
who humbled himself to share in our humanity.

Blessed are you, Lord God of all creation,
for through your goodness we have received
the wine we offer you:
fruit of the vine and work of human hands,
it will become our spiritual drink.
Blessed be God for ever.

With humble spirit and contrite heart
may we be accepted by you, O Lord,
and may our sacrifice in your sight this day
be pleasing to you, Lord God.

Wash me, O Lord, from my iniquity
and cleanse me from my sin.

Pray, brethren (brothers and sisters),
that my sacrifice and yours
may be acceptable to God,
the almighty Father.

May the Lord accept the sacrifice at your hands
for the praise and glory of his name,
for our good
and the good of all his holy Church.

PRAYER OVER THE OFFERINGS (Turn to the appropriate day)

EUCHARISTIC PRAYER
The Lord be with you.
And with your spirit.
Lift up your hearts.
We lift them up to the Lord.
Let us give thanks to the Lord our God.
It is right and just.

PREFACE
The celebrant chooses from among the possible prefaces corresponding to liturgical seasons and feasts. These prefaces are for use with Eucharistic Prayers 1-3. Eucharistic Prayer 4 has its own fixed preface.

PREFACE 1 OF ADVENT
It is truly right and just, our duty and our salvation,
always and everywhere to give you thanks,
Lord, holy Father, almighty and eternal God,
through Christ our Lord.

For he assumed at his first coming
the lowliness of human flesh,
and so fulfilled the design you formed long ago,
and opened for us the way to eternal salvation,
that, when he comes again in glory and majesty
and all is at last made manifest,
we who watch for that day

may inherit the great promise
in which now we dare to hope.

And so, with Angels and Archangels,
with Thrones and Dominions,
and with all the hosts and Powers of heaven,
we sing the hymn of your glory,
as without end we acclaim:
Holy, Holy, Holy Lord God of hosts... *(page 35)*

PREFACE 2 OF ADVENT

It is truly right and just, our duty and our salvation,
always and everywhere to give you thanks,
Lord, holy Father, almighty and eternal God,
through Christ our Lord.

For all the oracles of the prophets foretold him,
the Virgin Mother longed for him
with love beyond all telling,
John the Baptist sang of his coming
and proclaimed his presence when he came.

It is by his gift that already we rejoice
at the mystery of his Nativity,
so that he may find us watchful in prayer
and exultant in his praise.

And so, with Angels and Archangels,
with Thrones and Dominions,
and with all the hosts and Powers of heaven,
we sing the hymn of your glory,
as without end we acclaim:
Holy, Holy, Holy Lord God of hosts... *(page 35)*

PREFACE 1 OF THE NATIVITY OF THE LORD

It is truly right and just, our duty and our salvation,
always and everywhere to give you thanks,
Lord, holy Father, almighty and eternal God.

For in the mystery of the Word made flesh
a new light of your glory has shone upon the eyes of our mind,
so that, as we recognize in him God made visible,
we may be caught up through him in love of things invisible.

And so, with Angels and Archangels,
with Thrones and Dominions,
and with all the hosts and Powers of heaven,
we sing the hymn of your glory,
as without end we acclaim:
Holy, Holy, Holy Lord God of hosts... *(page 35)*

PREFACE 2 OF THE NATIVITY OF THE LORD

It is truly right and just, our duty and our salvation,
always and everywhere to give you thanks,
Lord, holy Father, almighty and eternal God,
through Christ our Lord.

For on the feast of this awe-filled mystery,
though invisible in his own divine nature,
he has appeared visibly in ours;
and begotten before all ages,
he has begun to exist in time;
so that, raising up in himself all that was cast down,
he might restore unity to all creation
and call straying humanity back to the heavenly Kingdom.

And so, with all the Angels, we praise you,
as in joyful celebration we acclaim:
Holy, Holy, Holy Lord God of hosts... (page 35)

PREFACE 3 OF THE NATIVITY OF THE LORD
It is truly right and just, our duty and our salvation,
always and everywhere to give you thanks,
Lord, holy Father, almighty and eternal God,
through Christ our Lord.

For through him the holy exchange that restores our life
has shone forth today in splendor:
when our frailty is assumed by your Word
not only does human mortality receive unending honor
but by this wondrous union we, too, are made eternal.

And so, in company with the choirs of Angels,
we praise you, and with joy we proclaim:
Holy, Holy, Holy Lord God of hosts... (page 35)

PREFACE OF THE EPIPHANY OF THE LORD
It is truly right and just, our duty and our salvation,
always and everywhere to give you thanks,
Lord, holy Father, almighty and eternal God.

For today you have revealed the mystery
of our salvation in Christ
as a light for the nations,
and, when he appeared in our mortal nature,
you made us new by the glory of his immortal nature.

And so, with Angels and Archangels,
with Thrones and Dominions,

and with all the hosts and Powers of heaven,
we sing the hymn of your glory,
as without end we acclaim:
Holy, Holy, Holy Lord God of hosts... *(page 35)*

PREFACE 1 OF LENT

It is truly right and just, our duty and our salvation,
always and everywhere to give you thanks,
Lord, holy Father, almighty and eternal God,
through Christ our Lord.

For by your gracious gift each year
your faithful await the sacred paschal feasts
with the joy of minds made pure,
so that, more eagerly intent on prayer
and on the works of charity,
and participating in the mysteries
by which they have been reborn,
they may be led to the fullness of grace
that you bestow on your sons and daughters.

And so, with Angels and Archangels,
with Thrones and Dominions,
and with all the hosts and Powers of heaven,
we sing the hymn of your glory,
as without end we acclaim:
Holy, Holy, Holy Lord God of hosts... *(page 35)*

PREFACE 2 OF LENT

It is truly right and just, our duty and our salvation,
always and everywhere to give you thanks,
Lord, holy Father, almighty and eternal God.

For you have given your children a sacred time
for the renewing and purifying of their hearts,
that, freed from disordered affections,
they may so deal with the things of this passing world
as to hold rather to the things that eternally endure.

And so, with all the Angels and Saints,
we praise you, as without end we acclaim:
Holy, Holy, Holy Lord God of hosts... (page 35)

PREFACE 3 OF LENT

It is truly right and just, our duty and our salvation,
always and everywhere to give you thanks,
Lord, holy Father, almighty and eternal God.

For you will that our self-denial should give you thanks,
humble our sinful pride,
contribute to the feeding of the poor,
and so help us imitate you in your kindness.

And so we glorify you with countless Angels,
as with one voice of praise we acclaim:
Holy, Holy, Holy Lord God of hosts... (page 35)

PREFACE 4 OF LENT

It is truly right and just, our duty and our salvation,
always and everywhere to give you thanks,
Lord, holy Father, almighty and eternal God.

For through bodily fasting you restrain our faults,
raise up our minds,
and bestow both virtue and its rewards,
through Christ our Lord.

Through him the Angels praise your majesty,
Dominions adore and Powers tremble before you.
Heaven and the Virtues of heaven and the blessed Seraphim
worship together with exultation.
May our voices, we pray, join with theirs
in humble praise, as we acclaim:
Holy, Holy, Holy Lord God of hosts... (page 35)

PREFACE 1 OF THE PASSION OF THE LORD
It is truly right and just, our duty and our salvation,
always and everywhere to give you thanks,
Lord, holy Father, almighty and eternal God.

For through the saving Passion of your Son
the whole world has received a heart
to confess the infinite power of your majesty,
since by the wondrous power of the Cross
your judgment on the world is now revealed
and the authority of Christ crucified.

And so, Lord, with all the Angels and Saints,
we, too, give you thanks, as in exultation we acclaim:
Holy, Holy, Holy Lord God of hosts... (page 35)

PREFACE 2 OF THE PASSION OF THE LORD
It is truly right and just, our duty and our salvation,
always and everywhere to give you thanks,
Lord, holy Father, almighty and eternal God,
through Christ our Lord.

For the days of his saving Passion
and glorious Resurrection are approaching,

by which the pride of the ancient foe is vanquished
and the mystery of our redemption in Christ is celebrated.

Through him the host of Angels adores your majesty
and rejoices in your presence for ever.
May our voices, we pray, join with theirs
in one chorus of exultant praise, as we acclaim:
Holy, Holy, Holy Lord God of hosts... *(page 35)*

PREFACE 1 OF EASTER
It is truly right and just, our duty and our salvation,
at all times to acclaim you, O Lord,
but (on this night / on this day / in this time) above all
to laud you yet more gloriously,
when Christ our Passover has been sacrificed.

For he is the true Lamb
who has taken away the sins of the world;
by dying he has destroyed our death,
and by rising, restored our life.

Therefore, overcome with paschal joy,
every land, every people exults in your praise
and even the heavenly Powers, with the angelic hosts,
sing together the unending hymn of your glory,
as they acclaim: ***Holy, Holy, Holy Lord God of hosts...*** *(page 35)*

PREFACE 2 OF EASTER
It is truly right and just, our duty and our salvation,
at all times to acclaim you, O Lord,
but in this time above all to laud you yet more gloriously,
when Christ our Passover has been sacrificed.

Through him the children of light rise to eternal life
and the halls of the heavenly Kingdom
are thrown open to the faithful;
for his Death is our ransom from death,
and in his rising the life of all has risen.

Therefore, overcome with paschal joy,
every land, every people exults in your praise
and even the heavenly Powers, with the angelic hosts,
sing together the unending hymn of your glory,
as they acclaim: ***Holy, Holy, Holy Lord God of hosts...*** *(page 35)*

PREFACE 3 OF EASTER

It is truly right and just, our duty and our salvation,
at all times to acclaim you, O Lord,
but in this time above all to laud you yet more gloriously,
when Christ our Passover has been sacrificed.

He never ceases to offer himself for us
but defends us and ever pleads our cause before you:
he is the sacrificial Victim who dies no more,
the Lamb, once slain, who lives for ever.

Therefore, overcome with paschal joy,
every land, every people exults in your praise
and even the heavenly Powers, with the angelic hosts,
sing together the unending hymn of your glory,
as they acclaim: ***Holy, Holy, Holy Lord God of hosts...*** *(page 35)*

PREFACE 4 OF EASTER

It is truly right and just, our duty and our salvation,
at all times to acclaim you, O Lord,

but in this time above all to laud you yet more gloriously,
when Christ our Passover has been sacrificed.

For, with the old order destroyed,
a universe cast down is renewed,
and integrity of life is restored to us in Christ.

Therefore, overcome with paschal joy,
every land, every people exults in your praise
and even the heavenly Powers, with the angelic hosts,
sing together the unending hymn of your glory,
as they acclaim: ***Holy, Holy, Holy Lord God of hosts...*** *(page 35)*

PREFACE 5 OF EASTER

It is truly right and just, our duty and our salvation,
at all times to acclaim you, O Lord,
but in this time above all to laud you yet more gloriously,
when Christ our Passover has been sacrificed.

By the oblation of his Body,
he brought the sacrifices of old to fulfillment
in the reality of the Cross
and, by commending himself to you for our salvation,
showed himself the Priest, the Altar, and the Lamb of sacrifice.

Therefore, overcome with paschal joy,
every land, every people exults in your praise
and even the heavenly Powers, with the angelic hosts,
sing together the unending hymn of your glory,
as they acclaim: ***Holy, Holy, Holy Lord God of hosts...*** *(page 35)*

PREFACE 1 OF THE ASCENSION OF THE LORD

It is truly right and just, our duty and our salvation,
always and everywhere to give you thanks,
Lord, holy Father, almighty and eternal God.

For the Lord Jesus, the King of glory,
conqueror of sin and death,
ascended (today) to the highest heavens,
as the Angels gazed in wonder.

Mediator between God and man,
judge of the world and Lord of hosts,
he ascended, not to distance himself from our lowly state
but that we, his members, might be confident of following
where he, our Head and Founder, has gone before.

Therefore, overcome with paschal joy,
every land, every people exults in your praise
and even the heavenly Powers, with the angelic hosts,
sing together the unending hymn of your glory,
as they acclaim: *Holy, Holy, Holy Lord God of hosts...* (page 35)

PREFACE 2 OF THE ASCENSION OF THE LORD

It is truly right and just, our duty and our salvation,
always and everywhere to give you thanks,
Lord, holy Father, almighty and eternal God,
through Christ our Lord.

For after his Resurrection
he plainly appeared to all his disciples
and was taken up to heaven in their sight,
that he might make us sharers in his divinity.

Therefore, overcome with paschal joy,
every land, every people exults in your praise
and even the heavenly Powers, with the angelic hosts,
sing together the unending hymn of your glory,
as they acclaim: *Holy, Holy, Holy Lord God of hosts...* *(page 35)*

PREFACE 1 OF THE SUNDAYS IN ORDINARY TIME

It is truly right and just, our duty and our salvation,
always and everywhere to give you thanks,
Lord, holy Father, almighty and eternal God,
through Christ our Lord.

For through his Paschal Mystery,
he accomplished the marvelous deed,
by which he has freed us from the yoke of sin and death,
summoning us to the glory of being now called
a chosen race, a royal priesthood,
a holy nation, a people for your own possession,
to proclaim everywhere your mighty works,
for you have called us out of darkness
into your own wonderful light.

And so, with Angels and Archangels,
with Thrones and Dominions,
and with all the hosts and Powers of heaven,
we sing the hymn of your glory,
as without end we acclaim:
Holy, Holy, Holy Lord God of hosts... *(page 35)*

PREFACE 2 OF THE SUNDAYS IN ORDINARY TIME

It is truly right and just, our duty and our salvation,
always and everywhere to give you thanks,

Lord, holy Father, almighty and eternal God,
through Christ our Lord.

For out of compassion for the waywardness that is ours,
he humbled himself and was born of the Virgin;
by the passion of the Cross he freed us from unending death,
and by rising from the dead he gave us life eternal.

And so, with Angels and Archangels,
with Thrones and Dominions,
and with all the hosts and Powers of heaven,
we sing the hymn of your glory,
as without end we acclaim:
Holy, Holy, Holy Lord God of hosts... (page 35)

PREFACE 3 OF THE SUNDAYS IN ORDINARY TIME

It is truly right and just, our duty and our salvation,
always and everywhere to give you thanks,
Lord, holy Father, almighty and eternal God.

For we know it belongs to your boundless glory,
that you came to the aid of mortal beings with your divinity
and even fashioned for us a remedy out of mortality itself,
that the cause of our downfall
might become the means of our salvation,
through Christ our Lord.

Through him the host of Angels adores your majesty
and rejoices in your presence for ever.
May our voices, we pray, join with theirs
in one chorus of exultant praise, as we acclaim:
Holy, Holy, Holy Lord God of hosts... (page 35)

PREFACE 4 OF THE SUNDAYS IN ORDINARY TIME
It is truly right and just, our duty and our salvation,
always and everywhere to give you thanks,
Lord, holy Father, almighty and eternal God,
through Christ our Lord.

For by his birth he brought renewal
to humanity's fallen state,
and by his suffering, canceled out our sins;
by his rising from the dead
he has opened the way to eternal life,
and by ascending to you, O Father,
he has unlocked the gates of heaven.

And so, with the company of Angels and Saints,
we sing the hymn of your praise,
as without end we acclaim:
Holy, Holy, Holy Lord God of hosts...   *(page 35)*

PREFACE 5 OF THE SUNDAYS IN ORDINARY TIME
It is truly right and just, our duty and our salvation,
always and everywhere to give you thanks,
Lord, holy Father, almighty and eternal God.

For you laid the foundations of the world
and have arranged the changing of times and seasons;
you formed man in your own image
and set humanity over the whole world in all its wonder,
to rule in your name over all you have made
and for ever praise you in your mighty works,
through Christ our Lord.

And so, with all the Angels, we praise you,
as in joyful celebration we acclaim:
Holy, Holy, Holy Lord God of hosts... (page 35)

PREFACE 6 OF THE SUNDAYS IN ORDINARY TIME
It is truly right and just, our duty and our salvation,
always and everywhere to give you thanks,
Lord, holy Father, almighty and eternal God.

For in you we live and move and have our being,
and while in this body
we not only experience the daily effects of your care,
but even now possess the pledge of life eternal.

For, having received the first fruits of the Spirit,
through whom you raised up Jesus from the dead,
we hope for an everlasting share in the Paschal Mystery.

And so, with all the Angels, we praise you,
as in joyful celebration we acclaim:
Holy, Holy, Holy Lord God of hosts... (page 35)

PREFACE 7 OF THE SUNDAYS IN ORDINARY TIME
It is truly right and just, our duty and our salvation,
always and everywhere to give you thanks,
Lord, holy Father, almighty and eternal God.

For you so loved the world
that in your mercy you sent us the Redeemer,
to live like us in all things but sin,
so that you might love in us what you loved in your Son,
by whose obedience we have been restored to those gifts of yours
that, by sinning, we had lost in disobedience.

And so, Lord, with all the Angels and Saints,
we, too, give you thanks, as in exultation we acclaim:
Holy, Holy, Holy Lord God of hosts... *(page 35)*

PREFACE 8 OF THE SUNDAYS IN ORDINARY TIME

It is truly right and just, our duty and our salvation,
always and everywhere to give you thanks,
Lord, holy Father, almighty and eternal God.

For, when your children were scattered afar by sin,
through the Blood of your Son and the power of the Spirit,
you gathered them again to yourself,
that a people, formed as one by the unity of the Trinity,
made the body of Christ and the temple of the Holy Spirit,
might, to the praise of your manifold wisdom,
be manifest as the Church.

And so, in company with the choirs of Angels,
we praise you, and with joy we proclaim:
Holy, Holy, Holy Lord God of hosts... *(page 35)*

PREFACE 1 OF THE MOST HOLY EUCHARIST

It is truly right and just, our duty and our salvation,
always and everywhere to give you thanks,
Lord, holy Father, almighty and eternal God,
through Christ our Lord.

For he is the true and eternal Priest,
who instituted the pattern of an everlasting sacrifice
and was the first to offer himself as the saving Victim,
commanding us to make this offering as his memorial.
As we eat his flesh that was sacrificed for us,

we are made strong,
and, as we drink his Blood that was poured out for us,
we are washed clean.

And so, with Angels and Archangels,
with Thrones and Dominions,
and with all the hosts and Powers of heaven,
we sing the hymn of your glory,
as without end we acclaim:
Holy, Holy, Holy Lord God of hosts... *(page 35)*

PREFACE 2 OF THE MOST HOLY EUCHARIST

It is truly right and just, our duty and our salvation,
always and everywhere to give you thanks,
Lord, holy Father, almighty and eternal God,
through Christ our Lord.

For at the Last Supper with his Apostles,
establishing for the ages to come the saving memorial of the Cross,
he offered himself to you as the unblemished Lamb,
the acceptable gift of perfect praise.

Nourishing your faithful by this sacred mystery,
you make them holy, so that the human race,
bounded by one world,
may be enlightened by one faith
and united by one bond of charity.

And so, we approach the table of this wondrous Sacrament,
so that, bathed in the sweetness of your grace,
we may pass over to the heavenly realities here foreshadowed.

Therefore, all creatures of heaven and earth
sing a new song in adoration,
and we, with all the host of Angels,
cry out, and without end we acclaim:
Holy, Holy, Holy Lord God of hosts... (page 35)

PREFACE 1 OF THE BLESSED VIRGIN MARY

It is truly right and just, our duty and our salvation,
always and everywhere to give you thanks,
Lord, holy Father, almighty and eternal God,
and to praise, bless, and glorify your name
(on the Solemnity of the Motherhood /
on the feast day / on the Nativity / in veneration)
of the Blessed ever-Virgin Mary.

For by the overshadowing of the Holy Spirit
she conceived your Only Begotten Son,
and without losing the glory of virginity,
brought forth into the world the eternal Light,
Jesus Christ our Lord.

Through him the Angels praise your majesty,
Dominions adore and Powers tremble before you.
Heaven and the Virtues of heaven and the blessed Seraphim
worship together with exultation.
May our voices, we pray, join with theirs
in humble praise, as we acclaim:
Holy, Holy, Holy Lord God of hosts... (page 35)

HOLY, HOLY, HOLY

Holy, Holy, Holy Lord God of hosts.
Heaven and earth are full of your glory.
Hosanna in the highest.
Blessed is he who comes in the name of the Lord.
Hosanna in the highest.

EUCHARISTIC PRAYER 1 *(page 35)*

EUCHARISTIC PRAYER 2 *(page 42)*

EUCHARISTIC PRAYER 3 *(page 45)*

EUCHARISTIC PRAYER 4 *(page 48)*

EUCHARISTIC PRAYER 1

To you, therefore, most merciful Father,
we make humble prayer and petition
through Jesus Christ, your Son, our Lord:
that you accept
and bless these gifts, these offerings,
these holy and unblemished sacrifices,
which we offer you firstly
for your holy catholic Church.
Be pleased to grant her peace,
to guard, unite and govern her
throughout the whole world,
together with your servant N. our Pope
and N. our Bishop,
and all those who, holding to the truth,
hand on the catholic and apostolic faith.

Remember, Lord, your servants N. and N.
and all gathered here,

whose faith and devotion are known to you.
For them, we offer you this sacrifice of praise
or they offer it for themselves
and all who are dear to them:
for the redemption of their souls,
in hope of health and well being,
and paying their homage to you,
the eternal God, living and true.

On the Nativity of the Lord and throughout the Octave add:
Celebrating the most sacred night (day)
on which blessed Mary the immaculate Virgin
brought forth the Savior for this world,
and

On the Epiphany of the Lord add:
Celebrating the most sacred day
on which your Only Begotten Son,
eternal with you in your glory,
appeared in a human body, truly sharing our flesh,
and

On Holy Thursday add:
Celebrating the most sacred day
on which our Lord Jesus Christ
was handed over for our sake,
and

From the Mass of the Easter Vigil until the Second Sunday
of Easter add:
Celebrating the most sacred night (day)

of the Resurrection of our Lord Jesus Christ in the flesh,
and

On the Ascension of the Lord add:
Celebrating the most sacred day
on which your Only Begotten Son, our Lord,
placed at the right hand of your glory
our weak human nature,
which he had united to himself,
and

On Pentecost Sunday add:
Celebrating the most sacred day of Pentecost,
on which the Holy Spirit
appeared to the Apostles in tongues of fire,
and

In communion with those whose memory we venerate,
especially the glorious ever-Virgin Mary,
Mother of our God and Lord, Jesus Christ,
and blessed Joseph, her Spouse,
your blessed Apostles and Martyrs,
Peter and Paul, Andrew,
(James, John,
Thomas, James, Philip,
Bartholomew, Matthew,
Simon and Jude;
Linus, Cletus, Clement, Sixtus,
Cornelius, Cyprian,
Lawrence, Chrysogonus,
John and Paul,
Cosmas and Damian)

and all your Saints;
we ask that through their merits and prayers,
in all things we may be defended
by your protecting help.
(Through Christ our Lord. Amen.)

Therefore, Lord, we pray:
graciously accept this oblation of our service,
that of your whole family;

> On Holy Thursday add:
> which we make to you
> as we observe the day
> on which our Lord Jesus Christ
> handed on the mysteries of his Body and Blood
> for his disciples to celebrate;

> From the Mass of the Easter Vigil until the Second Sunday
> of Easter add:
> which we make to you
> also for those to whom you have been pleased to give
> the new birth of water and the Holy Spirit,
> granting them forgiveness of all their sins;

order our days in your peace,
and command that we be delivered from eternal damnation
and counted among the flock of those you have chosen.
(Through Christ our Lord. Amen.)

Be pleased, O God, we pray,
to bless, acknowledge,
and approve this offering in every respect;
make it spiritual and acceptable,

so that it may become for us
the Body and Blood of your most beloved Son,
our Lord Jesus Christ.

On the day before he was to suffer,

> On Holy Thursday add:
> for our salvation and the salvation of all,
> that is today,

he took bread in his holy and venerable hands,
and with eyes raised to heaven
to you, O God, his almighty Father,
giving you thanks, he said the blessing,
broke the bread
and gave it to his disciples, saying:

TAKE THIS, ALL OF YOU, AND EAT OF IT,
FOR THIS IS MY BODY,
WHICH WILL BE GIVEN UP FOR YOU.

In a similar way, when supper was ended,
he took this precious chalice
in his holy and venerable hands,
and once more giving you thanks, he said the blessing
and gave the chalice to his disciples, saying:

TAKE THIS, ALL OF YOU, AND DRINK FROM IT,
FOR THIS IS THE CHALICE OF MY BLOOD,
THE BLOOD OF THE NEW AND ETERNAL COVENANT,
WHICH WILL BE POURED OUT FOR YOU AND FOR MANY
FOR THE FORGIVENESS OF SINS.

DO THIS IN MEMORY OF ME.

The mystery of faith.

① *We proclaim your Death, O Lord,*
and profess your Resurrection
until you come again.

② *When we eat this Bread and drink this Cup,*
we proclaim your Death, O Lord,
until you come again.

③ *Save us, Savior of the world,*
for by your Cross and Resurrection
you have set us free.

Therefore, O Lord,
as we celebrate the memorial of the blessed Passion,
the Resurrection from the dead,
and the glorious Ascension into heaven
of Christ, your Son, our Lord,
we, your servants and your holy people,
offer to your glorious majesty
from the gifts that you have given us,
this pure victim,
this holy victim,
this spotless victim,
the holy Bread of eternal life
and the Chalice of everlasting salvation.

Be pleased to look upon these offerings
with a serene and kindly countenance,
and to accept them,
as once you were pleased to accept
the gifts of your servant Abel the just,

the sacrifice of Abraham, our father in faith,
and the offering of your high priest Melchizedek,
a holy sacrifice, a spotless victim.

In humble prayer we ask you, almighty God:
command that these gifts be borne
by the hands of your holy Angel
to your altar on high
in the sight of your divine majesty,
so that all of us, who through this participation at the altar
receive the most holy Body and Blood of your Son,
may be filled with every grace and heavenly blessing.
(Through Christ our Lord. Amen.)

Remember also, Lord, your servants N. and N.,
who have gone before us with the sign of faith
and rest in the sleep of peace.
   (Pause)
Grant them, O Lord, we pray,
and all who sleep in Christ,
a place of refreshment, light and peace.
(Through Christ our Lord. Amen.)

To us, also, your servants, who, though sinners,
hope in your abundant mercies,
graciously grant some share
and fellowship with your holy Apostles and Martyrs:
with John the Baptist, Stephen,
Matthias, Barnabas,
(Ignatius, Alexander,
Marcellinus, Peter,
Felicity, Perpetua,

Agatha, Lucy,
Agnes, Cecilia, Anastasia)
and all your Saints;
admit us, we beseech you,
into their company,
not weighing our merits,
but granting us your pardon,
through Christ our Lord.

Through whom
you continue to make all these good things, O Lord;
you sanctify them, fill them with life,
bless them, and bestow them upon us.

Through him, and with him, and in him,
O God, almighty Father,
in the unity of the Holy Spirit,
all glory and honor is yours,
for ever and ever. *Amen.*

(Turn to the Lord's Prayer, page 53)

EUCHARISTIC PRAYER 2

PREFACE

It is truly right and just, our duty and our salvation,
always and everywhere to give you thanks, Father most holy,
through your beloved Son, Jesus Christ,
your Word through whom you made all things,
whom you sent as our Savior and Redeemer,
incarnate by the Holy Spirit and born of the Virgin.

Fulfilling your will and gaining for you a holy people,
he stretched out his hands as he endured his Passion,
so as to break the bonds of death and manifest the resurrection.

And so, with the Angels and all the Saints
we declare your glory,
as with one voice we acclaim:
Holy, Holy, Holy Lord God of hosts... (page 35)

You are indeed Holy, O Lord,
the fount of all holiness.

Make holy, therefore, these gifts, we pray,
by sending down your Spirit upon them like the dewfall,
so that they may become for us
the Body and Blood of our Lord Jesus Christ.

At the time he was betrayed
and entered willingly into his Passion,
he took bread and, giving thanks, broke it,
and gave it to his disciples, saying:

TAKE THIS, ALL OF YOU, AND EAT OF IT,
FOR THIS IS MY BODY,
WHICH WILL BE GIVEN UP FOR YOU.

In a similar way, when supper was ended,
he took the chalice
and, once more giving thanks,
he gave it to his disciples, saying:

TAKE THIS, ALL OF YOU, AND DRINK FROM IT,
FOR THIS IS THE CHALICE OF MY BLOOD,
THE BLOOD OF THE NEW AND ETERNAL COVENANT,

WHICH WILL BE POURED OUT FOR YOU AND FOR MANY
FOR THE FORGIVENESS OF SINS.

DO THIS IN MEMORY OF ME.

The mystery of faith.

We proclaim your Death, O Lord,
and profess your Resurrection
until you come again.

(For other acclamations, see page 40)

Therefore, as we celebrate
the memorial of his Death and Resurrection,
we offer you, Lord,
the Bread of life and the Chalice of salvation,
giving thanks that you have held us worthy
to be in your presence and minister to you.

Humbly we pray
that, partaking of the Body and Blood of Christ,
we may be gathered into one by the Holy Spirit.

Remember, Lord, your Church,
spread throughout the world,
and bring her to the fullness of charity,
together with N. our Pope and N. our Bishop
and all the clergy.

Remember also our brothers and sisters
who have fallen asleep in the hope of the resurrection,
and all who have died in your mercy:
welcome them into the light of your face.

Have mercy on us all, we pray,
that with the Blessed Virgin Mary, Mother of God,
with blessed Joseph, her Spouse,
with the blessed Apostles,
and all the Saints who have pleased you throughout the ages,
we may merit to be coheirs to eternal life,
and may praise and glorify you
through your Son, Jesus Christ.

Through him, and with him, and in him,
O God, almighty Father,
in the unity of the Holy Spirit,
all glory and honor is yours,
for ever and ever. *Amen.*

(Turn to the Lord's Prayer, page 53)

EUCHARISTIC PRAYER 3
You are indeed Holy, O Lord,
and all you have created
rightly gives you praise,
for through your Son our Lord Jesus Christ,
by the power and working of the Holy Spirit,
you give life to all things and make them holy,
and you never cease to gather a people to yourself,
so that from the rising of the sun to its setting
a pure sacrifice may be offered to your name.

Therefore, O Lord, we humbly implore you:
by the same Spirit graciously make holy
these gifts we have brought to you for consecration,

that they may become the Body and Blood
of your Son our Lord Jesus Christ,
at whose command we celebrate these mysteries.

For on the night he was betrayed
he himself took bread,
and, giving you thanks, he said the blessing,
broke the bread and gave it to his disciples, saying:

TAKE THIS, ALL OF YOU, AND EAT OF IT,
FOR THIS IS MY BODY,
WHICH WILL BE GIVEN UP FOR YOU.

In a similar way, when supper was ended,
he took the chalice,
and, giving you thanks, he said the blessing,
and gave the chalice to his disciples, saying:

TAKE THIS, ALL OF YOU, AND DRINK FROM IT,
FOR THIS IS THE CHALICE OF MY BLOOD,
THE BLOOD OF THE NEW AND ETERNAL COVENANT,
WHICH WILL BE POURED OUT FOR YOU AND FOR MANY
FOR THE FORGIVENESS OF SINS.

DO THIS IN MEMORY OF ME.

The mystery of faith.

When we eat this Bread and drink this Cup,
we proclaim your Death, O Lord,
until you come again.

(For other acclamations, see page 40)

Therefore, O Lord, as we celebrate the memorial
of the saving Passion of your Son,
his wondrous Resurrection
and Ascension into heaven,
and as we look forward to his second coming,
we offer you in thanksgiving
this holy and living sacrifice.

Look, we pray, upon the oblation of your Church
and, recognizing the sacrificial Victim by whose death
you willed to reconcile us to yourself,
grant that we, who are nourished
by the Body and Blood of your Son
and filled with his Holy Spirit,
may become one body, one spirit in Christ.

May he make of us
an eternal offering to you,
so that we may obtain an inheritance with your elect,
especially with the most Blessed Virgin Mary, Mother of God,
with blessed Joseph, her Spouse,
with your blessed Apostles and glorious Martyrs
(with Saint N.)
and with all the Saints,
on whose constant intercession in your presence
we rely for unfailing help.

May this Sacrifice of our reconciliation,
we pray, O Lord,
advance the peace and salvation of all the world.
Be pleased to confirm in faith and charity
your pilgrim Church on earth,

with your servant N. our Pope and N. our Bishop,
the Order of Bishops, all the clergy,
and the entire people you have gained for your own.

Listen graciously to the prayers of this family,
whom you have summoned before you:
in your compassion, O merciful Father,
gather to yourself all your children
scattered throughout the world.

To our departed brothers and sisters
and to all who were pleasing to you
at their passing from this life,
give kind admittance to your kingdom.
There we hope to enjoy for ever the fullness of your glory
through Christ our Lord,
through whom you bestow on the world all that is good.

Through him, and with him, and in him,
O God, almighty Father,
in the unity of the Holy Spirit,
all glory and honor is yours,
for ever and ever. *Amen.*

(Turn to the Lord's Prayer, page 53)

EUCHARISTIC PRAYER 4
PREFACE
It is truly right to give you thanks,
truly just to give you glory, Father most holy,
for you are the one God living and true,
existing before all ages and abiding for all eternity,

dwelling in unapproachable light;
yet you, who alone are good, the source of life,
have made all that is,
so that you might fill your creatures with blessings
and bring joy to many of them by the glory of your light.

And so, in your presence are countless hosts of Angels,
who serve you day and night
and, gazing upon the glory of your face,
glorify you without ceasing.

With them we, too, confess your name in exultation,
giving voice to every creature under heaven,
as we acclaim:
Holy, Holy, Holy Lord God of hosts... (page 35)

We give you praise, Father most holy,
for you are great
and you have fashioned all your works
in wisdom and in love.
You formed man in your own image
and entrusted the whole world to his care,
so that in serving you alone, the Creator,
he might have dominion over all creatures.

And when through disobedience he had lost your friendship,
you did not abandon him to the domain of death.
For you came in mercy to the aid of all,
so that those who seek might find you.
Time and again you offered them covenants
and through the prophets
taught them to look forward to salvation.

And you so loved the world, Father most holy,
that in the fullness of time
you sent your Only Begotten Son to be our Savior.
Made incarnate by the Holy Spirit
and born of the Virgin Mary,
he shared our human nature
in all things but sin.
To the poor he proclaimed the good news of salvation,
to prisoners, freedom,
and to the sorrowful of heart, joy.
To accomplish your plan,
he gave himself up to death,
and, rising from the dead,
he destroyed death and restored life.

And that we might live no longer for ourselves
but for him who died and rose again for us,
he sent the Holy Spirit from you, Father,
as the first fruits for those who believe,
so that, bringing to perfection his work in the world,
he might sanctify creation to the full.

Therefore, O Lord, we pray:
may this same Holy Spirit
graciously sanctify these offerings,
that they may become
the Body and Blood of our Lord Jesus Christ
for the celebration of this great mystery,
which he himself left us
as an eternal covenant.

For when the hour had come
for him to be glorified by you, Father most holy,
having loved his own who were in the world,
he loved them to the end:
and while they were at supper,
he took bread, blessed and broke it,
and gave it to his disciples, saying:

TAKE THIS, ALL OF YOU, AND EAT OF IT,
FOR THIS IS MY BODY,
WHICH WILL BE GIVEN UP FOR YOU.

In a similar way,
taking the chalice filled with the fruit of the vine,
he gave thanks,
and gave the chalice to his disciples, saying:

TAKE THIS, ALL OF YOU, AND DRINK FROM IT,
FOR THIS IS THE CHALICE OF MY BLOOD,
THE BLOOD OF THE NEW AND ETERNAL COVENANT,
WHICH WILL BE POURED OUT FOR YOU AND FOR MANY
FOR THE FORGIVENESS OF SINS.

DO THIS IN MEMORY OF ME.

The mystery of faith.

Save us, Savior of the world,
for by your Cross and Resurrection
you have set us free.

(For other acclamations, see page 40)

Therefore, O Lord,
as we now celebrate the memorial of our redemption,
we remember Christ's Death
and his descent to the realm of the dead,
we proclaim his Resurrection
and his Ascension to your right hand,
and, as we await his coming in glory,
we offer you his Body and Blood,
the sacrifice acceptable to you
which brings salvation to the whole world.

Look, O Lord, upon the Sacrifice
which you yourself have provided for your Church,
and grant in your loving kindness
to all who partake of this one Bread and one Chalice
that, gathered into one body by the Holy Spirit,
they may truly become a living sacrifice in Christ
to the praise of your glory.

Therefore, Lord, remember now
all for whom we offer this sacrifice:
especially your servant N. our Pope,
N. our Bishop, and the whole Order of Bishops,
all the clergy,
those who take part in this offering,
those gathered here before you,
your entire people,
and all who seek you with a sincere heart.

Remember also
those who have died in the peace of your Christ
and all the dead,

whose faith you alone have known.

To all of us, your children,
grant, O merciful Father,
that we may enter into a heavenly inheritance
with the Blessed Virgin Mary, Mother of God,
with blessed Joseph, her Spouse,
and with your Apostles and Saints in your kingdom.
There, with the whole of creation,
freed from the corruption of sin and death,
may we glorify you through Christ our Lord,
through whom you bestow on the world all that is good.

Through him, and with him, and in him,
O God, almighty Father,
in the unity of the Holy Spirit,
all glory and honor is yours,
for ever and ever. *Amen.*

COMMUNION RITE

LORD'S PRAYER
At the Savior's command
and formed by divine teaching,
we dare to say:

Our Father, who art in heaven,
hallowed be thy name;
thy kingdom come,
thy will be done

on earth as it is in heaven.
Give us this day our daily bread,
and forgive us our trespasses,
as we forgive those who trespass against us;
and lead us not into temptation,
but deliver us from evil.

Deliver us, Lord, we pray, from every evil,
graciously grant peace in our days,
that, by the help of your mercy,
we may be always free from sin
and safe from all distress,
as we await the blessed hope
and the coming of our Savior, Jesus Christ.

For the kingdom,
the power and the glory are yours
now and for ever.

SIGN OF PEACE

Lord Jesus Christ,
who said to your Apostles:
Peace I leave you, my peace I give you,
look not on our sins,
but on the faith of your Church,
and graciously grant her peace and unity
in accordance with your will.
Who live and reign for ever and ever. *Amen.*

The peace of the Lord be with you always.
And with your spirit.
Let us offer each other the sign of peace.

FRACTION OF THE BREAD

May this mingling of the Body and Blood
of our Lord Jesus Christ
bring eternal life to us who receive it.

Lamb of God, you take away the sins of the world,
    have mercy on us.
Lamb of God, you take away the sins of the world,
    have mercy on us.
Lamb of God, you take away the sins of the world,
    grant us peace.

Lord Jesus Christ, Son of the living God,
who, by the will of the Father
and the work of the Holy Spirit,
through your Death gave life to the world,
free me by this, your most holy Body and Blood,
from all my sins and from every evil;
keep me always faithful to your commandments,
and never let me be parted from you.

Or

May the receiving of your Body and Blood,
Lord Jesus Christ,
not bring me to judgment and condemnation,
but through your loving mercy
be for me protection in mind and body
and a healing remedy.

COMMUNION

Behold the Lamb of God,
behold him who takes away the sins of the world.
Blessed are those called to the supper of the Lamb.

Lord, I am not worthy
that you should enter under my roof,
but only say the word
and my soul shall be healed.

May the Body (Blood) of Christ
keep me safe for eternal life.

COMMUNION ANTIPHON (Turn to the appropriate day)

PRAYER AFTER COMMUNION (Turn to the appropriate day)

CONCLUDING RITES

BLESSING

On certain days or occasions, this blessing is preceded by a solemn
formula of blessing (see page 57) or prayer over the people.

The Lord be with you.
And with your spirit.
May almighty God bless you,
the Father, and the Son, and the Holy Spirit.
Amen.

DISMISSAL

1 Go forth, the Mass is ended.
Thanks be to God.

2 Go and announce the Gospel of the Lord.
Thanks be to God.

3 Go in peace, glorifying the Lord by your life.
Thanks be to God.

4 Go in peace.
Thanks be to God.

During the Easter Octave and on Pentecost Sunday, the double alleluia is added:

1 Go forth, the Mass is ended, alleluia, alleluia.
Thanks be to God, alleluia, alleluia.

2 Go in peace, alleluia, alleluia.
Thanks be to God, alleluia, alleluia.

OPTIONAL SOLEMN BLESSINGS

ADVENT

May the almighty and merciful God,
by whose grace you have placed your faith
in the First Coming of his Only Begotten Son
and yearn for his coming again,
sanctify you by the radiance of Christ's Advent
and enrich you with his blessing. *Amen.*

As you run the race of this present life,
may he make you firm in faith,
joyful in hope and active in charity. *Amen.*

So that, rejoicing now with devotion
at the Redeemer's coming in the flesh,
you may be endowed with the rich reward of eternal life
when he comes again in majesty. *Amen.*

And may the blessing of almighty God,
the Father, and the Son, and the Holy Spirit,
come down on you and remain with you for ever. *Amen.*

THE NATIVITY OF THE LORD

May the God of infinite goodness,
who by the Incarnation of his Son
    has driven darkness from the world
and by that glorious Birth has illumined
    this most holy night (day),
drive far from you the darkness of vice
and illumine your hearts with the light of virtue. *Amen.*

May God, who willed that the great joy
of his Son's saving Birth
be announced to shepherds by the Angel,
fill your minds with the gladness he gives
and make you heralds of his Gospel. *Amen.*

And may God, who by the Incarnation
brought together the earthly and heavenly realm,
fill you with the gift of his peace and favor
and make you sharers with the Church in heaven. *Amen.*

And may the blessing of almighty God,
the Father, and the Son, and the Holy Spirit,
come down on you and remain with you for ever. *Amen.*

THE BEGINNING OF THE YEAR
May God, the source and origin of all blessing,
grant you grace,
pour out his blessing in abundance,
and keep you safe from harm throughout the year. *Amen.*

May he give you integrity in the faith,
endurance in hope,
and perseverance in charity
with holy patience to the end. *Amen.*

May he order your days and your deeds in his peace,
grant your prayers in this and in every place,
and lead you happily to eternal life. *Amen.*

And may the blessing of almighty God,
the Father, and the Son, and the Holy Spirit,
come down on you and remain with you for ever. *Amen.*

THE EPIPHANY OF THE LORD
May God, who has called you
out of darkness into his wonderful light,
pour out in kindness his blessing upon you
and make your hearts firm
in faith, hope and charity. *Amen.*

And since in all confidence you follow Christ,
who today appeared in the world
as a light shining in darkness,
may God make you, too,
a light for your brothers and sisters. *Amen.*

And so when your pilgrimage is ended,
may you come to him
whom the Magi sought as they followed the star
and whom they found with great joy, the Light from Light,
who is Christ the Lord. *Amen.*

And may the blessing of almighty God,
the Father, and the Son, and the Holy Spirit,
come down on you and remain with you for ever. *Amen.*

THE PASSION OF THE LORD

May God, the Father of mercies,
who has given you an example of love
in the Passion of his Only Begotten Son,
grant that, by serving God and your neighbor,
you may lay hold of the wondrous gift of his blessing. *Amen.*

So that you may receive the reward of everlasting life from him,
through whose earthly Death
you believe that you escape eternal death. *Amen.*

And by following the example of his self-abasement,
may you possess a share in his Resurrection. *Amen.*

And may the blessing of almighty God,
the Father, and the Son, and the Holy Spirit,
come down on you and remain with you for ever. *Amen.*

EASTER TIME

May God, who by the Resurrection of his Only Begotten Son
was pleased to confer on you
the gift of redemption and of adoption,

give you gladness by his blessing. *Amen*.

May he, by whose redeeming work
you have received the gift of everlasting freedom,
make you heirs to an eternal inheritance. *Amen.*

And may you, who have already risen with Christ
in Baptism through faith,
by living in a right manner on this earth,
be united with him in the homeland of heaven. *Amen.*

And may the blessing of almighty God,
the Father, and the Son, and the Holy Spirit,
come down on you and remain with you for ever. *Amen.*

THE ASCENSION OF THE LORD
May almighty God bless you,
for on this very day his Only Begotten Son
pierced the heights of heaven
and unlocked for you the way
to ascend to where he is. *Amen.*

May he grant that,
as Christ after his Resurrection
was seen plainly by his disciples,
so when he comes as Judge
he may show himself merciful to you for all eternity. *Amen.*

And may you, who believe he is seated
with the Father in his majesty,
know with joy the fulfillment of his promise
to stay with you until the end of time. *Amen.*

And may the blessing of almighty God,
the Father, and the Son, and the Holy Spirit,
come down on you and remain with you for ever. *Amen.*

THE HOLY SPIRIT

May God, the Father of lights,
who was pleased to enlighten the disciples' minds
by the outpouring of the Spirit, the Paraclete,
grant you gladness by his blessing
and make you always abound with the gifts
    of the same Spirit. *Amen.*

May the wondrous flame that appeared above the disciples,
powerfully cleanse your hearts from every evil
and pervade them with its purifying light. *Amen.*

And may God, who has been pleased to unite many tongues
in the profession of one faith,
give you perseverance in that same faith
and, by believing, may you journey from hope
    to clear vision. *Amen.*

And may the blessing of almighty God,
the Father, and the Son, and the Holy Spirit,
come down on you and remain with you for ever. *Amen.*

THE BLESSED VIRGIN MARY

May God, who through the childbearing
    of the Blessed Virgin Mary
willed in his great kindness to redeem the human race,
be pleased to enrich you with his blessing. *Amen.*

May you know always and everywhere the protection of her,
through whom you have been found worthy
    to receive the author of life. *Amen.*

May you, who have devoutly gathered on this day,
carry away with you the gifts of spiritual joys
    and heavenly rewards. *Amen.*

And may the blessing of almighty God,
the Father, and the Son, and the Holy Spirit,
come down on you and remain with you for ever. *Amen.*

ALL SAINTS

May God, the glory and joy of the Saints,
who has caused you to be strengthened
by means of their outstanding prayers,
bless you with unending blessings. *Amen.*

Freed through their intercession from present ills
and formed by the example of their holy way of life,
may you be ever devoted
to serving God and your neighbor. *Amen.*

So that, together with all,
you may possess the joys of the homeland,
where Holy Church rejoices
that her children are admitted in perpetual peace
to the company of the citizens of heaven. *Amen.*

And may the blessing of almighty God,
the Father, and the Son, and the Holy Spirit,
come down on you and remain with you for ever. *Amen.*

Sunday Readings
& Prayers

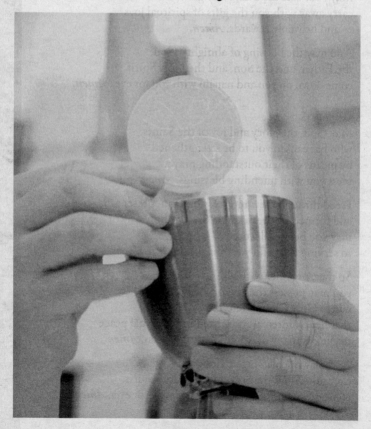

Christ lights our darkness

Advent (literally, "at the coming") prepares for the annual celebration of Jesus' birth at Christmas and his revelation to the nations at Epiphany. The Church year moves in a cycle of promise–fulfillment–proclamation, often using the images of darkness and light to accentuate the movement. With Advent we enter the first part of the cycle—promise—as, in our northern hemisphere, the dark period of the solar year begins. God's goodness gives us light, the light of the Messiah that dawns in the birth of Christ at Bethlehem and that will shine in its fullness at his coming again as King and Judge.

So in this Advent season as we begin a new Church year, we focus our attention on the demands of responding to the light of Jesus' presence. We desire to let his vision and values enlighten us and transform the darkness of our lives so that we may become a light that will lead others to God.

The lectionary focus for this year on Mark's gospel is particularly suited to enhance our experience of enlightenment for following this way of commitment, conversion, and cooperation in the saving work of Jesus for our world today.

As we live through the seasons of the Church year, we will learn that the way of Christian discipleship always leads through the darkness of suffering to the experience of new life in Christ. Preparing the way is the first step to which our Advent experience is directed.

Praying and living the Advent season

An Advent wreath can help you and your household focus on waiting for Christ. Create a wreath from evergreen boughs and four candles (three purple and one rose or white for the joyful third week). Use the following format each week.

INVITATION TO PRAYER *As you light the candles (one for each week of Advent), invite all to share in the response.*

Leader: We look for light, and lo, darkness;
for brightness, but we walk in gloom! *(Isaiah 59:9)*

All: You, Lord, give light to my lamp;
you brighten the darkness about me. *(Psalm 18:28)*

SCRIPTURE READING *When the candles are lit, read aloud one of the Scripture readings from the day or Sunday. Either reflect quietly or invite each household member to respond to these questions:*

- How do I want Jesus to be my light this Advent (tonight)?
- How do the words of this reading help me to wait for Jesus to come?

CLOSING PRAYER *(adapted from Ephesians 5:1-2, 8-14)*
O God of light, help us be imitators of you and live in love.
For we were once darkness, but now we are light in the Lord.
Help us live as children of light,
for light produces every kind of goodness and truth.
Help us learn what is pleasing to the Lord.
We want to take no part in the works of darkness
but rather to expose them.
Christ will give us light! Amen.

December 3

DEC 3

In this moment...

On the first Sunday of Advent, we as a Church enter a precious period of in-betweenness. It is a time of expectancy and longing, bated breath and watchful waiting. It is a time that calls us to explicitly reflect on the peculiarity of our position: our Lord has already come and we wait for him to come again. We return to the stories leading up to his birth each year, knowing that we are living in a kind of "already/not yet." We know our Beloved and still we yearn to see his face.

In the gospel today, we are called to be watchful: "Be watchful. Be alert!" "You do not know when the time will come." These insistent passages call us to be attentive in our every moment. When we are alert, we become attuned to the vibrancy of all that surrounds us; any movement could signal the arrival of the Beloved. It's a delightful kind of anticipation. Eighteenth-century Jesuit writer Jean Pierre de Caussade might invite us, in our anticipation, into what he called "the sacramentality of the present moment." What if every moment were one in which we might meet our God? What might we notice, then? How might we act? Let us pray for the grace to be receptive to God in every moment.

■ **KATE McGEE**

ENTRANCE ANTIPHON *(Cf. Psalm 25 [24]:1-3)*

To you, I lift up my soul, O my God. In you, I have trusted; let me not be put to shame. Nor let my enemies exult over me; and let none who hope in you be put to shame.

INTRODUCTORY RITES *(page 10)*

COLLECT

Grant your faithful, we pray, almighty God,
the resolve to run forth to meet your Christ
with righteous deeds at his coming,
so that, gathered at his right hand,
they may be worthy to possess the heavenly Kingdom.
Through our Lord Jesus Christ, your Son,
who lives and reigns with you in the unity of the Holy Spirit,
one God, for ever and ever. ***Amen.***

FIRST READING *(Isaiah 63:16b-17, 19b; 64:2-7)*

You, LORD, ✝ are our father,
   our redeemer you are named forever.
Why do you let us wander, O LORD, from your ways,
   and harden our hearts so that we fear you not?
Return for the sake of your servants,
   the tribes of your heritage.
Oh, that you would rend the heavens and come down,
   with the mountains quaking before you,
while you wrought awesome deeds we could not hope for,
   such as they had not heard of from of old.
No ear has ever heard, no eye ever seen, any God but you
   doing such deeds for those who wait for him.
Would that you might meet us doing right,
   that we were mindful of you in our ways!

Behold, you are angry, and we are sinful;
　all of us have become like unclean people,
　all our good deeds are like polluted rags;
we have all withered like leaves,
　and our guilt carries us away like the wind.
There is none who calls upon your name,
　who rouses himself to cling to you;
for you have hidden your face from us
　and have delivered us up to our guilt.
Yet, O Lord, you are our father;
　we are the clay and you the potter:
　we are all the work of your hands.
The word of the Lord. *Thanks be to God.*

RESPONSORIAL PSALM *(Psalm 80:2-3, 15-16, 18-19)*

℟ **Lord, make us turn to you; let us see your face and we shall
be saved.**

O shepherd of Israel, hearken,
　from your throne upon the cherubim,* shine forth.
Rouse your power,
　and come to save us. ℟

Once again, O Lord of hosts,
　look down from heaven, and see;
take care of this vine,
　and protect what your right hand has planted,
　the son of man whom you yourself made strong. ℟

May your help be with the man of your right hand,
　with the son of man whom you yourself made strong.
Then we will no more withdraw from you;
　give us new life, and we will call upon your name. ℟

SECOND READING *(1 Corinthians 1:3–9)*

Brothers and sisters: Grace to you and peace from God our Father and the Lord Jesus Christ.

I give thanks to my God always on your account for the grace of God bestowed on you in Christ Jesus, that in him you were enriched in every way, with all discourse and all knowledge, as the testimony to Christ was confirmed among you, so that you are not lacking in any spiritual gift as you wait for the revelation of our Lord Jesus Christ. He will keep you firm to the end, irreproachable on the day of our Lord Jesus Christ. God is faithful, and by him you were called to fellowship with his Son, Jesus Christ our Lord.

The word of the Lord. *Thanks be to God.*

ALLELUIA *(Psalm 85:8)*

Alleluia, alleluia. Show us, Lord, your love; and grant us your salvation. *Alleluia, alleluia.*

GOSPEL *(Mark 13:33–37)*

A reading from the holy Gospel according to Mark.
Glory to you, O Lord.

Jesus said to his disciples: "Be watchful! Be alert! You do not know when the time will come. It is like a man traveling abroad. He leaves home and places his servants in charge, each with his own work, and orders the gatekeeper to be on the watch. Watch, therefore; you do not know when the lord of the house is coming, whether in the evening, or at midnight, or at cockcrow, or in the morning. May he not come suddenly and find you sleeping. What I say to you, I say to all: 'Watch!'"

The Gospel of the Lord. *Praise to you, Lord Jesus Christ.*

PROFESSION OF FAITH *(page 13)*

PRAYER OF THE FAITHFUL

PREPARATION OF GIFTS *(page 16)*

PRAYER OVER THE OFFERINGS
Accept, we pray, O Lord, these offerings we make,
gathered from among your gifts to us,
and may what you grant us to celebrate devoutly here below
gain for us the prize of eternal redemption.
Through Christ our Lord. *Amen.*

PREFACE *(Advent 1, page 17)*

❖ TAKING A CLOSER LOOK ❖

✠ **LORD** The New American Bible, used for our Sunday Mass readings, uses Lord in small capital letters to indicate the sacred name of God revealed to Moses and the Israelites—*Yahweh*. This choice is appropriate for two reasons. First, Lord has the same number of letters as God's sacred name. Since the Hebrew language wrote only the consonants and not the vowels, God's name was written: YHWH (in English). Since God's name was so sacred, the Jews did not speak it aloud but would instead say *Adonai*, the Hebrew word for Lord. In the Bible, when God is addressed as "Lord Yahweh" (*Adonai YHWH*), God is put in small capital letters. So, when we see Lord or God in small capital letters in the text, we know that the original word is Yahweh, the unique personal name by which God wanted to be known.

COMMUNION ANTIPHON *(Psalm 85 [84]:13)*

The Lord will bestow his bounty, and our earth shall yield its increase.

PRAYER AFTER COMMUNION

May these mysteries, O Lord,
in which we have participated,
profit us, we pray,
for even now, as we walk amid passing things,
you teach us by them to love the things of heaven
and hold fast to what endures.
Through Christ our Lord. *Amen.*

SOLEMN BLESSING: ADVENT *(Optional, page 57)*

DISMISSAL *(page 57)* ✤

• RESPONDING TO THE WORD •

Isaiah asks why God lets us wander, and he yearns for God's return.	Paul thanks God, who has given many spiritual gifts.	Jesus warns us to "watch" and be alert.
➡ *Where has my spiritual wandering taken me this past year?*	➡ *Which spiritual gift stands out for me recently?*	➡ *What makes me less attentive to God's presence than I want?*

December 8

DEC 8

Lord, deepen my faith!

Conception without original sin and an elderly woman bearing a child: both of these marvels are possible for God. That is the message for us.

God's power works in us as well, making possible what seems to be impossible. We look at our obligations and wonder how we can fulfill them, but that will be possible for us if we call upon God. We look at our weaknesses and wonder how we can overcome them, but that too will be possible for us if we call upon God.

Let us pray that our hearts may be open to all that God wants to make possible for us today.

As we celebrate Mary's Immaculate Conception, we ask for a share in the purity that was Mary's from the first moment of her life. We ask for the faith to believe that God will cleanse us where we need to be cleansed, free us where we need to be freed, and strengthen us where we need to be strong. All of this is possible for God.

■ FR. KENNETH GRABNER, CSC

ENTRANCE ANTIPHON *(Isaiah 61:10)*

I rejoice heartily in the Lord, in my God is the joy of my soul; for he has clothed me with a robe of salvation, and wrapped me in a mantle of justice, like a bride adorned with her jewels.

INTRODUCTORY RITES *(page 10)*

COLLECT

O God, who by the Immaculate Conception of the Blessed Virgin prepared a worthy dwelling for your Son,
grant, we pray,
that, as you preserved her from every stain
by virtue of the Death of your Son, which you foresaw,
so, through her intercession,
we, too, may be cleansed and admitted to your presence.
Through our Lord Jesus Christ, your Son,
who lives and reigns with you in the unity of the Holy Spirit,
one God, for ever and ever. *Amen.*

FIRST READING *(Genesis 3:9–15, 20)*

After the man, Adam, had eaten of the tree, the LORD God called to the man and asked him, "Where are you?" He answered, "I heard you in the garden; but I was afraid, because I was naked, so I hid myself." Then he asked, "Who told you that you were naked? You have eaten, then, from the tree of which I had forbidden you to eat!" The man replied, "The woman whom you put here with me—she gave me fruit from the tree, and so I ate it." The LORD God then asked the woman, "Why did you do such a thing?" The woman answered, "The serpent tricked me into it, so I ate it."

Then the LORD God said to the serpent:

"Because you have done this, you shall be banned
    from all the animals
    and from all the wild creatures;
on your belly shall you crawl,
    and dirt shall you eat
    all the days of your life.
I will put enmity between you and the woman,
    and between your offspring and hers;
he will strike at your head,
    while you strike at his heel."

The man called his wife Eve, because she became the mother of all the living.

The word of the Lord. *Thanks be to God.*

RESPONSORIAL PSALM *(Psalm 98:1, 2–3ab, 3cd–4)*

R̷ **Sing to the Lord a new song, for he has done marvelous deeds.**

Sing to the Lord a new song,
    for he has done wondrous deeds;
His right hand has won victory for him,
    his holy arm. R̷
The Lord has made his salvation known:
    in the sight of the nations he has revealed his justice.
He has remembered his kindness and his faithfulness
    toward the house of Israel. R̷
All the ends of the earth have seen
    the salvation by our God.
Sing joyfully to the Lord, all you lands;
    break into song; sing praise. R̷

SECOND READING *(Ephesians 1:3-6, 11-12)*

Brothers and sisters: Blessed be the God and Father of our Lord Jesus Christ, who has blessed us in Christ with every spiritual blessing in the heavens, as he chose us in him, before the foundation of the world, to be holy and without blemish before him. In love he destined us for adoption to himself through Jesus Christ, in accord with the favor of his will, for the praise of the glory of his grace that he granted us in the beloved.

In him we were also chosen, destined in accord with the purpose of the One who accomplishes all things according to the intention of his will, so that we might exist for the praise of his glory, we who first hoped in Christ.

The word of the Lord. *Thanks be to God.*

ALLELUIA *(See Luke 1:28)*

Alleluia, alleluia. Hail, Mary, full of grace, the Lord is with you; blessed are you among women. *Alleluia, alleluia.*

GOSPEL *(Luke 1:26-38)*

A reading from the holy Gospel according to Luke.
Glory to you, O Lord.

The angel Gabriel was sent from God to a town of Galilee called Nazareth, to a virgin betrothed to a man named Joseph, of the house of David, and the virgin's name was Mary. And coming to her, he said, "**Hail, full of grace!**✝ The Lord is with you." But she was greatly troubled at what was said and pondered what sort of greeting this might be. Then the angel said to her, "Do not be afraid, Mary, for you have found favor with God. Behold, you will conceive in your womb and bear a son, and you shall name him Jesus. He will be great and will be called Son of the Most High, and the Lord God will give him the throne of David his father, and he will rule over the house of Jacob forever, and of his Kingdom there will be no end." But Mary said to the angel, "How can this be, since I have no relations with a man?" And the angel said to her in reply, "The Holy Spirit will come upon you, and the power of the Most High will overshadow you. Therefore the child to be born will be called holy, the Son of God. And behold, Elizabeth, your relative, has also conceived a son in her old age, and this is the sixth month for her who was called barren; for nothing will be impossible for God." Mary said, "Behold, I am the handmaid of the Lord. May it be done to me according to your word." Then the angel departed from her.

The Gospel of the Lord. *Praise to you, Lord Jesus Christ.*

PROFESSION OF FAITH *(page 13)*

PRAYER OF THE FAITHFUL

PREPARATION OF GIFTS *(page 16)*

PRAYER OVER THE OFFERINGS

Graciously accept the saving sacrifice
which we offer you, O Lord,
on the Solemnity of the Immaculate Conception
of the Blessed Virgin Mary,
and grant that, as we profess her,
on account of your prevenient grace,
to be untouched by any stain of sin,
so, through her intercession,
we may be delivered from all our faults.
Through Christ our Lord. *Amen.*

PREFACE: THE MYSTERY OF MARY AND THE CHURCH

It is truly right and just, our duty and our salvation,
always and everywhere to give you thanks,
Lord, holy Father, almighty and eternal God.

For you preserved the most Blessed Virgin Mary
from all stain of original sin,
so that in her, endowed with the rich fullness of your grace,
you might prepare a worthy Mother for your Son
and signify the beginning of the Church,
his beautiful Bride without spot or wrinkle.

She, the most pure Virgin, was to bring forth a Son,
the innocent Lamb who would wipe away our offenses;
you placed her above all others
to be for your people an advocate of grace
and a model of holiness.

And so, in company with the choirs of Angels,
we praise you, and with joy we proclaim:
Holy, Holy, Holy Lord God of hosts... *(page 35)*

COMMUNION ANTIPHON

Glorious things are spoken of you, O Mary, for from you arose
the sun of justice, Christ our God.

• TAKING A CLOSER LOOK •

✚ **Hail, full of grace!** Although we tend to hear these words as overflowing with theological meaning, note that they are a greeting that Mary finds perplexing. The sense is given by Gabriel, the messenger angel: "You have found favor with God." The basic meaning of the word grace (Greek, *charis*; Latin, *gratia*) describes a free gift that is bestowed not out of merit (then it would be owed rather than a true gift) but because the giver has found some reason to single out or favor the recipient. The choice of one recipient (a favorite) from many possible ones for the gift led to the common connection of grace and honor. As the text indicates, Mary's gift is that God is with her (as God also is with us!), which is indeed both a great favor and an honor.

PRAYER AFTER COMMUNION

May the Sacrament we have received,
O Lord our God,
heal in us the wounds of that fault
from which in a singular way
you preserved Blessed Mary in her Immaculate Conception.
Through Christ our Lord. *Amen.*

SOLEMN BLESSING: THE BLESSED VIRGIN MARY *(Optional, page 62)*

DISMISSAL *(page 57)* ✢

● RESPONDING TO THE WORD ●

Adam and Eve shirk their responsibility for sin and blame others.	Paul reminds us that we have been chosen to participate in God's plan of salvation.	Mary's "yes" to God is unconditional and puts her completely at God's service.
➡ *Whom have I blamed instead of taking responsibility for my actions?*	➡ *Where and to whom does it seem that God is directing me to serve today?*	➡ *What conditions do I try to set for what God seems to be asking me to be or do?*

December 10

**DEC
10**

Making room for Jesus

Remember the scene in *How the Grinch Stole Christmas* when the Grinch says: "That's one thing I hate! All the noise, noise, noise, NOISE!" Sometimes the lead-up to Christmas is like that: overtired, screaming toddlers in the mall; nonstop Christmas music everywhere; the incessant TV commercials. All this can bring out the Grinch in the best of us.

So I am especially grateful for the calming voices in today's readings that encourage us to focus on what's *really* important during these weeks before Christmas. Both Isaiah and John the Baptist remind us that this season of Advent is about preparing the way of the Lord. It's about clearing some space, making room for Jesus, and welcoming him into our lives in an ever-deeper way.

It might mean committing more time for prayer each day, even in the midst of the December hustle and bustle. Or giving the gift of presence to someone who is lonely or housebound in this festive season. Maybe it is something as simple as making a conscious effort to treat the harried cashier with courtesy and respect.

Today, prophetic voices reach out to us across the centuries. As we continue our Advent journey, may we have ears to hear their words and hearts to heed their call.

■ **TERESA WHALEN LUX**

ENTRANCE ANTIPHON *(Cf. Isaiah 30:19, 30)*

O people of Sion, behold, the Lord will come to save the nations, and the Lord will make the glory of his voice heard in the joy of your heart.

INTRODUCTORY RITES *(page 10)*

COLLECT

Almighty and merciful God,
may no earthly undertaking hinder those
who set out in haste to meet your Son,
but may our learning of heavenly wisdom
gain us admittance to his company.
Who lives and reigns with you in the unity of the Holy Spirit,
one God, for ever and ever. *Amen.*

FIRST READING *(Isaiah 40:1-5, 9-11)*

Comfort, give comfort to my people,
    says your God.
Speak tenderly to Jerusalem, and proclaim to her
        that her service is at an end,
        her guilt is expiated;
indeed, she has received from the hand of the LORD
        double for all her sins.

        A voice cries out:
In the desert prepare the way of the LORD!
        Make straight in the wasteland a highway for our God!
Every valley shall be filled in,
        every mountain and hill shall be made low;
the rugged land shall be made a plain,
        the rough country, a broad valley.

Then the glory of the LORD shall be revealed,
　　and all people shall see it together;
　　for the mouth of the LORD has spoken.

Go up on to a high mountain,
　　Zion,* herald of glad tidings;
cry out at the top of your voice,
　　Jerusalem, herald of good news!
Fear not to cry out
　　and say to the cities of Judah:
　　Here is your God!
Here comes with power
　　the Lord GOD,
　　who rules by his strong arm;
here is his reward with him,
　　his recompense before him.
Like a shepherd he feeds his flock;
　　in his arms he gathers the lambs,
carrying them in his bosom,
　　and leading the ewes with care.
The word of the Lord. *Thanks be to God.*

RESPONSORIAL PSALM *(Psalm 85:9-10, 11-12, 13-14)*
℟ Lord, let us see your kindness, and grant us your salvation.

I will hear what God proclaims;
　　the LORD—for he proclaims peace to his people.
Near indeed is his salvation to those who fear him,
　　glory dwelling in our land. ℟
Kindness and truth shall meet;
　　justice and peace shall kiss.
Truth shall spring out of the earth,

and justice shall look down from heaven.

℟ **Lord, let us see your kindness, and grant us your salvation.**

The LORD himself will give his benefits;

our land shall yield its increase.

Justice shall walk before him,

and prepare the way of his steps. ℟

SECOND READING *(2 Peter 3:8–14)*

Do not ignore this one fact, beloved, that with the Lord one day is like a thousand years and a thousand years like one day. The Lord does not delay his promise, as some regard "delay," but he is patient with you, not wishing that any should perish but that all should come to repentance. But the day of the Lord will come like a thief, and then the heavens will pass away with a mighty roar and the elements will be dissolved by fire, and the earth and everything done on it will be found out.

Since everything is to be dissolved in this way, what sort of persons ought you to be, conducting yourselves in holiness and devotion, waiting for and hastening the coming of the day of God, because of which the heavens will be dissolved in flames and the elements melted by fire. But according to his promise we await new heavens and a new earth in which righteousness dwells. Therefore, beloved, since you await these things, be eager to be found without spot or blemish before him, at peace.

The word of the Lord. ***Thanks be to God.***

ALLELUIA *(Luke 3:4, 6)*

Alleluia, alleluia. Prepare the way of the Lord, make straight his paths: all flesh shall see the salvation of God. *Alleluia, alleluia.*

GOSPEL *(Mark 1:1–8)*

A reading from the holy Gospel according to Mark.
Glory to you, O Lord.

The beginning of the gospel of Jesus Christ the Son of God. As it is written in Isaiah the prophet:

Behold, I am sending my messenger ahead of you;
he will prepare your way.
A voice of one crying out in the desert:
"Prepare the way of the Lord,
make straight his paths."

John the Baptist appeared in the desert proclaiming a baptism of **repentance**✠ for the forgiveness of sins. People of the whole Judean* countryside and all the inhabitants of Jerusalem were going out to him and were being baptized by him in the Jordan River as they acknowledged their sins. John was clothed in camel's hair, with a leather belt around his waist. He fed on locusts and wild honey. And this is what he proclaimed: "One mightier than I is coming after me. I am not worthy to stoop and loosen the thongs of his sandals. I have baptized you with water; he will baptize you with the Holy Spirit."

The Gospel of the Lord. *Praise to you, Lord Jesus Christ.*

PROFESSION OF FAITH *(page 13)*

PRAYER OF THE FAITHFUL

PREPARATION OF GIFTS *(page 16)*

PRAYER OVER THE OFFERINGS

Be pleased, O Lord, with our humble prayers and offerings,
and, since we have no merits to plead our cause,
come, we pray, to our rescue
with the protection of your mercy.
Through Christ our Lord. *Amen.*

PREFACE *(Advent 1, page 17)*

COMMUNION ANTIPHON *(Baruch 5:5; 4:36)*

Jerusalem, arise and stand upon the heights, and behold the joy
which comes to you from God.

• TAKING A CLOSER LOOK •

✢ **Repentance** Because we tend to limit the meaning of
repentance to being sorry for something, repentance is a somewhat
inadequate translation of the Greek word *metanoia*, which describes
a change of mind and heart and attitude demanded by personal conversion. It demands a re-forming of our self and our life by turning toward God and away from the evil forces that pervade our world. It is
a lifelong challenge to order ourselves and our world according to the
vision and values of Jesus and live out the obligations of belonging to
his community of disciples.

PRAYER AFTER COMMUNION
Replenished by the food of spiritual nourishment,
we humbly beseech you, O Lord,
that, through our partaking in this mystery,
you may teach us to judge wisely the things of earth
and hold firm to the things of heaven.
Through Christ our Lord. *Amen.*

SOLEMN BLESSING: ADVENT *(Optional, page 57)*

DISMISSAL *(page 57)* ✠

• RESPONDING TO THE WORD •

Isaiah encourages us to prepare the way of the Lord.

➡ *What preparations can I make to invite Jesus to be more present in my life this week?*

Paul tells us that God's timetable is not like ours.

➡ *When has God surprised me with the divine presence?*

John the Baptist invites us to repent—to turn from what separates us from God.

➡ *What most hinders my relationship with God now?*

December 17

Make straight the way of the Lord!

As Christians, we recognize the season of Advent as a time of great anticipation in which we prepare for the coming of the Lord. In today's gospel, John the Baptist calls us to "make straight the way of the Lord." This call to action is not easy in an ever-growing secular world.

Although it should be the very opposite, the season of Advent is perhaps the most difficult time of year to rise and meet John's call. More often than not, today's reality is one where the season of Advent is inundated with commercialism and anything but Christ. To remain focused while we await the coming of the Lord is increasingly difficult and requires humility, discipline, and patience. Deepening these qualities in ourselves requires a great deal of practice and prayer.

If we are to lead a virtuous Christian life then we must follow John's example: he displayed humility, discipline, and patience when responding to those who questioned him. In the midst of this heavily commercialized Advent season, let us persevere in prayer and practice as we celebrate and share the coming of the Lord with everyone we encounter.

■ DANA KENNY

ENTRANCE ANTIPHON *(Philippians 4:4–5)*

Rejoice in the Lord always; again I say, rejoice.
Indeed, the Lord is near.

INTRODUCTORY RITES *(page 10)*

COLLECT

O God, who see how your people
faithfully await the feast of the Lord's Nativity,
enable us, we pray,
to attain the joys of so great a salvation
and to celebrate them always
with solemn worship and glad rejoicing.
Through our Lord Jesus Christ, your Son,
who lives and reigns with you in the unity of the Holy Spirit,
one God, for ever and ever. *Amen.*

FIRST READING *(Isaiah 61:1-2a, 10-11)*

The spirit of the Lord GOD is upon me,
    because the LORD has anointed me;
he has sent me to bring glad tidings to the poor,
    to heal the brokenhearted,
to proclaim liberty to the captives
    and release to the prisoners,
to announce a year of favor from the LORD
    and a day of vindication by our God.

I rejoice heartily in the LORD,
    in my God is the joy of my soul;
for he has clothed me with a robe of salvation
    and wrapped me in a mantle of justice,
like a bridegroom adorned with a diadem,

like a bride bedecked with her jewels.
As the earth brings forth its plants,
    and a garden makes its growth spring up,
so will the Lord GOD make justice and praise
    spring up before all the nations.
The word of the Lord. *Thanks be to God.*

RESPONSORIAL PSALM *(Luke 1:46–48, 49–50, 53–54)*
℟ **My soul rejoices in my God.**

My soul proclaims the greatness of the Lord;
    my spirit rejoices in God my Savior,
for he has looked upon his lowly servant.
    From this day all generations will call me blessed. ℟
The Almighty has done great things for me,
    and holy is his Name.
He has mercy on those who fear him
    in every generation. ℟
He has filled the hungry with good things,
    and the rich he has sent away empty.
He has come to the help of his servant Israel
    for he has remembered his promise of mercy. ℟

SECOND READING *(1 Thessalonians 5:16–24)*

Brothers and sisters: Rejoice always. Pray without ceasing. In all circumstances give thanks, for this is the will of God for you in Christ Jesus. Do not quench the Spirit. Do not despise prophetic utterances. Test everything; retain what is good. Refrain from every kind of evil.

May the God of peace make you perfectly holy and may you entirely, **spirit, soul, and body,** ☩ be preserved blameless for the coming of our Lord Jesus Christ. The one who calls you is faithful, and he will also accomplish it.

The word of the Lord. *Thanks be to God.*

ALLELUIA *(Isaiah 61:1)*
Alleluia, alleluia. The Spirit of the Lord is upon me, because he has anointed me to bring glad tidings to the poor. *Alleluia, alleluia.*

GOSPEL *(John 1:6-8, 19-28)*
A reading from the holy Gospel according to Mark.
Glory to you, O Lord.

A man named John was sent from God. He came for testimony, to testify to the light, so that all might believe through him. He was not the light, but came to testify to the light.

And this is the testimony of John. When the Jews from Jerusalem sent priests and Levites* to him to ask him, "Who are you?" he admitted and did not deny it, but admitted, "I am not the Christ." So they asked him, "What are you then? Are you Elijah?" And he said, "I am not." "Are you the Prophet?" He answered, "No." So they said to him, "Who are you, so we can give an answer to those who sent us? What do you have to say for yourself?" He said:

"I am *the voice of one crying out in the desert,*
'make straight the way of the Lord,'
as Isaiah the prophet said." Some Pharisees were also sent. They asked him, "Why then do you baptize if you are not the Christ or Elijah or the Prophet?" John answered them, "I baptize with water; but there is one among you whom you do not recognize, the one who is coming after me, whose sandal strap I am not worthy to untie." This happened in Bethany* across the Jordan, where John was baptizing.

The Gospel of the Lord. *Praise to you, Lord Jesus Christ.*

PROFESSION OF FAITH *(page 13)*

PRAYER OF THE FAITHFUL

PREPARATION OF GIFTS *(page 16)*

PRAYER OVER THE OFFERINGS
May the sacrifice of our worship, Lord, we pray,
be offered to you unceasingly,
to complete what was begun in sacred mystery
and powerfully accomplish for us your saving work.
Through Christ our Lord. *Amen.*

PREFACE *(Advent 2, page 18)*

• TAKING A CLOSER LOOK •

✟ **Spirit, soul, and body** In our world, we normally describe a human being as composed of body and soul (in which we include all mental and emotional aspects). But Paul follows a slightly different Jewish tradition, identifying the entirety of a person as spirit, soul, and body. These are not three elements blended together, but rather three ways of understanding the entirety of a person in relation to the material or biological realm (Greek, *soma*, "body") and the vital energy for living (*psyche*, "soul"), which are breathed into us through God's Spirit (*pneuma*, "breath or wind," see Genesis 2:7), which then dwells in us and permeates all of these other aspects so that we live in the Spirit (Romans 8:9).

COMMUNION ANTIPHON *(Cf. Isaiah 35:4)*
Say to the faint of heart: Be strong and do not fear. Behold, our
God will come, and he will save us.

PRAYER AFTER COMMUNION
We implore your mercy, Lord,
that this divine sustenance may cleanse us of our faults
and prepare us for the coming feasts.
Through Christ our Lord. *Amen.*

SOLEMN BLESSING: ADVENT *(Optional, page 57)*

DISMISSAL *(page 57)* ⊹

• RESPONDING TO THE WORD •

Isaiah's life is changed because God's Spirit empowers him.	Paul advises us not to quench the Holy Spirit.	John urges us to "make straight the way of the Lord."
➡ *How has God's Spirit empowered me?*	➡ *How have I been hesitant to let God's Spirit work in me this Advent?*	➡ *What needs to be straightened so God can come more easily to me?*

December 24

God has a plan for each of us

"The Lord is with you." One can only imagine how Mary felt receiving this knowledge. Despite her lowliness, she was chosen to give birth to the Son of God. She was perplexed and moved by what she heard, yet Mary accepted the tremendous responsibility and proclaimed a joyful "yes." Mary's faithful response to God's call carried her through life when, years later, she watched her son be put to death. Even then she drew on God for strength.

Just as Mary felt perplexed by the angel's greeting, we too can feel overwhelmed by the intense love God has for us. Tomorrow, we gather at the crèche and celebrate that the Word of God took on human form to be present with us. And then, after dying for our sins on the cross, Jesus remains with us through the Eucharist. The Lord is always with us.

It is astonishing to think that, regardless of our failings, we are not alone. As Advent comes to a close, may we allow ourselves to find peace in the knowledge that God has a plan for each one of us and that the love of God will not lead us astray. God is with us every hour of the day, and we need only ask for the strength and hope that will allow us to overcome our challenges.

■ ELIZABETH CHESLEY-JEWELL

ENTRANCE ANTIPHON *(Cf. Isaiah 45:8)*

Drop down dew from above, you heavens, and let the clouds rain down the Just One; let the earth be opened and bring forth a Savior.

INTRODUCTORY RITES *(page 10)*

COLLECT

Pour forth, we beseech you, O Lord,
your grace into our hearts,
that we, to whom the Incarnation of Christ your Son
was made known by the message of an Angel,
may by his Passion and Cross
be brought to the glory of his Resurrection.
Who lives and reigns with you in the unity of the Holy Spirit,
one God, for ever and ever. *Amen.*

FIRST READING *(2 Samuel 7:1-5, 8b-12, 14a, 16)*

When King David was settled in his palace, and the LORD had given him rest from his enemies on every side, he said to Nathan the prophet, "Here I am living in a house of cedar, while **the ark of God dwells in a tent!**" Nathan answered the king, "Go, do whatever you have in mind, for the LORD is with you." But that night the LORD spoke to Nathan and said: "Go, tell my servant David, 'Thus says the LORD: Should you build me a house to dwell in?

" 'It was I who took you from the pasture and from the care of the flock to be commander of my people Israel. I have been with you wherever you went, and I have destroyed all your enemies before you. And I will make you famous like the great ones of the earth. I will fix a place for my people Israel; I will plant them so that they may dwell in their place without further disturbance.

Neither shall the wicked continue to afflict them as they did of old, since the time I first appointed judges over my people Israel. I will give you rest from all your enemies. The LORD also reveals to you that he will establish a house for you. And when your time comes and you rest with your ancestors, I will raise up your heir after you, sprung from your loins, and I will make his kingdom firm. I will be a father to him, and he shall be a son to me. Your house and your kingdom shall endure forever before me; your throne shall stand firm forever.'"

The word of the Lord. *Thanks be to God.*

RESPONSORIAL PSALM *(Psalm 24:1-2, 3-4, 5-6)*
℟ **For ever I will sing the goodness of the Lord.**

The promises of the LORD I will sing forever;
    through all generations my mouth shall proclaim
        your faithfulness.
For you have said, "My kindness is established forever";
    in heaven you have confirmed your faithfulness. ℟
"I have made a covenant with my chosen one,
    I have sworn to David my servant:
forever will I confirm your posterity
    and establish your throne for all generations." ℟
"He shall say of me, 'You are my father,
    my God, the Rock, my savior.'
Forever I will maintain my kindness toward him,
    and my covenant with him stands firm." ℟

SECOND READING *(Romans 16:25-27)*

Brothers and sisters: To him who can strengthen you, according to my gospel and the proclamation of Jesus Christ, according to the revelation of the mystery kept secret for long ages but now manifested through the prophetic writings and, according to the command of the eternal God, made known to all nations to bring about the obedience of faith, to the only wise God, through Jesus Christ be glory forever and ever. Amen.

The word of the Lord. *Thanks be to God.*

ALLELUIA *(Luke 1:38)*

Alleluia, alleluia. Behold, I am the handmaid of the Lord. May it be done to me according to your word. *Alleluia, alleluia.*

GOSPEL *(Luke 1:26–38)*

A reading from the holy Gospel according to Luke.
Glory to you, O Lord.

The angel Gabriel was sent from God to a town of Galilee called Nazareth, to a virgin betrothed to a man named Joseph, of the house of David, and the virgin's name was Mary. And coming to her, he said, "Hail, full of grace! The Lord is with you." But she was greatly troubled at what was said and pondered what sort of greeting this might be. Then the angel said to her, "Do not be afraid, Mary, for you have found favor with God.

"Behold, you will conceive in your womb and bear a son, and you shall name him Jesus. He will be great and will be called Son of the Most High, and the Lord God will give him the throne of David his father, and he will rule over the house of Jacob forever, and of his kingdom there will be no end." But Mary said to the angel, "How can this be, since I have no relations with a man?" And the angel said to her in reply, "The Holy Spirit will come upon you, and the power of the Most High will overshadow you. Therefore the child to be born will be called holy, the Son of God. And behold, Elizabeth, your relative, has also conceived a son in her old age, and this is the sixth month for her who was called barren; for nothing will be impossible for God." Mary said, "Behold, I am the handmaid of the Lord. May it be done to me according to your word." Then the angel departed from her.

The Gospel of the Lord. *Praise to you, Lord Jesus Christ.*

PROFESSION OF FAITH *(page 13)*

PRAYER OF THE FAITHFUL

PREPARATION OF GIFTS *(page 16)*

PRAYER OVER THE OFFERINGS

May the Holy Spirit, O Lord,
sanctify these gifts laid upon your altar,
just as he filled with his power the womb of the Blessed Virgin Mary.
Through Christ our Lord. *Amen.*

• TAKING A CLOSER LOOK •

✛ **The ark of God dwells in a tent** The ark was an ornate portable box containing the tablets of the covenant commandments (Exodus 25). It was also thought of as a throne for God to sit on when Moses and the people met with God in the tent of meeting. This tent was a movable dwelling for God until the people became settled and prosperous. Then it was replaced by the Jerusalem Temple that was God's permanent "house."

PREFACE *(Advent 2, page 18)*

COMMUNION ANTIPHON *(Isaiah 7:14)*

Behold, a Virgin shall conceive and bear a son; and his name will
be called Emmanuel.

PRAYER AFTER COMMUNION

Having received this pledge of eternal redemption,
we pray, almighty God,
that, as the feast day of our salvation draws ever nearer,
so we may press forward all the more eagerly
to the worthy celebration of the mystery of your Son's Nativity.
Who lives and reigns for ever and ever. *Amen.*

SOLEMN BLESSING: ADVENT *(Optional, page 57)*

DISMISSAL *(page 57)* ❖

❖ RESPONDING TO THE WORD ❖

God desires to dwell within us.	Paul gives praise to God for God's presence among us.	Mary gives herself completely to God's plans for her.
➡ *What can I do this week to prepare myself for God's indwelling?*	➡ *For what would I like to give praise to God?*	➡ *What is God inviting me to do to share in Christ's work now?*

Christ's light shines in the darkness

C hristmas celebrates God's becoming incarnate in time and history. The God who promised to be among us has come and continues to be with us, now and always, through Jesus and the Holy Spirit.

As the shortest days of the year end and the light of a new year begins, we celebrate Christ's presence with us to transform our world. The darkness of sin and the reign of evil now must confront the light of the nations and the reign of God. Where Christ's light is allowed to shine, the dark shadows of sin will be illumined, allowing us to live in the light. So each day, as the light intensifies, we proclaim that "Christ's light shines in the darkness, and the darkness has not overcome it" (John 1:5).

Like John the Baptist, we too are called "to testify to the light, so that all might believe through him" (John 1:7). Our testimony to Christ's light will be evident in our words and in our actions. As we are more and more enlightened by Christ, we become beacons of hope for others in a world still steeped in darkness.

Our lives are Christmas in miniature. We are invited to let God enlighten us so that we become "divinized" persons, full of the gift of the divine life and its power to change us completely. In us, God makes an appeal to all humanity to enter into this new life and live in God's light.

Praying and living the Christmas season

The twelve days between Christmas and Epiphany are a special time to celebrate Jesus as God's great gift to us and share gifts with one another. This reminds us that Eucharist (Greek for "thanksgiving") sums up our Christian lives. Let us focus our attention on God's everyday gifts to us and the gifts that we in turn receive and give. As we become more and more attentive to these gifts, we will also grow in our attitude of gratitude and be more aware of how much we have to be thankful for when we celebrate Eucharist.

Whenever your household gathers for a meal or your faith-sharing group meets, take time to thank God for being present in your daily lives. You may wish to do this as part of your grace (another word for "gift"!) before the meal.

INVITATION TO PRAYER

Leader: Jesus said, "I am the light of the world. Whoever follows me will not walk in darkness, but will have the light of life." *(John 8:12)*

All: Thanks be to God for this indescribable gift!

AROUND THE TABLE *Invite each member of the household or group to respond to these questions:*

- What gifts did I receive today from others? from God?
- How did I express my gratitude?
- What gifts did I give today to others? to God?

THINGS TO DO *Each day find one way to give a small gift of time, attention, or care for someone in the household, at work, or at school.*

December 25

The Word was made flesh...

It happened in the third year before his death. The year was 1223. The place: Greccio, Italy. Francis of Assisi wanted to awaken the faith and devotion of the people. He desired to celebrate with the greatest solemnity the memory of the birth of the Child Jesus and have the people experience the stable at Bethlehem.

Francis had a crib prepared with hay, an ox, and a donkey. The Friars gathered and the people of Greccio came with candles and lanterns, lighting up the night and singing as they arrived at the crib. Francis stood before the crib, filled with affection and overflowing with joy.

Mass was celebrated, and Francis, as deacon, read the gospel and preached with fervor about the humility of Jesus, whom he called the Child of Bethlehem. Francis spoke with such tenderness and power that it became evident it was not he but the Spirit of God who was speaking.

It is said that Francis of Assisi went over to the crib and picked up the figure of the child Jesus, and it seemed to wake from sleep. The continuation of Francis' re-enactment of the birth of Jesus still awakens a love for the Child Jesus in the hearts of people.

"And the Word became flesh and made his dwelling among us."

■ FRIAR ED DEBONO, OFM CONV.

MASS DURING THE NIGHT

ENTRANCE ANTIPHON *(Psalm 2:7)*

The Lord said to me: You are my Son. It is I who have begotten you this day.

Or

Let us all rejoice in the Lord, for our Savior has been born in the world. Today true peace has come down to us from heaven.

INTRODUCTORY RITES *(page 10)*

COLLECT

O God, who have made this most sacred night
radiant with the splendor of the true light,
grant, we pray, that we, who have known the mysteries of his
   light on earth,
may also delight in his gladness in heaven.
Who lives and reigns with you in the unity of the Holy Spirit,
one God, for ever and ever. *Amen.*

FIRST READING *(Isaiah 9:1-6)*

The people who walked in darkness
   have seen a great light;
upon those who dwelt in the land of gloom
   a light has shone.
You have brought them abundant joy
   and great rejoicing,
as they rejoice before you as at the harvest,
   as people make merry when dividing spoils.
For the yoke that burdened them,
   the pole on their shoulder,

and the rod of their taskmaster
    you have smashed, as on the day of Midian.*
For every boot that tramped in battle,
    every cloak rolled in blood,
    will be burned as fuel for flames.
For a child is born to us, a son is given us;
    upon his shoulder dominion rests.
They name him Wonder-Counselor, God-Hero,
    Father-Forever, Prince of Peace.
His dominion is vast
    and forever peaceful,
from David's throne, and over his kingdom,
    which he confirms and sustains
by judgment and justice,
    both now and forever.
The zeal of the LORD of hosts will do this!
The word of the Lord. *Thanks be to God.*

RESPONSORIAL PSALM *(Psalm 96:1-2, 2-3, 11-12, 13)*
℟ **Today is born our Savior, Christ the Lord.**

Sing to the LORD a new song;
    sing to the LORD, all you lands.
Sing to the LORD; bless his name. ℟
Announce his salvation, day after day.
    Tell his **glory**✠ among the nations;
    among all peoples, his wondrous deeds. ℟
Let the heavens be glad and the earth rejoice;
    let the sea and what fills it resound;
    let the plains be joyful and all that is in them!
Then shall all the trees of the forest exult. ℟

They shall exult before the LORD, for he comes;
for he comes to rule the earth.
He shall rule the world with justice
and the peoples with his constancy. ℟

SECOND READING *(Titus 2:11-14)*

Beloved: The grace of God has appeared, saving all and training us to reject godless ways and worldly desires and to live temperately, justly, and devoutly in this age, as we await the blessed hope, the appearance of the **glory**✝ of our great God and savior Jesus Christ, who gave himself for us to deliver us from all lawlessness and to cleanse for himself a people as his own, eager to do what is good.

The word of the Lord. *Thanks be to God.*

ALLELUIA *(Luke 2:10-11)*
Alleluia, alleluia. I proclaim to you good news of great joy: today a Savior is born for us, Christ the Lord. *Alleluia, alleluia.*

GOSPEL *(Luke 2:1-14)*
A reading from the holy Gospel according to Luke.
Glory to you, O Lord.

In those days a decree went out from Caesar* Augustus that the whole world should be enrolled. This was the first enrollment, when Quirinius* was governor of Syria. So all went to be enrolled, each to his own town. And Joseph too went up from Galilee from the town of Nazareth to Judea, to the city of David that is called Bethlehem, because he was of the house and family of David, to be enrolled with Mary, his betrothed, who was with child. While they were there, the time came for her to have her child, and she gave birth to her firstborn son. She wrapped him in swaddling clothes and laid him in a manger, because there was no room for them in the inn.

Now there were shepherds in that region living in the fields and keeping the night watch over their flock. The angel of the Lord appeared to them and the glory of the Lord shone around them, and they were struck with great fear. The angel said to them, "Do not be afraid; for behold, I proclaim to you good news of great joy that will be for all the people. For today in the city of David a savior has been born for you who is Christ and Lord. And this will be a sign for you: you will find an infant wrapped in swaddling clothes and lying in a manger." And suddenly there was a multitude of the heavenly host with the angel, praising God and saying:

"**Glory** ✣ to God in the highest
   and on earth peace to those on whom his favor rests."
The Gospel of the Lord. ***Praise to you, Lord Jesus Christ.***

PROFESSION OF FAITH *(page 13)*

PRAYER OF THE FAITHFUL

PREPARATION OF GIFTS *(page 16)*

PRAYER OVER THE OFFERINGS
May the oblation of this day's feast

⸳⸳⸳⸳⸳⸳⸳⸳⸳⸳⸳⸳⸳⸳⸳⸳⸳⸳⸳⸳ ● TAKING A CLOSER LOOK ● ⸳⸳⸳⸳⸳⸳⸳⸳⸳⸳⸳⸳⸳⸳⸳⸳⸳⸳⸳⸳

✣ **Glory** In Hebrew, the word "glory" describes someone's inner worth or importance. When applied to humans, it can be associated with what gives a person dignity and commands respect, such as honor, wealth, or wisdom. When glory is associated with God, the meaning becomes more complex. Glory describes the essence of God's divinity that requires us to respect and honor God. But glory also points to the visible manifestation of God's invisible presence, for example in the cloud and pillar of fire leading the Hebrews during the Exodus. In today's second reading, Paul awaits the glory or reappearance of the risen Christ.

be pleasing to you, O Lord, we pray,
that through this most holy exchange
we may be found in the likeness of Christ,
in whom our nature is united to you.
Who lives and reigns for ever and ever. *Amen.*

PREFACE *(Nativity of the Lord 1–3, pages 19–20)*

COMMUNION ANTIPHON *(John 1:14)*
The Word became flesh, and we have seen his glory.

PRAYER AFTER COMMUNION
Grant us, we pray, O Lord our God,
that we, who are gladdened by participation
in the feast of our Redeemer's Nativity,
may through an honorable way of life become worthy of union
    with him.
Who lives and reigns for ever and ever. *Amen.*

SOLEMN BLESSING: THE NATIVITY OF THE LORD *(Optional, page 58)*

DISMISSAL *(page 57)* ✵

• RESPONDING TO THE WORD •

Isaiah understands how God's presence, like light in darkness, changes the way we see everything.

➦ How has knowing Christ made my life seem clearer?

Paul understands how accepting Christ means rejecting godless ways.

➦ What unhelpful behaviors have I rejected to follow Christ's ways?

God's revelation of Jesus to his family and to the shepherds changed them completely.

➦ How has Jesus' entrance into my life changed me?

MASS AT DAWN

ENTRANCE ANTIPHON *(Cf. Isaiah 9:1, 5; Luke 1:33)*

Today a light will shine upon us, for the Lord is born for us;
and he will be called Wondrous God, Prince of peace, Father of
future ages; and his reign will be without end.

INTRODUCTORY RITES *(page 10)*

COLLECT

Grant, we pray, almighty God,
that, as we are bathed in the new radiance of your incarnate Word,
the light of faith, which illumines our minds,
may also shine through in our deeds.
Through our Lord Jesus Christ, your Son,
who lives and reigns with you in the unity of the Holy Spirit,
one God, for ever and ever. *Amen.*

FIRST READING *(Isaiah 62:11-12)*

See, the LORD proclaims
to the ends of the earth:
say to daughter Zion,*
your savior comes!
Here is his reward with him,
his recompense before him.
They shall be called the holy people,
the redeemed of the LORD,
and you shall be called "Frequented,"
a city that is not forsaken.
The word of the Lord. *Thanks be to God.*

RESPONSORIAL PSALM *(Psalm 97:1, 6, 11–12)*

℞ A light will shine on us this day: the Lord is born for us.

The LORD is king; let the earth rejoice;
　　let the many isles be glad.
The heavens proclaim his justice,
　　and all peoples see his glory. ℞

Light dawns for the just;
　　and gladness, for the upright of heart.
Be glad in the LORD, you just,
　　and give thanks to his holy name. ℞

SECOND READING *(Titus 3:4–7)*

Beloved:
　　When the kindness and generous love
of God our savior appeared,
not because of any righteous deeds we had done
　　but because of his mercy,
he saved us through the bath of rebirth
　　and renewal by the Holy Spirit,
whom he richly poured out on us
　　through Jesus Christ our savior,
so that we might be justified by his grace
　　and become heirs in hope of eternal life.
　　The word of the Lord. *Thanks be to God.*

ALLELUIA *(Luke 2:14)*

Alleluia, alleluia. Glory to God in the highest, and on earth
peace to those on whom his favor rests. *Alleluia, alleluia.*

GOSPEL *(Luke 2:15–20)*

A reading from the holy Gospel according to Luke.
Glory to you, O Lord.

When the angels went away from them to heaven, the shepherds said to one another, "Let us go, then, to Bethlehem to see this thing that has taken place, which the Lord has made known to us." So they went in haste and found Mary and Joseph, and the infant lying in the manger. When they saw this, they made known the message that had been told them about this child. All who heard it were amazed by what had been told them by the shepherds. And Mary kept all these things, reflecting on them in her **heart**.✠ Then the shepherds returned, glorifying and praising God for all they had heard and seen, just as it had been told to them.

The Gospel of the Lord. *Praise to you, Lord Jesus Christ.*

PROFESSION OF FAITH *(page 13)*

PRAYER OF THE FAITHFUL

PREPARATION OF GIFTS *(page 16)*

PRAYER OVER THE OFFERINGS
May our offerings be worthy, we pray, O Lord,

• TAKING A CLOSER LOOK •

✠ **Heart** For biblical people, the heart did not just identify the physical organ but rather the psychological activity associated with it. Since the heart was associated with emotional changes (speeding up when we are excited) and physical life (ceasing to beat when we die), "heart" became a general word to identify the location of the distinctively human activities of feeling, thinking, and deciding. Today we might describe this as the "self." So Mary reflects deeply within her "self" about these wondrous experiences arising from her mysterious relationship with Jesus.

of the mysteries of the Nativity this day,
that, just as Christ was born a man and also shone forth as God,
so these earthly gifts may confer on us what is divine.
Through Christ our Lord. *Amen.*

PREFACE *(Nativity of the Lord 1–3, pages 19–20)*

COMMUNION ANTIPHON *(Cf. Zechariah 9:9)*

Rejoice, O Daughter Sion; lift up praise, Daughter Jerusalem:
Behold, your King will come, the Holy One and Savior of the
world.

PRAYER AFTER COMMUNION

Grant us, Lord, as we honor with joyful devotion
the Nativity of your Son,
that we may come to know with fullness of faith
the hidden depths of this mystery
and to love them ever more and more.
Through Christ our Lord. *Amen.*

SOLEMN BLESSING: THE NATIVITY OF THE LORD *(Optional, page 58)*

DISMISSAL *(page 57)* ✦

✦ RESPONDING TO THE WORD ✦

God's presence brings salvation and makes us a holy people.	Paul reminds us we are reborn in the Holy Spirit.	Mary treasured her spiritual experience in her heart.
▸ *How have I grown in holiness this past year?*	▸ *How has the power of God's Holy Spirit made me feel more full of spiritual energy?*	▸ *How will I make more time to treasure my spiritual experience in prayer this year?*

MASS DURING THE DAY

ENTRANCE ANTIPHON *(Cf. Isaiah 9:5)*

A child is born for us, and a son is given to us; his scepter of power rests upon his shoulder, and his name will be called Messenger of great counsel.

INTRODUCTORY RITES *(page 10)*

COLLECT

O God, who wonderfully created the dignity of human nature
and still more wonderfully restored it,
grant, we pray,
that we may share in the divinity of Christ,
who humbled himself to share in our humanity.
Who lives and reigns with you in the unity of the Holy Spirit,
one God, for ever and ever. ***Amen.***

FIRST READING *(Isaiah 52:7–10)*

How beautiful upon the mountains
are the feet of him who brings glad tidings,
announcing peace, bearing good news,
announcing salvation, and saying to Zion,*
"Your God is King!"

Hark! Your sentinels raise a cry,
together they shout for joy,
for they see directly, before their eyes,
the LORD restoring Zion.
Break out together in song,
O ruins of Jerusalem!
For the LORD comforts his people,

he redeems Jerusalem.
The LORD has bared his holy arm
  in the sight of all the nations;
all the ends of the earth will behold
  the salvation of our God.
The word of the Lord. *Thanks be to God.*

RESPONSORIAL PSALM *(Psalm 98:1, 2-3, 3-4, 5-6)*

℟ **All the ends of the earth have seen the saving power of God.**

Sing to the LORD a new song,
  for he has done wondrous deeds;
his right hand has won victory for him,
  his holy arm. ℟
The LORD has made his salvation known:
  in the sight of the nations he has revealed his justice.
He has remembered his kindness and his faithfulness
  toward the house of Israel. ℟
All the ends of the earth have seen
  the salvation by our God.
Sing joyfully to the LORD, all you lands;
  break into song; sing praise. ℟
Sing praise to the LORD with the harp,
  with the harp and melodious song.
With trumpets and the sound of the horn
  sing joyfully before the King, the LORD. ℟

SECOND READING *(Hebrews 1:1-6)*

Brothers and sisters: In times past, God spoke in partial and various ways to our ancestors through the prophets; in these last days, he has spoken to us through the Son, whom he made heir of all things and through whom he created the universe,

who is the refulgence of his glory, the very imprint of his being,
and who sustains all things by his mighty word.
When he had accomplished purification from sins,
he took his seat at the right hand of the Majesty on high,
as far superior to the angels
as the name he has inherited is more excellent than theirs.

For to which of the angels did God ever say:
You are my son; this day I have begotten you?
Or again:
I will be a father to him, and he shall be a son to me?
And again, when he leads the firstborn into the world, he says:
Let all the angels of God worship him.
The word of the Lord. *Thanks be to God.*

ALLELUIA
Alleluia, alleluia. A holy day has dawned upon us. Come, you
nations, and adore the Lord. For today a great light has come
upon the earth. *Alleluia, alleluia.*

GOSPEL *(John 1:1–18)*
For the shorter reading, omit the indented parts in brackets.

A reading from the holy Gospel according to John.
Glory to you, O Lord.

In the beginning was the Word,
and the Word was with God,
and the Word was God.
He was in the beginning with God.
All things came to be through him,
and without him nothing came to be.
What came to be through him was life,

and this life was the light of the human race;
the light shines in the darkness,
    and the darkness has not overcome it.
[A man named John was sent from God. He came for testimony, to testify to the light, so that all might believe through him. He was not the light, but came to testify to the light.]
The true light, which enlightens everyone, was coming into the world.

He was in the world,
    and the world came to be through him,
    but the world did not know him.
He came to what was his own,
    but his own people did not accept him.

But to those who did accept him he gave power to become children of God, to those who believe in his name, who were born not by natural generation nor by human choice nor by a man's decision but of God.

And the Word became **flesh** ✛
    and made his dwelling among us,
    and we saw his glory,
    the glory as of the Father's only Son,
    full of grace and truth.
[John testified to him and cried out, saying, "This was he of whom I said, 'The one who is coming after me ranks ahead of me because he existed before me.'" From his fullness we have all received, grace in place of grace, because while the law was given through Moses, grace and truth came through Jesus Christ. No one has ever seen God. The only Son, God, who is at the Father's side, has revealed him.]
The Gospel of the Lord. *Praise to you, Lord Jesus Christ.*

PROFESSION OF FAITH *(page 13)*

PRAYER OF THE FAITHFUL

PREPARATION OF GIFTS *(page 16)*

PRAYER OVER THE OFFERINGS

Make acceptable, O Lord, our oblation on this solemn day,
when you manifested the reconciliation
that makes us wholly pleasing in your sight
and inaugurated for us the fullness of divine worship.
Through Christ our Lord. *Amen.*

PREFACE *(Nativity of the Lord 1–3, pages 19–20)*

● TAKING A CLOSER LOOK ●

✢ **Flesh** The word "flesh" does not just refer to the skin but is often used to describe the whole living human body (hence "flesh and blood" to describe a whole living person). But flesh also describes what is corruptible (for we all die) and prone to sin (for we are not perfect). Because "flesh" describes the reality of human existence, it is appropriate to highlight Jesus' becoming human. But because "flesh" points to that which moves us toward sin and alienation from God, it is startling to apply this to Jesus. Normally, God and flesh would not go together, but in the divine-human reality of Jesus they must.

COMMUNION ANTIPHON *(Cf. Psalm 98 [97]:3)*
All the ends of the earth have seen the salvation of our God.

PRAYER AFTER COMMUNION
Grant, O merciful God,
that, just as the Savior of the world, born this day,
is the author of divine generation for us,
so he may be the giver even of immortality.
Who lives and reigns for ever and ever. *Amen.*

SOLEMN BLESSING: THE NATIVITY OF THE LORD *(Optional, page 58)*

DISMISSAL *(page 57)* ✤

• RESPONDING TO THE WORD •

Isaiah foresees a time when God will restore relationships broken by sin.	As God's Word, Jesus summarizes in himself all that God wants to tell us about God's hidden self.	Jesus is the human image of God.
➡ What might I need to do to restore a broken relationship in my life?	➡ How might I listen more attentively to Jesus' words this year?	➡ What particular aspect of God has Jesus revealed to me during this Advent?

December 31

With God, we are more than prepared

I have read all the "what-to-expect" books. Yet nothing prepared me for how utterly *unprepared* I felt as our family-of-now-three walked out of the maternity ward of the hospital.

I did eventually figure out things like diapering and feeding. However, I never felt ready as a parent. I was not ready for the rush of love at my son's first smile, the gripping fear I experienced during a late-night hospital visit, or the overwhelming emotion washing over me as I saw him climb onto the yellow bus on his first day of school. That's the funny thing about parenting. Once you think you have figured it out, the kids are already onto the next stage: crawling, walking, running, driving, dating.

Only now, 22 years later, have I realized only one checklist matters. We read it in today's gospel. Jesus' formative years are summed up in seventeen words: "The child grew and became strong, filled with wisdom; and the favor of God was upon him."

Reflect today on what helps you and your loved ones grow strong in character, rich in wisdom, and eager for God's favor. Know that whatever role or task God doles out, with God we are more than prepared.

■ CAROLINE PIGNAT

ENTRANCE ANTIPHON *(Luke 2:16)*

The shepherds went in haste, and found Mary and
Joseph and the Infant lying in a manger.

INTRODUCTORY RITES *(page 10)*

COLLECT

O God, who were pleased to give us
the shining example of the Holy Family,
graciously grant that we may imitate them
in practicing the virtues of family life and in the bonds of charity,
and so, in the joy of your house,
delight one day in eternal rewards.
Through our Lord Jesus Christ, your Son,
who lives and reigns with you in the unity of the Holy Spirit,
one God, for ever and ever. *Amen.*

*These are the readings for Year B. The first reading, psalm, and second
reading for Year A (Sirach 3:2-6, 12-14; Psalm 128:1-2, 3, 4-5; Colossians
3:12-21 or 3:12-17) may also be used.*

FIRST READING *(Genesis 15:1-6; 21:1-3)*

The word of the LORD came to Abram in a vision, saying:
    "Fear not, Abram!
        I am your shield;
        I will make your reward very great."
But Abram said, "O Lord GOD, what good will your gifts be, if
I keep on being childless and have as my heir the steward of my
house, Eliezer?" Abram continued, "See, you have given me no
offspring, and so one of my servants will be my heir." Then the
word of the LORD came to him: "No, that one shall not be your

heir; your own issue shall be your heir." The LORD took Abram outside and said, "Look up at the sky and count the stars, if you can. Just so," he added, "shall your descendants be." Abram put his faith in the LORD, who credited it to him as an act of righteousness.

The LORD took note of Sarah as he had said he would; he did for her as he had promised. Sarah became pregnant and bore Abraham a son in his old age, at the set time that God had stated. Abraham gave the name Isaac to this son of his whom Sarah bore him.

The word of the Lord. ***Thanks be to God.***

RESPONSORIAL PSALM *(Psalm 105:1-2, 3-4, 6-7, 8-9)*

℟ **The Lord remembers his covenant forever.**

Give thanks to the LORD, invoke his name;
    make known among the nations his deeds.
Sing to him, sing his praise,
    proclaim all his wondrous deeds. ℟

Glory in his holy name;
    rejoice, O hearts that seek the LORD!
Look to the Lord in his strength;
    constantly seek his face. ℟

You descendants of Abraham, his servants,
    sons of Jacob, his chosen ones!
He, the LORD, is our God;
    throughout the earth his judgments prevail. ℟

He remembers forever his covenant
    which he made binding for a thousand generations
which he entered into with Abraham
    and by his oath to Isaac. ℟

SECOND READING *(Hebrews 11:8, 11-12, 17-19)*

Brothers and sisters: By faith Abraham obeyed when he was called to go out to a place that he was to receive as an inheritance; he went out, not knowing where he was to go. By faith he received power to generate, even though he was past the normal age—and Sarah herself was sterile—for he thought that the one who had made the promise was trustworthy. So it was that there came forth from one man, himself as good as dead, descendants as numerous as the stars in the sky and as countless as the sands on the seashore.

By faith Abraham, when put to the test, offered up Isaac, and he who had received the promises was ready to offer his only son, of whom it was said, "Through Isaac descendants shall bear your name." He reasoned that God was able to raise even from the dead, and he received Isaac back as a symbol.

The word of the Lord. *Thanks be to God.*

ALLELUIA *(Hebrews 1:1-2)*

Alleluia, alleluia. In the past God spoke to our ancestors through the prophets; in these last days, he has spoken to us through the Son. *Alleluia, alleluia.*

GOSPEL *(Luke 2:22-40)*

For the shorter version, omit the indented parts in brackets.

A reading from the holy Gospel according to Luke.
Glory to you, O Lord.

When the days were completed for their **purification**✝ according to the law of Moses, they took him up to Jerusalem to present him to the Lord.

[just as it is written in the law of the Lord, *Every male that opens the womb shall be consecrated to the Lord*, and to offer the sacrifice of *a pair of turtledoves or two young pigeons,* in accordance with the dictate in the law of the Lord.

Now there was a man in Jerusalem whose name was Simeon. This man was righteous and devout, awaiting the consolation of Israel, and the Holy Spirit was upon him. It had been revealed to him by the Holy Spirit that he should not see death before he had seen the Christ of the Lord. He came in the Spirit into the temple; and when the parents brought in the child Jesus to perform the custom of the law in regard to him, he took him into his arms and blessed God, saying:

"Now, Master, you may let your servant go
in peace, according to your word,
for my eyes have seen your salvation,
which you prepared in sight of all the peoples,
a light for revelation to the Gentiles,
and glory for your people Israel."

The child's father and mother were amazed at what was said about him; and Simeon blessed them and said to Mary his mother, "Behold, this child is destined for the fall and rise of many in Israel, and to be a sign that will be contradicted—and you yourself a sword will pierce—so that the thoughts of many hearts may be revealed." There was also a prophetess, Anna, the daughter of Phanuel, of the tribe of Asher. She was advanced in years, having lived seven years with her husband after her marriage, and then as a widow until she was eighty-four. She never left the temple, but worshiped night and day with fasting and prayer. And coming forward at that very time, she gave thanks to God and spoke about the child to all who were awaiting the redemption of Jerusalem.]

When they had fulfilled all the prescriptions of the law of the Lord, they returned to Galilee, to their own town of Nazareth. The child grew and became strong, filled with wisdom; and the favor of God was upon him.

The Gospel of the Lord. ***Praise to you, Lord Jesus Christ.***

PROFESSION OF FAITH *(page 13)*

PRAYER OF THE FAITHFUL

PREPARATION OF GIFTS *(page 16)*

PRAYER OVER THE OFFERINGS

We offer you, Lord, the sacrifice of conciliation,
humbly asking that,
through the intercession of the Virgin Mother of God
    and Saint Joseph,
you may establish our families firmly in your grace and your peace.
Through Christ our Lord. ***Amen.***

PREFACE *(Nativity of the Lord 1–3, pages 19–20)*

• TAKING A CLOSER LOOK •

✚ **Purification** Like many ancient peoples, the Jews had a carefully devised system of meanings that identified and kept order in their lives. When something or someone violated that system, they were "unclean" for a specified time and could not participate in worship until a blessing or a purification rite would reinstate them to the proper relationship with the community. So a mother who gave birth to a boy was ritually "unclean" for forty days (see Leviticus 12:1-8) at which time she brought her purification gift to the priest. Luke reveals that Joseph and Mary fulfill all the ritual obligations of the Jewish law and, from their gift, that they are poor because they could not afford the usual offering of a lamb.

COMMUNION ANTIPHON *(Baruch 3:38)*

Our God has appeared on the earth, and lived among us.

PRAYER AFTER COMMUNION

Bring those you refresh with this heavenly Sacrament,
most merciful Father,
to imitate constantly the example of the Holy Family,
so that, after the trials of this world,
we may share their company for ever.
Through Christ our Lord. *Amen.*

BLESSING & DISMISSAL *(page 56)* ✦

• RESPONDING TO THE WORD •

Abraham's faith and trust created the right relationship with God.	Simeon and Anna rejoice because Jesus has come to them.	Abraham obeyed God even though he did not know where he was going.
➡ *How might I express my trust in God today?*	➡ *How can I share with others how Jesus' presence has changed me and my life?*	➡ *How is God calling me to something new today?*

January 1

Our model of trust in the Lord

Mary, the Mother of God, is honored on this day as well as on many others. Joseph is her spouse, protector, and provider—and foster father to the Son of God. How was it that in spite of all of God's graces poured upon them, all details of God's plan were not known to them?

Our culture fosters a fierce autonomy. It has led to pride, to an independence from God our Father. The way back is difficult because it is frightening for us to live without being in complete control. Yet Mary and Joseph lived in the fullness of the Spirit even though if not in the fullness of knowledge. Mary humbly "kept all these things, reflecting on them in her heart" and continued to live a life trusting in God.

God condescended to become human so that we could enter into God's love through God's humility. The Eucharist exemplifies God's humility and love. Can we live lives of such profound humility? Profound dependence? Can we honor God our Father and Jesus our Lord by remembering the grace of God is alive within us most fully when we live like Mary?

JOHANNE BROWNRIGG

ENTRANCE ANTIPHON

Hail, Holy Mother, who gave birth to the King who rules heaven and earth for ever.

Or *(Cf. Isaiah 9:1, 5; Luke 1:33)*
Today a light will shine upon us, for the Lord is born for us;
and he will be called Wondrous God, Prince of peace, Father of
future ages: and his reign will be without end.

INTRODUCTORY RITES *(page 10)*

COLLECT

O God, who through the fruitful virginity of Blessed Mary
bestowed on the human race
the grace of eternal salvation,
grant, we pray,
that we may experience the intercession of her,
through whom we were found worthy
to receive the author of life,
our Lord Jesus Christ, your Son.
Who lives and reigns with you in the unity of the Holy Spirit,
one God, for ever and ever. *Amen.*

FIRST READING *(Numbers 6:22-27)*

The LORD said to Moses: "Speak to Aaron and his sons and tell
them: This is how you shall bless the Israelites. Say to them:
The LORD bless you and keep you!
The LORD let his face shine upon you, and be gracious to you!
The LORD look upon you kindly and give you peace!
So shall they invoke my name upon the Israelites, and I will bless them."
The word of the Lord. *Thanks be to God.*

RESPONSORIAL PSALM *(Psalm 67:2–3, 5, 6, 8)*
℟ **May God bless us in his mercy.**

May God have pity on us and bless us;
 may he let his face shine upon us.
So may your way be known upon earth;
 among all nations, your salvation. ℟
May the nations be glad and exult
 because you rule the peoples in equity;
 the nations on the earth you guide. ℟
May the peoples praise you, O God;
 may all the peoples praise you!
May God bless us,
 and may all the ends of the earth fear him! ℟

SECOND READING *(Galatians 4:1-7)*

Brothers and sisters: When the fullness of time had come, God sent his Son, born of a woman, born under the law, to ransom those under the law, so that we might receive adoption as sons. As proof that you are sons, God sent the Spirit of his Son into our hearts, crying out, **"Abba,**✣ Father!" So you are no longer a slave but a son, and if a son then also an heir, through God.

 The word of the Lord. *Thanks be to God.*

ALLELUIA *(Hebrews 1:1-2)*
Alleluia, alleluia. In the past God spoke to our ancestors through the prophets; in these last days, he has spoken to us through the Son. *Alleluia, alleluia.*

GOSPEL *(Luke 2:16-21)*
A reading from the holy Gospel according to Luke.
Glory to you, O Lord.

The shepherds went in haste to Bethlehem and found Mary and Joseph, and the infant lying in the manger. When they saw this, they made known the message that had been told them about this child. All who heard it were amazed by what had been told them by the shepherds. And Mary kept all these things, reflecting on them in her heart. Then the shepherds returned, glorifying and praising God for all they had heard and seen, just as it had been told to them.

When eight days were completed for his circumcision, he was named Jesus, the name given him by the angel before he was conceived in the womb.

The Gospel of the Lord. ***Praise to you, Lord Jesus Christ.***

PROFESSION OF FAITH *(page 13)*

PRAYER OF THE FAITHFUL

PREPARATION OF GIFTS *(page 16)*

PRAYER OVER THE OFFERINGS
O God, who in your kindness begin all good things
and bring them to fulfillment,

• TAKING A CLOSER LOOK •

✚ **Abba** This is the Aramaic (the spoken language of Jews in the Holy Land in Jesus' time) word for "father." It is a more familiar form than the common but slightly more formal Greek word for "father," and thus represents the more intimate and close relationship that Jesus has with God. Paul does not expect the Galatians to know its meaning, so he connects the Aramaic term with its Greek translation: "Abba, Father."

grant to us, who find joy in the Solemnity of the holy Mother of God,
that, just as we glory in the beginnings of your grace,
so one day we may rejoice in its completion.
Through Christ our Lord. *Amen.*

PREFACE (*Blessed Virgin Mary 1, page 34*)

COMMUNION ANTIPHON (*Hebrews 13:8*)
Jesus Christ is the same yesterday, today, and for ever.

PRAYER AFTER COMMUNION
We have received this heavenly Sacrament with joy, O Lord:
grant, we pray,
that it may lead us to eternal life,
for we rejoice to proclaim the blessed ever-Virgin Mary
Mother of your Son and Mother of the Church.
Through Christ our Lord. *Amen.*

SOLEMN BLESSING: THE BEGINNING OF THE YEAR (*Optional, page 59*)
   OR THE BLESSED VIRGIN MARY (*Optional, page 62*)

DISMISSAL (*page 57*) ✠

• RESPONDING TO THE WORD •

Moses blesses the people, hoping that God's face will shine on them.	**Paul reminds us that we are all brothers and sisters of Jesus.**	**Mary reflected in her heart about her experience with Jesus.**
⇨ *When have I felt God's loving gaze on me?*	⇨ *Who is someone I find difficult to think of as a brother or sister in Christ? Why?*	⇨ *How might I find more time for prayer in the coming year?*

January 7

Share the light of God's love

"Your light has come," Isaiah says. He calls us to know God's presence, God's light on and around us, and he commands us to spread that light.

Isaiah tells the people of Israel that the light of God's blessing shines on them and beyond them. He sees nations streaming to them, attracted by God's light. Some Israelites thought God's favor was exclusively theirs. But God's light can be shared without diminishing it.

Every year at Easter, the paschal candle, the Light of Christ, comes into a dark church, and its light is shared so the whole church glows. We proclaim a light divided but never dimmed.

Epiphany celebrates God's light being revealed to all nations. The gospel, Paul says, has spread to the Gentiles. They have seen and received the light of Christ. Matthew tells of even earlier Gentile observers of that light, the Magi: "We saw his star at its rising, and have come to do him homage."

The light that shone on the Magi shines on us. Jesus shares his light with us, and asks us to share it. The light of our faith may seem fragile, but a small light can set the world on fire! Sharing the light of God's love, God's blessing does not diminish it—it grows in strength as it is shared. Let's keep it burning brightly!

DINAH SIMMONS

MASS DURING THE DAY

·····················

ENTRANCE ANTIPHON *(Cf. Malachi 3:1; 1 Chronicles 29:12)*
Behold, the Lord, the Mighty One, has come; and
kingship is in his grasp, and power and dominion.

INTRODUCTORY RITES *(page 10)*

COLLECT
O God, who on this day
revealed your Only Begotten Son to the nations
by the guidance of a star,
grant in your mercy
that we, who know you already by faith,
may be brought to behold the beauty of your sublime glory.
Through our Lord Jesus Christ, your Son,
who lives and reigns with you in the unity of the Holy Spirit,
one God, for ever and ever. *Amen.*

FIRST READING *(Isaiah 60:1-6)*

Rise up in splendor, Jerusalem! Your light has come,
the glory of the Lord shines upon you.
See, darkness covers the earth,
    and thick clouds cover the peoples;
but upon you the LORD shines,
    and over you appears his glory.
Nations shall walk by your light,
    and kings by your shining radiance.
Raise your eyes and look about;
    they all gather and come to you:
your sons come from afar,
    and your daughters in the arms of their nurses.

Then you shall be radiant at what you see,
  your heart shall throb and overflow,
for the riches of the sea shall be emptied out before you,
  the wealth of nations shall be brought to you.
Caravans of camels shall fill you,
  dromedaries from Midian* and Ephah;*
all from Sheba* shall come
  bearing gold and frankincense,
  and proclaiming the praises of the LORD.
The word of the Lord. ***Thanks be to God.***

RESPONSORIAL PSALM *(Psalm 72:1-2, 7-8, 10-11, 12-13)*
R̷ **Lord, every nation on earth will adore you.**

O God, with your judgment endow the king,
  and with your justice, the king's son;
he shall govern your people with justice
  and your afflicted ones with judgment. R̷
Justice shall flower in his days,
  and profound peace, till the moon be no more.
May he rule from sea to sea,
  and from the River to the ends of the earth. R̷
The kings of Tarshish* and the Isles shall offer gifts;
  the kings of Arabia and Seba* shall bring tribute.
All kings shall pay him homage,
  all nations shall serve him. R̷
For he shall rescue the poor when he cries out,
  and the afflicted when he has no one to help him.
He shall have pity for the lowly and the poor;
  the lives of the poor he shall save. R̷

SECOND READING *(Ephesians 3:2-3a, 5-6)*

Brothers and sisters: You have heard of the stewardship of God's grace that was given to me for your benefit, namely, that the **mystery**† was made known to me by revelation. It was not made known to people in other generations as it has now been revealed to his holy apostles and prophets by the Spirit: that the Gentiles are coheirs, members of the same body, and copartners in the promise in Christ Jesus through the gospel.

The word of the Lord. *Thanks be to God.*

ALLELUIA *(Matthew 2:2)*

Alleluia, alleluia. We saw his star at its rising and have come to do him homage. *Alleluia, alleluia.*

GOSPEL *(Matthew 2:1-12)*

A reading from the holy Gospel according to Matthew.
Glory to you, O Lord.

When Jesus was born in Bethlehem of Judea, in the days of King Herod, behold, magi from the east arrived in Jerusalem, saying, "Where is the newborn king of the Jews? We saw his star at its rising and have come to do him homage." When King Herod heard this, he was greatly troubled, and all Jerusalem with him. Assembling all the chief priests and the scribes of the people, he inquired of them where the Christ was to be born. They said to him, "In Bethlehem of Judea, for thus it has been written through the prophet:

And you, Bethlehem, land of Judah,
are by no means least among the rulers of Judah;
since from you shall come a ruler,
who is to shepherd my people Israel."

Then Herod called the magi secretly and ascertained from them the time of the star's appearance. He sent them to Bethlehem and said, "Go and search diligently for the child. When you have found him, bring me word, that I too may go and do him homage." After their audience with the king they set out. And behold, the star that they had seen at its rising preceded them, until it came and stopped over the place where the child was. They were overjoyed at seeing the star, and on entering the house they saw the child with Mary his mother. They prostrated themselves and did him homage. Then they opened their treasures and offered him gifts of gold, frankincense, and myrrh.* And having been warned in a dream not to return to Herod, they departed for their country by another way.

The Gospel of the Lord. ***Praise to you, Lord Jesus Christ.***

PROFESSION OF FAITH *(page 13)*

PRAYER OF THE FAITHFUL

PREPARATION OF GIFTS *(page 16)*

PRAYER OVER THE OFFERINGS
Look with favor, Lord, we pray,
on these gifts of your Church,

• TAKING A CLOSER LOOK •

✛ **Mystery** In the Greek world of early Christianity, "mystery" (singular) referred to that which is hidden or secret and cannot be talked about openly. For Christians like Paul, a mystery points to what is hidden unless God reveals it. Paul identifies this revealed mystery as God's desire to unite all humanity—both Jew and Gentile—into one community in Christ. This becomes the core of Paul's Christian message. In later theological terminology, a mystery (such as the Trinity or the Incarnation) is a revealed truth about God that can be affirmed in faith but never completely and adequately expressed in abstract concepts or rational explanations.

in which are offered now not gold or frankincense or myrrh,
but he who by them is proclaimed,
sacrificed and received, Jesus Christ.
Who lives and reigns for ever and ever. *Amen.*

PREFACE *(Epiphany, page 20)*

COMMUNION ANTIPHON *(Cf. Matthew 2:2)*
We have seen his star in the East, and have come with gifts to
adore the Lord.

PRAYER AFTER COMMUNION
Go before us with heavenly light, O Lord,
always and everywhere,
that we may perceive with clear sight
and revere with true affection
the mystery in which you have willed us to participate.
Through Christ our Lord. *Amen.*

SOLEMN BLESSING: THE EPIPHANY OF THE LORD *(Optional, page 59)*

DISMISSAL *(page 57)* ✦

✦ RESPONDING TO THE WORD

Isaiah rejoices that God's light banishes the world's darkness.	The mystery of God's love for us has been made known in Jesus.	The magi followed a star to find Jesus.
➡ When has God's light lifted the shadows of my heart?	➡ How can I share that message with those around me this week?	➡ Like the magi, how willing am I to "go the extra mile" to find Jesus in my daily life?

January 14

Come and see

In today's gospel, John the Baptist proclaims that Jesus is the Lamb of God, the one who takes away our sins, the Promised One of God. When the two disciples run up to Jesus, he asks them, "What are you looking for?"

I believe Jesus asks the same question of you and me. How do we answer him? Maybe we can't answer that question, unless we face a deeper question: *what is God asking of me?* Am I truly letting that question shape me? Are you and I ready, like Samuel, to say: "Speak Lord, for your servant is listening"? Can we accept God's invitation to discipleship, to love and serve God?

Today is World Day of Migrants and Refugees, and we are invited to "come and see" the faithful and courageous works of so many volunteers, organizations, and parishes serving migrants and refugees. As strong advocates with a commitment to care for others, these "disciples" put the gospel into action. They show us—and those they serve—the working hands, feet, and heart of our merciful and loving Messiah. Like Samuel, John, and the first disciples, will you and I "come and see," trusting in the Lord's love and saving power that is given to us and through us for others?

■ JULIE CACHIA

ENTRANCE ANTIPHON *(Psalm 66 [65]:4)*

All the earth shall bow down before you, O God,
and shall sing to you, shall sing to your name,
O Most High!

INTRODUCTORY RITES *(page 10)*

COLLECT

Almighty ever-living God,
who govern all things,
both in heaven and on earth,
mercifully hear the pleading of your people
and bestow your peace on our times.
Through our Lord Jesus Christ, your Son,
who lives and reigns with you in the unity of the Holy Spirit,
one God, for ever and ever. *Amen.*

FIRST READING *(1 Samuel 3:3b–10, 19)*

Samuel was sleeping in the temple of the LORD where the ark
of God was. The LORD called to Samuel, who answered, "Here
I am." Samuel ran to Eli and said, "Here I am. You called me." "I
did not call you," Eli said. "Go back to sleep." So he went back to
sleep. Again the LORD called Samuel, who rose and went to Eli.
"Here I am," he said. "You called me." But Eli answered, "I did
not call you, my son. Go back to sleep."

At that time Samuel was not familiar with the LORD, because
the LORD had not revealed anything to him as yet. The LORD
called Samuel again, for the third time. Getting up and going to
Eli, he said, "Here I am. You called me." Then Eli understood that
the LORD was calling the youth. So he said to Samuel, "Go to
sleep, and if you are called, reply, Speak, LORD, for your servant
is listening." When Samuel went to sleep in his place, the LORD

came and revealed his presence, calling out as before, "Samuel, Samuel!" Samuel answered, "Speak, for your servant is listening."

Samuel grew up, and the LORD was with him, not permitting any word of his to be without effect.

The word of the Lord. ***Thanks be to God.***

RESPONSORIAL PSALM *(Psalm 40:2, 4, 7-8, 8-9, 10)*

℞ **Here am I, Lord; I come to do your will.**

I have waited, waited for the LORD,
    and he stooped toward me and heard my cry.
And he put a new song into my mouth,
    a hymn to our God. ℞

Sacrifice or offering you wished not,
    but ears open to obedience you gave me.
Holocausts or sin-offerings† you sought not;
    then said I, "Behold I come." ℞

"In the written scroll it is prescribed for me,
to do your will, O my God, is my delight,
    and your law is within my heart!" ℞

I announced your justice in the vast assembly;
    I did not restrain my lips, as you, O Lord, know. ℞

SECOND READING *(1 Corinthians 6:13c–15a, 17-20)*

Brothers and sisters: The body is not for immorality, but for the Lord, and the Lord is for the body; God raised the Lord and will also raise us by his power.

Do you not know that your bodies are members of Christ? But whoever is joined to the Lord becomes one Spirit with him. Avoid immorality. Every other sin a person commits is outside the body, but the immoral person sins against his own body. Do you not know that your body is a temple of the Holy Spirit within you, whom you have from God, and that you are not your own? For you have been purchased at a price. Therefore glorify God in your body.

The word of the Lord. *Thanks be to God.*

ALLELUIA *(John 1:41, 17b)*
Alleluia, alleluia. We have found the Messiah: Jesus Christ, who brings us truth and grace. *Alleluia, alleluia.*

GOSPEL *(John 1:35–42)*
A reading from the holy Gospel according to John.
Glory to you, O Lord.

John was standing with two of his disciples, and as he watched Jesus walk by, he said, "Behold, the Lamb of God." The two disciples heard what he said and followed Jesus. Jesus turned and saw them following him and said to them, "What are you looking for?" They said to him, "Rabbi"—which translated means Teacher—, "where are you staying?" He said to them, "Come, and you will see." So they went and saw where Jesus was staying, and they stayed with him that day. It was about four in the afternoon. Andrew, the brother of Simon Peter, was one of the two who heard John and followed Jesus. He first found his own brother Simon and told him, "We have found the Messiah"—which is translated Christ. Then he brought him to Jesus. Jesus looked at him and said, "You are Simon the son of John; you will be called Cephas*"—which is translated Peter.

The Gospel of the Lord. *Praise to you, Lord Jesus Christ.*

PROFESSION OF FAITH *(page 13)*

PRAYER OF THE FAITHFUL

PREPARATION OF GIFTS *(page 16)*

PRAYER OVER THE OFFERINGS
Grant us, O Lord, we pray,
that we may participate worthily in these mysteries,
for whenever the memorial of this sacrifice is celebrated
the work of our redemption is accomplished.
Through Christ our Lord. *Amen.*

PREFACE *(Sundays in Ordinary Time, pages 28-32)*

• TAKING A CLOSER LOOK •

✚ **Holocausts or sin-offerings** Sacrifice in the biblical world was a way of expressing one's relationship with God by setting apart something for God (thus making it "holy") and offering it as a gift to God. To show the complete character of the gift, it would be burned so that the giver could not take the gift back. This whole burnt offering is a *holocaust* (from the Greek words meaning a complete burning). A sin-offering was a gift offered to God that would help to restore the relationship when it was threatened by unintentional (rather than deliberate) sins.

COMMUNION ANTIPHON *(Cf. Psalm 23 [22]:5)*
You have prepared a table before me, and how precious is the
chalice that quenches my thirst.

Or *(1 John 4:16)*
We have come to know and to believe in the love that God has
for us.

PRAYER AFTER COMMUNION
Pour on us, O Lord, the Spirit of your love,
and in your kindness
make those you have nourished
by this one heavenly Bread
one in mind and heart.
Through Christ our Lord. *Amen.*

BLESSING & DISMISSAL *(page 56)* ✢

• RESPONDING TO THE WORD •

Once he learned how to listen, Samuel responded generously to God's call.

➡ *How can I pay closer attention to the surprising ways God might be calling me?*

Jesus reminds us that our bodies also belong to God.

➡ *What difference might it make in my attitudes or behavior to accept my body as God's gift?*

The disciples search out Jesus but are not sure what they want from him.

➡ *How would I answer if Jesus asked me, "What are you looking for?"*

January 21

Making God our priority

The Ninevites' conversion is astounding in its brevity and sweeping success. Such an immediate and all-encompassing turning away from sin in this wicked and non-Israelite city toward a faith in God akin to Abraham's or that of Moses was a testament to God's power and a telling criticism of Israel's infidelity.

Our God, the source of such salvation, is described in today's psalm. This is the God we know in Jesus of Nazareth, who dwelt among us and who offers us fullness of life. Today's readings encourage us to follow the example of those who have given to God a complete and unreserved response of faith.

The first disciples demonstrate such readiness and resolve, leaving behind their thriving business ventures, family, and employees. They follow Jesus regardless of the cost. Their actions are not a counsel to shirk life's responsibilities, but to make God our priority. St. Paul also advises living with this perspective, always ready to follow Jesus, making his way our own. May such unity in willing discipleship be a gift for us and for the entire Christian family.

■ CHRISTINE MADER

JAN 21

ENTRANCE ANTIPHON *(Cf. Psalm 96 [95]:1, 6)*

O sing a new song to the Lord; sing to the Lord, all the earth. In his presence are majesty and splendor, strength and honor in his holy place.

INTRODUCTORY RITES *(page 10)*

COLLECT

Almighty ever-living God,
direct our actions according to your good pleasure,
that in the name of your beloved Son
we may abound in good works.
Through our Lord Jesus Christ, your Son,
who lives and reigns with you in the unity of the Holy Spirit,
one God, for ever and ever. *Amen.*

FIRST READING *(Jonah 3:1-5, 10)*

The word of the Lord came to Jonah, saying: "Set out for the great city of Nineveh, and announce to it the message that I will tell you." So Jonah made ready and went to Nineveh, according to the Lord's bidding. Now Nineveh was an enormously large city; it took three days to go through it. Jonah began his journey through the city, and had gone but a single day's walk announcing, "Forty days more and Nineveh shall be destroyed," when the people of Nineveh believed God; they proclaimed a fast and all of them, great and small, put on sackcloth.

When God saw by their actions how they turned from their evil way, he repented of the evil that he had threatened to do to them; he did not carry it out.

The word of the Lord. *Thanks be to God.*

RESPONSORIAL PSALM *(Psalm 25:4-5, 6-7, 8-9)*
℟ **Teach me your ways, O Lord.**

Your ways, O LORD, make known to me;
    teach me your paths,
guide me in your truth and teach me,
    for you are God my savior. ℟
Remember that your compassion, O LORD,
    and your love are from of old.
In your kindness remember me,
    because of your goodness, O LORD. ℟
Good and upright is the LORD;
    thus he shows sinners the way.
He guides the humble to justice
    and teaches the humble his way. ℟

SECOND READING *(1 Corinthians 7:29-31)*

I tell you, brothers and sisters, the time is running out. From now on, let those having wives act as not having them, those weeping as not weeping, those rejoicing as not rejoicing, those buying as not owning, those using the world as not using it fully. For the world in its present form is passing away.

    The word of the Lord. *Thanks be to God.*

ALLELUIA *(Mark 1:15)*
Alleluia, alleluia. The kingdom of God is at hand. Repent and believe in the Gospel. *Alleluia, alleluia.*

GOSPEL *(Mark 1:14–20)*
A reading from the holy Gospel according to Mark.
Glory to you, O Lord.

After John had been arrested, Jesus came to Galilee proclaiming the gospel of God: "This is the time of fulfillment. The **kingdom of God**✝ is at hand. Repent, and believe in the gospel."

As he passed by the Sea of Galilee, he saw Simon and his brother Andrew casting their nets into the sea; they were fishermen. Jesus said to them, "Come after me, and I will make you fishers of men." Then they abandoned their nets and followed him. He walked along a little farther and saw James, the son of Zebedee, and his brother John. They too were in a boat mending their nets. Then he called them. So they left their father Zebedee in the boat along with the hired men and followed him.

The Gospel of the Lord. *Praise to you, Lord Jesus Christ.*

PROFESSION OF FAITH *(page 13)*

PRAYER OF THE FAITHFUL

PREPARATION OF GIFTS *(page 16)*

PRAYER OVER THE OFFERINGS
Accept our offerings, O Lord, we pray,
and in sanctifying them
grant that they may profit us for salvation.
Through Christ our Lord. *Amen.*

PREFACE *(Sundays in Ordinary Time, pages 28–32)*

COMMUNION ANTIPHON *(Cf. Psalm 34 [33]:6)*

Look toward the Lord and be radiant; let your faces not be abashed.

Or *(John 8:12)*

I am the light of the world, says the Lord; whoever follows me will not walk in darkness, but will have the light of life.

✤ TAKING A CLOSER LOOK ✤

✚ **Kingdom of God** In his teaching and preaching, Jesus identifies God's ideal community as the kingdom of God—both the place where God rules and the people who live as God desires. This community is to be characterized by a new way of living together that includes everyone (both Jew and Gentile), who as brothers and sisters will relate to God as their father and as a king whose benevolent rule over them guides every moment of their lives. The kingdom is inaugurated by Jesus and continues today in the Christian community that daily strives to make God's ideal of community a reality.

PRAYER AFTER COMMUNION
Grant, we pray, almighty God,
that, receiving the grace
by which you bring us to new life,
we may always glory in your gift.
Through Christ our Lord. *Amen.*

BLESSING & DISMISSAL *(page 56)* ❖

• RESPONDING TO THE WORD •

Jonah is surprised when he shares God's message with others.

➡ What has happened when I shared God's good news?

Paul knows that Jesus makes all things new.

➡ What is the biggest change going on in my life now because of Christ and his message?

Jesus calls disciples to use their skills for building God's kingdom community.

➡ Which gift or skill do I bring to the building of this community?

January 28

A new teaching with authority!

In today's gospel reading, the people "were amazed and asked one another, 'What is this? A new teaching with authority. He commands even the unclean spirits and they obey him.'"

You will notice that Jesus' teaching is always consistent. There are no flip-flops. And there is no division between his words and his actions. Jesus lived as he taught, and whatever he said and did was a reflection of his love. No wonder his contemporaries were amazed. Jesus' authority came from his consistent reflection of his Father's love

and from the harmony that existed between his words and actions. Those are the compelling reasons that draw our hearts to follow him in faith.

May our actions be in harmony with our words, as Jesus' actions were with God's. Let us pray that God gives us the strength to be consistent as Jesus was; let us pray that Jesus shows us how to imitate him according to his plan for each of us, so that we may become who we were created to be.

◼ Fr. Kenneth E. Grabner, CSC

ENTRANCE ANTIPHON *(Psalm 106 (105):47)*

Save us, O Lord our God! And gather us from the
nations, to give thanks to your holy name, and make
it our glory to praise you.

INTRODUCTORY RITES *(page 10)*

COLLECT

Grant us, Lord our God,
that we may honor you with all our mind,
and love everyone in truth of heart.
Through our Lord Jesus Christ, your Son,
who lives and reigns with you in the unity of the Holy Spirit,
one God, for ever and ever. *Amen.*

FIRST READING *(Deuteronomy 18:15-20)*

Moses spoke to all the people, saying: "A prophet like me
will the LORD, your God, raise up for you from among
your own kin; to him you shall listen. This is exactly what you
requested of the LORD, your God, at Horeb* on the day of the
assembly, when you said, 'Let us not again hear the voice of the
LORD, our God, nor see this great fire any more, lest we die.'
And the LORD said to me, 'This was well said. I will raise up
for them a prophet like you from among their kin, and will put
my words into his mouth; he shall tell them all that I command
him. Whoever will not listen to my words which he speaks in my
name, I myself will make him answer for it. But if a prophet pre-
sumes to speak in my name an oracle that I have not commanded
him to speak, or speaks in the name of other gods, he shall die.'"

The word of the Lord. *Thanks be to God.*

RESPONSORIAL PSALM *(Psalm 95:1–2, 6–7, 7–9)*

℟ **If today you hear his voice, harden not your hearts.**

Come, let us sing joyfully to the LORD;
 let us acclaim the rock of our salvation.
Let us come into his presence with thanksgiving;
 let us joyfully sing psalms to him. ℟
Come, let us bow down in worship;
 let us kneel before the LORD who made us.
For he is our God,
 and we are the people he shepherds, the flock he guides. ℟
Oh, that today you would hear his voice:
 "Harden not your hearts as at Meribah,*
 as in the day of Massah* in the desert,
where your fathers tempted me;
 they tested me though they had seen my works." ℟

SECOND READING *(1 Corinthians 7:32–35)*

Brothers and sisters: I should like you to be free of anxieties. An unmarried man is anxious about the things of the Lord, ☩ how he may please the Lord. But a married man is anxious about the things of the world, how he may please his wife, and he is divided. An unmarried woman or a virgin is anxious about the things of the Lord, so that she may be holy in both body and spirit. A married woman, on the other hand, is anxious about the things of the world, how she may please her husband. I am telling you this for your own benefit, not to impose a restraint upon you, but for the sake of propriety and adherence to the Lord without distraction.

The word of the Lord. *Thanks be to God.*

ALLELUIA *(Matthew 4:16)*

Alleluia, alleluia. The people who sit in darkness have seen a great light; on those dwelling in a land overshadowed by death, light has arisen. *Alleluia, alleluia.*

GOSPEL *(Mark 1:21–28)*

A reading from the holy Gospel according to Mark.
Glory to you, O Lord.

Then they came to Capernaum,* and on the sabbath Jesus entered the synagogue and taught. The people were astonished at his teaching, for he taught them as one having authority and not as the scribes. In their synagogue was a man with an unclean spirit; he cried out, "What have you to do with us, Jesus of Nazareth? Have you come to destroy us? I know who you are—the Holy One of God!" Jesus rebuked him and said, "Quiet! Come out of him!" The unclean spirit convulsed him and with a loud cry came out of him. All were amazed and asked one another, "What is this? A new teaching with authority. He commands even the unclean spirits and they obey him." His fame spread everywhere throughout the whole region of Galilee.

The Gospel of the Lord. *Praise to you, Lord Jesus Christ.*

PROFESSION OF FAITH *(page 13)*

PRAYER OF THE FAITHFUL

PREPARATION OF GIFTS *(page 16)*

PRAYER OVER THE OFFERINGS

O Lord, we bring to your altar
these offerings of our service:
be pleased to receive them, we pray,
and transform them
into the Sacrament of our redemption.
Through Christ our Lord. *Amen.*

PREFACE *(Sundays in Ordinary Time, pages 28–32)*

COMMUNION ANTIPHON *(Cf. Psalm 31 (30):17-18)*

Let your face shine on your servant. Save me in your merciful
love. O Lord, let me never be put to shame, for I call on you.

Or *(Matthew 5:3-4)*

Blessed are the poor in spirit, for theirs is the Kingdom of
Heaven. Blessed are the meek, for they shall possess the land.

• TAKING A CLOSER LOOK •

✦ **Lord** Since God's personal name, *Yahweh* (Lord printed in small
capital letters as LORD in our Bible), which was revealed to Moses and the
Israelites (Exodus 3:14) was so sacred, the Jews did not speak it aloud but
would instead often say Adonai, the Hebrew word for "Lord." Thus "Lord"
(Greek, *Kyrios*; Latin, *Dominus*) describes the exalted status of God—higher in power, honor, and glory than any creature. When Christians began
to recognize that Jesus did most of the things that God did (except to create, which God the Father alone did), they reasoned that since Jesus did
what God did, Jesus must also be divine and hence worthy of the name
"Lord." As St. Paul realized, although God the Father remains Lord, the
name "Lord" is now also honorably bestowed on Jesus (see Philippians
2:6-11, Palm Sunday), who thus becomes Our Lord Jesus Christ.

PRAYER AFTER COMMUNION
Nourished by these redeeming gifts,
we pray, O Lord,
that through this help to eternal salvation
true faith may ever increase.
Through Christ our Lord. *Amen.*

BLESSING & DISMISSAL *(page 56)* ✦

✦ RESPONDING TO THE WORD ✦

God promises to send prophets who will reveal God's presence among us.

➡ *Who has shown me where God is hidden in our midst?*

Paul encourages us to be free of anxieties in our relationships.

➡ *How has my anxiety about a relationship influenced my behavior toward God or others?*

Jesus' mastery of unclean spirits shows he is reordering the world for God.

➡ *How has my life been reordered because of my faith in Christ?*

February 4

No time to waste!

This year we listen to the Evangelist Mark. His is the shortest of the four Gospels. In today's few verses, Mark reveals the intensity and urgency of Jesus.

Jesus was compelled to share the good news as deeply and broadly as possible. Look at the work he accomplishes in one day. First, he teaches in the synagogue and frees a man from an unclean spirit. Then, in Simon's home, he heals Simon's mother-in-law of a serious fever. And then, he spends the evening healing the sick and casting out demons. Mark tells us that the whole town was gathered at the door!

After all that intense effort, Jesus is up the next morning before sunrise and goes away to pray alone. His energy is renewed in prayer with his Father, and then he sets out again, moving from one town to the next, proclaiming the loving mercy of God. And let us remember, he walked everywhere he went.

Jesus knew his mission. He had no time to waste.

Do we dare ask for that grace of urgency? Yes! Start each day in prayer, deliberately treat everyone you meet as brothers and sisters of Jesus Christ, and stay alert for God's invitations to live ever more deeply in God's love and mercy.

■ **MARILYN SWEET**

ENTRANCE ANTIPHON *(Psalm 95 [94]:6-7)*

O come, let us worship God and bow low before the
God who made us, for he is the Lord our God.

INTRODUCTORY RITES *(page 10)*

COLLECT

Keep your family safe, O Lord, with unfailing care,
that, relying solely on the hope of heavenly grace,
they may be defended always by your protection.
Through our Lord Jesus Christ, your Son,
who lives and reigns with you in the unity of the Holy Spirit,
one God, for ever and ever. *Amen.*

FIRST READING *(Job 7:1-4, 6-7)*

Job spoke, saying:
Is not man's life on earth a drudgery?
    Are not his days those of hirelings?
He is a slave who longs for the shade,
    a hireling who waits for his wages.
So I have been assigned months of misery,
    and troubled nights have been allotted to me.
If in bed I say, "When shall I arise?"
    then the night drags on;
    I am filled with restlessness until the dawn.
My days are swifter than a weaver's shuttle;
    they come to an end without hope.
Remember that my life is like the wind;
    I shall not see happiness again.
The word of the Lord. *Thanks be to God.*

RESPONSORIAL PSALM *(Psalm 147:1-2, 3-4, 5-6)*

℟ **Praise the Lord who heals the brokenhearted.** *Or* **Alleluia.**

Praise the LORD, for he is good;
  sing praise to our God, for he is gracious;
  it is fitting to praise him.
The LORD rebuilds Jerusalem;
  the dispersed of Israel he gathers. ℟
He heals the brokenhearted
  and binds up their wounds.
He tells the number of the stars;
  he calls each by name. ℟
Great is our LORD and mighty in power;
  to his wisdom there is no limit.
The LORD sustains the lowly;
  the wicked he casts to the ground. ℟

SECOND READING *(1 Corinthians 9:16-19, 22-23)*

Brothers and sisters: If I preach the gospel, this is no reason for me to boast, for an obligation has been imposed on me, and woe to me if I do not preach it! If I do so willingly, I have a recompense, but if unwillingly, then I have been entrusted with a stewardship. What then is my recompense? That, when I preach, I offer the gospel free of charge so as not to make full use of my right in the gospel.

Although I am free in regard to all, I have made myself a slave to all so as to win over as many as possible. To the weak I became weak, to win over the weak. I have become all things to all, to save at least some. All this I do for the sake of the gospel, so that I too may have a share in it.

The word of the Lord. *Thanks be to God.*

ALLELUIA *(Matthew 8:17)*

Alleluia, alleluia. Christ took away our infirmities and bore our diseases. *Alleluia, alleluia.*

GOSPEL *(Mark 1:29-39)*

A reading from the holy Gospel according to Mark.
Glory to you, O Lord.

On leaving the **synagogue**✠ Jesus entered the house of Simon and Andrew with James and John. Simon's mother-in-law lay sick with a fever. They immediately told him about her. He approached, grasped her hand, and helped her up. Then the fever left her and she waited on them.

When it was evening, after sunset, they brought to him all who were ill or possessed by demons. The whole town was gathered at the door. He cured many who were sick with various diseases, and he drove out many demons, not permitting them to speak because they knew him.

Rising very early before dawn, he left and went off to a deserted place, where he prayed. Simon and those who were with him pursued him and on finding him said, "Everyone is looking for you." He told them, "Let us go on to the nearby villages that I may preach there also. For this purpose have I come." So he went into their synagogues, preaching and driving out demons throughout the whole of Galilee.

The Gospel of the Lord. *Praise to you, Lord Jesus Christ.*

PROFESSION OF FAITH *(page 13)*

PRAYER OF THE FAITHFUL

PREPARATION OF GIFTS *(page 16)*

PRAYER OVER THE OFFERINGS

O Lord our God,
who once established these created things
to sustain us in our frailty,
grant, we pray,
that they may become for us now
the Sacrament of eternal life.
Through Christ our Lord. *Amen.*

PREFACE *(Sundays in Ordinary Time, pages 28-32)*

COMMUNION ANTIPHON *(Cf. Psalm 107 [106]:8-9)*

Let them thank the Lord for his mercy, his wonders for the
children of men, for he satisfies the thirsty soul, and the hungry
he fills with good things.

Or *(Matthew 5:5-6)*

Blessed are those who mourn, for they shall be consoled. Blessed
are those who hunger and thirst for righteousness, for they shall
have their fill.

• TAKING A CLOSER LOOK •

✣ **Synagogue** The synagogue was not, like the Temple in
Jerusalem, a place where God dwelt and where Jews worshipped and
offered sacrifices. It was primarily a meeting place for community prayer
and for the study and discussion of the Scriptures. Hence, it was not
organized and run by priests but by lay people, in particular the elders
of the community. Synagogues became even more important after the
Jerusalem Temple was destroyed in 70 AD by the Romans and sacrifices
ceased to be offered. Synagogues also helped affirm Jewish identity and
community belonging when Jews emigrated to other nations.

PRAYER AFTER COMMUNION

O God, who have willed that we be partakers
in the one Bread and the one Chalice,
grant us, we pray, so to live
that, made one in Christ,
we may joyfully bear fruit
for the salvation of the world.
Through Christ our Lord. *Amen.*

BLESSING & DISMISSAL *(page 56)* ✣

• RESPONDING TO THE WORD •

Job recognizes the difficulties of life and how they push us to give up hope.	Paul feels compelled to share the gospel message.	Despite his busy ministry, Jesus prayed alone in the morning.
➡ *How does Christ's presence in my life offer hope?*	➡ *What makes Jesus' good news so good that I want to share it?*	➡ *When can I find time each day to pray and be alone with God?*

February 11

Accept Jesus' challenge!

The leper in today's gospel story violated the religious rules laid out in the Book of Leviticus—he broke the Law and approached a clean man. Even then, Jesus did not send the leper away.

Rather, Our Lord was so moved with pity that he touched the leper (yet another religious violation) and healed him. Jesus also insisted that the man present himself to the priests so that he could be declared officially clean and then fully reintegrated into the community.

The lesson is that we must constantly opt to serve our brothers and sisters in need. Sometimes social and economic problems seem too big and complex for us to handle. Oftentimes, it is just plain easier to settle for inaction.

But Jesus shows us the best response: "I will do it. Be made clean."

In this story, leprosy could be viewed as a metaphor for brokenness. Can we recognize that we, as well as our society, suffer from various sorts of brokenness? Might we also need to kneel before Jesus requesting the deepest healing for which humanity yearns? Is today a new opportunity for each of us to choose to accept Jesus' challenge to fully love our neighbor?

■ JOE GUNN

ENTRANCE ANTIPHON *(Cf. Psalm 31 [30]:3-4)*

Be my protector, O God, a mighty stronghold to save me. For you are my rock, my stronghold! Lead me, guide me, for the sake of your name.

INTRODUCTORY RITES *(page 10)*

COLLECT

O God, who teach us that you abide
in hearts that are just and true,
grant that we may be so fashioned by your grace
as to become a dwelling pleasing to you.
Through our Lord Jesus Christ, your Son,
who lives and reigns with you in the unity of the Holy Spirit,
one God, for ever and ever. *Amen.*

FIRST READING *(Leviticus 13:1-2, 44-46)*

The LORD said to Moses and Aaron, "If someone has on his skin a scab or pustule or blotch which appears to be the sore of leprosy, he shall be brought to Aaron, the priest, or to one of the priests among his descendants. If the man is leprous and unclean, the priest shall declare him unclean by reason of the sore on his head.

"The one who bears the sore of leprosy shall keep his garments rent and his head bare, and shall muffle his beard; he shall cry out, 'Unclean, unclean!' As long as the sore is on him he shall declare himself unclean, since he is in fact unclean. He shall dwell apart, making his abode outside the camp."

The word of the Lord. *Thanks be to God.*

RESPONSORIAL PSALM *(Psalm 32:1-2, 5, 11)*

℟ **I turn to you, Lord, in time of trouble, and you fill me with the joy of salvation.**

Blessed is he whose fault is taken away,
  whose sin is covered.
Blessed the man to whom the LORD imputes not guilt,
  in whose spirit there is no guile.

R. **I turn to you, Lord, in time of trouble, and you fill me
  with the joy of salvation.**

Then I acknowledged my sin to you,
  my guilt I covered not.
I said, "I confess my faults to the LORD,"
  and you took away the guilt of my sin. R.
Be glad in the LORD and rejoice, you just;
  exult, all you upright of heart. R.

SECOND READING *(1 Corinthians 10:31—11:1)*

Brothers and sisters, whether you eat or drink, or whatever
you do, do everything for the glory of God. Avoid giving
offense, whether to the Jews or Greeks or the church of God, just
as I try to please everyone in every way, not seeking my own benefit but that of the many, that they may be saved. Be imitators of
me, as I am of Christ.

  The word of the Lord. *Thanks be to God.*

ALLELUIA *(Luke 7:16)*

Alleluia, alleluia. A great prophet has arisen in our midst, God
has visited his people. *Alleluia, alleluia.*

GOSPEL *(Mark 1:40-45)*

A reading from the holy Gospel according to Mark.
Glory to you, O Lord.

A leper came to Jesus and kneeling down begged him and said,
"If you wish, you can make me clean." Moved with pity, he
stretched out his hand, touched him, and said to him, "I do will it.

Be made clean." The **leprosy** ✢ left him immediately, and he was made clean. Then, warning the him sternly, he dismissed him at once.

He said to him, "See that you tell no one anything, but go, show yourself to the priest and offer for your cleansing what Moses prescribed; that will be proof for them."

The man went away and began to publicize the whole matter. He spread the report abroad so that it was impossible for Jesus to enter a town openly. He remained outside in deserted places, and people kept coming to him from everywhere.

The Gospel of the Lord. *Praise to you, Lord Jesus Christ.*

PROFESSION OF FAITH (page 13)

PRAYER OF THE FAITHFUL

PREPARATION OF GIFTS (page 16)

PRAYER OVER THE OFFERINGS
May this oblation, O Lord, we pray,
cleanse and renew us
and may it become for those who do your will

● TAKING A CLOSER LOOK ●

✢ **Leprosy** In the Bible, leprosy did not always mean just the modern illness (also known as Hansen's Disease) but also included other skin problems such as fungal infections, eczema, or psoriasis. The priest decided whether a skin eruption was leprous. If the disease progressed, the person was declared ritually "unclean." Since ritual impurity jeopardized the pure life and worship of the community, the lepers were separated from the community. This prevented any normal way of making a living and impeded human companionship, other than that of their fellow lepers. Bands of lepers often traveled about together, begging for charity.

the source of eternal reward.
Through Christ our Lord. *Amen.*

PREFACE *(Sundays in Ordinary Time, pages 28–32)*

COMMUNION ANTIPHON *(Cf. Psalm 78 [77]:29–30)*
They ate and had their fill, and what they craved the Lord gave
them; they were not disappointed in what they craved.

Or *(John 3:16)*
God so loved the world that he gave his Only Begotten Son,
so that all who believe in him may not perish, but may have
eternal life.

PRAYER AFTER COMMUNION
Having fed upon these heavenly delights,
we pray, O Lord,
that we may always long
for that food by which we truly live.
Through Christ our Lord. *Amen.*

BLESSING & DISMISSAL *(page 56)* ✦

✦ RESPONDING TO THE WORD ✦

In Moses' time, sick people were separated from the community.	Paul knows that Christian behavior imitates Christ's example.	The leper trusts that Christ can make him well.
➡ *How can I help someone who is sick to feel more a part of the community?*	➡ *Who has been an important model of the Christian life for me?*	➡ *From what might I ask Jesus to heal me today?*

Christ lights our darkness

We may be surprised to hear that the Church's liturgy reminds us that Lent is meant to be a joyful season.

> For by your gracious gift each year
> your faithful await the sacred paschal feasts
> with the joy of minds made pure...
> PREFACE 1 OF LENT

The season of Lent finds its meaning and origin in Easter, the annual celebration of our Lord's resurrection and our salvation. As the Church's time to prepare for the high point of the Christian year, it is the most appropriate time for persons to enter into Christ's new life through baptism. How can it not be a time of joy?

Over the centuries, Lent has become a special time for fasting, abstinence, communal and private prayer, self-discipline, serving others, study, reflection, and penance. With the whole Church we re-examine our priorities, leaving sin and self behind and intensifying our love and service of God and our neighbors.

The joy of this time of preparation is all about the surprise of new life coming from what may have appeared dead—just as fresh buds break through each spring on trees that seemed dead during the long winter.

If we use these forty days of Lent for honest examination and careful "pruning" of our lives, we will be ready to celebrate the great feast of Easter with our risen Lord and to be joyful witnesses of the power of his resurrection in our world so broken by sin.

Praying and living the Lenten season

It's a common practice to "give things up" for Lent. But when we give something up, we create an empty space into which we must then put some new form of loving behavior.

Give yourself and each household member an index card. Either divide the card into five weeks or, better, use a new card each week. Invite everyone to write on one side what they want to give up to create space for something new, and on the other side what they want to fill the space with.

For example, giving up calories by fasting creates a space for feeling a little of the hunger that haunts millions of the world's poor. The money we save from fasting can also be donated to groups that help feed the hungry. Giving up some television time as a household creates space for spending time together in conversation, prayer, or even playing games. Giving up an attitude of complaining makes space for a more cooperative approach to fixing dinners or doing chores.

When everyone is finished, take the cards and place them in the center of the dinner table or in your household Lenten prayer space. Light a candle and pray together:

God, giver of all gifts,
you have given us so much.
Now we want to give up something
so that we might experience
the emptiness that reminds us
how much we want to be filled
by your loving presence.
May our sacrifice show our willingness
to change our lives this Lent. Amen.

February 14

Here and now

The opening of today's first reading and the end of the second both contain a small but resonant word that can easily be overlooked. The word is *"now."* This little word, I think, captures both the hope and the urgency of the opportunity offered to us in Lent.

"Even now, says the LORD, return to me with your whole heart." My interpretation is that it is never too late for repentance and conversion. Even in the face of the baggage from the past that may be weighing us down—our bad choices, our failures, our sinfulness—"even now" God gently but insistently invites us back.

In Paul's letter to the Corinthians, he is even more insistent: "Behold, now is a very acceptable time." Lent calls us to examine and renew our relationship with God and with one another here, *now,* not at some vague future date, when I might have more time or when my life is more organized.

As we enter into our Lenten observance this year, let us take to heart God's call to repentance, prayer, integrity, and wholeness. May neither regret nor procrastination prevent us from responding to that call—*now!*

◼ KRYSTYNA HIGGINS

If the blessing and distribution of ashes take place outside Mass, it is appropriate that the complete Liturgy of the Word precede it, using texts assigned to the Mass of Ash Wednesday.

ENTRANCE ANTIPHON *(Wisdom 11:24, 25, 27)*
You are merciful to all, O Lord, and despise nothing that you have made. You overlook people's sins, to bring them to repentance, and you spare them, for you are the Lord our God.

INTRODUCTORY RITES *(page 10)*

COLLECT
Grant, O Lord, that we may begin with holy fasting
this campaign of Christian service,
so that, as we take up battle against spiritual evils,
we may be armed with weapons of self-restraint.
Through our Lord Jesus Christ, your Son,
who lives and reigns with you in the unity of the Holy Spirit,
one God, for ever and ever. *Amen.*

FIRST READING *(Joel 2:12-18)*
Even now, says the LORD,
    return to me with your whole heart,
        with fasting, and weeping, and mourning;
Rend your hearts, not your garments,
        and return to the LORD, your God.
For gracious and merciful is he,
        slow to anger, rich in kindness,
        and relenting in punishment.
Perhaps he will again relent
        and leave behind him a blessing,

Offerings and libations
    for the LORD, your God.

Blow the trumpet in Zion!*
    proclaim a fast,
    call an assembly;
Gather the people,
    notify the congregation;
Assemble the elders,
    gather the children
    and the infants at the breast;
Let the bridegroom quit his room
    and the bride her chamber.
Between the porch and the altar
    let the priests, the ministers of the LORD, weep,
And say, "Spare, O LORD, your people,
    and make not your heritage a reproach,
    with the nations ruling over them!
Why should they say among the peoples,
    'Where is their God?' "

Then the LORD was stirred to concern for his land
    and took pity on his people.
    The word of the Lord. *Thanks be to God.*

RESPONSORIAL PSALM *(Psalm 51:3-4, 5-6ab, 12-13, 14, 17)*
R̸ **Be merciful, O Lord, for we have sinned.**

Have mercy on me, O God, in your goodness;
    in the greatness of your compassion wipe out my offense.

Thoroughly wash me from my guilt
    and of my sin cleanse me.
℟ **Be merciful, O Lord, for we have sinned.**
For I acknowledge my offense,
    and my sin is before me always:
"Against you only have I sinned,
    and done what is evil in your sight." ℟
A clean heart create for me, O God,
    and a steadfast spirit renew within me.
Cast me not out from your presence,
    and your Holy Spirit take not from me. ℟
Give me back the joy of your salvation,
    and a willing spirit sustain in me.
O Lord, open my lips,
    and my mouth shall proclaim your praise. ℟

SECOND READING *(2 Corinthians 5:20–6:2)*

Brothers and sisters: We are ambassadors for Christ, as if God were appealing through us. We implore you on behalf of Christ, be reconciled to God. For our sake he made him to be sin who did not know sin, so that we might become the righteousness of God in him.

    Working together, then, we appeal to you not to receive the grace of God in vain. For he says:
    In an acceptable time I heard you,
        and on the day of salvation I helped you.
Behold, now is a very acceptable time; behold, now is the day of salvation.

    The word of the Lord. ***Thanks be to God.***

VERSE BEFORE THE GOSPEL *(See Psalm 95:8)*
Glory and praise to you, Lord Jesus Christ! If today you hear his voice, harden not your hearts. *Glory and praise to you, Lord Jesus Christ!*

GOSPEL *(Matthew 6:1-6, 16-18)*
A reading from the holy Gospel according to Matthew.
Glory to you, O Lord.

Jesus said to his disciples: "Take care not to perform righteous deeds in order that people may see them; otherwise, you will have no recompense from your heavenly Father. When you give alms, do not blow a trumpet before you, as the **hypocrites**⁺ do in the synagogues and in the streets to win the praise of others. Amen, I say to you, they have received their reward. But when you give alms, do not let your left hand know what your right is doing, so that your almsgiving may be secret. And your Father who sees in secret will repay you.

"When you pray, do not be like the hypocrites, who love to stand and pray in the synagogues and on street corners so that others may see them. Amen, I say to you, they have received their reward. But when you pray, go to your inner room, close the door, and pray to your Father in secret. And your Father who sees in secret will repay you.

"When you fast, do not look gloomy like the hypocrites. They neglect their appearance, so that they may appear to others to be fasting. Amen, I say to you, they have received their reward. But when you fast, anoint your head and wash your face, so that you may not appear to be fasting, except to your Father who is hidden. And your Father who sees what is hidden will repay you."

The Gospel of the Lord. *Praise to you, Lord Jesus Christ.*

BLESSING AND DISTRIBUTION OF ASHES

After the homily, the priest, standing with hands joined, says:

Dear brethren (brothers and sisters), let us humbly ask God
   our Father
that he be pleased to bless with the abundance of his grace
these ashes, which we will put on our heads in penitence.

After a brief prayer in silence he continues:

O God, who are moved by acts of humility
and respond with forgiveness to works of penance,
lend your merciful ear to our prayers
and in your kindness pour out the grace of your blessing
on your servants who are marked with these ashes,
that, as they follow the Lenten observances,
they may be worthy to come with minds made pure
to celebrate the Paschal Mystery of your Son.
Who lives and reigns for ever and ever. *Amen.*

Or

O God, who desire not the death of sinners,
but their conversion,
mercifully hear our prayers
and in your kindness be pleased to bless these ashes,
which we intend to receive upon our heads,
that we, who acknowledge we are but ashes
and shall return to dust,
may, through a steadfast observance of Lent,
gain pardon for sins and newness of life
after the likeness of your Risen Son.
Who lives and reigns for ever and ever. *Amen.*

The priest sprinkles the ashes with holy water, places ashes on the heads of all those present who come to him, and says to each one:

Repent, and believe in the Gospel.

Or

Remember that you are dust, and to dust you shall return.

PRAYER OF THE FAITHFUL

PREPARATION OF GIFTS *(page 16)*

PRAYER OVER THE OFFERINGS

As we solemnly offer
the annual sacrifice for the beginning of Lent,
we entreat you, O Lord,
that, through works of penance and charity,
we may turn away from harmful pleasures
and, cleansed from our sins, may become worthy
to celebrate devoutly the Passion of your Son.
Who lives and reigns for ever and ever. *Amen.*

• TAKING A CLOSER LOOK •

✠ **Hypocrites**   *Hypokrites* is a Greek word for an actor in the theater. Since Greek plays were performed outdoors and the audience was at a distance, actors wore large stereotyped masks to identify their characters. So in popular usage, a hypocrite was someone who pretended to be something that he or she was not, and hypocrisy described the general mismatch between one's external appearance and one's internal attitudes or intentions. Just as the actor hid behind a mask and performed a role, so the hypocrite hides something behind a pleasing external appearance.

PREFACE (*Lent 3–4, page 22*)

COMMUNION ANTIPHON (*Cf. Psalm 1:2–3*)
He who ponders the law of the Lord day and night will yield
fruit in due season.

PRAYER AFTER COMMUNION
May the Sacrament we have received sustain us, O Lord,
that our Lenten fast may be pleasing to you
and be for us a healing remedy.
Through Christ our Lord. *Amen.*

PRAYER OVER THE PEOPLE
Pour out a spirit of compunction, O God,
on those who bow before your majesty,
and by your mercy may they merit the rewards you promise
to those who do penance.
Through Christ our Lord. *Amen.*

DISMISSAL (*page 57*) ✠

• RESPONDING TO THE WORD •

Joel wants us to change on the inside and not just externally.	**Paul says that now is the acceptable time to be an ambassador of Christ.**	**Jesus warns against hypocritical behavior.**
➡ *What change of attitude do I most want to make this Lent?*	➡ *With whom will I share the good news of salvation today?*	➡ *What do I need to do to match my words with my actions?*

February 18

An unconditional offering

The more pain and sacrifice you experience on your journey, the more satisfying your arrival at your destination. Athletes who train excessively will say that the victory, the medal is well worth the extra work. Students who hit the books instead of going to a party have as their reward the satisfaction of knowing that they have achieved the best grade possible.

Jesus was thrust into the wilderness for 40 long days and was constantly tempted by Satan. We know, of course, that he did not succumb to any temptation, and he was provided divine, angelic support in his struggle.

The athlete and the student who choose to sacrifice have a specific end goal in mind. Their self-oblation is driven by the long-range reward of achieving a medal or a diploma. When they see their friends or classmates enjoying the things that they deny themselves, they are sustained by thoughts of the final victory.

Like Jesus, we are expected to endure our forty-day fast as an unconditional offering to God, not because of the promise of reward when the summit is finally reached. But still, when the time of our sacrifice and commitment is fulfilled, the inherent bounty is that the kingdom of God is nearer!

◼ **FRANK CAMPBELL**

Parishes engaged in the Rite of Christian Initiation of Adults (RCIA) may celebrate the Rite of Election today.

ENTRANCE ANTIPHON *(Cf. Psalm 91 [90]:15-16)*
When he calls on me, I will answer him; I will deliver him and give him glory, I will grant him length of days.

INTRODUCTORY RITES *(page 10)*

COLLECT
Grant, almighty God,
through the yearly observances of holy Lent,
that we may grow in understanding
of the riches hidden in Christ
and by worthy conduct pursue their effects.
Through our Lord Jesus Christ, your Son,
who lives and reigns with you in the unity of the Holy Spirit,
one God, for ever and ever. *Amen.*

FIRST READING *(Genesis 9:8-15)*
God said to Noah and to his sons with him: "See, I am now establishing my **covenant**✝ with you and your descendants after you and with every living creature that was with you: all the birds, and the various tame and wild animals that were with you and came out of the ark. I will establish my covenant with you, that never again shall all bodily creatures be destroyed by the waters of a flood; there shall not be another flood to devastate the earth." God added: "This is the sign that I am giving for all ages to come, of the covenant between me and you and every living creature with you: I set my bow in the clouds to serve as a sign of the covenant between me and the earth. When I bring clouds over the earth, and the bow appears in the clouds, I will recall the covenant I have

made between me and you and all living beings, so that the waters shall never again become a flood to destroy all mortal beings."

The word of the Lord. *Thanks be to God.*

RESPONSORIAL PSALM *(Psalm 25:4-5, 6-7, 8-9)*

℟ **Your ways, O Lord, are love and truth to those who keep your covenant.**

Your ways, O LORD, make known to me;
  teach me your paths.
Guide me in your truth and teach me,
  for you are God my savior. ℟

Remember that your compassion, O LORD,
  and your love are from of old.
In your kindness remember me,
  because of your goodness, O LORD. ℟

Good and upright is the LORD,
  thus he shows sinners the way.
He guides the humble to justice,
  and he teaches the humble his way. ℟

SECOND READING *(1 Peter 3:18-22)*

Beloved: Christ suffered for sins once, the righteous for the sake of the unrighteous, that he might lead you to God. Put to death in the flesh, he was brought to life in the Spirit. In it he also went to preach to the spirits in prison, who had once been disobedient while God patiently waited in the days of Noah during the building of the ark, in which a few persons, eight in all, were saved through water. This prefigured baptism, which saves you now. It is not a removal of dirt from the body but an appeal to God for a clear conscience, through the resurrection of Jesus Christ, who has gone into heaven and is at the right hand of

God, with angels, authorities, and powers subject to him.

The word of the Lord. ***Thanks be to God.***

VERSE BEFORE THE GOSPEL *(Matthew 4:4b)*
Glory and praise to you, Lord Jesus Christ! One does not live on bread alone, but on every word that comes forth from the mouth of God. *Glory and praise to you, Lord Jesus Christ!*

GOSPEL *(Mark 1:12-15)*
A reading from the holy Gospel according to Mark.
Glory to you, O Lord.

The Spirit drove Jesus out into the desert, and he remained in the desert for forty days, tempted by Satan. He was among wild beasts, and the angels ministered to him.

After John had been arrested, Jesus came to Galilee proclaiming the gospel of God: "This is the time of fulfillment. The kingdom of God is at hand. Repent, and believe in the gospel."

The Gospel of the Lord. ***Praise to you, Lord Jesus Christ.***

RITE OF ELECTION

PROFESSION OF FAITH *(page 13)*

PRAYER OF THE FAITHFUL

PREPARATION OF GIFTS *(page 16)*

PRAYER OVER THE OFFERINGS
Give us the right dispositions, O Lord, we pray,
to make these offerings,
for with them we celebrate the beginning
of this venerable and sacred time.
Through Christ our Lord. ***Amen.***

PREFACE: THE TEMPTATION OF THE LORD

It is truly right and just, our duty and our salvation,
always and everywhere to give you thanks,
Lord, holy Father, almighty and eternal God,
through Christ our Lord.

By abstaining forty long days from earthly food,
he consecrated through his fast
the pattern of our Lenten observance
and, by overturning all the snares of the ancient serpent,
taught us to cast out the leaven of malice,
so that, celebrating worthily the Paschal Mystery,
we might pass over at last to the eternal paschal feast.

And so, with the company of Angels and Saints,
we sing the hymn of your praise,
as without end we acclaim:
Holy, Holy, Holy Lord God of hosts... *(page 35)*

COMMUNION ANTIPHON *(Matthew 4:4)*

One does not live by bread alone, but by every word that comes
forth from the mouth of God.

Or *(Cf. Psalm 91 [90]:4)*

The Lord will conceal you with his pinions, and under his wings
you will trust.

PRAYER AFTER COMMUNION
Renewed now with heavenly bread,
by which faith is nourished, hope increased,
and charity strengthened,
we pray, O Lord,
that we may learn to hunger for Christ,
the true and living Bread,
and strive to live by every word
which proceeds from your mouth.
Through Christ our Lord. *Amen.*

• TAKING A CLOSER LOOK •

✚ **Covenant** A covenant is a formal agreement between two persons or parties that spells out the obligations of their relationship. In the biblical world, the general expectations were modeled on the customs that guided relationships between persons of unequal honor, status, and wealth. These relationships were voluntary and freely entered into and were not required by law. The covenant bound the parties in mutual and reciprocal obligations. The "patron" or more powerful person (like God) promised to provide for and protect the less powerful "clients" (from the Latin word for dependents). In return, to enhance the honor and reputation of the patron, the clients offered respect, praise, and gratitude, and other favors when requested.

PRAYER OVER THE PEOPLE

May bountiful blessing, O Lord, we pray,
come down upon your people,
that hope may grow in tribulation,
virtue be strengthened in temptation,
and eternal redemption be assured.
Through Christ our Lord. *Amen.*

DISMISSAL *(page 57)* ❖

• RESPONDING TO THE WORD •

The rainbow was Noah's reminder of God's covenant with all creation.

➡ *What, like the rainbow, reminds me of God's loving care for creation?*

Peter reminds us it is not outer dirt but the inner spirit that needs cleansing.

➡ *What inner renewal do I most desire this Lent?*

Jesus' desert experience led to a new ministry for others.

➡ *How might my Lenten changes make me a better announcer for God's good news?*

February 25

Rising from death

A central focus of our Lenten journey is dealing with the tension between life and death. Like the disciples at the transfiguration, we too try to reconcile death with the glory of God. We ask, "What does this 'rising from the dead' mean?"

Occasionally we have a dramatic "rising from the dead" experience when we, like Isaac in our first reading, walk away from a near-to-death experience.

More commonly, though, it means rising above the despair, hardships, and poverties that St. Paul lists in his letter to the Romans in the verse following today's reading (v. 35). After weighing the troubles of life against the glory of God, Paul concludes a few verses later: "In all these things we conquer overwhelmingly through him who loved us" (v. 27).

But eventually for Jesus and for each one of us as baptized Christians, "rising from the dead" means passing from this life to the next. It is this dying and rising again that we celebrate at every baptism, each confession, and every time we gather around the altar to receive Christ at Mass.

Like the transfiguration, Holy Eucharist draws us into the paschal mystery. As we receive anew the blessed and broken body of Christ, let us give thanks for God's gift of eternal life.

■ BEVERLY ILLAUQ

ENTRANCE ANTIPHON *(Cf. Psalm 27 [26]:8-9)*

Of you my heart has spoken: Seek his face. It is your face, O Lord, that I seek; hide not your face from me.

Or *(Cf. Psalm 25 [24]:6, 2, 22)*

Remember your compassion, O Lord, and your merciful love, for they are from of old. Let not our enemies exult over us. Redeem us, O God of Israel, from all our distress.

INTRODUCTORY RITES *(page 10)*

COLLECT

O God, who have commanded us
to listen to your beloved Son,
be pleased, we pray,
to nourish us inwardly by your word,
that, with spiritual sight made pure,
we may rejoice to behold your glory.
Through our Lord Jesus Christ, your Son,
who lives and reigns with you in the unity of the Holy Spirit,
one God, for ever and ever. ***Amen.***

FIRST READING *(Genesis 22:1-2, 9a, 10-13, 15-18)*

God put Abraham to the test. He called to him, "Abraham!" "Here I am!" he replied. Then God said: "Take your son Isaac, your only one, whom you love, and go to the land of Moriah.* There you shall offer him up as a holocaust on a height that I will point out to you."

When they came to the place of which God had told him, Abraham built an altar there and arranged the wood on it. Then he reached out and took the knife to slaughter his son. But the LORD's messenger called to him from heaven, "Abraham, Abraham!" "Here I am!" he answered. "Do not lay your hand on the boy," said the messenger. "Do not do the least thing to him. I know now how devoted you are to God, since you did not withhold from me your own beloved son." As Abraham looked about, he spied a ram caught by its horns in the thicket. So he went and took the ram and offered it up as a holocaust in place of his son.

Again the LORD's messenger called to Abraham from heaven and said: "I swear by myself, declares the LORD, that because you acted as you did in not withholding from me your beloved son, I will bless you abundantly and make your descendants as countless as the stars of the sky and the sands of the seashore; your descendants shall take possession of the gates of their enemies, and in your descendants all the nations of the earth shall find blessing—all this because you obeyed my command."

The word of the Lord. ***Thanks be to God.***

RESPONSORIAL PSALM *(Psalm 116:10, 15, 16-17, 18-19)*
℟ **I will walk before the Lord, in the land of the living.**

I believed, even when I said,
  "I am greatly afflicted."
Precious in the eyes of the LORD
  is the death of his faithful ones. ℟
O LORD, I am your servant;
  I am your servant, the son of your handmaid;
  you have loosed my bonds.
To you will I offer sacrifice of thanksgiving,
  and I will call upon the name of the LORD. ℟
My vows to the LORD I will pay

in the presence of all his people,
in the courts of the house of the LORD,
in your midst, O Jerusalem. ℟

SECOND READING *(Romans 8:31b-34)*

Brothers and sisters: If God is for us, who can be against us? He who did not spare his own Son but handed him over for us all, how will he not also give us everything else along with him?

Who will bring a charge against God's chosen ones? It is God who acquits us, who will condemn? Christ Jesus it is who died—or, rather, was raised—who also is at the right hand of God, who indeed intercedes for us.

The word of the Lord. *Thanks be to God.*

VERSE BEFORE THE GOSPEL *(See Matthew 17:5)*

Glory and praise to you, Lord Jesus Christ! From the shining cloud the Father's voice is heard: This is my beloved Son, listen to him. *Glory and praise to you, Lord Jesus Christ!*

GOSPEL *(Mark 9:2-10)*

A reading from the holy Gospel according to Mark.
Glory to you, O Lord.

Jesus took Peter, James, and John and led them up a high mountain apart by themselves. And he was **transfigured**✝ before them, and his clothes became dazzling white, such as no fuller on earth could bleach them. Then Elijah appeared to them along with Moses, and they were conversing with Jesus. Then Peter said to Jesus in reply, "Rabbi, it is good that we are here! Let us make three tents: one for you, one for Moses, and one for Elijah." He hardly knew what to say, they were so terrified. Then a cloud came, casting a shadow over them; from the cloud came a voice, "This is my beloved Son. Listen to him." Suddenly, looking around, they no longer saw anyone but Jesus alone with them.

As they were coming down from the mountain, he charged them not to relate what they had seen to anyone, except when the Son of Man had risen from the dead. So they kept the matter to themselves, questioning what rising from the dead meant.

The Gospel of the Lord. *Praise to you, Lord Jesus Christ.*

PROFESSION OF FAITH *(page 13)*

PRAYER OF THE FAITHFUL

PREPARATION OF GIFTS *(page 16)*

PRAYER OVER THE OFFERINGS
May this sacrifice, O Lord, we pray,
cleanse us of our faults
and sanctify your faithful in body and mind
for the celebration of the paschal festivities.
Through Christ our Lord. *Amen.*

PREFACE: THE TRANSFIGURATION OF THE LORD
It is truly right and just, our duty and our salvation,
always and everywhere to give you thanks,
Lord, holy Father, almighty and eternal God,
through Christ our Lord.

For after he had told the disciples of his coming Death,
on the holy mountain he manifested to them his glory,
to show, even by the testimony of the law and the prophets,
that the Passion leads to the glory of the Resurrection.

And so, with the Powers of heaven,
we worship you constantly on earth,
and before your majesty
without end we acclaim:
Holy, Holy, Holy Lord God of hosts... *(page 35)*

COMMUNION ANTIPHON *(Matthew 17:5)*
This is my beloved Son, with whom I am well pleased; listen
to him.

PRAYER AFTER COMMUNION
As we receive these glorious mysteries,
we make thanksgiving to you, O Lord,
for allowing us while still on earth
to be partakers even now of the things of heaven.
Through Christ our Lord. ***Amen.***

• TAKING A CLOSER LOOK •

✣ **Transfigured** Although the Greek word here (*metamorphosis*)
commonly described a change in form or appearance that a god might
make to appear to humans, the gospel writers suggest a completely new
meaning. The transfiguration is a glimpse of God's glory breaking forth
from Jesus' human form. After revealing to the disciples that, as Messiah,
he would have to suffer, Jesus' changed appearance previews the change
that he will undergo at his resurrection. The dazzling light, the divine voice
of approval, and the support of the whole Jewish tradition represented
by Moses (the Jewish Law) and Elijah (the prophets) signal that Jesus'
messianic suffering is the fulfillment of God's plan for salvation.

PRAYER OVER THE PEOPLE

Bless your faithful, we pray, O Lord,
with a blessing that endures for ever,
and keep them faithful
to the Gospel of your Only Begotten Son,
so that they may always desire and at last attain
that glory whose beauty he showed in his own Body,
to the amazement of his Apostles.
Through Christ our Lord. *Amen.*

DISMISSAL *(page 57)* ✦

• RESPONDING TO THE WORD •

Abraham was asked to sacrifice what was most dear to him—his beloved son.	Paul feels that God is for us, bringing new life through Christ.	Jesus' baptism affirms that he is God's beloved son.
➡ *What might I need to give up to live more closely with God?*	➡ *What sign gives me confidence that God is for me?*	➡ *What evidence from my life shows that I am God's beloved child?*

March 4

It's never too late!

Our Lenten journey is well underway. Has the enthusiasm with which we welcomed Ash Wednesday, at the start of a season of inner growth, flourished? Or has it dimmed? Lent is a time to deepen our relationship with God. Has our progress been a source of delight to God? If not, it's never too late to begin!

Today's first reading reviews the Ten Commandments. God has expectations of us. Jesus later summarized the lot into two all-encompassing commandments: love God and love one another. Are our relationships with others life-giving?

In today's gospel, we see Jesus in the temple as Passover approaches. He is outraged that his "Father's house" is being used as a trading center. He restores it to a prayerful state. Are we striving for wholeness? Are our souls in need of spring-cleaning?

We might ask ourselves today: what cobwebs might we wipe away before we celebrate Easter? Does pride distance us from God or others? Do we judge, criticize, or fail to recognize the needs of others? In the silence of our hearts, do we hear God whispering, "Come back to me"? We are temples of the Spirit, called to holiness and to the joy of eternal life. How blessed we are!

■ BARBARA D'ARTOIS

Parishes engaged in the Rite of Christian Initiation of Adults (RCIA) may celebrate the First Scrutiny today (see page 196).

ENTRANCE ANTIPHON *(Cf. Psalm 25 [24]:15–16)*

My eyes are always on the Lord, for he rescues my feet from the snare. Turn to me and have mercy on me, for I am alone and poor.

INTRODUCTORY RITES *(page 10)*

COLLECT

O God, author of every mercy and of all goodness,
who in fasting, prayer and almsgiving
have shown us a remedy for sin,
look graciously on this confession of our lowliness,
that we, who are bowed down by our conscience,
may always be lifted up by your mercy.
Through our Lord Jesus Christ, your Son,
who lives and reigns with you in the unity of the Holy Spirit,
one God, for ever and ever. ***Amen.***

These are the readings for Year B. The readings for Year A may also be used (see page 196).

FIRST READING *(Exodus 20:1–17)*
For the shorter version, omit the indented parts in brackets.

In those days, God delivered all these commandments: "I, the LORD, am your God, who brought you out of the land of Egypt, that place of slavery. You shall not have other gods besides me.
[You shall not carve idols for yourselves in the shape of anything in the sky above or on the earth below or in the waters

beneath the earth; you shall not bow down before them or worship them. For I, the LORD, your God, am a jealous God, inflicting punishment for their fathers' wickedness on the children of those who hate me, down to the third and fourth generation; but bestowing mercy down to the thousandth generation on the children of those who love me and keep my commandments.]

"You shall not take the name of the LORD, your God, in vain. For the LORD will not leave unpunished the one who takes his name in vain.

"Remember to keep holy the sabbath day.

[Six days you may labor and do all your work, but the seventh day is the sabbath of the LORD, your God. No work may be done then either by you, or your son or daughter, or your male or female slave, or your beast, or by the alien who lives with you. In six days the LORD made the heavens and the earth, the sea and all that is in them; but on the seventh day he rested. That is why the LORD has blessed the sabbath day and made it holy.]

"Honor your father and your mother, that you may have a long life in the land which the LORD, your God, is giving you. You shall not kill. You shall not commit adultery. You shall not steal. You shall not bear false witness against your neighbor. You shall not covet your neighbor's house. You shall not covet your neighbor's wife, nor his male or female slave, nor his ox or ass, nor anything else that belongs to him."

The word of the Lord. ***Thanks be to God.***

RESPONSORIAL PSALM *(Psalm 19:8, 9, 10, 11)*
℟ **Lord, you have the words of everlasting life.**

The law of the LORD is perfect,
  refreshing the soul;
the decree of the LORD is trustworthy,
  giving wisdom to the simple. ℟

The precepts of the LORD are right,
  rejoicing the heart;
the command of the LORD is clear,
  enlightening the eye. ℟

The fear of the LORD is pure,
  enduring forever;
the ordinances of the LORD are true,
  all of them just. ℟

They are more precious than gold,
  than a heap of purest gold;
sweeter also than syrup
  or honey from the comb. ℟

SECOND READING *(1 Corinthians 1:22-25)*

Brothers and sisters: Jews demand signs and Greeks look for wisdom, but we proclaim Christ crucified, a stumbling block to Jews and foolishness to Gentiles, but to those who are called, Jews and Greeks alike, Christ the power of God and the wisdom of God. For the foolishness of God is wiser than human wisdom, and the weakness of God is stronger than human strength.

The word of the Lord. ***Thanks be to God.***

VERSE BEFORE THE GOSPEL *(John 3:16)*
Glory and praise to you, Lord Jesus Christ! God so loved the world that he gave his only Son, so that everyone who believes in

him might have eternal life. ***Glory and praise to you, Lord Jesus Christ!***

GOSPEL *(John 2:13–25)*

A reading from the holy Gospel according to John.
Glory to you, O Lord.

Since the Passover of the Jews was near, Jesus went up to Jerusalem. He found in the temple area those who sold oxen, sheep, and doves, as well as the **money changers**✝ seated there. He made a whip out of cords and drove them all out of the temple area, with the sheep and oxen, and spilled the coins of the money changers and overturned their tables, and to those who sold doves he said, "Take these out of here, and stop making my Father's house a marketplace." His disciples recalled the words of Scripture, *Zeal for your house will consume me.* At this the Jews answered and said to him, "What sign can you show us for doing this?" Jesus answered and said to them, "Destroy this temple and in three days I will raise it up." The Jews said, "This temple has been under construction for forty-six years, and you will raise it up in three days?" But he was speaking about the temple of his body. Therefore, when he was raised from the dead, his disciples remembered that he had said this, and they came to believe the Scripture and the word Jesus had spoken.

While he was in Jerusalem for the feast of Passover, many began to believe in his name when they saw the signs he was doing. But Jesus would not trust himself to them because he knew them all, and did not need anyone to testify about human nature. He himself understood it well.

The Gospel of the Lord. ***Praise to you, Lord Jesus Christ.***

PROFESSION OF FAITH *(page 13)*

PRAYER OF THE FAITHFUL

PREPARATION OF GIFTS *(page 16)*

PRAYER OVER THE OFFERINGS
Be pleased, O Lord, with these sacrificial offerings,
and grant that we who beseech pardon for our own sins,
may take care to forgive our neighbor.
Through Christ our Lord. *Amen.*

PREFACE *(Lent 1–2, page 21)*

COMMUNION ANTIPHON *(Cf. John 4:13–14)*
For anyone who drinks it, says the Lord, the water I shall give will
become in him a spring welling up to eternal life.

• TAKING A CLOSER LOOK •

✦ **Money changers** The Jerusalem temple was not merely a
place of worship but also a market where sacrificial animals were sold
and a bank where the state treasury was kept (recall the widow who
is contributing to the treasury in Mark 12:41-44). Jews throughout the
world were obligated to pay a special tax each year to provide for the
upkeep of the temple. But since Roman and Greek coins were stamped
with images of their gods and emperors, these coins could not be used
to pay the temple tax. Thus money changers congregated in the outer
court of the temple and exchanged these pagan coins for Jewish coins
that could be used for temple business.

PRAYER AFTER COMMUNION

As we receive the pledge
of things yet hidden in heaven
and are nourished while still on earth
with the Bread that comes from on high,
we humbly entreat you, O Lord,
that what is being brought about in us in mystery
may come to true completion.
Through Christ our Lord. *Amen.*

PRAYER OVER THE PEOPLE

Direct, O Lord, we pray, the hearts of your faithful,
and in your kindness grant your servants this grace:
that, abiding in the love of you and their neighbor,
they may fulfill the whole of your commands.
Through Christ our Lord. *Amen.*

DISMISSAL *(page 57)* ✣

• RESPONDING TO THE WORD •

God's commandments reveal the way for us to have a good community.	Jesus' crucifixion as a criminal was a stumbling block for many.	Jesus disrupts the non-religious activities in the temple.
▸ *Which commandment is hardest for me to observe now in my life?*	▸ *What stumbling block makes it hard for me to accept Jesus today?*	▸ *What might I need to disrupt to restore a more religious attitude when I go to Mass?*

CHRISTIAN INITIATION: FIRST SCRUTINY

*The Mass prayers and readings below are for use
in parishes celebrating the First Scrutiny.*

ENTRANCE ANTIPHON *(Ezekiel 36.23-26)*

When I prove my holiness among you, I will gather you from
all the foreign lands and I will pour clean water upon you and
cleanse you from all your impurities, and I will give you a new
spirit, says the Lord.

Or *(Cf. Isaiah 55:1)*

Come to the waters, you who are thirsty, says the Lord; you who
have no money, come and drink joyfully.

COLLECT

Grant, we pray, O Lord,
that these chosen ones may come worthily and wisely
to the confession of your praise,
so that in accordance with that first dignity
which they lost by original sin
they may be fashioned anew through your glory.
Through our Lord Jesus Christ, your Son,
who lives and reigns with you in the unity of the Holy Spirit,
one God, for ever and ever. *Amen.*

FIRST READING *(Exodus 17:3-7)*

In those days, in their thirst for water, the people grumbled against
Moses, saying, "Why did you ever make us leave Egypt? Was it
just to have us die here of thirst with our children and our live-
stock?" So Moses cried out to the LORD, "What shall I do with this

people? A little more and they will stone me!" The LORD answered Moses, "Go over there in front of the people, along with some of the elders of Israel, holding in your hand, as you go, the staff with which you struck the river. I will be standing there in front of you on the rock in Horeb.* Strike the rock, and the water will flow from it for the people to drink." This Moses did, in the presence of the elders of Israel. The place was called Massah* and Meribah,* because the Israelites quarreled there and tested the LORD, saying, "Is the LORD in our midst or not?"

The word of the Lord. *Thanks be to God.*

RESPONSORIAL PSALM *(Psalm 95:1-2, 6-7, 8-9)*

℟ **If today you hear his voice, harden not your hearts.**

Come, let us sing joyfully to the LORD;
  let us acclaim the Rock of our salvation.
Let us come into his presence with thanksgiving;
  let us joyfully sing psalms to him. ℟
Come, let us bow down in worship;
  let us kneel before the LORD who made us.
For he is our God,
  and we are the people he shepherds, the flock he guides. ℟
Oh, that today you would hear his voice:
  "Harden not your hearts as at Meribah,*
  as in the day of Massah* in the desert,
where your fathers tempted me;
  they tested me though they had seen my works." ℟

SECOND READING *(Romans 5:1-2, 5-8)*

Brothers and sisters: Since we have been justified by faith, we have peace with God through our Lord Jesus Christ, through whom we have gained access by faith to this grace in which we stand, and we boast in hope of the glory of God.

And hope does not disappoint, because the love of God has been poured out into our hearts through the Holy Spirit who has been given to us. For Christ, while we were still helpless, died at the appointed time for the ungodly. Indeed, only with difficulty does one die for a just person, though perhaps for a good person one might even find courage to die. But God proves his love for us in that while we were still sinners Christ died for us.

The word of the Lord. *Thanks be to God.*

VERSE BEFORE THE GOSPEL *(See John 4:42, 15)*
Glory and praise to you, Lord Jesus Christ! Lord, you are truly the Savior of the world; give me living water, that I may never thirst again. *Glory and praise to you, Lord Jesus Christ!*

GOSPEL *(John 4:5–42)*
For the shorter version, omit the indented parts in brackets.

A reading from the holy Gospel according to John.
Glory to you, O Lord.

Jesus came to a town of Samaria* called Sychar,* near the plot of land that Jacob had given to his son Joseph. Jacob's well was there. Jesus, tired from his journey, sat down there at the well. It was about noon.

A woman of Samaria came to draw water. Jesus said to her, "Give me a drink." His disciples had gone into the town to buy food. The Samaritan woman said to him, "How can you, a Jew, ask me, a Samaritan woman, for a drink?"—For Jews use nothing in common with Samaritans.—Jesus answered and said to her, "If you knew the gift of God and who is saying to you, 'Give me a drink,' you would have asked him and he would have given you living water." The woman said to him, "Sir, you do not even have a bucket and the cistern is deep; where then can you get this living water? Are you greater than our father Jacob, who gave us this cistern and drank from it himself with his children and his flocks?" Jesus answered and said to her, "Everyone who drinks this water will be thirsty again; but whoever drinks the water I shall give will never thirst; the water I shall give will become in him a spring of water welling up to eternal life." The woman said to him, "Sir, give me this water, so that I may not be thirsty or have to keep coming here to draw water."

[Jesus said to her, "Go call your husband and come back." The woman answered and said to him, "I do not have a husband." Jesus answered her, "You are right in saying, 'I do not have a husband.' For you have had five husbands, and the one you have now is not your husband. What you have said is true." The woman said to him, "Sir,] "I can see that you are a prophet. Our ancestors worshiped on this mountain; but you people say that the place to worship is in Jerusalem." Jesus said to her, "Believe me, woman, the hour is coming when you will worship the Father neither on this mountain nor in Jerusalem. You people worship what you do not understand; we worship what we understand, because salvation is from the Jews. But the hour is coming, and is now here, when true worshipers will worship the Father in Spirit and truth; and indeed the Father seeks such people to worship him. God is Spirit, and those who worship him must worship in Spirit and truth." The woman said to him, "I know that the Messiah is coming, the one called the Christ; when he comes, he will tell us everything." Jesus said to her, "I am he, the one speaking with you."

[At that moment his disciples returned, and were amazed that he was talking with a woman, but still no one said, "What are you looking for?" or "Why are you talking with her?" The woman left her water jar and went into the town and said to the people, "Come see a man who told me everything I have done. Could he possibly be the Christ?" They went out of the town and came to him. Meanwhile, the disciples urged him, "Rabbi, eat." But he said to them, "I have food to eat of which you do not know." So the disciples said to one another, "Could someone have brought him something to eat?" Jesus said to them, "My food is to do the will of the one who sent me and to finish his work. Do you not say, 'In four months the harvest will be here'? I tell you, look up and see the fields ripe for the harvest. The reaper is already receiving payment and gathering crops for eternal life, so that the sower and reaper can rejoice together. For here the saying is verified that 'One sows and another reaps.' I sent you to reap what you have not worked for; others have done the work, and you are sharing the fruits of their work."]

Many of the Samaritans of that town began to believe in him [because of the word of the woman who testified, "He told me everything I have done."]

When the Samaritans came to him, they invited him to stay with them; and he stayed there two days. Many more began to believe in him because of his word, and they said to the woman, "We no longer believe because of your word; for we have heard for ourselves, and we know that this is truly the savior of the world."

The Gospel of the Lord. ***Praise to you, Lord Jesus Christ.***

PRAYER OVER THE OFFERINGS

May your merciful grace prepare your servants, O Lord,
for the worthy celebration of these mysteries
and lead them to it by a devout way of life.
Through Christ our Lord. *Amen.*

PREFACE : THE SAMARITAN WOMAN

It is truly right and just, our duty and our salvation,
always and everywhere to give you thanks,
Lord, holy Father, almighty and eternal God,
through Christ our Lord.

For when he asked the Samaritan woman for water to drink,
he had already created the gift of faith within her
and so ardently did he thirst for her faith,
that he kindled in her the fire of divine love.

And so we, too, give you thanks
and with the Angels
praise your mighty deeds, as we acclaim:
Holy, Holy, Holy Lord God of hosts... *(page 35)*

COMMUNION ANTIPHON *(Cf. John 4:13-14)*

For anyone who drinks it, says the Lord, the water I shall give will
become in him a spring welling up to eternal life.

PRAYER AFTER COMMUNION

Give help, O Lord, we pray,
by the grace of your redemption
and be pleased to protect and prepare
those you are to initiate
through the Sacraments of eternal life.
Through Christ our Lord. *Amen.* ✤

March 11

Love is the way

While it may seem odd, I look forward to Lent all year because it permits me the luxury of meditating on the rich tradition of lament that is often forgotten or ignored altogether. Lament is the action of truly mourning the incompleteness of our lives, our society, and our world in the sight of God. There is a wealth of emotions bubbling in the reading from Chronicles as the destruction of Jerusalem and the Temple has effectively terminated the sacred worship space of the Jewish people. Psalm 137 reiterates the destruction and one is drawn into the devastation through the psalmist's plaintive words.

John's gospel shows a way out of the lament and devastation: "God so loved the world that he gave his only Son." Love is the path out of lament and devastation. The unconditional love that God has for us is something freely given and can never be earned. Through this ultimate sacrifice on our behalf, we become people of the light, forever abandoning the darkness that threatens to overshadow hope.

■ **MARILYN-ANN ELPHICK**

*Parishes engaged in the Rite of Christian Initiation of
Adults (RCIA) may celebrate the Second Scrutiny today
(see page 209).*

ENTRANCE ANTIPHON *(Cf. Isaiah 66:10–11)*

Rejoice, Jerusalem, and all who love her. Be joyful,
all who were in mourning; exult and be satisfied at
her consoling breast.

INTRODUCTORY RITES *(page 10)*

COLLECT

O God, who through your Word
reconcile the human race to yourself in a wonderful way,
grant, we pray,
that with prompt devotion and eager faith
the Christian people may hasten
toward the solemn celebrations to come.
Through our Lord Jesus Christ, your Son,
who lives and reigns with you in the unity of the Holy Spirit,
one God, for ever and ever. ***Amen.***

*These are the readings for Year B. The readings for Year A may also be
used (see page 209).*

FIRST READING *(2 Chronicles 36:14–16, 19–23)*

I n those days, all the princes of Judah, the priests, and the
people added infidelity to infidelity, practicing all the abomi-
nations of the nations and polluting the LORD's temple which he
had consecrated in Jerusalem.

Early and often did the LORD, the God of their fathers, send
his messengers to them, for he had compassion on his people

and his dwelling place. But they mocked the messengers of God, despised his warnings, and scoffed at his prophets, until the anger of the LORD against his people was so inflamed that there was no remedy. Their enemies burnt the house of God, tore down the walls of Jerusalem, set all its palaces afire, and destroyed all its precious objects. Those who escaped the sword were carried captive to Babylon,* where they became servants of the king of the Chaldeans* and his sons until the kingdom of the Persians came to power. All this was to fulfill the word of the LORD spoken by Jeremiah: "Until the land has retrieved its lost sabbaths, during all the time it lies waste it shall have rest while seventy years are fulfilled."

In the first year of Cyrus, king of Persia, in order to fulfill the word of the LORD spoken by Jeremiah, the LORD inspired King Cyrus of Persia to issue this proclamation throughout his kingdom, both by word of mouth and in writing: "Thus says Cyrus, king of Persia: All the kingdoms of the earth the LORD, the God of heaven, has given to me, and he has also charged me to build him a house in Jerusalem, which is in Judah. Whoever, therefore, among you belongs to any part of his people, let him go up, and may his God be with him!"

The word of the Lord. *Thanks be to God.*

RESPONSORIAL PSALM *(Psalm 137:1-2, 3, 4-5, 6)*
R. Let my tongue be silenced, if I ever forget you!

By the streams of Babylon*
    we sat and wept
    when we remembered Zion.*
On the aspens of that land
    we hung up our harps. R.
For there our captors asked of us

the lyrics of our songs,
and our despoilers urged us to be joyous:
    "Sing for us the songs of Zion!" ℟
How could we sing a song of the LORD
    in a foreign land?
If I forget you, Jerusalem,
    may my right hand be forgotten! ℟
May my tongue cleave to my palate
    if I remember you not,
if I place not Jerusalem
    ahead of my joy. ℟

SECOND READING (*Ephesians 2:4-10*)

Brothers and sisters: God, who is rich in **mercy**,✝ because
of the great love he had for us, even when we were dead in
our transgressions, brought us to life with Christ—by grace you
have been saved—, raised us up with him, and seated us with
him in the heavens in Christ Jesus, that in the ages to come he
might show the immeasurable riches of his grace in his kindness
to us in Christ Jesus. For by grace you have been saved through
faith, and this is not from you; it is the gift of God; it is not from
works, so no one may boast. For we are his handiwork, created
in Christ Jesus for the good works that God has prepared in
advance, that we should live in them.

The word of the Lord. *Thanks be to God.*

VERSE BEFORE THE GOSPEL (*John 3:16*)

Glory and praise to you, Lord Jesus Christ! God so loved the
world that he gave his only Son, so everyone who believes in him
might have eternal life. *Glory and praise to you, Lord Jesus
Christ!*

GOSPEL *(John 3:14–21)*

A reading from the holy Gospel according to John.

Glory to you, O Lord.

Jesus said to Nicodemus: "Just as Moses lifted up the serpent in the desert, so must the Son of Man be lifted up, so that everyone who believes in him may have eternal life."

For God so loved the world that he gave his only Son, so that everyone who believes in him might not perish but might have eternal life. For God did not send his Son into the world to condemn the world, but that the world might be saved through him. Whoever believes in him will not be condemned, but whoever does not believe has already been condemned, because he has not believed in the name of the only Son of God. And this is the verdict, that the light came into the world, but people preferred darkness to light, because their works were evil. For everyone who does wicked things hates the light and does not come toward the light, so that his works might not be exposed. But whoever lives the truth comes to the light, so that his works may be clearly seen as done in God.

The Gospel of the Lord. *Praise to you, Lord Jesus Christ.*

PROFESSION OF FAITH *(page 13)*

PRAYER OF THE FAITHFUL

PREPARATION OF GIFTS *(page 16)*

PRAYER OVER THE OFFERINGS

We place before you with joy these offerings,
which bring eternal remedy, O Lord,
praying that we may both faithfully revere them
and present them to you, as is fitting,
for the salvation of all the world.
Through Christ our Lord. *Amen.*

PREFACE *(Lent 1-2, page 21)*

COMMUNION ANTIPHON *(Cf. Psalm 122 [121]:3-4)*

Jerusalem is built as a city bonded as one together. It is there that
the tribes go up, the tribes of the Lord,
to praise the name of the Lord.

• TAKING A CLOSER LOOK •

✤ **Mercy** In the Old Testament, mercy usually identifies a complex
Hebrew idea that describes God's special covenant love. God's attitude of love or attachment to the covenant partners includes aspects
of loyalty, dependability, trustworthiness, and an eagerness to help
when situations turn bad. Paul echoes this fierce fidelity by describing
God's eagerness to rescue or save us when we were alienated by sin.
God's desire to be in relationship with us keeps God alert to our cries
for help and eager to deliver us from what separates us from God.

PRAYER AFTER COMMUNION

O God, who enlighten everyone who comes into this world,
illuminate our hearts, we pray,
with the splendor of your grace,
that we may always ponder
what is worthy and pleasing to your majesty
and love you in all sincerity.
Through Christ our Lord. *Amen.*

PRAYER OVER THE PEOPLE

Look upon those who call to you, O Lord,
and sustain the weak;
give life by your unfailing light
to those who walk in the shadow of death,
and bring those rescued by your mercy from every evil
to reach the highest good.
Through Christ our Lord. *Amen.*

DISMISSAL *(page 57)* ❖

• RESPONDING TO THE WORD •

God sends messengers to invite the people to change their ways.

➡ *Who is God sending me to help me make my Lenten changes?*

Our salvation or right relationship with God is God's gift to us.

➡ *How might I express my gratitude for this divine gift?*

Jesus is the light that drives away the shadows in our hearts.

➡ *What shadowy areas in me has Christ's light been shining into this Lent?*

CHRISTIAN INITIATION: SECOND SCRUTINY

*The Mass prayers and readings below are for use
in parishes celebrating the Second Scrutiny.*

ENTRANCE ANTIPHON *(Cf. Psalm 25 [24]:15-16)*

My eyes are always on the Lord, for he rescues my feet from the snare. Turn to me and have mercy on me, for I am alone and poor.

COLLECT

Almighty ever-living God,
give to your Church an increase in spiritual joy,
so that those once born of earth
may be reborn as citizens of heaven.
Through our Lord Jesus Christ, your Son,
who lives and reigns with you in the unity of the Holy Spirit,
one God, for ever and ever. *Amen.*

FIRST READING *(1 Samuel 16:1b, 6-7, 10-13a)*

The Lord said to Samuel: "Fill your horn with oil, and be on your way. I am sending you to Jesse of Bethlehem, for I have chosen my king from among his sons."

As Jesse and his sons came to the sacrifice, Samuel looked at Eliab and thought, "Surely the Lord's anointed is here before him." But the Lord said to Samuel: "Do not judge from his appearance or from his lofty stature, because I have rejected him. Not as man sees does God see, because man sees the appearance but the Lord looks into the heart." In the same way Jesse presented seven sons before Samuel, but Samuel said to Jesse,

"The LORD has not chosen any one of these." Then Samuel asked Jesse, "Are these all the sons you have?" Jesse replied, "There is still the youngest, who is tending the sheep." Samuel said to Jesse, "Send for him; we will not begin the sacrificial banquet until he arrives here." Jesse sent and had the young man brought to them. He was ruddy, a youth handsome to behold and making a splendid appearance. The LORD said, "There—anoint him, for this is the one!" Then Samuel, with the horn of oil in hand, anointed David in the presence of his brothers; and from that day on, the spirit of the LORD rushed upon David.

The word of the Lord. *Thanks be to God.*

RESPONSORIAL PSALM *(Psalm 23:1–3a, 3b–4, 5, 6)*
℞ **The Lord is my shepherd; there is nothing I shall want.**

The LORD is my shepherd; I shall not want.
    In verdant pastures he gives me repose;
beside restful waters he leads me;
    he refreshes my soul. ℞
He guides me in right paths
    for his name's sake.
Even though I walk in the dark valley
    I fear no evil; for you are at my side
with your rod and your staff
    that give me courage. ℞
You spread the table before me
    in the sight of my foes;
you anoint my head with oil;
    my cup overflows. ℞
Only goodness and kindness follow me
    all the days of my life;

and I shall dwell in the house of the LORD

for years to come. ℟

SECOND READING (*Ephesians 5:8-14*)

Brothers and sisters: You were once darkness, but now you are light in the Lord. Live as children of light, for light produces every kind of goodness and righteousness and truth. Try to learn what is pleasing to the Lord. Take no part in the fruitless works of darkness; rather expose them, for it is shameful even to mention the things done by them in secret; but everything exposed by the light becomes visible, for everything that becomes visible is light. Therefore, it says:

"Awake, O sleeper,

and arise from the dead,

and Christ will give you light."

The word of the Lord. *Thanks be to God.*

VERSE BEFORE THE GOSPEL (*John 8:12*)

Glory and praise to you, Lord Jesus Christ! I am the light of the world, says the Lord; whoever follows me will have the light of life. *Glory and praise to you, Lord Jesus Christ!*

GOSPEL (*John 9:1-41*)

For the shorter version, omit the indented parts in brackets.

A reading from the holy Gospel according to John.
Glory to you, O Lord.

As Jesus passed by he saw a man blind from birth. [His disciples asked him, "Rabbi, who sinned, this man or his parents, that he was born blind?" Jesus answered, "Neither he nor his parents sinned; it is so that the works of God might be made visible through him. We have to do the works of the

one who sent me while it is day. Night is coming when no
one can work. While I am in the world, I am the light of the
world." When he had said this,]
he spat on the ground and made clay with the saliva, and
smeared the clay on his eyes, and said to him, "Go wash in the
Pool of Siloam*"—which means Sent—. So he went and washed,
and came back able to see.

His neighbors and those who had seen him earlier as a beggar
said, "Isn't this the one who used to sit and beg?" Some said, "It
is," but others said, "No, he just looks like him." He said, "I am."
[So they said to him, "How were your eyes opened?" He replied, "The man called Jesus made clay and anointed my eyes
and told me, 'Go to Siloam and wash.' So I went there and
washed and was able to see." And they said to him, "Where is
he?" He said, "I don't know."]

They brought the one who was once blind to the Pharisees. Now
Jesus had made clay and opened his eyes on a sabbath. So then
the Pharisees also asked him how he was able to see. He said to
them, "He put clay on my eyes, and I washed, and now I can
see." So some of the Pharisees said, "This man is not from God,
because he does not keep the sabbath." But others said, "How
can a sinful man do such signs?" And there was a division among
them. So they said to the blind man again, "What do you have
to say about him, since he opened your eyes?" He said, "He is a
prophet."

[Now the Jews did not believe that he had been blind and
gained his sight until they summoned the parents of the one
who had gained his sight. They asked them, "Is this your son,
who you say was born blind? How does he now see?" His
parents answered and said, "We know that this is our son and

that he was born blind. We do not know how he sees now, nor do we know who opened his eyes. Ask him, he is of age; he can speak for himself." His parents said this because they were afraid of the Jews, for the Jews had already agreed that if anyone acknowledged him as the Christ, he would be expelled from the synagogue. For this reason his parents said, "He is of age; question him."

So a second time they called the man who had been blind and said to him, "Give God the praise! We know that this man is a sinner." He replied, "If he is a sinner, I do not know. One thing I do know is that I was blind and now I see." So they said to him, "What did he do to you? How did he open your eyes?" He answered them, "I told you already and you did not listen. Why do you want to hear it again? Do you want to become his disciples, too?" They ridiculed him and said, "You are that man's disciple; we are disciples of Moses! We know that God spoke to Moses, but we do not know where this one is from." The man answered and said to them, "This is what is so amazing, that you do not know where he is from, yet he opened my eyes. We know that God does not listen to sinners, but if one is devout and does his will, he listens to him. It is unheard of that anyone ever opened the eyes of a person born blind. If this man were not from God, he would not be able to do anything."]

They answered and said to him, "You were born totally in sin, and are you trying to teach us?" Then they threw him out.

When Jesus heard that they had thrown him out, he found him and said, "Do you believe in the Son of Man?" He answered and said, "Who is he, sir, that I may believe in him?" Jesus said to him, "You have seen him, the one speaking with you is he." He said, "I do believe, Lord," and he worshiped him.

[Then Jesus said, "I came into this world for judgment, so that those who do not see might see, and those who do see might become blind."

Some of the Pharisees who were with him heard this and said to him, "Surely we are not also blind, are we?" Jesus said to them, "If you were blind, you would have no sin; but now you are saying, 'We see,' so your sin remains."]

The Gospel of the Lord. *Praise to you, Lord Jesus Christ.*

PRAYER OVER THE OFFERINGS

We place before you with joy these offerings,
which bring eternal remedy, O Lord,
praying that we may both faithfully revere them
and present them to you, as is fitting,
for those who seek salvation.
Through Christ our Lord. *Amen.*

PREFACE: THE MAN BORN BLIND

It is truly right and just, our duty and our salvation,
always and everywhere to give you thanks,
Lord, holy Father, almighty and eternal God,
through Christ our Lord.

By the mystery of the Incarnation,
he has led the human race that walked in darkness
into the radiance of the faith
and has brought those born in slavery to ancient sin
through the waters of regeneration
to make them your adopted children.

Therefore, all creatures of heaven and earth
sing a new song in adoration,
and we, with all the host of Angels,
cry out, and without end acclaim:
Holy, Holy, Holy Lord God of hosts... *(page 35)*

COMMUNION ANTIPHON *(Cf. John 9:11, 38)*
The Lord anointed my eyes; I went, I washed, I saw and
I believed in God.

PRAYER AFTER COMMUNION
Sustain your family always in your kindness,
O Lord, we pray,
correct them, set them in order,
graciously protect them under your rule,
and in your unfailing goodness
direct them along the way of salvation.
Through Christ our Lord. *Amen.* ✢

March 18

The divine love is revealed

Jeremiah believed that God was fully aware of sin in human history and so came up with a new strategy for addressing the problem: a new covenant that would make it possible for human beings to be faithful. In this loving plan, a lasting and intimate bond between God and God's people would be formed when the law was written directly on people's hearts (minds and wills), and past sins would be forgiven and forgotten.

The Hebrews reading insists Jesus understood life's difficulties. Though the author knows Jesus was the Son and sinless, he insists the Son did not go through life without feeling the temptations and sufferings we all do. Faced with his imminent death, Jesus experienced his own agony. Indeed, Jesus could become the source of eternal salvation in part because he shared our humanity.

Jesus' death is the moment in which the divine love for human beings—and the new covenant in his blood—is most powerfully revealed. It is the means by which a new and intimate communion between God and believers, facilitated by God's Holy Spirit, is inaugurated. Happily, then, we ask for clean hearts and blotted out transgressions so that our solidarity with Christ can shine forth fully for others' sake.

■ **CHRISTINE MADER**

Parishes engaged in the Rite of Christian Initiation of Adults (RCIA) may celebrate the Third Scrutiny today (see page 222).

ENTRANCE ANTIPHON *(Cf. Psalm 43 [42]:1-2)*
Give me justice, O God, and plead my cause against a nation that is faithless. From the deceitful and cunning rescue me, for you, O God, are my strength.

INTRODUCTORY RITES *(page 10)*

COLLECT
By your help, we beseech you, Lord our God,
may we walk eagerly in that same charity
with which, out of love for the world,
your Son handed himself over to death.
Through our Lord Jesus Christ, your Son,
who lives and reigns with you in the unity of the Holy Spirit,
one God, for ever and ever. *Amen.*

These are the readings for Year B. The readings for Year A may also be used (see page 222).

FIRST READING *(Jeremiah 31:31-34)*

The days are coming, says the LORD, when I will make a new covenant with the house of Israel and the house of Judah. It will not be like the covenant I made with their fathers the day I took them by the hand to lead them forth from the land of Egypt; for they broke my covenant, and I had to show myself their master, says the LORD. But this is the covenant that I will make with the house of Israel after those days, says the LORD. I will place my law within them and write it upon their hearts; I will be their God, and they shall be my people. No longer will they have need to teach their friends and relatives how to know the LORD. All, from least to greatest, shall know me, says the LORD, for I will forgive their evildoing and remember their sin no more.

The word of the Lord. ***Thanks be to God.***

RESPONSORIAL PSALM *(Psalm 51:3-4, 12-13, 14-15)*

R̸ **Create a clean heart in me, O God.**

Have mercy on me, O God, in your goodness;
    in the greatness of your compassion wipe out my offense.
Thoroughly wash me from my guilt
    and of my sin cleanse me. R̸
A clean heart create for me, O God,
    and a steadfast spirit renew within me.
Cast me not out from your presence,
    and your Holy Spirit take not from me. R̸
Give me back the joy of your salvation,
    and a willing spirit sustain in me.
I will teach transgressors your ways,
    and sinners shall return to you.

R̸ **Create a clean heart in me, O God.**

SECOND READING *(Hebrews 5:7-9)*

In the days when Christ Jesus was in the flesh, he offered prayers and supplications with loud cries and tears to the one who was able to save him from death, and he was heard because of his reverence. Son though he was, he learned obedience from what he suffered; and when he was made perfect, he became the source of eternal salvation for all who obey him.

The word of the Lord. ***Thanks be to God.***

VERSE BEFORE THE GOSPEL *(John 12:26)*
Glory and praise to you, Lord Jesus Christ! Whoever serves me must follow me, says the Lord; and where I am, there also will my servant be. *Glory and praise to you, Lord Jesus Christ!*

GOSPEL *(John 12:20–33)*
A reading from the holy Gospel according to John.
Glory to you, O Lord.

Some Greeks who had come to worship at the Passover Feast came to Philip, who was from Bethsaida* in Galilee, and asked him, "Sir, we would like to see Jesus." Philip went and told Andrew; then Andrew and Philip went and told Jesus. Jesus answered them, "The hour has come for the Son of Man to be glorified. **Amen,**✝ amen, I say to you, unless a grain of wheat falls to the ground and dies, it remains just a grain of wheat; but if it dies, it produces much fruit. Whoever loves his life loses it, and whoever hates his life in this world will preserve it for eternal life. Whoever serves me must follow me, and where I am, there also will my servant be. The Father will honor whoever serves me.

"I am troubled now. Yet what should I say? 'Father, save me from this hour'? But it was for this purpose that I came to this hour. Father, glorify your name." Then a voice came from heaven, "I have glorified it and will glorify it again." The crowd there heard it and said it was thunder; but others said, "An angel has spoken to him." Jesus answered and said, "This voice did not come for my sake but for yours. Now is the time of judgment on this world; now the ruler of this world will be driven out. And when I am lifted up from the earth, I will draw everyone to myself." He said this indicating the kind of death he would die.

The Gospel of the Lord. *Praise to you, Lord Jesus Christ.*

PROFESSION OF FAITH *(page 13)*

PRAYER OF THE FAITHFUL

PREPARATION OF GIFTS *(page 16)*

PRAYER OVER THE OFFERINGS
Hear us, almighty God,
and, having instilled in your servants
the teachings of the Christian faith,
graciously purify them
by the working of this sacrifice.
Through Christ our Lord. *Amen.*

PREFACE *(Lent 1–2, page 21)*

COMMUNION ANTIPHON *(John 12:24)*
Amen, amen I say to you: Unless a grain of wheat falls to the
ground and dies, it remains a single grain. But if it dies, it bears
much fruit.

• Taking a Closer Look •

✢ **Amen** "Amen" is a Hebrew word that affirms what has been
said—"It is true!" It appears often throughout the Bible both in normal speech and in prayer whenever people want to signal their acceptance and affirmation. So it is used at Mass as the people's affirmation of what the priest has prayed in their name. In the gospels,
Jesus often begins his teaching with the phrase "Amen, I say to you"
to emphasize the importance of what follows. And in John's gospel,
when Jesus wants to really stress the importance of what he is about
to say, he uses the curious double "Amen, amen" to invite his audience to pay close attention to his message.

PRAYER AFTER COMMUNION
We pray, almighty God,
that we may always be counted among the members of Christ,
in whose Body and Blood we have communion.
Who lives and reigns for ever and ever. *Amen.*

PRAYER OVER THE PEOPLE
Bless, O Lord, your people,
who long for the gift of your mercy,
and grant that what, at your prompting, they desire
they may receive by your generous gift.
Through Christ our Lord. *Amen.*

DISMISSAL *(page 57)* ✥

⁂ RESPONDING TO THE WORD ⁂

Jeremiah foresees a time when God's law will be written on our hearts.	Jesus' suffering led to a deeper relationship with God.	Jesus connects death and service because for us to live, some other animals and plants must die.
➲ What new experience of God's loving guidance have I felt this Lent?	➲ How has my suffering helped me to discover new dimensions of God's love?	➲ What little deaths of service have I experienced during this Lenten season?

CHRISTIAN INITIATION:
THIRD SCRUTINY

*The Mass prayers and readings below are for use
in parishes celebrating the Third Scrutiny.*

ENTRANCE ANTIPHON *(Cf. Psalm 18 [17]:5-7)*

The waves of death rose about me; the pains of the netherworld surrounded me. In my anguish I called to the Lord; and from his holy temple he heard my voice.

COLLECT

Grant, O Lord, to these chosen ones
that, instructed in the holy mysteries,
they may receive new life at the font of Baptism
and be numbered among the members of your Church.
Through our Lord Jesus Christ, your Son,
who lives and reigns with you in the unity of the Holy Spirit,
one God, for ever and ever. *Amen.*

FIRST READING *(Ezekiel 37:12-14)*

Thus says the Lord GOD: O my people, I will open your graves and have you rise from them, and bring you back to the land of Israel. Then you shall know that I am the LORD, when I open your graves and have you rise from them, O my people! I will put my spirit in you that you may live, and I will settle you upon your land; thus you shall know that I am the LORD. I have promised, and I will do it, says the LORD.

The word of the Lord. ***Thanks be to God.***

RESPONSORIAL PSALM *(Psalm 130:1-2, 3-4, 5-6, 7-8)*

℟. With the Lord there is mercy and fullness of redemption.

Out of the depths I cry to you, O LORD;
 LORD, hear my voice!
Let your ears be attentive
 to my voice in supplication. ℟.

If you, O LORD, mark iniquities,
 LORD, who can stand?
But with you is forgiveness,
 that you may be revered. ℟.

I trust in the LORD;
 my soul trusts in his word.
More than sentinels wait for the dawn,
 let Israel wait for the LORD. ℟.

For with the LORD is kindness
 and with him is plenteous redemption;
and he will redeem Israel
 from all their iniquities. ℟.

SECOND READING *(Romans 8:8-11)*

Brothers and sisters: Those who are in the flesh cannot please God. But you are not in the flesh; on the contrary, you are in the spirit, if only the Spirit of God dwells in you. Whoever does not have the Spirit of Christ does not belong to him. But if Christ is in you, although the body is dead because of sin, the spirit is alive because of righteousness. If the Spirit of the One who raised Jesus from the dead dwells in you, the One who raised Christ from the dead will give life to your mortal bodies also, through his Spirit dwelling in you.

 The word of the Lord. *Thanks be to God.*

VERSE BEFORE THE GOSPEL *(John 11:25, 26)*

Glory and praise to you, Lord Jesus Christ! I am the resurrection and the life, says the Lord; whoever believes in me, even if he dies, will never die. ***Glory and praise to you, Lord Jesus Christ!***

GOSPEL *(John 11:1–45)*

For the shorter version, omit the indented text in brackets and add words in parentheses.

A reading from the holy Gospel according to John.

Glory to you, O Lord.

[Now a man was ill, Lazarus from Bethany,* the village of Mary and her sister Martha. Mary was the one who had anointed the Lord with perfumed oil and dried his feet with her hair; it was her brother Lazarus who was ill. So] The sisters (of Lazarus) sent word to Jesus saying, "Master, the one you love is ill." When Jesus heard this he said, "This illness is not to end in death, but is for the glory of God, that the Son of God may be glorified through it." Now Jesus loved Martha and her sister and Lazarus. So when he heard that he was ill, he remained for two days in the place where he was. Then after this he said to his disciples, "Let us go back to Judea."

[The disciples said to him, "Rabbi, the Jews were just trying to stone you, and you want to go back there?" Jesus answered, "Are there not twelve hours in a day? If one walks during the day, he does not stumble, because he sees the light of this world. But if one walks at night, he stumbles, because the light is not in him." He said this, and then told them, "Our friend Lazarus is asleep, but I am going to awaken him." So the disciples said to him, "Master, if he is asleep, he will be saved." But Jesus was talking about his death, while they thought that he meant ordinary sleep. So then Jesus said to them clearly, "Lazarus has died. And I am glad for you that I was not there, that you may believe. Let us go to him." So Thomas, called Didymus,* said to his fellow disciples, "Let us also go to die with him."]

When Jesus arrived, he found that Lazarus had already been in the tomb for four days.

[Now Bethany was near Jerusalem, only about two miles away. And many of the Jews had come to Martha and Mary to comfort them about their brother.]

When Martha heard that Jesus was coming, she went to meet him; but Mary sat at home. Martha said to Jesus, "Lord, if you had been here, my brother would not have died. But even now I know that whatever you ask of God, God will give you." Jesus said to her, "Your brother will rise." Martha said to him, "I know he will rise, in the resurrection on the last day." Jesus told her, "I am the resurrection and the life; whoever believes in me, even if he dies, will live, and everyone who lives and believes in me will never die. Do you believe this?" She said to him, "Yes, Lord. I have come to believe that you are the Christ, the Son of God, the one who is coming into the world."

[When she had said this, she went and called her sister Mary secretly, saying, "The teacher is here and is asking for you." As soon as she heard this, she rose quickly and went to him. For Jesus had not yet come into the village, but was still where Martha had met him. So when the Jews who were with her in the house comforting her saw Mary get up quickly and go out, they followed her, presuming that she was going to the tomb to weep there. When Mary came to where Jesus was and saw him, she fell at his feet and said to him, "Lord, if you had been here, my brother would not have died." When Jesus saw her weeping and the Jews who had come with her weeping,] He became perturbed and deeply troubled, and said, "Where have you laid him?" They said to him, "Sir, come and see." And Jesus wept. So the Jews said, "See how he loved him." But some of them said, "Could not the one who opened the eyes of the blind man have done something so that this man would not have died?"

So Jesus, perturbed again, came to the tomb. It was a cave, and a stone lay across it. Jesus said, "Take away the stone." Martha, the dead man's sister, said to him, "Lord, by now there will be a stench; he has been dead for four days." Jesus said to her, "Did I not tell you that if you believe you will see the glory of God?" So they took away the stone. And Jesus raised his eyes and said, "Father, I thank you for hearing me. I know that you always hear me; but because of the crowd here I have said this, that they may believe that you sent me." And when he had said this, He cried out in a loud voice, "Lazarus, come out!" The dead man came out, tied hand and foot with burial bands, and his face was wrapped in a cloth. So Jesus said to them, "Untie him and let him go."

Now many of the Jews who had come to Mary and seen what he had done began to believe in him.

The Gospel of the Lord. *Praise to you, Lord Jesus Christ.*

PRAYER OVER THE OFFERINGS

Hear us, almighty God,
and, having instilled in your servants
the first fruits of the Christian faith,
graciously purify them by the working of this sacrifice.
Through Christ our Lord. *Amen.*

PREFACE: LAZARUS

It is truly right and just, our duty and our salvation,
always and everywhere to give you thanks,
Lord, holy Father, almighty and eternal God,
through Christ our Lord.

For as true man he wept for Lazarus his friend
and as eternal God raised him from the tomb,
just as, taking pity on the human race,
he leads us by sacred mysteries to new life.

Through him the host of Angels adores your majesty
and rejoices in your presence for ever.
May our voices, we pray, join with theirs
in one chorus of exultant praise, as we acclaim:
Holy, Holy, Holy Lord God of hosts... (page 35)

COMMUNION ANTIPHON (Cf. John 11:26)

Everyone who lives and believes in me will not die for ever, says
the Lord.

PRAYER AFTER COMMUNION

May your people be at one, O Lord, we pray,
and in wholehearted submission to you
may they obtain this grace:
that, safe from all distress,
they may readily live out their joy at being saved
and remember in loving prayer those to be reborn.
Through Christ our Lord. *Amen.* ✤

So let us spread before his feet, not garments or soulless olive branches, which delight the eye for a few hours and then wither, but ourselves, clothed in his grace, or rather, clothed completely in him. We who have been baptized into Christ must ourselves be the garments that we spread before him. Let our souls take the place of the welcoming branches as we join in the holy song: "Blessed is he who comes in the name of the Lord. Blessed is the King of Israel."

ST. ANDREW OF CRETE

March 25

**MAR
25**

Jesus gave himself for us

"Turn the other cheek." Many people identify this as a central teaching from Jesus, but it only appears in the Gospels of Matthew and Luke. Nevertheless, Mark's narrative of Jesus' passion and death illustrates what this saying means. Jesus does not resist when they arrest him, and he rebukes those who fight on his behalf. He doesn't defend himself at trial. He simply acknowledges his true identity, then submits to mockery, crucifixion and death.

The Old Testament tells us about individuals suffering for the sake of their faith. Second Isaiah presents God's servant, who submitted to physical attacks knowing that God was with him, and in Psalm 22 an individual describes his persecution and suffering but in the end is confident that God will deliver him. However, Paul tells us that Jesus sacrificed even more, emptying himself of his divinity to become one of us in order to die on the cross for us.

This is the paschal mystery we celebrate at every Eucharist. Jesus gave himself over to death so that we can have life. As we share the bread and wine, we remember his sacrifice and celebrate its effect in our lives today.

■ JOHN L. McLAUGHLIN

THE COMMEMORATION OF THE LORD'S ENTRANCE INTO JERUSALEM

FIRST FORM: THE PROCESSION

INTRODUCTION

The assembly, carrying palm branches, gather in a place distinct from the church to which the procession will move. They may sing Hosanna! or another hymn.

Dear brethren (brothers and sisters),
since the beginning of Lent until now
we have prepared our hearts by penance and charitable works.
Today we gather together to herald with the whole Church
the beginning of the celebration
of our Lord's Paschal Mystery,
that is to say, of his Passion and Resurrection.
For it was to accomplish this mystery
that he entered his own city of Jerusalem.
Therefore, with all faith and devotion,
let us commemorate
the Lord's entry into the city for our salvation,
following in his footsteps,
so that, being made by his grace partakers of the Cross,
we may have a share also in his Resurrection and in his life.

Let us pray:

Almighty ever-living God,
sanctify these branches with your blessing,
that we, who follow Christ the King in exultation,

may reach the eternal Jerusalem through him.
Who lives and reigns for ever and ever. *Amen.*

Or

Increase the faith of those who place their hope in you, O God,
and graciously hear the prayers of those who call on you,
that we, who today hold high these branches
to hail Christ in his triumph,
may bear fruit for you by good works accomplished in him.
Who lives and reigns for ever and ever. *Amen.*

An alternate reading follows.

GOSPEL *(Mark 11:1-10)*
A reading from the holy Gospel according to Mark.
Glory to you, O Lord.

When Jesus and his disciples drew near to Jerusalem, to Bethphage* and Bethany* at the Mount of Olives, he sent two of his disciples and said to them, "Go into the village opposite you, and immediately on entering it, you will find a colt tethered on which no one has ever sat. Untie it and bring it here. If anyone should say to you, 'Why are you doing this?' reply, 'The Master has need of it and will send it back here at once.'" So they went off and found a colt tethered at a gate outside on the street, and they untied it. Some of the bystanders said to them, "What are you doing, untying the colt?" They answered them just as Jesus had told them to, and they permitted them to do it. So they brought the colt to Jesus and put their cloaks over it. And he sat on it. Many people spread their cloaks on the road, and others spread leafy branches that they had cut from the fields. Those preceding him as well as those following kept crying out:

"Hosanna!
Blessed is he who comes in the name of the Lord!
Blessed is the kingdom of our father David that is to come!
Hosanna in the highest!"
The Gospel of the Lord. ***Praise to you, Lord Jesus Christ.***

Or

GOSPEL (*John 12:12–16*)
A reading from the holy Gospel according to John.
Glory to you, O Lord.

When the great crowd that had come to the feast heard that
Jesus was coming to Jerusalem, they took palm branches
and went out to meet him, and cried out:
"Hosanna!
Blessed is he who comes in the name of the Lord,
the king of Israel.
Jesus found an ass and sat upon it, as is written:
Fear no more, O daughter Zion; *
see, your king comes, seated upon an ass's colt.
His disciples did not understand this at first, but when Jesus had
been glorified they remembered that these things were written
about him and that they had done this for him.
The Gospel of the Lord. ***Praise to you, Lord Jesus Christ.***

PROCESSION
Dear brethren (brothers and sisters),
like the crowds who acclaimed Jesus in Jerusalem,
let us go forth in peace.

All process to the church singing a hymn in honor of Christ the King.
Mass continues with the Collect.

SECOND FORM: THE SOLEMN ENTRANCE

The blessing of branches and proclamation of the gospel take place, as above, but in the church. After the gospel, the celebrant moves solemnly through the church to the sanctuary, while all sing. Mass continues with the Collect.

THIRD FORM: THE SIMPLE ENTRANCE

The people gather in the church as usual. While the celebrant goes to the altar, the following entrance antiphon or a suitable hymn is sung.

ENTRANCE ANTIPHON *(Cf. John 12:1, 12-13; Psalm 24 [23]:9-10)*
Six days before the Passover, when the Lord came into the city of Jerusalem, the children ran to meet him; in their hands they carried palm branches and with a loud voice cried out: Hosanna in the highest! Blessed are you, who have come in your abundant mercy! O gates, lift high your heads; grow higher, ancient doors. Let him enter, the king of glory! Who is this king of glory? He, the Lord of hosts, he is the king of glory. Hosanna in the highest! Blessed are you, who have come in your abundant mercy!

INTRODUCTORY RITES *(page 10)*

COLLECT
Almighty ever-living God,
who as an example of humility for the human race to follow
caused our Savior to take flesh and submit to the Cross,
graciously grant that we may heed his lesson of patient suffering
and so merit a share in his Resurrection.
Who lives and reigns with you in the unity of the Holy Spirit,
one God, for ever and ever. ***Amen.***

FIRST READING *(Isaiah 50:4-7)*

The Lord GOD has given me
    a well-trained tongue,
that I might know how to speak to the weary
    a word that will rouse them.
Morning after morning
    he opens my ear that I may hear;
and I have not rebelled,
    have not turned back.
I gave my back to those who beat me,
    my cheeks to those who plucked my beard;
my face I did not shield
    from buffets and spitting.

The Lord GOD is my help,
    therefore I am not disgraced;
I have set my face like flint,
    knowing that I shall not be put to shame.
The word of the Lord. *Thanks be to God.*

RESPONSORIAL PSALM *(Psalm 22:8-9, 17-18, 19-20, 23-24)*
℟ **My God, my God, why have you abandoned me?**

All who see me scoff at me;
    they mock me with parted lips, they wag their heads:
"He relied on the LORD; let him deliver him,
    let him rescue him, if he loves him." ℟
Indeed, many dogs surround me,
    a pack of evildoers closes in upon me;
they have pierced my hands and my feet;
    I can count all my bones. ℟
They divide my garments among them,

and for my vesture they cast lots.
But you, O LORD, be not far from me;
   O my help, hasten to aid me. ℟
I will proclaim your name to my brethren;
   in the midst of the assembly I will praise you:
"You who fear the LORD, praise him;
   all you descendants of Jacob, give glory to him;
   revere him, all you descendants of Israel!" ℟

SECOND READING *(Philippians 2:6-11)*

Christ Jesus, though he was in the form of God,
   did not regard equality with God
   something to be grasped.
Rather, he emptied himself,
   taking the form of a slave,
   coming in human likeness;
   and found human in appearance,
   he humbled himself,
   becoming obedient to the point of death,
   even death on a cross.
Because of this, God greatly exalted him
   and bestowed on him the name
   which is above every name,
   that at the name of Jesus
   every knee should bend,
   of those in heaven and on earth and under the earth,
   and every tongue confess that
   Jesus Christ is Lord,
   to the glory of God the Father.
The word of the Lord. *Thanks be to God.*

VERSE BEFORE THE GOSPEL *(Philippians 2:8–9)*
Glory and praise to you, Lord Jesus Christ! Christ became obedient to the point of death, even death on a cross. Because of this, God greatly exalted him and bestowed on him the name which is above every name. *Glory and praise to you, Lord Jesus Christ!*

GOSPEL *(Mark 14:1–15:47 or 15:1–39)*
Several readers may proclaim the passion narrative today. (**N**) *indicates the narrator,* (✝) *the words of Jesus,* (**V**) *a voice, and* (**C**) *the crowd. The shorter version begins (page 242) and ends (page 246) at the asterisks.*

N The Passion of our Lord Jesus Christ according to Mark.
    The **Passover**✝ and the **Feast of Unleavened Bread**✝ were to take place in two days' time. So the chief priests and the scribes were seeking a way to arrest him by treachery and put him to death. They said,

C "Not during the festival, for fear that there may be a riot among the people."

N When he was in Bethany* reclining at table in the house of Simon the leper, a woman came with an alabaster jar of perfumed oil, costly genuine spikenard. She broke the alabaster jar and poured it on his head. There were some who were indignant.

C "Why has there been this waste of perfumed oil? It could have been sold for more than three hundred days' wages and the money given to the poor."

N They were infuriated with her. Jesus said,

✝ "Let her alone. Why do you make trouble for her? She has done a good thing for me. The poor you will always have with you, and whenever you wish you can do good to them, but you will not always have me. She has done what she could. She has anticipated anointing my body for burial. Amen, I say to you, wherever the gospel is proclaimed to the whole world, what she has done will be told in memory of her."

N Then Judas Iscariot, one of the Twelve, went off to the chief priests to hand him over to them. When they heard him they were pleased and promised to pay him money. Then he looked for an opportunity to hand him over.

On the first day of the Feast of Unleavened Bread, when they sacrificed the Passover lamb, his disciples said to him,

C "Where do you want us to go and prepare for you to eat the Passover?"

N He sent two of his disciples and said to them,

✝ "Go into the city and a man will meet you, carrying a jar of water. Follow him. Wherever he enters, say to the master of the house, 'The Teacher says, "Where is my guest room where I may eat the Passover with my disciples?" ' Then he will show you a large upper room furnished and ready. Make the preparations for us there."

N The disciples then went off, entered the city, and found it just as he had told them; and they prepared the Passover.

When it was evening, he came with the Twelve. And as they reclined at table and were eating, Jesus said,

† "Amen, I say to you, one of you will betray me, one who is eating with me."

N They began to be distressed and to say to him, one by one,

V "Surely it is not I?"

N He said to them,

† "One of the Twelve, the one who dips with me into the dish. For the Son of Man indeed goes, as it is written of him, but woe to that man by whom the Son of Man is betrayed. It would be better for that man if he had never been born."

N While they were eating, he took bread, said the blessing, broke it, and gave it to them, and said,

† "Take it; this is my body."

N Then he took a cup, gave thanks, and gave it to them, and they all drank from it. He said to them,

† "This is my blood of the covenant, which will be shed for many. Amen, I say to you, I shall not drink again the fruit of the vine until the day when I drink it new in the kingdom of God."

N Then, after singing a hymn, they went out to the Mount of Olives. Then Jesus said to them,

† "All of you will have your faith shaken, for it is written:

> *I will strike the shepherd,*
> *and the sheep will be dispersed.*

But after I have been raised up, I shall go before you to Galilee."

N Peter said to him,

V "Even though all should have their faith shaken, mine will not be."

N Then Jesus said to him,

† "Amen, I say to you, this very night before the cock crows twice you will deny me three times."

N But he vehemently replied,

V "Even though I should have to die with you, I will not deny you."

N And they all spoke similarly.

Then they came to a place named Gethsemane,* and he said to his disciples,

† "Sit here while I pray."

N He took with him Peter, James, and John, and began to be troubled and distressed. Then he said to them,

† "My soul is sorrowful even to death. Remain here and keep watch."

N He advanced a little and fell to the ground and prayed that if it were possible the hour might pass by him; he said,

† "Abba, Father, all things are possible to you. Take this cup away from me, but not what I will but what you will."

N When he returned he found them asleep. He said to Peter,

† "Simon, are you asleep? Could you not keep watch for one hour? Watch and pray that you may not undergo the test. The spirit is willing but the flesh is weak."

N Withdrawing again, he prayed, saying the same thing. Then he returned once more and found them asleep, for they could not keep their eyes open and did not know what to answer him. He returned a third time and said to them,

† "Are you still sleeping and taking your rest? It is enough. The hour has come. Behold, the Son of Man is to be handed over to sinners. Get up, let us go. See, my betrayer is at hand."

N Then, while he was still speaking, Judas, one of the Twelve, arrived, accompanied by a crowd with swords and clubs who had come from the chief priests, the scribes, and the elders. His betrayer had arranged a signal with them, saying,

V "The man I shall kiss is the one; arrest him and lead him away securely."

N He came and immediately went over to him and said,

V "Rabbi."

N And he kissed him. At this they laid hands on him and arrested him. One of the bystanders drew his sword, struck the high priest's servant, and cut off his ear. Jesus said to them in reply,

† "Have you come out as against a robber, with swords and clubs, to seize me? Day after day I was with you teaching in the temple area, yet you did not arrest me; but that the Scriptures may be fulfilled."

N And they all left him and fled. Now a young man followed him wearing nothing but a linen cloth about his body. They seized him, but he left the cloth behind and ran off naked.

They led Jesus away to the high priest, and all the chief priests and the elders and the scribes came together. Peter followed him at a distance into the high priest's courtyard and was seated with the guards, warming himself at the fire. The chief priests and the entire Sanhedrin* kept trying to obtain testimony against Jesus in order to put him to death, but they found none. Many gave false witness against him, but their testimony did not agree. Some took the stand and testified falsely against him, alleging,

C "We heard him say, 'I will destroy this temple made with hands and within three days I will build another not made with hands.'"

N Even so their testimony did not agree. The high priest rose before the assembly and questioned Jesus, saying,

V "Have you no answer? What are these men testifying against you?"

N But he was silent and answered nothing. Again the high priest asked him and said to him,

V "Are you the Christ, the son of the Blessed One?"

N Then Jesus answered,

† "I am;
    and 'you will see the Son of Man
        seated at the right hand of the Power
        and coming with the clouds of heaven.'"

N At that the high priest tore his garments and said,

V "What further need have we of witnesses? You have heard the blasphemy. What do you think?"

N They all condemned him as deserving to die. Some began to spit on him. They blindfolded him and struck him and said to him,

C "Prophesy!"

N And the guards greeted him with blows.

While Peter was below in the courtyard, one of the high priest's maids came along. Seeing Peter warming himself, she looked intently at him and said,

C "You too were with the Nazarene, Jesus."

N But he denied it saying,

V "I neither know nor understand what you are talking about."

N So he went out into the outer court. Then the cock crowed. The maid saw him and began again to say to the bystanders,

C "This man is one of them."

N Once again he denied it. A little later the bystanders said to Peter once more,

C "Surely you are one of them; for you too are a Galilean."

N He began to curse and to swear,

V "I do not know this man about whom you are talking."

N And immediately a cock crowed a second time. Then Peter remembered the word that Jesus had said to him, "Before the cock crows twice you will deny me three times." He broke down and wept.

✳ ✳ ✳

N As soon as morning came, the chief priests with the elders and the scribes, that is, the whole Sanhedrin, held a council. They bound Jesus, led him away, and handed him over to Pilate. Pilate questioned him,

V "Are you the king of the Jews?"

N He said to him in reply,

† "You say so."

N The chief priests accused him of many things. Again Pilate questioned him,

V "Have you no answer? See how many things they accuse you of."

N Jesus gave him no further answer, so that Pilate was amazed.
  Now on the occasion of the feast he used to release to them one prisoner whom they requested. A man called Barabbas* was then in prison along with the rebels who had committed murder in a rebellion. The crowd came forward and began to ask him to do for them as he was accustomed. Pilate answered,

V "Do you want me to release to you the king of the Jews?"

N For he knew that it was out of envy that the chief priests had handed him over. But the chief priests stirred up the crowd to have him release Barabbas for them instead. Pilate again said to them in reply,

V "Then what do you want me to do with the man you call the king of the Jews?"

N They shouted again,

C "Crucify him."

N Pilate said to them,

V "Why? What evil has he done?"

N They only shouted the louder,

C "Crucify him."

N So Pilate, wishing to satisfy the crowd, released Barabbas to them and, after he had Jesus scourged, handed him over to be crucified.

    The soldiers led him away inside the palace, that is, the praetorium,* and assembled the whole cohort. They clothed him in purple and, weaving a crown of thorns, placed it on him. They began to salute him with,

C "Hail, King of the Jews!"

N and kept striking his head with a reed and spitting upon him. They knelt before him in homage. And when they had mocked him, they stripped him of the purple cloak, dressed him in his own clothes, and led him out to crucify him.

    They pressed into service a passer-by, Simon, a Cyrenian,* who was coming in from the country, the father of Alexander and Rufus, to carry his cross.

    They brought him to the place of Golgotha*—which is translated Place of the Skull—. They gave him wine drugged with myrrh,* but he did not take it. Then they crucified him and divided his garments by casting lots for them to see what each should take. It was nine o'clock in the morning when they crucified him. The inscription of the charge against him read, "The King of the Jews." With him they crucified two revolutionaries, one on his right and one on his left. Those passing by reviled him, shaking their heads and saying,

C "Aha! You who would destroy the temple and rebuild it in three days, save yourself by coming down from the cross."

N Likewise the chief priests, with the scribes, mocked him among themselves and said,

C "He saved others; he cannot save himself. Let the Christ, the King of Israel, come down now from the cross that we may see and believe."

N Those who were crucified with him also kept abusing him.

At noon darkness came over the whole land until three in the afternoon. And at three o'clock Jesus cried out in a loud voice,

† *"Eloi, Eloi, lema sabachthani?"**

N which is translated,

† "My God, my God, why have you forsaken me?"

N Some of the bystanders who heard it said,

C "Look, he is calling Elijah."

N One of them ran, soaked a sponge with wine, put it on a reed and gave it to him to drink saying,

V "Wait, let us see if Elijah comes to take him down."

N Jesus gave a loud cry and breathed his last.

(Here all kneel and pause for a short time.)

N The veil of the sanctuary was torn in two from top to bottom. When the centurion who stood facing him saw how he breathed his last he said,

V "Truly this man was the Son of God!"

* * *

N There were also women looking on from a distance. Among them were Mary Magdalene, Mary the mother of the younger James and of Joses, and Salome.* These women had followed him when he was in Galilee and ministered to him. There were also many other women who had come up with him to Jerusalem.

When it was already evening, since it was the day of preparation, the day before the sabbath, Joseph of Arimathea,* a distinguished member of the council, who was himself awaiting the kingdom of God, came and courageously went to Pilate and asked for the body of Jesus. Pilate was amazed that he was already dead. He summoned the centurion and asked him if Jesus had already died. And when he learned of it from the centurion, he gave the body to Joseph. Having bought a linen cloth, he took him down, wrapped him in the linen cloth, and laid him in a tomb that had been hewn out of the rock. Then he rolled a stone against the entrance to the tomb. Mary Magdalene and Mary the mother of Joses watched where he was laid.

The Gospel of the Lord. ***Praise to you, Lord Jesus Christ.***

PROFESSION OF FAITH *(page 13)*

PRAYER OF THE FAITHFUL

PREPARATION OF GIFTS *(page 16)*

PRAYER OVER THE OFFERINGS

Through the Passion of your Only Begotten Son, O Lord,
may our reconciliation with you be near at hand,
so that, though we do not merit it by our own deeds,
yet by this sacrifice made once for all,
we may feel already the effects of your mercy.
Through Christ our Lord. *Amen.*

PREFACE: THE PASSION OF THE LORD

It is truly right and just, our duty and our salvation,
always and everywhere to give you thanks,
Lord, holy Father, almighty and eternal God,
through Christ our Lord.

For, though innocent, he suffered willingly for sinners
and accepted unjust condemnation to save the guilty.
His Death has washed away our sins,
and his Resurrection has purchased our justification.

And so, with all the Angels,
we praise you, as in joyful celebration we acclaim:
Holy, Holy, Holy Lord God of hosts... (page 35)

COMMUNION ANTIPHON *(Matthew 26:42)*

Father, if this chalice cannot pass without my drinking it, your will be done.

PRAYER AFTER COMMUNION

Nourished with these sacred gifts,
we humbly beseech you, O Lord,
that, just as through the death of your Son
you have brought us to hope for what we believe,
so by his Resurrection
you may lead us to where you call.
Through Christ our Lord. *Amen.*

✦ TAKING A CLOSER LOOK ✦

✚ Passover / Feast of Unleavened Bread

Passover (Greek, *ta pascha*) was the annual Jewish family celebration remembering God's deliverance of Israel from Egypt. In particular, the term recalls God's striking down of every Egyptian firstborn, both children and animals, and "passing over" the Hebrews whose houses were marked with lamb's blood (see Exodus 12). To this feast was joined an eight-day period when only unleavened bread could be eaten. Their leaven was not like our powdered yeast, but rather a fermentation agent as is used in making sourdough bread today. Thus leavened bread contained a corrupting agent that would render it "unclean" for ritual use on this most sacred feast.

PRAYER OVER THE PEOPLE

Look, we pray, O Lord, on this your family,
for whom our Lord Jesus Christ
did not hesitate to be delivered into the hands of the wicked
and submit to the agony of the Cross.
Who lives and reigns for ever and ever. *Amen.*

DISMISSAL *(page 57)* ✣

• RESPONDING TO THE WORD •

Isaiah describes God's faithful servant, who suffers but is later rewarded.	Paul's hymn characterizes Jesus' earthly career as self-emptying service.	In Mark's gospel, Jesus is abandoned by everybody to die alone.
➡ *What has been the hardest aspect of my Lenten time?*	➡ *What self-emptying service have I experienced this Lent?*	➡ *How have I felt abandoned and alone when I had to suffer?*

The Triduum (Latin for "three days") comes at the end of Holy Week and comprises the three-day period of prayer leading to the Easter feast, the fulfillment of the whole liturgical year.

Holy Thursday

On Holy Thursday (also called Maundy Thursday), the Church celebrates the Lord's Supper and the institution of the Eucharist. The word "Maundy" stems from the Latin word *mandatum*, meaning "commandment," and refers to the new commandment of love that Jesus gave his disciples that night.

Most parishes now observe the custom of foot-washing, recalling how Jesus washed his disciples' feet at the Last Supper (John 13:1-20). After the liturgy, the consecrated bread is transferred to a side altar and kept in the tabernacle of repose. Then the altar is stripped.

Good Friday

Good Friday is the only day of the year on which Mass is not celebrated. The altar is bare, and the liturgy consists of proclaiming John's passion account, intercessions, veneration of the cross, and a communion service.

Many churches, in addition to the liturgy of Good Friday, have a meditation on the Way of the Cross commemorating the events of Jesus' passion. Some parishes have also introduced Good Friday meditations on the seven last words of Christ on the cross, taken from all four gospels.

The Great Vigil of Easter

Only the Eucharist itself is older than the liturgy of the Easter Vigil. This service reenacts the passage from death into life. On this night, we celebrate our deliverance by Christ our Passover and look forward to the day when we shall see him face to face. During the Easter Vigil, as the sacramentary explains, "the Church keeps watch, awaiting the resurrection of Christ and celebrating it in the sacraments."

The liturgy begins outside a darkened church. The paschal candle is lighted as the "Light of Christ" is proclaimed and praised. In many churches, small candles held by the worshipers are lighted from the paschal candle, and the candles provide the only light for this part of the service.

Then several readings from the Old Testament summarize the story of salvation, telling of God's work of creation, the calling of the Hebrews to be God's people, their deliverance in the Exodus, and God's constant care until Christ came. An air of expectancy surrounds the prayers and singing of canticles that follow each reading.

Then the altar candles are lighted from the paschal candle, and, in a blaze of light and triumphant music, the first Easter Eucharist begins. Our risen Lord comes, in word and sacrament, into the darkness of our lives with the light of his risen life.

Baptisms follow the Scripture readings. Easter Eve has always been the traditional time for baptisms and, in ancient times, for the laying-on of hands by the bishop. If there are no candidates for baptism, the congregation may join in the renewal of baptismal promises. Thus is recalled the time when we "died and were buried with Christ" and were raised with him to newness of life.

Praying and living Holy Week

When a Jewish household gathers for its Passover meal, the youngest child begins the reminiscing by asking: "Why is this night different from all other nights?" So likewise, we Christians might ask, "Why are these three days different from all other days?" The answer, of course, is that they encapsulate the deepest meaning of the story of our salvation. Through his death and resurrection, Jesus brings us all into the right relationships with God and with others.

During Holy Week and the Triduum, in order to recall the story of our salvation, individuals and family members might read the Scriptures appointed for each day or, if there are young children, read the events of Holy Week from a Bible storybook.

But knowing the story is only half the challenge. We need to connect its life-giving possibilities with our own lives. Use the following questions (based on Exodus 14:15–15:1, see page 305) as a way for household members to discover the "exodus" character of their own lives.

- Tell a story of your experience of freedom and deliverance. What part did God play in this experience?

- When did you escape your own form of slavery and head for the promised land of freedom?

- When did you pass through the waters of your Red Sea and dance like Miriam on the other side?

- Tell a story of your passing over from some form of death to new life.

March 29

Accept God's gentle humility

"You will never wash my feet!" I wonder how many of us say something like this to God, especially at critical moments in our lives? "This is not what I expected! This is not what I wanted!"

Peter, like us, has listened to Jesus, seen his power, and acknowledged him as Messiah. But he reacts strongly to his Lord and Messiah humbling himself!

Most of us, I suspect, are not overly thrilled with the idea of God's humility. We want a "bigger" God, an "action" God. Indeed, many people today reject God because God does not meet their expectations or demands.

Nonetheless, the Eucharist is the pinnacle of God's gentle humility, of letting go of divinity to become human, to become food for a starving people. In this peaceful oasis we encounter our humble, incarnate, healing God, reaching out to us in love and offering us the Spirit—and asking us to trust in in Jesus.

"Do this in remembrance of me" is not just a memory; it is the beginning of a daily prayer: "Lord, I accept that you wash my feet; help me wash the feet of my brothers and sisters to become more like you."

▪ Fr. Mark Miller, CSsR

ENTRANCE ANTIPHON *(Cf. Galatians 6:14)*

We should glory in the Cross of our Lord Jesus Christ, in whom is our salvation, life and resurrection, through whom we are saved and delivered.

INTRODUCTORY RITES *(page 10)*

COLLECT

O God, who have called us to participate
in this most sacred Supper,
in which your Only Begotten Son,
when about to hand himself over to death,
entrusted to the Church a sacrifice new for all eternity,
the banquet of his love,
grant, we pray,
that we may draw from so great a mystery,
the fullness of charity and of life.
Through our Lord Jesus Christ, your Son,
who lives and reigns with you in the unity of the Holy Spirit,
one God, for ever and ever. *Amen.*

FIRST READING *(Exodus 12:1-8, 11-14)*

The LORD said to Moses and Aaron in the land of Egypt, "This month shall stand at the head of your calendar; you shall reckon it the first month of the year. Tell the whole community of Israel: On the tenth of this month every one of your families must procure for itself a lamb, one apiece for each household. If a family is too small for a whole lamb, it shall join the nearest household in procuring one and shall share in the lamb in proportion to the number of persons who partake of it. The lamb must be a year-old male and without blemish. You may take it from either the sheep or the goats. You shall keep it until the fourteenth day of this month, and then, with the whole assembly of Israel present, it shall be slaughtered during the evening twilight. They shall take some of its blood and apply it to the two doorposts and the lintel of every house in which they partake of the lamb. That same night they shall eat its roasted flesh with unleavened bread and bitter herbs.

"This is how you are to eat it: with your loins girt, sandals on your feet and your staff in hand, you shall eat like those who are in flight. It is the Passover of the LORD. For on this same night I will go through Egypt, striking down every firstborn of the land, both man and beast, and executing judgment on all the gods of Egypt—I, the LORD! But the blood will mark the houses where you are. Seeing the blood, I will pass over you; thus, when I strike the land of Egypt, no destructive blow will come upon you.

"This day shall be a memorial feast for you, which all your generations shall celebrate with pilgrimage to the LORD, as a perpetual institution."

The word of the Lord. *Thanks be to God.*

RESPONSORIAL PSALM *(Psalm 116:12-13, 15-16bc, 17-18)*

R. **Our blessing-cup is a communion with the Blood of Christ.**

How shall I make a return to the LORD
    for all the good he has done for me?
The cup of salvation I will take up,
    and I will call upon the name of the LORD. R.
Precious in the eyes of the LORD
    is the death of his faithful ones.
I am your servant, the son of your handmaid;
    you have loosed my bonds. R.
To you will I offer sacrifice of thanksgiving,

and I will call upon the name of the LORD.
My vows to the LORD I will pay
in the presence of all his people.

℞ **Our blessing-cup is a communion with the Blood of Christ.**

SECOND READING *(1 Corinthians 11:23–26)*

Brothers and sisters: I received from the Lord what I also handed on to you, that the Lord Jesus, on the night he was handed over, took bread, and, after he had given thanks, broke it and said, "This is my body that is for you. Do this in remembrance of me." In the same way also the cup, after supper, saying, "This cup is the new covenant in my blood. Do this, as often as you drink it, in remembrance of me." For as often as you eat this bread and drink the cup, you proclaim the death of the Lord until he comes.

The word of the Lord. *Thanks be to God.*

VERSE BEFORE THE GOSPEL *(John 13:34)*

Glory and praise to you, Lord Jesus Christ! I give you a new commandment, says the Lord: love one another as I have loved you. *Glory and praise to you, Lord Jesus Christ!*

GOSPEL *(John 13:1–15)*

A reading from the holy Gospel according to John.
Glory to you, O Lord.

Before the feast of Passover, Jesus knew that his hour had come to pass from this world to the Father. He loved his own in the world and he loved them to the end. The devil had already induced Judas, son of Simon the Iscariot, to hand him over. So, during supper, fully aware that the Father had put everything into his power and that he had come from God and was returning to God, he rose from supper and took off his outer garments. He took a towel and tied it around his waist. Then he poured water into a basin and began to **wash the disciples' feet**[+] and dry them with the towel around his waist. He came to Simon Peter, who said to him, "Master, are you going to wash my feet?" Jesus answered and said to him, "What I am doing, you do not understand now, but you will understand later." Peter said to him, "You will never wash my feet." Jesus answered him, "Unless I wash you, you will have no inheritance with me." Simon Peter said to him, "Master, then not only my feet, but my hands and head as well." Jesus said to him, "Whoever has bathed has no need except to have his feet washed, for he is clean all over; so you are clean, but not all." For he knew who would betray him; for this reason, he said, "Not all of you are clean."

So when he had washed their feet and put his garments back on and reclined at table again, he said to them, "Do you realize what I have done for you? You call me 'teacher' and 'master,' and rightly so, for indeed I am. If I, therefore, the master and teacher, have washed your feet, you ought to wash one another's feet. I have given you a model to follow, so that as I have done for you, you should also do."

The Gospel of the Lord. *Praise to you, Lord Jesus Christ.*

THE WASHING OF FEET

During the washing of feet, the assembly may sing an appropriate song.

PRAYER OF THE FAITHFUL

PREPARATION OF GIFTS *(page 16)*

PRAYER OVER THE OFFERINGS

Grant us, O Lord, we pray,
that we may participate worthily in these mysteries,
for whenever the memorial of this sacrifice is celebrated

the work of our redemption is accomplished.
Through Christ our Lord. *Amen.*

PREFACE *(Most Holy Eucharist 1, page 32)*

COMMUNION ANTIPHON *(f1:24–25)*
This is the Body that will be given up for you; this is the Chalice
of the new covenant in my Blood, says the Lord; do this, whenever you receive it, in memory of me.

PRAYER AFTER COMMUNION
Grant, almighty God,
that, just as we are renewed
by the Supper of your Son in this present age,
so we may enjoy his banquet for all eternity.
Who lives and reigns for ever and ever. *Amen.*

• TAKING A CLOSER LOOK •

✛ **The washing of feet** Footwashing was not part of the
Passover ritual, but for John it is clearly an acting out of the deepest
meaning of the Eucharist—giving oneself in loving service for others. In
the biblical world, sandals that protected the bottom of the foot did not
keep the dirt away, so a customary sign of hospitality upon entering a
house was to provide water for a guest to wash their feet. This was usually the task of a servant. So, when Jesus assumes the role of the servant
instead of the master that he is, what would normally be considered
undignified and humiliating becomes a sign of love for his disciples.

The Blessing and Dismissal are omitted tonight.

TRANSFER OF THE MOST BLESSED SACRAMENT

The consecrated eucharistic bread is carried through the church in procession to the place of reposition. During the procession, the hymn "Pange lingua" or another eucharistic song is sung.

When the procession reaches the place of reposition, the celebrant incenses the eucharistic bread, while the "Tantum ergo" (stanzas 5-6 of the "Pange lingua") is sung. The tabernacle of repose is then closed.

After a few moments of silent adoration, the priests and ministers of the altar leave. The faithful are encouraged to continue adoration before the Blessed Sacrament for a suitable period of time through the evening and night, but there should be no solemn adoration after midnight. ⁑

• RESPONDING TO THE WORD •

At the Passover, the Jews remembered God's powerful presence that transformed their oppression into freedom.

➡ *How has God freed me from some oppression this Lent?*

At the Eucharist, we remember Christ's powerful presence that is always transforming us.

➡ *How might I express my gratitude to Christ for what he has done for me?*

In John's gospel, Jesus' footwashing is the model of eucharistic service.

➡ *What service for others might I undertake to show my thanks to Christ for his gift of life to me?*

March 30

The Way of the Cross

Alone. Abandoned. Forsaken. How must it have felt for Jesus on that fateful Friday? The day that we have come to call "good"; the first day in the celebration of the Lord's passion. Taken prisoner the night before, handed over to the Romans, and betrayed by someone close to him, he faced horrible torture and death.

His crime? He healed the sick, he embraced the poor, he made the lame walk and blind see; he spoke of love, justice, and mercy. The Way of the Cross is a journey that each of us will make in our own way. For some, it has been one that called them to sacrifice their lives to be tortured and imprisoned for the sake of justice, so that others might live free from oppression. But for most of us, our Way is often that of keeping vigil over loved ones in palliative care, or struggling to ensure that there is food on the table and a decent place for our children to live, or helping others who struggle to live day-by-day.

Good Friday reminds us that Jesus is our rock, our refuge, our safe harbor (Psalm 31). He knows what suffering and feeling helpless means. We need only call on him to find the strength and the grace to help us on our way (Hebrews 4:15).

■ Jack Panozzo

No Mass is celebrated today. The celebration of the Lord's Passion consists of three parts: the Liturgy of the Word, the Adoration of the Holy Cross, and the Reception of Holy Communion.

PRAYER

Remember your mercies, O Lord,
and with your eternal protection sanctify your servants,
for whom Christ your Son,
by the shedding of his Blood,
established the Paschal Mystery.
Who lives and reigns for ever and ever. *Amen.*

Or

O God, who by the Passion of Christ your Son, our Lord,
abolished the death inherited from ancient sin
by every succeeding generation,
grant that just as, being conformed to him,
we have borne by the law of nature
the image of the man of earth,
so by the sanctification of grace
we may bear the image of the Man of heaven.
Through Christ our Lord. *Amen.*

LITURGY OF THE WORD

FIRST READING *(Isaiah 52:13–53:12)*

See, my servant shall prosper,
he shall be raised high and greatly exalted.

Even as many were amazed at him—
    so marred was his look beyond human semblance
    and his appearance beyond that of the sons of man—
so shall he startle many nations,
    because of him kings shall stand speechless;
for those who have not been told shall see,
    those who have not heard shall ponder it.

Who would believe what we have heard?
    To whom has the arm of the LORD been revealed?
He grew up like a sapling before him,
    like a shoot from the parched earth;
there was in him no stately bearing to make us look at him,
    nor appearance that would attract us to him.
He was spurned and avoided by people,
    a man of suffering, accustomed to infirmity,
one of those from whom people hide their faces,
    spurned, and we held him in no esteem.

Yet it was our infirmities that he bore,
    our sufferings that he endured,
while we thought of him as stricken,
    as one smitten by God and afflicted.
But he was pierced for our offenses,
    crushed for our sins;
upon him was the chastisement that makes us whole,
    by his stripes we were healed.
We had all gone astray like sheep,
    each following his own way;
but the LORD laid upon him
    the guilt of us all.

Though he was harshly treated, he submitted
    and opened not his mouth;
like a lamb led to the slaughter
    or a sheep before the shearers,
    he was silent and opened not his mouth.
Oppressed and condemned, he was taken away,
    and who would have thought any more of his destiny?
When he was cut off from the land of the living,
    and smitten for the sin of his people,
a grave was assigned him among the wicked
    and a burial place with evildoers,
though he had done no wrong
    nor spoken any falsehood.
But the LORD was pleased
    to crush him in infirmity.

If he gives his life as an offering for sin,
    he shall see his descendants in a long life,
    and the will of the LORD shall be accomplished through him.

Because of his affliction
    he shall see the light in fullness of days;
through his suffering, my servant shall justify many,
    and their guilt he shall bear.
Therefore I will give him his portion among the great,
    and he shall divide the spoils with the mighty,
because he surrendered himself to death
    and was counted among the wicked;
and he shall take away the sins of many,
    and win pardon for their offenses.
The word of the Lord. ***Thanks be to God.***

RESPONSORIAL PSALM (*Psalm 31:2, 6, 12-13, 15-16, 17, 25*)

℟ **Father, into your hands I commend my spirit.**

In you, O LORD, I take refuge;
  let me never be put to shame.
In your justice rescue me.
Into your hands I commend my spirit;
  you will redeem me, O LORD, O faithful God. ℟
For all my foes I am an object of reproach,
  a laughingstock to my neighbors, and a dread to my friends;
  they who see me abroad flee from me.
I am forgotten like the unremembered dead;
  I am like a dish that is broken. ℟
But my trust is in you, O LORD;
  I say, "You are my God.
In your hands is my destiny; rescue me
  from the clutches of my enemies and my persecutors." ℟
Let your face shine upon your servant;
  save me in your kindness.
Take courage and be stouthearted,
  all you who hope in the Lord. ℟

SECOND READING (*Hebrews 4:14-16; 5:7-9*)

Brothers and sisters: Since we have a great high priest who has passed through the heavens, Jesus, the Son of God, let us hold fast to our confession. For we do not have a high priest who is unable to sympathize with our weaknesses, but one who has similarly been tested in every way, yet without sin. So let us confidently approach the throne of grace to receive mercy and to find grace for timely help.

  In the days when Christ was in the flesh, he offered prayers and supplications with loud cries and tears to the one who was able to save him from death, and he was heard because of his reverence. Son though he was, he learned obedience from what he suffered; and when he was made perfect, he became the source of eternal salvation for all who obey him.

The word of the Lord. *Thanks be to God.*

VERSE BEFORE THE GOSPEL *(Philippians 2:8–9)*
Glory and praise to you, Lord Jesus Christ! Christ became obedient to the point of death, even death on a cross. Because of this, God greatly exalted him and bestowed on him the name which is above every other name. *Glory and praise to you, Lord Jesus Christ!*

GOSPEL *(John 18:1–19:42)*
*Several readers may proclaim the passion narrative today. (***N***) indicates the narrator, (***✝***) the words of Jesus, (***V***) a voice, and (***C***) the crowd.*

N The Passion of our Lord Jesus Christ according to John.

Jesus went out with his disciples across the Kidron* valley to where there was a garden, into which he and his disciples entered. Judas his betrayer also knew the place, because Jesus had often met there with his disciples. So Judas got a band of soldiers and guards from the chief priests and the Pharisees and went there with lanterns, torches, and weapons. Jesus, knowing everything that was going to happen to him, went out and said to them,

✝ "Whom are you looking for?"

N They answered him,

C "Jesus the Nazorean.*"

N He said to them,

† "I AM."✠

N Judas his betrayer was also with them. When he said to them, "I AM," they turned away and fell to the ground. So he again asked them,

† "Whom are you looking for?"

N They said,

C "Jesus the Nazorean."

N Jesus answered,

† "I told you that I AM. So if you are looking for me, let these men go."

N This was to fulfill what he had said, "I have not lost any of those you gave me." Then Simon Peter, who had a sword, drew it, struck the high priest's slave, and cut off his right ear. The slave's name was Malchus.* Jesus said to Peter,

† "Put your sword into its scabbard. Shall I not drink the cup that the Father gave me?"

N So the band of soldiers, the tribune, and the Jewish guards seized Jesus, bound him, and brought him to Annas first. He was the father-in-law of Caiaphas,* who was high priest that year. It was Caiaphas who had counseled the Jews that it was better that one man should die rather than the people.

Simon Peter and another disciple followed Jesus. Now the other disciple was known to the high priest, and he entered the courtyard of the high priest with Jesus. But Peter stood at the gate outside. So the other disciple, the acquaintance of the high priest, went out and spoke to the gatekeeper and brought Peter in. Then the maid who was the gatekeeper said to Peter,

C **"You are not one of this man's disciples, are you?"**

N He said,

V "I am not."

N Now the slaves and the guards were standing around a charcoal fire that they had made, because it was cold, and were warming themselves. Peter was also standing there keeping warm.

The high priest questioned Jesus about his disciples and about his doctrine. Jesus answered him,

✝ "I have spoken publicly to the world. I have always taught in a synagogue or in the temple area where all the Jews gather, and in secret I have said nothing. Why ask me? Ask those who heard me what I said to them. They know what I said."

N When he had said this, one of the temple guards standing there struck Jesus and said,

V "Is this the way you answer the high priest?"

N Jesus answered him,

✝ "If I have spoken wrongly, testify to the wrong; but if I have spoken rightly, why do you strike me?"

N Then Annas sent him bound to Caiaphas the high priest.

Now Simon Peter was standing there keeping warm. And they said to him,

C "You are not one of his disciples, are you?"

N He denied it and said,

V "I am not."

N One of the slaves of the high priest, a relative of the one whose ear Peter had cut off, said,

C "Didn't I see you in the garden with him?"

N Again Peter denied it. And immediately the cock crowed.
Then they brought Jesus from Caiaphas to the praetorium.*
It was morning. And they themselves did not enter the praetorium, in order not to be defiled so that they could eat the Passover. So Pilate came out to them and said,

V "What charge do you bring against this man?"

N They answered and said to him,

C "If he were not a criminal, we would not have handed him over to you."

N At this, Pilate said to them,

V "Take him yourselves, and judge him according to your law."

N The Jews answered him,

C "We do not have the right to execute anyone,"

N in order that the word of Jesus might be fulfilled that he said indicating the kind of death he would die. So Pilate went back into the praetorium and summoned Jesus and said to him,

V "Are you the King of the Jews?"

N Jesus answered,

✝ "Do you say this on your own or have others told you about me?"

N Pilate answered,

V "I am not a Jew, am I? Your own nation and the chief priests handed you over to me. What have you done?"

N Jesus answered,

✝ "My kingdom does not belong to this world. If my kingdom did belong to this world, my attendants would be fighting to keep me from being handed over to the Jews. But as it is, my kingdom is not here."

N So Pilate said to him,

V "Then you are a king?"

N Jesus answered,

✝ "You say I am a king. For this I was born and for this I came into the world, to testify to the truth. Everyone who belongs to the truth listens to my voice."

N Pilate said to him,

V "What is truth?"

N When he had said this, he again went out to the Jews and said to them,

V "I find no guilt in him. But you have a custom that I release one prisoner to you at Passover. Do you want me to release to you the King of the Jews?"

N They cried out again,

C "Not this one but Barabbas!*"

N Now Barabbas was a revolutionary.

Then Pilate took Jesus and had him scourged. And the soldiers wove a crown out of thorns and placed it on his head, and clothed him in a purple cloak, and they came to him and said,

C "Hail, King of the Jews!"

N And they struck him repeatedly. Once more Pilate went out and said to them,

V "Look, I am bringing him out to you, so that you may know that I find no guilt in him."

N So Jesus came out, wearing the crown of thorns and the purple cloak. And Pilate said to them,

V "Behold, the man!"

N When the chief priests and the guards saw him they cried out,

C "Crucify him, crucify him!"

N Pilate said to them,

V "Take him yourselves and crucify him. I find no guilt in him."

N The Jews answered,

C "We have a law, and according to that law he ought to die, because he made himself the Son of God."

N Now when Pilate heard this statement, he became even more afraid, and went back into the praetorium and said to Jesus,

V "Where are you from?"

N Jesus did not answer him. So Pilate said to him,

V "Do you not speak to me? Do you not know that I have power to release you and I have power to crucify you?"

N Jesus answered him,

☩ "You would have no power over me if it had not been given to you from above. For this reason the one who handed me over to you has the greater sin."

N Consequently, Pilate tried to release him; but the Jews cried out,

C "If you release him, you are not a Friend of Caesar.* Everyone who makes himself a king opposes Caesar."

N When Pilate heard these words he brought Jesus out and seated him on the judge's bench in the place called Stone Pavement, in Hebrew, Gabbatha.* It was preparation day for Passover, and it was about noon. And he said to the Jews,

V "Behold, your king!"

N They cried out,

C "Take him away, take him away! Crucify him!"

N Pilate said to them,

V "Shall I crucify your king?"

N The chief priests answered,

C "We have no king but Caesar."

N Then he handed him over to them to be crucified.

So they took Jesus, and, carrying the cross himself, he went out to what is called the Place of the Skull, in Hebrew, Golgotha.* There they crucified him, and with him two others, one on either side, with Jesus in the middle. Pilate also had an inscription written and put on the cross. It read, "Jesus the Nazorean, the King of the Jews." Now many of the Jews read this inscription, because the place where Jesus was crucified was near the city; and it was written in Hebrew, Latin, and Greek. So the chief priests of the Jews said to Pilate,

C "Do not write 'The King of the Jews,' but that he said, 'I am the King of the Jews.'"

N Pilate answered,

V "What I have written, I have written."

N When the soldiers had crucified Jesus, they took his clothes and divided them into four shares, a share for each soldier. They also took his tunic, but the tunic was seamless, woven in one piece from the top down. So they said to one another,

C "Let's not tear it, but cast lots for it to see whose it will be,"

N in order that the passage of Scripture might be fulfilled that says:
> They divided my garments among them,
> and for my vesture they cast lots.

N This is what the soldiers did. Standing by the cross of Jesus were his mother and his mother's sister, Mary the wife of Clopas, and Mary of Magdala. When Jesus saw his mother and the disciple there whom he loved he said to his mother,

† "Woman, behold, your son."

N Then he said to the disciple,

† "Behold, your mother."

N And from that hour the disciple took her into his home.
　　After this, aware that everything was now finished, in order that the Scripture might be fulfilled, Jesus said,

† "I thirst."

N There was a vessel filled with common wine. So they put a sponge soaked in wine on a sprig of hyssop* and put it up to his mouth. When Jesus had taken the wine, he said,

† "It is finished."

N And bowing his head, he handed over the spirit.

(Here all kneel and pause for a short time.)

N Now since it was preparation day, in order that the bodies might not remain on the cross on the sabbath, for the sabbath day of that week was a solemn one, the Jews asked Pilate that their legs be broken and that they be taken down. So the soldiers came and broke the legs of the first and then of the other one who was crucified with Jesus. But when they came to Jesus and saw that he was already dead, they did not break his legs, but one soldier thrust his lance into his side, and immediately blood and water flowed out. An eyewitness has testified, and his testimony is true; he knows that he is speaking the truth, so that you also may come to believe. For this happened so that the Scripture passage might be fulfilled:

Not a bone of it will be broken.

And again another passage says:

They will look upon him whom they have pierced.

After this, Joseph of Arimathea,* secretly a disciple of Jesus for fear of the Jews, asked Pilate if he could remove the body of Jesus. And Pilate permitted it. So he came and took his body. Nicodemus, the one who had first come to him at night, also came bringing a mixture of myrrh and aloes weighing about one hundred pounds. They took the body of Jesus and bound it with burial cloths along with the spices, according to the Jewish burial custom. Now in the place where he had been crucified there was a garden, and in the garden a new tomb, in which no one had yet been buried. So they laid Jesus there because of the Jewish preparation day; for the tomb was close by. The Gospel of the Lord. ***Praise to you, Lord Jesus Christ.***

PRAYER OF THE FAITHFUL
For Holy Church
Let us pray, dearly beloved, for the holy Church of God,
that our God and Lord be pleased to give her peace,
to guard her and to unite her throughout the whole world
and grant that, leading our life in tranquility and quiet,
we may glorify God the Father almighty.
(Prayer in silence.)
Almighty ever-living God,
who in Christ revealed your glory to all the nations,
watch over the works of your mercy,

that your Church, spread throughout all the world,
may persevere with steadfast faith in confessing your name.
Through Christ our Lord. *Amen.*

For the Pope

Let us pray also for our most Holy Father Pope N.,
that our God and Lord,
who chose him for the Order of Bishops,
may keep him safe and unharmed for the Lord's holy Church,
to govern the holy People of God.

(Prayer in silence.)

Almighty ever-living God,
by whose decree all things are founded,
look with favor on our prayers
and in your kindness protect the Pope chosen for us,
that, under him, the Christian people,
governed by you their maker,
may grow in merit by reason of their faith.
Through Christ our Lord. *Amen.*

For all orders and degrees of the faithful

Let us pray also for our Bishop N.,
for all Bishops, Priests, and Deacons of the Church
and for the whole of the faithful people.

(Prayer in silence.)

Almighty ever-living God,
by whose Spirit the whole body of the Church
is sanctified and governed,
hear our humble prayer for your ministers,
that, by the gift of your grace,

all may serve you faithfully.
Through Christ our Lord. *Amen.*

For catechumens

Let us pray also for (our) catechumens,
that our God and Lord
may open wide the ears of their inmost hearts
and unlock the gates of his mercy,
that, having received forgiveness of all their sins
through the waters of rebirth,
they, too, may be one with Christ Jesus our Lord.
(Prayer in silence.)
Almighty ever-living God,
who make your Church ever fruitful with new offspring,
increase the faith and understanding of (our) catechumens,
that, reborn in the font of Baptism,
they may be added to the number of your adopted children.
Through Christ our Lord. *Amen.*

For the unity of Christians

Let us pray also for all our brothers and sisters who believe in Christ,
that our God and Lord may be pleased,
as they live the truth,
to gather them together and keep them in his one Church.
(Prayer in silence.)
Almighty ever-living God,
who gather what is scattered
and keep together what you have gathered,
look kindly on the flock of your Son,
that those whom one Baptism has consecrated

may be joined together by integrity of faith
and united in the bond of charity.
Through Christ our Lord. *Amen.*

For the Jewish people

Let us pray also for the Jewish people,
to whom the Lord our God spoke first,
that he may grant them to advance in love of his name
and in faithfulness to his covenant.
(Prayer in silence.)
Almighty ever-living God,
who bestowed your promises on Abraham and his descendants,
graciously hear the prayers of your Church,
that the people you first made your own
may attain the fullness of redemption.
Through Christ our Lord. *Amen.*

For those who do not believe in Christ

Let us pray also for those who do not believe in Christ,
that, enlightened by the Holy Spirit,
they, too, may enter on the way of salvation.
(Prayer in silence.)
Almighty ever-living God,
grant to those who do not confess Christ
that, by walking before you with a sincere heart,
they may find the truth
and that we ourselves, being constant in mutual love
and striving to understand more fully the mystery of your life,
may be made more perfect witnesses to your love in the world.
Through Christ our Lord. *Amen.*

For those who do not believe in God
Let us pray also for those who do not acknowledge God,
that, following what is right in sincerity of heart,
they may find the way to God himself.
(Prayer in silence.)
Almighty ever-living God,
who created all people
to seek you always by desiring you
and, by finding you, come to rest,
grant, we pray,
that, despite every harmful obstacle,
all may recognize the signs of your fatherly love
and the witness of the good works
done by those who believe in you,
and so in gladness confess you,
the one true God and Father of our human race.
Through Christ our Lord. *Amen.*

For those in public office
Let us pray also for those in public office,
that our God and Lord
may direct their minds and hearts according to his will
for the true peace and freedom of all.
(Prayer in silence.)
Almighty ever-living God,
in whose hand lies every human heart
and the rights of peoples,
look with favor, we pray,
on those who govern with authority over us,
that throughout the whole world,
the prosperity of peoples,

the assurance of peace,
and freedom of religion
may through your gift be made secure.
Through Christ our Lord. *Amen.*

For those in tribulation
Let us pray, dearly beloved,
to God the Father almighty,
that he may cleanse the world of all errors,
banish disease, drive out hunger,
unlock prisons, loosen fetters,
granting to travelers safety, to pilgrims return,
health to the sick, and salvation to the dying.
(Prayer in silence.)
Almighty ever-living God,
comfort of mourners, strength of all who toil,
may the prayers of those who cry out in any tribulation
come before you,
that all may rejoice,
because in their hour of need
your mercy was at hand.
Through Christ our Lord. *Amen.*

ADORATION OF THE HOLY CROSS

Three times the celebrant invites the assembly to proclaim its faith:

Behold the wood of the Cross,
on which hung the salvation of the world.
Come, let us adore.

After each response all venerate the cross briefly in silence. After the third response, the people approach to venerate the cross. They make a simple genuflection or perform some other appropriate sign of reverence according to local custom.

During the veneration, appropriate songs may be sung. All who have venerated the cross return to their places and sit. Where large numbers of people make individual veneration difficult, the celebrant may raise the cross briefly for all to venerate in silence.

HOLY COMMUNION

THE LORD'S PRAYER *(page 53)*

PRAYER AFTER COMMUNION
Almighty ever-living God,
who have restored us to life
by the blessed Death and Resurrection of your Christ,

• Taking a Closer Look •

✤ **I AM** These words have multiple levels of meaning. In everyday conversation, Jesus' statement "I am he" (John 4:26) would simply identify him as the one sought. The "I AM" of Exodus 3:14 (in capital letters) is God's personal name, *Yahweh*, which was closely related to the verb "I am." When Jesus says these words, his adversaries understand their deeper meaning, that Jesus shares God's power and, as Jesus says later to Pilate (John 19:11), they have no power over him unless he willingly permits it. It also accounts for the response of the soldiers and guards who fall to the ground, indicating that something more was being understood (John 18:3-6).

preserve in us the work of your mercy,
that, by partaking of this mystery,
we may have a life unceasingly devoted to you.
Through Christ our Lord. *Amen.*

PRAYER OVER THE PEOPLE
May abundant blessing, O Lord, we pray,
descend upon your people,
who have honored the Death of your Son
in the hope of their resurrection:
may pardon come,
comfort be given,
holy faith increase,
and everlasting redemption be made secure.
Through Christ our Lord. *Amen.*

All depart in silence. ⸭

• RESPONDING TO THE WORD •

The suffering of God's servant is hard for Isaiah to understand.	Jesus shares our human weakness but never lets that create a separation from God.	John's narrative contrasts Jesus and the other characters—including Peter, the Jewish leaders, Pilate, and the crowds.
▶ How does suffering make me more aware of who I am and of who God is for me?	▶ What weakness or suffering has tempted me to question God's love for me?	▶ Which of these other characters do I feel most like today?

March 31

We are Easter people!

The history of God's people recounted in tonight's Liturgy of the Word is bookended by two particularly powerful readings. The Genesis 1 story shows God creating and delighting in all that is. From dark emptiness the Master Artist calls forth light, land and sea, vegetation, animals, and humanity, and "God saw how good it was."

In Mark's resurrection account, the focus narrows to a dark and empty tomb. The dominant feeling here is fear, as the women confront the inexplicable. And yet this scene is as cosmically significant as the Creation story. For in rising from the dead Jesus has overcome our greatest enemy, death itself.

But the story does not end here. In a world still crying out for wholeness and healing, we are continually called to cooperate with God in the *ongoing* work of creation and redemption. In his encyclical *Laudato si'*, Pope Francis reminds us of our duty to care for both our planet and our brothers and sisters, especially those who are in most need. This is what it means to be an Easter people. As we rejoice in the resurrection, we cannot give in to complacency. May the risen Jesus renew in us the courage and faith needed to be co-creators and co-redeemers with our God in the light of the Holy Spirit.

■ **Krystyna Higgins**

There is no Mass celebrated during the day on Holy Saturday. But during the night, we anticipate Jesus' resurrection with one of the most ancient rites—a solemn vigil, which leads into the celebration of the 50 days of the Easter Season.

The Easter Vigil is arranged in four parts: the Service of Light (Lucernarium), the Liturgy of the Word, the Liturgy of Baptism, and the Liturgy of the Eucharist.

LUCERNARIUM

BLESSING OF THE FIRE

Dear brethren (brothers and sisters),
on this most sacred night,
in which our Lord Jesus Christ
passed over from death to life,
the Church calls upon her sons and daughters,
scattered throughout the world,
to come together to watch and pray.
If we keep the memorial
of the Lord's paschal solemnity in this way,
listening to his word and celebrating his mysteries,
then we shall have the sure hope
of sharing his triumph over death
and living with him in God.

Let us pray.

O God, who through your Son
bestowed upon the faithful the fire of your glory,
sanctify this new fire, we pray,
and grant that,
by these paschal celebrations,
we may be so inflamed with heavenly desires,
that with minds made pure
we may attain festivities of unending splendor.
Through Christ our Lord. *Amen.*

PREPARATION OF THE CANDLE

*The celebrant cuts a cross in the Easter candle and traces the Greek letters
alpha (A) and omega (Ω) and the numerals 2018, saying:*

Christ yesterday and today;
the Beginning and the End;
the Alpha; and the Omega.
All time belongs to him;
and all the ages.
To him be glory and power;
through every age and for ever. Amen.

*When the marks have been made, the celebrant may insert five grains of
incense in the candle, saying:*

By his holy and glorious wounds,
may Christ the Lord guard us and protect us. Amen.

LIGHTING OF THE CANDLE

The celebrant lights the Easter candle from the new fire, saying:

May the light of Christ rising in glory
dispel the darkness of our hearts and minds.

PROCESSION WITH THE EASTER CANDLE

The priest or deacon takes the Easter candle and, three times during the procession to the altar, lifts it high and sings alone. Then the people respond.

The Light of Christ.
Thanks be to God.

EASTER PROCLAMATION (Exultet)

For the shorter version, omit the indented parts in brackets.

Exult, let them exult, the hosts of heaven,
exult, let Angel ministers of God exult,
let the trumpet of salvation
sound aloud our mighty King's triumph!
Be glad, let earth be glad, as glory floods her,
ablaze with light from her eternal King,
let all corners of the earth be glad,
knowing an end to gloom and darkness.
Rejoice, let Mother Church also rejoice,
arrayed with the lightning of his glory,
let this holy building shake with joy,
filled with the mighty voices of the peoples.

> [(Therefore, dearest friends,
> standing in the awesome glory of this holy light,
> invoke with me, I ask you,
> the mercy of God almighty,
> that he, who has been pleased to number me,
> though unworthy, among the Levites,
> may pour into me his light unshadowed,
> that I may sing this candle's perfect praises).]

(The Lord be with you.
And with your spirit.)
Lift up your hearts.
We lift them up to the Lord.
Let us give thanks to the Lord our God.
It is right and just.

It is truly right and just,
with ardent love of mind and heart
and with devoted service of our voice,
to acclaim our God invisible, the almighty Father,
and Jesus Christ, our Lord, his Son, his Only Begotten.

Who for our sake paid Adam's debt to the eternal Father,
and, pouring out his own dear Blood,
wiped clean the record of our ancient sinfulness.

These then are the feasts of Passover,
in which is slain the Lamb, the one true Lamb,
whose Blood anoints the doorposts of believers.

This is the night,
when once you led our forebears, Israel's children,
from slavery in Egypt
and made them pass dry-shod through the Red Sea.

This is the night
that with a pillar of fire
banished the darkness of sin.

This is the night
that even now, throughout the world,
sets Christian believers apart from worldly vices

and from the gloom of sin,
leading them to grace
and joining them to his holy ones.

This is the night,
when Christ broke the prison-bars of death
and rose victorious from the underworld.

[Our birth would have been no gain,
had we not been redeemed.]
O wonder of your humble care for us!
O love, O charity beyond all telling,
to ransom a slave you gave away your Son!

O truly necessary sin of Adam,
destroyed completely by the Death of Christ!

O happy fault
that earned so great, so glorious a Redeemer!

[O truly blessed night,
worthy alone to know the time and hour
when Christ rose from the underworld!

This is the night
of which it is written:
The night shall be as bright as day,
dazzling is the night for me,
and full of gladness.]

The sanctifying power of this night
dispels wickedness, washes faults away,
restores innocence to the fallen, and joy to mourners,
[drives out hatred, fosters concord, and brings down the mighty.]

The longer version ending:

On this, your night of grace, O holy Father,
accept this candle, a solemn offering,
the work of bees and of your servants' hands,
an evening sacrifice of praise,
this gift from your most holy Church.

But now we know the praises of this pillar,
which glowing fire ignites for God's honor,
a fire into many flames divided,
yet never dimmed by sharing of its light,
for it is fed by melting wax,
drawn out by mother bees
to build a torch so precious.

O truly blessed night,
when things of heaven are wed to those of earth,
and divine to the human.

Therefore, O Lord,
we pray you that this candle,
hallowed to the honor of your name,
may persevere undimmed,
to overcome the darkness of this night.
Receive it as a pleasing fragrance,
and let it mingle with the lights of heaven.
May this flame be found still burning
by the Morning Star:
the one Morning Star who never sets,
Christ your Son,
who, coming back from death's domain,

has shed his peaceful light on humanity,
and lives and reigns for ever and ever. ***Amen.***

The shorter version ending:

O truly blessed night,
when things of heaven are wed to those of earth
and divine to the human.

On this, your night of grace, O holy Father,
accept this candle, a solemn offering,
the work of bees and of your servants' hands,
an evening sacrifice of praise,
this gift from your most holy Church.

Therefore, O Lord,
we pray you that this candle,
hallowed to the honor of your name,
may persevere undimmed,
to overcome the darkness of this night.
Receive it as a pleasing fragrance,
and let it mingle with the lights of heaven.
May this flame be found still burning
by the Morning Star:
the one Morning Star who never sets,
Christ your Son,
who, coming back from death's domain,
has shed his peaceful light on humanity,
and lives and reigns for ever and ever. ***Amen.***

LITURGY OF THE WORD

....

Dear brethren (brothers and sisters),
now that we have begun our solemn Vigil,
let us listen with quiet hearts to the Word of God.
Let us meditate on how God in times past saved his people
and in these, the last days, has sent us his Son as our Redeemer.
Let us pray that our God may complete this paschal work
   of salvation
by the fullness of redemption.

FIRST READING *(Genesis 1:1–2:2)*
For the shorter version, omit the indented parts in brackets.

In the beginning, when God created the heavens and the earth,
[the earth was a formless wasteland, and darkness covered the
abyss, while a mighty wind swept over the waters.

   Then God said, "Let there be light," and there was light. God
saw how good the light was. God then separated the light from
the darkness. God called the light "day," and the darkness he
called "night." Thus evening came, and morning followed—the
first day.

   Then God said, "Let there be a dome in the middle of the
waters, to separate one body of water from the other." And so
it happened: God made the dome, and it separated the water
above the dome from the water below it. God called the dome
"the sky." Evening came, and morning followed—the second
day.

   Then God said, "Let the water under the sky be gathered
into a single basin, so that the dry land may appear." And so
it happened: the water under the sky was gathered into its

basin, and the dry land appeared. God called the dry land "the earth," and the basin of the water he called "the sea." God saw how good it was. Then God said, "Let the earth bring forth vegetation: every kind of plant that bears seed and every kind of fruit tree on earth that bears fruit with its seed in it." And so it happened: the earth brought forth every kind of plant that bears seed and every kind of fruit tree on earth that bears fruit with its seed in it. God saw how good it was. Evening came, and morning followed—the third day.

Then God said: "Let there be lights in the dome of the sky, to separate day from night. Let them mark the fixed times, the days and the years, and serve as luminaries in the dome of the sky, to shed light upon the earth." And so it happened: God made the two great lights, the greater one to govern the day, and the lesser one to govern the night; and he made the stars. God set them in the dome of the sky, to shed light upon the earth, to govern the day and the night, and to separate the light from the darkness. God saw how good it was. Evening came, and morning followed—the fourth day.

Then God said, "Let the water teem with an abundance of living creatures, and on the earth let birds fly beneath the dome of the sky." And so it happened: God created the great sea monsters and all kinds of swimming creatures with which the water teems, and all kinds of winged birds. God saw how good it was, and God blessed them, saying, "Be fertile, multiply, and fill the water of the seas; and let the birds multiply on the earth." Evening came, and morning followed—the fifth day.

Then God said, "Let the earth bring forth all kinds of living creatures: cattle, creeping things, and wild animals of all kinds." And so it happened: God made all kinds of wild animals, all kinds of cattle, and all kinds of creeping things of the earth. God saw how good it was. Then]

God said: "Let us make man in our image, after our likeness. Let them have dominion over the fish of the sea, the birds of the air, and the cattle, and over all the wild animals and all the creatures that crawl on the ground."

God created man in his image;
> in the image of God he created him;
> male and female he created them.

God blessed them, saying: "Be fertile and multiply; fill the earth and subdue it. Have dominion over the fish of the sea, the birds of the air, and all the living things that move on the earth." God also said: "See, I give you every seed-bearing plant all over the earth and every tree that has seed-bearing fruit on it to be your food; and to all the animals of the land, all birds of the air, and all the living creatures that crawl on the ground, I give all the green plants for food." And so it happened. God looked at everything he had made, and he found it very good.

[Evening came, and morning followed—the sixth day.

Thus the heavens and the earth and all their array were completed. Since on the seventh day God was finished with the work he had been doing, he rested on the seventh day from all the work he had undertaken.]

The word of the Lord. *Thanks be to God.*

An alternate psalm follows.

RESPONSORIAL PSALM *(Psalm 104:1-2, 5-6, 10, 12, 13-14, 24, 35)*
℟ Lord, send out your Spirit, and renew the face of the earth.

Bless the LORD, O my soul!

O LORD, my God, you are great!
You are clothed with majesty and glory,
    robed in light as with a cloak. ℟
You fixed the earth upon its foundation,
    not to be moved forever;
with the ocean, as with a garment, you covered it;
    above the mountains the waters stood. ℟
You send forth springs into the watercourses
    that wind among the mountains.
Beside them the birds of heaven dwell;
    from among the branches they send forth their song. ℟
You water the mountains from your palace;
    the earth is replete with the fruit of your works.
You raise grass for the cattle,
    and vegetation for man's use,
producing bread from the earth. ℟
How manifold are your works, O LORD!
    In wisdom you have wrought them all—
the earth is full of your creatures.
    Bless the LORD, O my soul! ℟

OR

RESPONSORIAL PSALM *(Psalm 33:4-5, 6-7, 12-13, 20 and 22)*
℟ **The earth is full of the goodness of the Lord.**

Upright is the word of the LORD,
    and all his works are trustworthy.
He loves justice and right;
    of the kindness of the LORD the earth is full. ℟
By the word of the LORD the heavens were made;
    by the breath of his mouth all their host.

He gathers the waters of the sea as in a flask;
  in cellars he confines the deep.

R︎ **The earth is full of the goodness of the Lord.**

Blessed the nation whose God is the Lord,
  the people he has chosen for his own inheritance.

From heaven the Lord looks down;
  he sees all mankind. R︎

Our soul waits for the Lord,
  who is our help and our shield.

May your kindness, O Lord, be upon us
  who have put our hope in you. R︎

PRAYER

Almighty ever-living God,
who are wonderful in the ordering of all your works,
may those you have redeemed understand
that there exists nothing more marvelous
than the world's creation in the beginning
except that, at the end of the ages,
Christ our Passover has been sacrificed.
Who lives and reigns for ever and ever. *Amen.*

Or

O God, who wonderfully created human nature
and still more wonderfully redeemed it,
grant us, we pray,
to set our minds against the enticements of sin,
that we may merit to attain eternal joys.
Through Christ our Lord. *Amen.*

SECOND READING *(Genesis 22:1–18)*
For the shorter version, omit the indented parts in brackets.

God put Abraham to the test. He called to him, "Abraham!" "Here I am," he replied. Then God said: "Take your son Isaac, your only one, whom you love, and go to the land of Moriah.* There you shall offer him up as a holocaust on a height that I will point out to you."

[Early the next morning Abraham saddled his donkey, took with him his son Isaac and two of his servants as well, and with the wood that he had cut for the holocaust, set out for the place of which God had told him.

On the third day Abraham got sight of the place from afar. Then he said to his servants: "Both of you stay here with the donkey, while the boy and I go on over yonder. We will worship and then come back to you." Thereupon Abraham took the wood for the holocaust and laid it on his son Isaac's shoulders, while he himself carried the fire and the knife. As the two walked on together, Isaac spoke to his father Abraham: "Father!" Isaac said. "Yes, son," he replied. Isaac continued, "Here are the fire and the wood, but where is the sheep for the holocaust?" "Son," Abraham answered, "God himself will provide the sheep for the holocaust." Then the two continued going forward.]

When they came to the place of which God had told him, Abraham built an altar there and arranged the wood on it.

[Next he tied up his son Isaac, and put him on top of the wood on the altar.]

Then he reached out and took the knife to slaughter his son. But the LORD's messenger called to him from heaven, "Abraham, Abraham!" "Here I am," he answered. "Do not lay your hand on the boy," said the messenger. "Do not do the least thing to him.

I know now how devoted you are to God, since you did not withhold from me your own beloved son." As Abraham looked about, he spied a ram caught by its horns in the thicket. So he went and took the ram and offered it up as a holocaust in place of his son.

[Abraham named the site Yahweh-yireh;* hence people now say, "On the mountain the LORD will see."]

Again the LORD's messenger called to Abraham from heaven and said: "I swear by myself, declares the LORD, that because you acted as you did in not withholding from me your beloved son, I will bless you abundantly and make your descendants as countless as the stars of the sky and the sands of the seashore; your descendants shall take possession of the gates of their enemies, and in your descendants all the nations of the earth shall find blessing—all this because you obeyed my command."

The word of the Lord. ***Thanks be to God.***

RESPONSORIAL PSALM *(Psalm 16:5, 8, 9-10, 11)*

℟ **You are my inheritance, O Lord.**

O LORD, my allotted portion and my cup,
     you it is who hold fast my lot.
I set the LORD ever before me;
     with him at my right hand I shall not be disturbed. ℟

Therefore my heart is glad and my soul rejoices,
     my body, too, abides in confidence;
because you will not abandon my soul to the netherworld,
     nor will you suffer your faithful one to undergo corruption. ℟

You will show me the path to life,
     fullness of joys in your presence,
     the delights at your right hand forever. ℟

PRAYER

O God, supreme Father of the faithful,
who increase the children of your promise
by pouring out the grace of adoption
throughout the whole world
and who through the Paschal Mystery
make your servant Abraham father of nations,
as once you swore,
grant, we pray,
that your peoples may enter worthily
into the grace to which you call them.
Through Christ our Lord. *Amen.*

THIRD READING *(Exodus 14:15—15:1)*

The LORD said to Moses, "Why are you crying out to me? Tell the Israelites to go forward. And you, lift up your staff and, with hand outstretched over the sea, split the sea in two, that the Israelites may pass through it on dry land. But I will make the Egyptians so obstinate that they will go in after them. Then I will receive glory through Pharaoh and all his army, his chariots and charioteers. The Egyptians shall know that I am the LORD, when I receive glory through Pharaoh and his chariots and charioteers."

The angel of God, who had been leading Israel's camp, now moved and went around behind them. The column of cloud also, leaving the front, took up its place behind them, so that it came between the camp of the Egyptians and that of Israel. But the cloud now became dark, and thus the night passed without the rival camps coming any closer together all night long. Then Moses stretched out his hand over the sea, and the LORD swept the sea with a strong east wind throughout the night and so turned it into dry land. When the water was thus divided, the

Israelites marched into the midst of the sea on dry land, with the water like a wall to their right and to their left.

The Egyptians followed in pursuit; all Pharaoh's horses and chariots and charioteers went after them right into the midst of the sea. In the night watch just before dawn the LORD cast through the column of the fiery cloud upon the Egyptian force a glance that threw it into a panic; and he so clogged their chariot wheels that they could hardly drive. With that the Egyptians sounded the retreat before Israel, because the LORD was fighting for them against the Egyptians.

Then the LORD told Moses, "Stretch out your hand over the sea, that the water may flow back upon the Egyptians, upon their chariots and their charioteers." So Moses stretched out his hand over the sea, and at dawn the sea flowed back to its normal depth. The Egyptians were fleeing head on toward the sea, when the LORD hurled them into its midst. As the water flowed back, it covered the chariots and the charioteers of Pharaoh's whole army which had followed the Israelites into the sea. Not a single one of them escaped. But the Israelites had marched on dry land through the midst of the sea, with the water like a wall to their right and to their left. Thus the LORD saved Israel on that day from the power of the Egyptians. When Israel saw the Egyptians lying dead on the seashore and beheld the great power that the LORD had shown against the Egyptians, they feared the LORD and believed in him and in his servant Moses.

Then Moses and the Israelites sang this song to the LORD:
I will sing to the LORD, for he is gloriously triumphant;
horse and chariot he has cast into the sea.

The word of the Lord. ***Thanks be to God.***

RESPONSORIAL CANTICLE *(Exodus 15:1-2, 3-4, 5-6, 17-18)*
℟ Let us sing to the Lord; he has covered himself in glory.

I will sing to the LORD, for he is gloriously triumphant;
　　horse and chariot he has cast into the sea.
My strength and my courage is the LORD,
　　and he has been my savior.
He is my God, I praise him;
　　the God of my father, I extol him. ℟
The LORD is a warrior,
　　LORD is his name!
Pharaoh's chariots and army he hurled into the sea;
　　the elite of his officers were submerged in the Red Sea. ℟
The flood waters covered them,
　　they sank into the depths like a stone.
Your right hand, O LORD, magnificent in power,
　　your right hand, O LORD, has shattered the enemy. ℟
You brought in the people you redeemed
　　and planted them on the mountain of your inheritance—
the place where you made your seat, O LORD,
　　the sanctuary, LORD, which your hands established.
The LORD shall reign forever and ever. ℟

PRAYER
O God, whose ancient wonders
remain undimmed in splendor even in our day,
for what you once bestowed on a single people,
freeing them from Pharaoh's persecution
by the power of your right hand,
now you bring about as the salvation of the nations
through the waters of rebirth,

grant, we pray, that the whole world
may become children of Abraham
and inherit the dignity of Israel's birthright.
Through Christ our Lord. *Amen.*

Or

O God, who by the light of the New Testament
have unlocked the meaning
of wonders worked in former times,
so that the Red Sea prefigures the sacred font
and the nation delivered from slavery
foreshadows the Christian people,
grant, we pray, that all nations,
obtaining the privilege of Israel by merit of faith,
may be reborn by partaking of your Spirit.
Through Christ our Lord. *Amen.*

FOURTH READING (Isaiah 54:5-14)

The One who has become your husband is your Maker;
his name is the LORD of hosts;
your redeemer is the Holy One of Israel,
called God of all the earth.
The LORD calls you back,
like a wife forsaken and grieved in spirit,
a wife married in youth and then cast off,
says your God.
For a brief moment I abandoned you,
but with great tenderness I will take you back.
In an outburst of wrath, for a moment
I hid my face from you;
but with enduring love I take pity on you,

says the LORD, your redeemer.
This is for me like the days of Noah,
    when I swore that the waters of Noah
    should never again deluge the earth;
so I have sworn not to be angry with you,
    or to rebuke you.
Though the mountains leave their place
    and the hills be shaken,
my love shall never leave you
    nor my covenant of peace be shaken,
    says the LORD, who has mercy on you.
O afflicted one, storm-battered and unconsoled,
    I lay your pavements in carnelians,
    and your foundations in sapphires;
I will make your battlements of rubies,
    your gates of carbuncles,
    and all your walls of precious stones.
All your children shall be taught by the LORD,
    and great shall be the peace of your children.
In justice shall you be established,
    far from the fear of oppression,
    where destruction cannot come near you.
The word of the Lord. ***Thanks be to God.***

RESPONSORIAL PSALM *(Psalm 30:2, 4, 5-6, 11-12, 13)*
℟ **I will praise you, Lord, for you have rescued me.**

I will extol you, O LORD, for you drew me clear
    and did not let my enemies rejoice over me.
O LORD, you brought me up from the netherworld;
    you preserved me from among those going down into the pit. ℟

Sing praise to the LORD, you his faithful ones,
    and give thanks to his holy name.
For his anger lasts but a moment;
    a lifetime, his good will.
At nightfall, weeping enters in,
    but with the dawn, rejoicing.
℟ **I will praise you, Lord, for you have rescued me.**
Hear, O LORD, and have pity on me;
    O LORD, be my helper.
You changed my mourning into dancing;
    O LORD, my God, forever will I give you thanks. ℟

PRAYER
Almighty ever-living God,
surpass, for the honor of your name,
what you pledged to the Patriarchs by reason of their faith,
and through sacred adoption increase the children of your promise,
so that what the Saints of old never doubted would come to pass
your Church may now see in great part fulfilled.
Through Christ our Lord. *Amen.*

FIFTH READING *(Isaiah 55:1-11)*

Thus says the LORD:
    All you who are thirsty,
    come to the water!
You who have no money,
    come, receive grain and eat;
come, without paying and without cost,
    drink wine and milk!
Why spend your money for what is not bread,
    your wages for what fails to satisfy?

Heed me, and you shall eat well,
    you shall delight in rich fare.
Come to me heedfully,
    listen, that you may have life.
I will renew with you the everlasting covenant,
    the benefits assured to David.
As I made him a witness to the peoples,
    a leader and commander of nations,
so shall you summon a nation you knew not,
    and nations that knew you not shall run to you,
because of the LORD, your God,
    the Holy One of Israel, who has glorified you.

Seek the LORD while he may be found,
    call him while he is near.
Let the scoundrel forsake his way,
    and the wicked man his thoughts;
let him turn to the LORD for mercy;
    to our God, who is generous in forgiving.
For my thoughts are not your thoughts,
    nor are your ways my ways, says the LORD.
As high as the heavens are above the earth,
    so high are my ways above your ways
    and my thoughts above your thoughts.

For just as from the heavens
    the rain and snow come down
and do not return there
    till they have watered the earth,
    making it fertile and fruitful,
giving seed to the one who sows

and bread to the one who eats,
so shall my word be
    that goes forth from my mouth;
my word shall not return to me void,
    but shall do my will,
    achieving the end for which I sent it.
The word of the Lord. *Thanks be to God.*

RESPONSORIAL CANTICLE *(Isaiah 12:2-3, 4, 5-6)*
℟ **You will draw water joyfully from the springs of salvation.**

God indeed is my savior;
    I am confident and unafraid.
My strength and my courage is the LORD,
    and he has been my savior.
With joy you will draw water
    at the fountain of salvation. ℟
Give thanks to the LORD, acclaim his name;
    among the nations make known his deeds,
    proclaim how exalted is his name. ℟
Sing praise to the LORD for his glorious achievement;
    let this be known throughout all the earth.
Shout with exultation, O city of Zion,*
    for great in your midst
    is the Holy One of Israel! ℟

PRAYER
Almighty ever-living God,
sole hope of the world,
who by the preaching of your Prophets
unveiled the mysteries of this present age,
graciously increase the longing of your people,

for only at the prompting of your grace
do the faithful progress in any kind of virtue.
Through Christ our Lord. *Amen.*

SIXTH READING *(Baruch 3:9-15, 32–4:4)*

Hear, O Israel, the commandments of life:
listen, and know prudence!
How is it, Israel,
    that you are in the land of your foes,
    grown old in a foreign land,
defiled with the dead,
    accounted with those destined for the netherworld?
You have forsaken the fountain of wisdom!
    Had you walked in the way of God,
    you would have dwelt in enduring peace.
Learn where prudence is,
    where strength, where understanding;
that you may know also
    where are length of days, and life,
    where light of the eyes, and peace.
Who has found the place of wisdom,
    who has entered into her treasuries?

The One who knows all things knows her;
    he has probed her by his knowledge—
The One who established the earth for all time,
    and filled it with four-footed beasts;
he who dismisses the light, and it departs,
    calls it, and it obeys him trembling;
before whom the stars at their posts
    shine and rejoice;

when he calls them, they answer, "Here we are!"
    shining with joy for their Maker.
Such is our God;
    no other is to be compared to him:
he has traced out the whole way of understanding,
    and has given her to Jacob, his servant,
    to Israel, his beloved son.

Since then she has appeared on earth,
    and moved among people.
She is the book of the precepts of God,
    the law that endures forever;
all who cling to her will live,
    but those will die who forsake her.
Turn, O Jacob, and receive her:
    walk by her light toward splendor.
Give not your glory to another,
    your privileges to an alien race.
Blessed are we, O Israel;
    for what pleases God is known to us!
The word of the Lord. ***Thanks be to God.***

RESPONSORIAL PSALM *(Psalm 19:8, 9, 10, 11)*
℞ **Lord, you have the words of everlasting life.**

The law of the LORD is perfect,
    refreshing the soul;
the decree of the LORD is trustworthy,
    giving wisdom to the simple. ℞
The precepts of the LORD are right,
    rejoicing the heart;
the command of the LORD is clear,

enlightening the eye. ℟

The fear of the LORD is pure,
    enduring forever;
the ordinances of the LORD are true,
    all of them just. ℟

They are more precious than gold,
    than a heap of purest gold;
sweeter also than syrup
    or honey from the comb. ℟

PRAYER

O God, who constantly increase your Church
by your call to the nations,
graciously grant
to those you wash clean in the waters of Baptism
the assurance of your unfailing protection.
Through Christ our Lord. *Amen.*

SEVENTH READING *(Ezekiel 36:16–17a, 18–28)*

The word of the LORD came to me, saying: Son of man, when the house of Israel lived in their land, they defiled it by their conduct and deeds. Therefore I poured out my fury upon them because of the blood that they poured out on the ground, and because they defiled it with idols. I scattered them among the nations, dispersing them over foreign lands; according to their conduct and deeds I judged them. But when they came among the nations wherever they came, they served to profane my holy name, because it was said of them: "These are the people of the LORD, yet they had to leave their land." So I have relented because of my holy name which the house of Israel profaned among the nations where they came. Therefore say to the house of Israel: Thus says the Lord GOD: Not for your sakes do I act, house of Israel, but for the sake of my holy name, which you profaned among the nations to which you came. I will prove the holiness of my great name, profaned among the nations, in whose midst you have profaned it. Thus the nations shall know that I am the LORD, says the Lord GOD, when in their sight I prove my holiness through you. For I will take you away from among the nations, gather you from all the foreign lands, and bring you back to your own land. I will sprinkle clean water upon you to cleanse you from all your impurities, and from all your idols I will cleanse you. I will give you a new heart and place a new spirit within you, taking from your bodies your stony hearts and giving you natural hearts. I will put my spirit within you and make you live by my statutes, careful to observe my decrees. You shall live in the land I gave your fathers; you shall be my people, and I will be your God.

The word of the Lord. *Thanks be to God.*

When baptism is celebrated, sing Psalm 42/43 (below); when baptism is not celebrated, sing Isaiah 12 (from after the Fifth Reading, page 304) or Psalm 51 (next page).

RESPONSORIAL PSALM *(Psalm 42:3, 5; 43:3, 4)*
℟ Like a deer that longs for running streams,
   my soul longs for you, my God.

Athirst is my soul for God, the living God.
   When shall I go and behold the face of God? ℟
I went with the throng
   and led them in procession to the house of God,
amid loud cries of joy and thanksgiving,

with the multitude keeping festival. ℟
Send forth your light and your fidelity;
    they shall lead me on
and bring me to your holy mountain,
    to your dwelling-place. ℟
Then will I go in to the altar of God,
    the God of my gladness and joy;
then will I give you thanks upon the harp,
    O God, my God! ℟

OR

RESPONSORIAL PSALM *(Psalm 51:12-13, 14-15, 18-19)*
℟ **Create a clean heart in me, O God.**

A clean heart create for me, O God,
    and a steadfast spirit renew within me.
Cast me not out from your presence,
    and your Holy Spirit take not from me. ℟
Give me back the joy of your salvation,
    and a willing spirit sustain in me.
I will teach transgressors your ways,
    and sinners shall return to you. ℟
For you are not pleased with sacrifices;
    should I offer a holocaust, you would not accept it.
My sacrifice, O God, is a contrite spirit;
    a heart contrite and humbled, O God, you will not spurn. ℟

PRAYER

O God of unchanging power and eternal light,
look with favor on the wondrous mystery of the whole Church
and serenely accomplish the work of human salvation,

which you planned from all eternity;
may the whole world know and see
that what was cast down is raised up,
what had become old is made new,
and all things are restored to integrity through Christ,
just as by him they came into being.
Who lives and reigns for ever and ever. *Amen.*

Or

O God, who by the pages of both Testaments
instruct and prepare us to celebrate the Paschal Mystery,
grant that we may comprehend your mercy,
so that the gifts we receive from you this night
may confirm our hope of the gifts to come.
Through Christ our Lord. *Amen.*

GLORY TO GOD *(page 12)*

COLLECT

O God, who make this most sacred night radiant
with the glory of the Lord's Resurrection,
stir up in your Church a spirit of adoption,
so that, renewed in body and mind,
we may render you undivided service.
Through our Lord Jesus Christ, your Son,
who lives and reigns with you in the unity of the Holy Spirit,
one God, for ever and ever. *Amen.*

EPISTLE *(Romans 6:3–11)*

Brothers and sisters: Are you unaware that we who were
baptized into Christ Jesus were baptized into his death? We
were indeed buried with him through baptism into death, so

that, just as Christ was raised from the dead by the glory of the Father, we too might live in newness of life.

For if we have grown into union with him through a death like his, we shall also be united with him in the **resurrection**.✝ We know that our old self was crucified with him, so that our sinful body might be done away with, that we might no longer be in slavery to sin. For a dead person has been absolved from sin. If, then, we have died with Christ, we believe that we shall also live with him. We know that Christ, raised from the dead, dies no more; death no longer has power over him. As to his death, he died to sin once and for all; as to his life, he lives for God. Consequently, you too must think of yourselves as being dead to sin and living for God in Christ Jesus.

The word of the Lord. *Thanks be to God.*

RESPONSORIAL PSALM *(Psalm 118:1–2, 16–17, 22–23)*
℟ Alleluia, alleluia, alleluia.

Give thanks to the LORD, for he is good,
    for his mercy endures forever.
Let the house of Israel say,
    "His mercy endures forever." ℟
The right hand of the LORD has struck with power;
    the right hand of the LORD is exalted.
I shall not die, but live,
    and declare the works of the LORD. ℟
The stone which the builders rejected
    has become the cornerstone.
By the LORD has this been done;
    it is wonderful in our eyes. ℟

GOSPEL *(Mark 16:1–7)*

A reading from the holy Gospel according to Mark.

Glory to you, O Lord.

When the sabbath was over, Mary Magdalene, Mary, the mother of James, and Salome* bought spices so that they might go and anoint him. Very early when the sun had risen, on the first day of the week, they came to the tomb. They were saying to one another, "Who will roll back the stone for us from the entrance to the tomb?" When they looked up, they saw that the stone had been rolled back; it was very large. On entering the tomb they saw a young man sitting on the right side, clothed in a white robe, and they were utterly amazed. He said to them, "Do not be amazed! You seek Jesus of Nazareth, the crucified. He has been raised; he is not here. Behold the place where they laid him. But go and tell his disciples and Peter, 'He is going before you to Galilee; there you will see him, as he told you.' "

The Gospel of the Lord. *Praise to you, Lord Jesus Christ.*

LITURGY OF BAPTISM

....

INVITATION

When baptism is celebrated:

Dearly beloved,
with one heart and one soul, let us by our prayers
come to the aid of these our brothers and sisters
    in their blessed hope,
so that, as they approach the font of rebirth,
the almighty Father may bestow on them
all his merciful help.

When baptism is not celebrated, but the font is blessed:

Dearly beloved,
let us humbly invoke upon this font
the grace of God the almighty Father,
that those who from it are born anew
may be numbered among the children of adoption in Christ.

*If baptism is not celebrated and the font is not blessed, proceed to the
blessing of the water outside of baptism (page 317).*

LITANY OF SAINTS

Lord, have mercy. ***Lord, have mercy.***
Christ, have mercy. ***Christ, have mercy.***
Lord, have mercy. ***Lord, have mercy.***

Holy Mary, Mother of God, ***pray for us.***

Saint Michael,
Holy Angels of God,
Saint John the Baptist,
Saint Joseph,
Saint Peter and Saint Paul,
Saint Andrew,
Saint John,
Saint Mary Magdalene,
Saint Stephen,
Saint Ignatius of Antioch,
Saint Lawrence,
Saint Perpetua
    and Saint Felicity,
Saint Agnes,

Saint Gregory,
Saint Augustine,
Saint Athanasius,
Saint Basil,
Saint Martin,
Saint Benedict,
Saint Francis
    and Saint Dominic,
Saint Francis Xavier,
Saint John Vianney,
Saint Catherine of Siena,
Saint Teresa of Jesus,
All holy men and women,
    Saints of God,

Lord, be merciful.
Lord, deliver us, we pray.
From all evil,
From every sin,
From everlasting death,
By your Incarnation,
By your Death and Resurrection,
By the outpouring of the Holy Spirit,

Be merciful to us sinners,
Lord, we ask you, hear our prayer.

When baptism is celebrated add:

Bring these chosen ones to new birth through the grace of Baptism,
Lord, we ask you, hear our prayer.

Or, when baptism is not celebrated:

Make this font holy by your grace for the new birth of your children.
Lord, we ask you, hear our prayer.

Jesus, Son of the living God
Lord, we ask you, hear our prayer.
Christ, hear us.
Christ, hear us.
Christ, graciously hear us.
Christ, graciously hear us.

When baptism is celebrated, the priest prays:

Almighty ever-living God,
be present by the mysteries of your great love
and send forth the spirit of adoption
to create the new peoples
brought to birth for you in the font of Baptism,
so that what is to be carried out by our humble service
may be brought to fulfillment by your mighty power.
Through Christ our Lord. *Amen.*

BLESSING OF BAPTISMAL WATER

O God, who by invisible power
accomplish a wondrous effect
through sacramental signs
and who in many ways have prepared water, your creation,
to show forth the grace of Baptism;

O God, whose Spirit
in the first moments of the world's creation

hovered over the waters,
so that the very substance of water
would even then take to itself the power to sanctify;

O God, who by the outpouring of the flood
foreshadowed regeneration,
so that from the mystery of one and the same element of water
would come an end to vice and a beginning of virtue;

O God, who caused the children of Abraham
to pass dry-shod through the Red Sea,
so that the chosen people,
set free from slavery to Pharaoh,
would prefigure the people of the baptized;

O God, whose Son,
baptized by John in the waters of the Jordan,
was anointed with the Holy Spirit,
and, as he hung upon the Cross,
gave forth water from his side along with blood,
and after his Resurrection, commanded his disciples:

"Go forth, teach all nations, baptizing them
in the name of the Father and of the Son and of the Holy Spirit,"
look now, we pray, upon the face of your Church
and graciously unseal for her the fountain of Baptism.

May this water receive by the Holy Spirit
the grace of your Only Begotten Son,
so that human nature, created in your image
and washed clean through the Sacrament of Baptism
from all the squalor of the life of old,
may be found worthy to rise to the life of newborn children

through water and the Holy Spirit.

May the power of the Holy Spirit,
O Lord, we pray,
come down through your Son
into the fullness of this font,
so that all who have been buried with Christ
by Baptism into death
may rise again to life with him.
Who lives and reigns with you in the unity of the Holy Spirit,
one God, for ever and ever. *Amen.*

Springs of water, bless the Lord;
praise and exalt him above all for ever.

Baptism is now conferred. Adults are then confirmed immediately afterward.

If there is no baptism and the font is not blessed, the priest blesses the
water and invites the assembly to renew their baptismal commitment:

THE BLESSING OF WATER *(OUTSIDE OF BAPTISM)*
Dear brothers and sisters,
let us humbly beseech the Lord our God
to bless this water he has created,
which will be sprinkled upon us
as a memorial of our Baptism.
May he graciously renew us,
that we may remain faithful to the Spirit
whom we have received.

Lord our God,
in your mercy be present to your people
who keep vigil on this most sacred night,

and, for us who recall the wondrous work of our creation
and the still greater work of our redemption,
graciously bless this water.
For you created water to make the fields fruitful
and to refresh and cleanse our bodies.
You also made water the instrument of your mercy:
for through water you freed your people from slavery
and quenched their thirst in the desert;
through water the Prophets proclaimed the new covenant
you were to enter upon with the human race;
and last of all,
through water, which Christ made holy in the Jordan,
you have renewed our corrupted nature
in the bath of regeneration.

Therefore, may this water be for us
a memorial of the Baptism we have received,
and grant that we may share
in the gladness of our brothers and sisters,
who at Easter have received their Baptism.
Through Christ our Lord. *Amen.*

*When the Rite of Baptism (and Confirmation) has been completed or, if
this has not taken place, after the blessing of water, all stand, holding
lighted candles in their hands, and renew the promise of baptismal faith,
unless this has already been done together with those to be baptized.*

RENEWAL OF BAPTISMAL PROMISES

Dear brethren (brothers and sisters), through the Paschal Mystery
we have been buried with Christ in Baptism,
so that we may walk with him in newness of life.

And so, now that our Lenten observance is concluded,
let us renew the promises of Holy Baptism,
by which we once renounced Satan and his works
and promised to serve God in the holy Catholic Church.
And so I ask you:

1 Do you renounce Satan? *I do.*
   And all his works? *I do.*
   And all his empty show? *I do.*

2 Do you renounce sin,
   so as to live in the freedom of the children of God? *I do.*
   Do you renounce the lure of evil,
   so that sin may have no mastery over you? *I do.*
   Do you renounce Satan,
   the author and prince of sin? *I do.*

PROFESSION OF FAITH

Do you believe in God, the Father almighty,
Creator of heaven and earth? *I do.*

Do you believe in Jesus Christ, his only Son, our Lord,
who was born of the Virgin Mary,
suffered death and was buried,
rose again from the dead
and is seated at the right hand of the Father? *I do.*

Do you believe in the Holy Spirit,
the holy Catholic Church,
the communion of saints,
the forgiveness of sins,
the resurrection of the body,
and life everlasting? *I do.*

And may almighty God, the Father of our Lord Jesus Christ,
who has given us new birth by water and the Holy Spirit
and bestowed on us forgiveness of our sins,
keep us by his grace,
in Christ Jesus our Lord,
for eternal life. *Amen.*

SPRINKLING WITH BAPTISMAL WATER

*The priest sprinkles all the people with the blessed baptismal water, while
an appropriate song may be sung.*

PRAYER OF THE FAITHFUL

LITURGY OF THE EUCHARIST

PREPARATION OF GIFTS *(page 16)*

PRAYER OVER THE OFFERINGS
Accept, we ask, O Lord,
the prayers of your people
with the sacrificial offerings,
that what has begun in the paschal mysteries
may, by the working of your power,
bring us to the healing of eternity.
Through Christ our Lord. *Amen.*

PREFACE *(Easter 1, page 24)*

COMMUNION ANTIPHON *(1 Corinthians 5:7-8)*

Christ our Passover has been sacrificed; therefore let us keep the feast with the unleavened bread of purity and truth, alleluia.

PRAYER AFTER COMMUNION

Pour out on us, O Lord, the Spirit of your love,
and in your kindness make those you have nourished
by this paschal Sacrament
one in mind and heart.
Through Christ our Lord. *Amen.*

SOLEMN BLESSING: MASS OF THE EASTER VIGIL

May almighty God bless you
through today's Easter Solemnity
and, in his compassion,
defend you from every assault of sin. *Amen.*

• TAKING A CLOSER LOOK •

✠ **Resurrection** What happened on Easter was a complete surprise to the disciples. The Jesus that they had known and who had died was suddenly experienced as alive again. This new life, described as resurrection, was not just a restoration of one's former life—a resuscitation from the dead. The prophets Elijah and Elisha had brought people back to this life, as had Jesus for the daughter of Jairus, the son of the widow of Nain, and Jesus' beloved friend Lazarus. Although their return from the dead left them temporarily alive, they would die again. Jesus' resurrection was a new life that would not be subject to death again. It was eternal life, permanent and undying existence in the presence of God forever.

And may he, who restores you to eternal life
in the Resurrection of his Only Begotten,
endow you with the prize of immortality. *Amen.*

Now that the days of the Lord's Passion have drawn to a close,
may you who celebrate the gladness of the Paschal Feast
come with Christ's help, and exulting in spirit,
to those feasts that are celebrated in eternal joy. *Amen.*

And may the blessing of almighty God,
the Father, and the Son, and the Holy Spirit,
come down on you and remain with you for ever. *Amen.*

DISMISSAL *(page 57)* ✤

• RESPONDING TO THE WORD •

The Old Testament readings recall the whole story of God's desire to create a covenant community that would follow God's guidelines.

➡ *What word, phrase, or idea in these readings most interested me tonight?*

Paul reminds us that, through our relationship with Jesus, we are drawn into the mystery of life and death and new life.

➡ *What hint of new life is beginning in me at this Easter time?*

The three women do not find Jesus' body, but they are told he is risen and where to meet him.

➡ *Where have I met or experienced the risen Jesus most clearly in my life?*

April 1

Rejoice in a promise fulfilled!

Reading today's gospel, on this most holy day, I marvel at Mary Magdalene's tenacity in seeking Jesus and her transformation when she sees his promise fulfilled.

As you hear the gospel proclaimed today, imagine her blinding grief. She watched her beloved Rabbi being tortured, witnessed his crucifixion, and finds his tomb empty. Notice how she comes so early in the morning that it is still dark, and she is the only one there. How greatly must she love him to go to the tomb alone, unafraid when all the others were? Her faith is a wondrous thing. Even in grief and bewilderment, Mary comes to the tomb.

Don't we all encounter these moments in our life, when we need God but do not feel God's presence? Mary Magdalene's unwavering faith teaches us discipleship—that we will find God if we seek with love and faith. Mary's faith transforms her grief to joy when she meets the risen Christ, and she becomes an apostle to the apostles.

This Easter, let us remember that we are here to rejoice in a promise fulfilled and the transformative power of God, who draws us close in love.

■ SASKIA SIVANANTHAN

ENTRANCE ANTIPHON *(Cf. Psalm 139 (138):18, 5-6)*

I have risen, and I am with you still, alleluia. You have laid your hand upon me, alleluia. Too wonderful for me, this knowledge, alleluia, alleluia.

Or *(Luke 24:34; cf. Revelation 1:6)*

The Lord is truly risen, alleluia. To him be glory and power for all the ages of eternity, alleluia, alleluia.

INTRODUCTORY RITES *(page 10)*

COLLECT

O God, who on this day,
through your Only Begotten Son,
have conquered death
and unlocked for us the path to eternity,
grant, we pray, that we who keep
the solemnity of the Lord's Resurrection
may, through the renewal brought by your Spirit,
rise up in the light of life.
Through our Lord Jesus Christ, your Son,
who lives and reigns with you in the unity of the Holy Spirit,
one God, for ever and ever. *Amen.*

FIRST READING *(Acts 10:34a, 37-43)*

Peter proceeded to speak and said: "You know what has hap-pened all over Judea, beginning in Galilee after the baptism that John preached, how God anointed Jesus of Nazareth with the Holy Spirit and power. He went about doing good and heal-ing all those oppressed by the devil, for God was with him. We are witnesses of all that he did both in the country of the Jews and in Jerusalem. They put him to death by hanging him on a tree. This man God raised on the third day and granted that he be visible, not to all the people, but to us, the witnesses chosen by God in advance, who ate and drank with him after he rose from the dead. He commissioned us to preach to the people and testify that he is the one appointed by God as judge of the living and the dead. To him all the prophets bear witness, that everyone who believes in him will receive forgiveness of sins through his name."

The word of the Lord. *Thanks be to God.*

RESPONSORIAL PSALM *(Psalm 118:1-2, 16-17, 22-23)*

R̶ **This is the day the Lord has made; let us rejoice and be glad.**
  Or **Alleluia.**

Give thanks to the LORD, for he is good,
  for his mercy endures forever.
Let the house of Israel say,
  "His mercy endures forever." R̶

"The right hand of the LORD has struck with power;
  the right hand of the LORD is exalted.
I shall not die, but live,
  and declare the works of the LORD." R̶

The stone which the builders rejected
  has become the cornerstone.
By the LORD has this been done;
  it is wonderful in our eyes. R̶

An alternate reading follows.

SECOND READING *(Colossians 3:1–4)*

Brothers and sisters: If then you were raised with Christ, seek what is above, where Christ is seated at the right hand of God. Think of what is above, not of what is on earth. For you have died, and your life is hidden with Christ in God. When Christ your life appears, then you too will appear with him in glory.

The word of the Lord. ***Thanks be to God.***

OR

SECOND READING *(1 Corinthians 5:6b–8)*

Brothers and sisters: Do you not know that a little yeast leavens all the dough? Clear out the old yeast, so that you may become a fresh batch of dough, inasmuch as you are unleavened. For our paschal lamb, Christ, has been sacrificed. Therefore, let us celebrate the feast, not with the old yeast, the yeast of malice and wickedness, but with the unleavened bread of sincerity and truth.

The word of the Lord. ***Thanks be to God.***

SEQUENCE

Christians, to the Paschal Victim
    Offer your thankful praises!
A Lamb the sheep redeems;
    Christ, who only is sinless,
    Reconciles sinners to the Father.
Death and life have contended in that combat stupendous:
    The Prince of life, who died, reigns immortal.
Speak, Mary, declaring
    What you saw, wayfaring.
"The tomb of Christ, who is living,
    The glory of Jesus' resurrection;

Bright angels attesting,
    The shroud and napkin resting.
Yes, Christ my hope is arisen;
    To Galilee he goes before you."
Christ indeed from death is risen, our new life obtaining.
    Have mercy, victor King, ever reigning!
    Amen. Alleluia.

ALLELUIA *(See 1 Corinthians 5:7b–8a)*
Alleluia, alleluia. Christ, our paschal lamb, has been sacrificed;
let us then feast with joy in the Lord. *Alleluia, alleluia.*

*The gospel from the Easter Vigil (Mark 16:1-7, page 312) may be read
instead. For an afternoon or evening Mass, Luke 24:13-35 (next page)
may be used.*

GOSPEL *(John 20:1–9)*
A reading from the holy Gospel according to John.
Glory to you, O Lord.

On the first day of the week, Mary of Magdala came to
the tomb✝ early in the morning, while it was still dark,
and saw the stone removed from the tomb. So she ran and went
to Simon Peter and to the other disciple whom Jesus loved, and
told them, "They have taken the Lord from the tomb, and we
don't know where they put him." So Peter and the other disciple
went out and came to the tomb. They both ran, but the other
disciple ran faster than Peter and arrived at the tomb first; he
bent down and saw the burial cloths there, but did not go in.
When Simon Peter arrived after him, he went into the tomb and
saw the burial cloths there, and the cloth that had covered his
head, not with the burial cloths but rolled up in a separate place.

Then the other disciple also went in, the one who had arrived at the tomb first, and he saw and believed. For they did not yet understand the Scripture that he had to rise from the dead.

The Gospel of the Lord. *Praise to you, Lord Jesus Christ.*

Alternate reading for an afternoon or evening Mass:

GOSPEL *(Luke 24:13-35)*

A reading from the holy Gospel according to Luke.
Glory to you, Lord.

That very day, the first day of the week, two of Jesus' disciples were going to a village seven miles from Jerusalem called Emmaus, and they were conversing about all the things that had occurred. And it happened that while they were conversing and debating, Jesus himself drew near and walked with them, but their eyes were prevented from recognizing him. He asked them, "What are you discussing as you walk along?" They stopped, looking downcast. One of them, named Cleopas, said to him in reply, "Are you the only visitor to Jerusalem who does not know of the things that have taken place there in these days?" And he replied to them, "What sort of things?" They said to him, "The things that happened to Jesus the Nazarene, who was a prophet mighty in deed and word before God and all the people, how our chief priests and rulers both handed him over to a sentence of death and crucified him. But we were hoping that he would be the one to redeem Israel; and besides all this, it is now the third day since this took place. Some women from our group, however, have astounded us: they were at the tomb early in the morning and did not find his body; they came back and reported that they had indeed seen a vision of angels who announced that he was alive.

Then some of those with us went to the tomb and found things just as the women had described, but him they did not see." And he said to them, "Oh, how foolish you are! How slow of heart to believe all that the prophets spoke! Was it not necessary that the Christ should suffer these things and enter into his glory?" Then beginning with Moses and all the prophets, he interpreted to them what referred to him in all the Scriptures. As they approached the village to which they were going, he gave the impression that he was going on farther. But they urged him, "Stay with us, for it is nearly evening and the day is almost over." So he went in to stay with them. And it happened that, while he was with them at table, he took bread, said the blessing, broke it, and gave it to them. With that their eyes were opened and they recognized him, but he vanished from their sight. Then they said to each other, "Were not our hearts burning within us while he spoke to us on the way and opened the Scriptures to us?" So they set out at once and returned to Jerusalem where they found gathered together the eleven and those with them who were saying, "The Lord has truly been raised and has appeared to Simon!" Then the two recounted what had taken place on the way and how he was made known to them in the breaking of bread.

The Gospel of the Lord. *Praise to you, Lord Jesus Christ.*

RENEWAL OF BAPTISMAL PROMISES AND PROFESSION OF FAITH
(See page 318)
In Easter Sunday Masses, the rite of the renewal of baptismal promises may take place after the homily, according to the text used at the Easter Vigil.

PRAYER OF THE FAITHFUL

PREPARATION OF GIFTS *(page 16)*

PRAYER OVER THE OFFERINGS
Exultant with paschal gladness, O Lord,
we offer the sacrifice
by which your Church
is wondrously reborn and nourished.
Through Christ our Lord. ***Amen.***

PREFACE *(Easter 1, page 24)*

• Taking a Closer Look •

✛ **The tomb** What is most apparent from the resurrection accounts in the gospels is that the meaning of the event was not immediately intelligible. The empty tomb was not proof of the resurrection but a fact whose meaning needed to be discovered. Finding the empty tomb made Jesus' followers bewildered and confused, grasping for various possible answers to account for it. Only when the disciples experienced the risen Lord did the meaning of the empty tomb become clear. The stone was rolled back not so Jesus could get out, but so we could get in and be assured that his tomb of death will remain empty forever. He is risen!

COMMUNION ANTIPHON *(1 Corinthians 5:7-8)*

Christ our Passover has been sacrificed, alleluia; therefore let us keep the feast with the unleavened bread of purity and truth, alleluia, alleluia.

PRAYER AFTER COMMUNION

Look upon your Church, O God,
with unfailing love and favor,
so that, renewed by the paschal mysteries,
she may come to the glory of the resurrection.
Through Christ our Lord. *Amen.*

SOLEMN BLESSING: MASS OF THE EASTER VIGIL *(Optional, page 321)*

DISMISSAL *(page 57)* ✛

• RESPONDING TO THE WORD •

Peter summarizes the Christian motive for mission: when we experience the risen Christ, we proclaim this message to others.

➡ *How might I share my belief in Jesus' resurrection with others today?*

Our connection to the risen Christ influences all our behavior.

➡ *What is the biggest change that Christ's presence to me this Lent has made in my life?*

The risen Christ is always present with us but not always noticed.

➡ *How can I be more attentive to Christ's presence now?*

These fifty days are like one great Sunday

The season of Easter is actually a celebration of fifty days, from Easter until Pentecost. The word "Pentecost" means "fiftieth" and is the Greek translation of the Hebrew word *Shavuot*. *Shavuot*, the Jewish Feast of Weeks, began as a harvest festival in Canaan, coming approximately seven weeks after the first day of Passover.

What Sunday is to our Christian week, the Easter season is to the whole liturgical year. The fifty days of Easter have been observed longer than any other season of the Christian year. In the early Church, it was celebrated as an "unbroken Sunday," a week of weeks (7 times 7, or 49 days) plus the eighth day of the new creation. During these fifty days of joy, we are called upon in our life and worship to proclaim the lordship of Jesus revealed through his resurrection and ascension, and the outpouring of the Holy Spirit.

This season is a time to grow in our understanding of the paschal mystery and to make it part of our lives through our renewed attentiveness to God's word that we hear each Sunday and talk about in our households, through our fuller participation in the Eucharist, and through our renewed dedication to acts of charity and justice.

As we celebrate this season, we become more deeply aware of Christ's abiding but hidden presence with us that is daily transforming us into the image of Jesus.

Praying and living the Easter season

Since the Easter season is fifty days long, it will take some effort on our part to extend its celebration for the full seven weeks until Pentecost.

As Christians we each share in the Easter experience because we have in one way or another met the risen Christ and so become connected to the community that witnesses to the good news of his resurrection.

One way to make Easter into a season of celebrations and keep its spirit alive is to adopt the daily practice of using the Collect for Sunday as the gathering prayer for a household meal.

Another practice is to connect ourselves to the long chain of Christian witnesses that have preceded us. Gather your household or faith-sharing group and explain that when Paul locates himself in the Christian tradition, he creates a chain of witnesses connecting those who experienced Christ's first Easter appearance to himself.

Invite the household to bring this chain of witnesses from Paul's time down to our present time by naming those who have been most important in handing on the living tradition (e.g., family, relatives, friends, mentors, spiritual persons you have admired, patron saints, etc.).

Write down the names to create your household's or group's unique connection to the Easter tradition. To express your solidarity, share a sign of peace with one another. Then conclude by praying the Lord's Prayer together.

April 8

Can we hear Jesus' voice today?

One cold, gray Argentine morning, amidst rubbish piles a small, scruffy child bent over a small fire trying to mend the strap on one of his plastic sandals. This is only one of a thousand mental images I have, of the poverty and brokenness in our world today. Aren't we called to something better?

Thomas felt the mercy and forgiveness of Jesus, whom he had followed so eagerly but doubted so quickly. We all need the comfort of knowing we can be forgiven over and over again when we fail to take to heart his commandments.

Yet still we doubt. We vainly try to tightly hold on to what earthly riches we have, knowing full well that material possessions will not bring us closer to our ultimate goal. Simple lessons like *the more we give, the more we will receive* just do not seem to stick and need to be re-learned over and over again.

The early Christian community recognized the best path. "There was no needy person among them" because they shared their wealth.

The risen Jesus entered the locked room and said, "Peace be with you." Can we hear his voice today? "And the victory that conquers the world is our faith."

■ **MICHAEL DOUGHERTY**

ENTRANCE ANTIPHON *(1 Peter 2:2)*

Like newborn infants, you must long for the pure, spiritual milk, that in him you may grow to salvation, alleluia.

Or *(4 Esdras 2:36-37)*

Receive the joy of your glory, giving thanks to God, who has called you into the heavenly kingdom, alleluia.

INTRODUCTORY RITES *(page 10)*

COLLECT

God of everlasting mercy,
who in the very recurrence of the paschal feast
kindle the faith of the people you have made your own,
increase, we pray, the grace you have bestowed,
that all may grasp and rightly understand
in what font they have been washed,
by whose Spirit they have been reborn,
by whose Blood they have been redeemed.
Through our Lord Jesus Christ, your Son,
who lives and reigns with you in the unity of the Holy Spirit,
one God, for ever and ever. *Amen.*

FIRST READING *(Acts 4:32-35)*

The community of believers was of one heart and mind, and no one claimed that any of his possessions was his own, but they had everything in common. With great power the apostles bore witness to the resurrection of the Lord Jesus, and great favor was accorded them all. There was no needy person among them, for those who owned property or houses would sell them, bring the proceeds of the sale, and put them at the feet of the

apostles, and they were distributed to each according to need.
The word of the Lord. *Thanks be to God.*

RESPONSORIAL PSALM *(Psalm 118:2-4, 13-15, 22-24)*

℟ **Give thanks to the Lord for he is good, his love is
    everlasting.** *Or* **Alleluia.**

Let the house of Israel say,
    "His **mercy endures forever.**"
Let the house of Aaron say,
    "His mercy endures forever."
Let those who fear the LORD say,
    "His mercy endures forever." ℟

I was hard pressed and was falling,
    but the LORD helped me.
My strength and my courage is the LORD,
    and he has been my savior.
The joyful shout of victory
    in the tents of the just. ℟

The stone which the builders rejected
    has become the cornerstone.
By the LORD has this been done;
    it is wonderful in our eyes.
This is the day the LORD has made;
    let us be glad and rejoice in it. ℟

SECOND READING *(1 John 5:1-6)*

Beloved: Everyone who believes that Jesus is the Christ
is begotten by God, and everyone who loves the Father
loves also the one begotten by him. In this way we know that
we love the children of God when we love God and obey his

commandments. For the love of God is this, that we keep his commandments. And his commandments are not burdensome, for whoever is begotten by God conquers the world. And the victory that conquers the world is our faith. Who indeed is the victor over the world but the one who believes that Jesus is the Son of God?

This is the one who came through water and blood, Jesus Christ, not by water alone, but by water and blood. The Spirit is the one that testifies, and the Spirit is truth.

The word of the Lord. *Thanks be to God.*

ALLELUIA *(John 20:29)*
Alleluia, alleluia. You believe in me, Thomas, because you have seen me, says the Lord; blessed are they who have not seen me, but still believe! *Alleluia, alleluia.*

GOSPEL *(John 20:19–31)*
A reading from the holy Gospel according to John.
Glory to you, O Lord.

On the evening of that first day of the week, when the doors were locked, where the disciples were, for fear of the Jews, Jesus came and stood in their midst and said to them, "Peace be with you." When he had said this, he showed them his hands and his side. The disciples rejoiced when they saw the Lord. Jesus said to them again, "Peace be with you. As the Father has sent me, so I send you." And when he had said this, he breathed on them and said to them, "Receive the Holy Spirit. Whose sins you forgive are forgiven them, and whose sins you retain are retained."

Thomas, called Didymus,* one of the Twelve, was not with them when Jesus came. So the other disciples said to him, "We have seen the Lord." But he said to them, "Unless I see the mark of the nails in his hands and put my finger into the nailmarks and put my hand into his side, I will not believe."

Now a week later his disciples were again inside and Thomas was with them. Jesus came, although the doors were locked, and stood in their midst and said, "Peace be with you." Then he said to Thomas, "Put your finger here and see my hands, and bring your hand and put it into my side, and do not be unbelieving, but believe." Thomas answered and said to him, "My Lord and my God!" Jesus said to him, "Have you come to believe because you have seen me? Blessed are those who have not seen and have believed."

Now Jesus did many other signs in the presence of his disciples that are not written in this book. But these are written that you may come to believe that Jesus is the Christ, the Son of God, and that through this belief you may have life in his name.

The Gospel of the Lord. *Praise to you, Lord Jesus Christ.*

PROFESSION OF FAITH *(page 13)*

PRAYER OF THE FAITHFUL

PREPARATION OF GIFTS *(page 16)*

PRAYER OVER THE OFFERINGS

Accept, O Lord, we pray,
the oblations of your people
(and of those you have brought to new birth),
that, renewed by confession of your name and by Baptism,
they may attain unending happiness.
Through Christ our Lord. *Amen.*

PREFACE *(Easter 1, page 24)*

● TAKING A CLOSER LOOK ●

✝ **Mercy endures forever** In the Old Testament, mercy (Hebrew, *hesed*) usually identifies a complex Hebrew idea that describes God's special covenant love. God's desire to be in communion with us as covenant partners reveals an attitude of divine love and faithfulness that includes loyalty, compassion, dependability, trustworthiness, and an eagerness to help when situations turn bad. And once God commits to the people in covenant fidelity, there is no question of God ever retracting that commitment. So God's covenant love will never end—hence it can aptly be described as enduring forever, as in the words of today's psalm.

COMMUNION ANTIPHON *(Cf. John 20:27)*

Bring your hand and feel the place of the nails, and do not be
unbelieving but believing, alleluia.

PRAYER AFTER COMMUNION

Grant, we pray, almighty God,
that our reception of this paschal Sacrament
may have a continuing effect
in our minds and hearts.
Through Christ our Lord. *Amen.*

SOLEMN BLESSING: EASTER TIME *(Optional, page 60)*

DISMISSAL *(page 57)*

● RESPONDING TO THE WORD

The earliest Christian community was distinguished by its sharing of goods.

➡ *What sharing of my goods might I undertake this week?*

John knows that love can make obedience much easier.

➡ *How has love made keeping God's commandments easier at times for me?*

Thomas wanted proof rather than relying on the word of the other disciples.

➡ *When has it been difficult for me to trust the word of others about Jesus?*

April 15

APR
15

Preparing for our mission

Imagine being one of the disciples in today's gospel. You have just heard of Jesus' appearance on the road to Emmaus, which, along with the amazing story of the tomb, has given you a surge of hope. However, the grief and fear you felt during the crucifixion still remain in your heart. You want to believe that Jesus has risen as he said, but a pall of paralyzing uncertainty hangs over everything.

Suddenly, he's in the room, standing right in front of you. Of course, he knows what you are feeling. "Why are you troubled? And why do questions arise in your hearts?" he asks. "Touch me and see."

You do see.

Appearing before the disciples, Jesus gave them precisely what they needed for the next phase of their mission. He reassured and strengthened them by replacing their fear and uncertainty with peace and joy. He made the Scriptures intelligible to them so that they'd be able to pass on his wisdom.

Why do fear and doubt arise in our hearts when Jesus calls us to something new? His death was the ultimate proof that his love for us knows no bounds. Just as he prepared the disciples for their mission, so he will prepare us for ours.

■ KATE LARSON

ENTRANCE ANTIPHON *(Cf. Psalm 66 [65]:1-2)*
Cry out with joy to God, all the earth; O sing to the glory of his name. O render him glorious praise, alleluia.

INTRODUCTORY RITES *(page 10)*

COLLECT
May your people exult for ever, O God,
in renewed youthfulness of spirit,
so that, rejoicing now in the restored glory of our adoption,
we may look forward in confident hope
to the rejoicing of the day of resurrection.
Through our Lord Jesus Christ, your Son,
who lives and reigns with you in the unity of the Holy Spirit,
one God, for ever and ever. *Amen.*

FIRST READING *(Acts 3:13-15, 17-19)*
Peter said to the people: "The God of Abraham, the God of Isaac, and the God of Jacob, the God of our fathers, has glorified his servant Jesus, whom you handed over and denied in Pilate's presence when he had decided to release him. You denied the Holy and Righteous One and asked that a murderer be released to you. The author of life you put to death, but God raised him from the dead; of this we are witnesses. Now I know, brothers, that you acted out of ignorance, just as your leaders did; but God has thus brought to fulfillment what he had announced beforehand through the mouth of all the prophets, that his Christ would suffer. Repent, therefore, and be converted, that your sins may be wiped away."
The word of the Lord. *Thanks be to God.*

RESPONSORIAL PSALM *(Psalm 4:2, 4, 7-8, 9)*

℟ **Lord, let your face shine on us.** *Or* **Alleluia.**

When I call, answer me, O my just God,
  you who relieve me when I am in distress;
    have pity on me, and hear my prayer! ℟
Know that the LORD does wonders for his faithful one;
  the LORD will hear me when I call upon him. ℟
O LORD, let the light of your countenance shine upon us!
  You put gladness into my heart. ℟
As soon as I lie down, I fall peacefully asleep,
  for you alone, O LORD,
    bring security to my dwelling. ℟

SECOND READING *(1 John 2:1-5a)*

My children, I am writing this to you so that you may not
commit sin. But if anyone does sin, we have an Advocate
with the Father, Jesus Christ the righteous one. He is expiation
for our sins, and not for our sins only but for those of the whole
world. The way we may be sure that we know him is to keep his
commandments. Those who say, "I know him," but do not keep
his commandments are liars, and the truth is not in them. But
whoever keeps his word, the love of God is truly perfected in him.

  The word of the Lord. *Thanks be to God.*

ALLELUIA *(Luke 24:32)*

Alleluia, alleluia. Lord Jesus, open the Scriptures to us; make
our hearts burn while you speak to us. *Alleluia, alleluia.*

GOSPEL *(Luke 24:35–48)*

A reading from the holy Gospel according to Luke.

Glory to you, O Lord.

The two disciples recounted what had taken place on the way, and how Jesus was made known to them in the breaking of bread.

While they were still speaking about this, he stood in their midst and said to them, "Peace be with you." But they were startled and terrified and thought that they were seeing a ghost. Then he said to them, "Why are you troubled? And why do questions arise in your hearts? Look at my hands and my feet, that it is I myself. Touch me and see, because a ghost does not have flesh and bones as you can see I have." And as he said this, he showed them his hands and his feet. While they were still incredulous for joy and were amazed, he asked them, "Have you anything here to eat?" They gave him a piece of baked fish; he took it and ate it in front of them.

He said to them, "These are my words that I spoke to you while I was still with you, that everything written about me **in the law of Moses and in the prophets and psalms**✝ must be fulfilled." Then he opened their minds to understand the Scriptures. And he said to them, "Thus it is written that the Christ would suffer and rise from the dead on the third day and that repentance, for the forgiveness of sins, would be preached in his name to all the nations, beginning from Jerusalem. You are witnesses of these things."

The Gospel of the Lord. *Praise to you, Lord Jesus Christ.*

PROFESSION OF FAITH *(page 13)*

PRAYER OF THE FAITHFUL

PREPARATION OF GIFTS *(page 16)*

PRAYER OVER THE OFFERINGS
Receive, O Lord, we pray,
these offerings of your exultant Church,
and, as you have given her cause for such great gladness,
grant also that the gifts we bring
may bear fruit in perpetual happiness.
Through Christ our Lord. *Amen.*

PREFACE *(Easter 1–5, pages 24–26)*

⸱ TAKING A CLOSER LOOK ⸱

✢ In the Law of Moses and in the prophets and psalms

This phrase summarizes the three general categories of Jewish sacred texts. The Law (Hebrew *Torah,* "instruction") consisted of the first five books of the Old Testament that tell of God's search for an appropriate covenant partner. The Prophets (*Nevi'im*) collected the prophetic stories and God's messages to the community. The Writings (*Ketuvim*) was a catch-all for everything else. It included the song book of the Psalms and wisdom writings for living a happy life. The first letter of each of these categories in Hebrew, T-N-K forms the acronym that identifies the Jewish Scriptures as TaNaKh.

COMMUNION ANTIPHON (Luke 24:35)

The disciples recognized the Lord Jesus in the breaking of the bread, alleluia.

Or Optional for Year B: (Luke 24:46–47)

The Christ had to suffer and on the third day rise from the dead; in his name repentance and remission of sins must be preached to all the nations, alleluia.

PRAYER AFTER COMMUNION

Look with kindness upon your people, O Lord,
and grant, we pray,
that those you were pleased to renew by eternal mysteries
may attain in their flesh
the incorruptible glory of the resurrection.
Through Christ our Lord. *Amen.*

SOLEMN BLESSING: EASTER TIME (Optional, page 60)

DISMISSAL (page 57) ✠

• RESPONDING TO THE WORD •

Peter encourages repentance—changing our lives to relate in a new way to God.	John joins together knowing Jesus and keeping his commandments.	Jesus invites us to be witnesses of what we have experienced with him.
⮕ How can I continue the changes I began during Lent and grow in my relationships to God and others?	⮕ How has my attempt to keep Jesus' commands helped me understand him better?	⮕ How might I share my love for Jesus with others today?

April 22

God's love will never fade

Today's readings are especially poignant to the Western world. Our culture is over-saturated with marketing. Advertisers promote the message that buying their products will make us happy. But most of us have experienced the disappointment of a newly purchased item falling short of our expectations.

Today's readings, especially the gospel, contrast God's true love with worldly promises of love that fade. Jesus uses the analogy of the Good Shepherd to compare his love for his flock with that of the hired help who only care about their pay check. They flee the scene at the first sign of danger, leaving the sheep to fend for themselves.

This message is also present in the other readings. In the reading from Acts, Peter says: "There is no salvation through anyone else." Putting our faith in others, whether they be advertisers or celebrities, will likely lead to disappointment. In Psalm 118, the psalmist praises God, who has protected him when all else failed.

God promises us a greater love than we can imagine. As the ultimate sign of this, God sent Jesus into the world to save us. During this Easter season, we pray that Jesus' message will be embraced by all people searching for immortal and timeless love.

◼ **ANDREW HUME**

ENTRANCE ANTIPHON *(Cf. Psalm 33 [32]:5-6)*
The merciful love of the Lord fills the earth; by the word of the
Lord the heavens were made, alleluia.

INTRODUCTORY RITES *(page 10)*

COLLECT
Almighty ever-living God,
lead us to a share in the joys of heaven,
so that the humble flock may reach
where the brave Shepherd has gone before.
Who lives and reigns with you in the unity of the Holy Spirit,
one God, for ever and ever. *Amen.*

FIRST READING *(Acts 4:8-12)*

Peter, filled with the Holy Spirit, said: "Leaders of the people
and elders: If we are being examined today about a good
deed done to a cripple, namely, by what means he was saved,
then all of you and all the people of Israel should know that
it was in the name of Jesus Christ the Nazorean* whom you
crucified, whom God raised from the dead; in his name this
man stands before you healed. He is *the stone rejected by you, the
builders, which has become the cornerstone.* There is no salvation
through anyone else, nor is there any other name under heaven
given to the human race by which we are to be saved."

The word of the Lord. *Thanks be to God.*

RESPONSORIAL PSALM *(Psalm 118:1, 8-9, 21-23, 26, 28, 29)*

℟ **The stone rejected by the builders has become the**
  cornerstone. *Or* **Alleluia.**

Give thanks to the LORD, for he is good,
  for his mercy endures for ever.
It is better to take refuge in the LORD
  than to trust in man.
It is better to take refuge in the LORD
  than to trust in princes. ℟

I will give thanks to you, for you have answered me
  and have been my savior.
The stone which the builders rejected
  has become the cornerstone.
By the LORD has this been done;
  it is wonderful in our eyes. ℟

Blessed is he who comes in the name of the LORD;
  we bless you from the house of the LORD.
I will give thanks to you, for you have answered me
  and have been my savior.
Give thanks to the LORD, for he is good;
  for his kindness endures for ever. ℟

SECOND READING *(1 John 3:1-2)*

Beloved: See what love the Father has bestowed on us that
we may be called the children of God. Yet so we are. The
reason **the world**✝ does not know us is that it did not know him.
Beloved, we are God's children now; what we shall be has not yet
been revealed. We do know that when it is revealed we shall be
like him, for we shall see him as he is.
  The word of the Lord. *Thanks be to God.*

ALLELUIA *(John 10:14)*
Alleluia, alleluia. I am the good shepherd, says the Lord;
I know my sheep, and mine know me. *Alleluia, alleluia.*

GOSPEL *(John 10:11-18)*
A reading from the holy Gospel according to John.
Glory to you, O Lord.

Jesus said: "I am the good shepherd. A good shepherd lays
down his life for the sheep. A hired man, who is not a shepherd and whose sheep are not his own, sees a wolf coming and
leaves the sheep and runs away, and the wolf catches and scatters
them. This is because he works for pay and has no concern for
the sheep. I am the good shepherd, and I know mine and mine
know me, just as the Father knows me and I know the Father;
and I will lay down my life for the sheep. I have other sheep that
do not belong to this fold. These also I must lead, and they will
hear my voice, and there will be one flock, one shepherd. This
is why the Father loves me, because I lay down my life in order
to take it up again. No one takes it from me, but I lay it down
on my own. I have power to lay it down, and power to take it up
again. This command I have received from my Father."

The Gospel of the Lord. *Praise to you, Lord Jesus Christ.*

PROFESSION OF FAITH *(page 13)*

PRAYER OF THE FAITHFUL

PREPARATION OF GIFTS *(page 16)*

PRAYER OVER THE OFFERINGS

Grant, we pray, O Lord,
that we may always find delight in these paschal mysteries,
so that the renewal constantly at work within us
may be the cause of our unending joy.
Through Christ our Lord. *Amen.*

PREFACE *(Easter 1-5, pages 24-26)*

COMMUNION ANTIPHON

The Good Shepherd has risen, who laid down his life for his
sheep and willingly died for his flock, alleluia.

• TAKING A CLOSER LOOK •

✣ **The world** As so often in John's gospel and letters, many terms
have two levels of meaning. Usually "the world" (Greek, *cosmos*) would
describe the ordered quality of God's creation. But since John also sees
a spiritual dimension to all of our existence, he uses "the world" as a
shorthand way to refer to the forces that we often experience that resist
the ordering power of God and so stand in opposition to Jesus and the
Christian community. Though the world is hostile to God, God is not
hostile to the world but sends Jesus "into the world" for its salvation.

PRAYER AFTER COMMUNION
Look upon your flock, kind Shepherd,
and be pleased to settle in eternal pastures
the sheep you have redeemed
by the Precious Blood of your Son.
Who lives and reigns for ever and ever. *Amen.*

SOLEMN BLESSING: EASTER TIME *(Optional, page 60)*

DISMISSAL *(page 57)* ✣

● RESPONDING TO THE WORD ●

Peter knows that Jesus has the power to heal us.	**John recognizes that we are all God's children.**	**Jesus knows our uniqueness just like a shepherd knows his sheep.**
➡ *What thanks can I give to Jesus for my healing (whether spiritual, physical, or emotional)?*	➡ *How might this awareness change the way I deal with a difficult person at work or at school this week?*	➡ *How does it change me to know that Jesus loves me the way I am, and that he can help me be the person God wants me to be?*

April 29

APR
29

Open your hearts!

God calls us daily into an intimate union. Today's readings remind us of this and that our souls thirst for God's love. God is the only source of eternal life, and apart from God we will never be satisfied.

In this Easter season, we rejoice in the Lord's resurrection and we continue to reflect on his unfailing and everlasting love for us. Today, we are called to go deeper in our relationship with Jesus and surrender our lives to him so we can be who we were created to be. As the branch needs to be attached to the vine, we need to be attached to Jesus to produce fruit. As we grow in faith and love for others, God will prune us so we can produce more fruit.

The more time we spend with Jesus, the more we will learn to love others and ourselves as he does. We will be faithful to his commandments and abide in him.

Today, let us open our hearts to receive Jesus and his love. Let's take today's readings home and meditate on them—especially the gospel. It's a great passage to use for a *Lectio Divina* with family or friends.

◼ **Sarah Escobar**

ENTRANCE ANTIPHON *(Cf. Psalm 98 [97]:1-2)*
O sing a new song to the Lord, for he has worked wonders; in
the sight of the nations he has shown his deliverance, alleluia.

INTRODUCTORY RITES *(page 10)*

COLLECT
Almighty ever-living God,
constantly accomplish the Paschal Mystery within us,
that those you were pleased to make new in Holy Baptism
may, under your protective care, bear much fruit
and come to the joys of life eternal.
Through our Lord Jesus Christ, your Son,
who lives and reigns with you in the unity of the Holy Spirit,
one God, for ever and ever. *Amen.*

FIRST READING *(Acts 9:26-31)*
When Saul arrived in Jerusalem he tried to join the disciples,
but they were all afraid of him, not believing that he was a
disciple. Then Barnabas took charge of him and brought him to
the apostles, and he reported to them how he had seen the Lord,
and that he had spoken to him, and how in Damascus he had
spoken out boldly in the name of Jesus. He moved about freely
with them in Jerusalem, and spoke out boldly in the name of the
Lord. He also spoke and debated with the **Hellenists**,✝ but they
tried to kill him. And when the brothers learned of this, they
took him down to Caesarea* and sent him on his way to Tarsus.

The church throughout all Judea, Galilee, and Samaria* was at
peace. It was being built up and walked in the fear of the Lord,
and with the consolation of the Holy Spirit it grew in numbers.

The word of the Lord. *Thanks be to God.*

RESPONSORIAL PSALM *(Psalm 22:26–27, 28, 30, 31–32)*

℟ **I will praise you, Lord, in the assembly of your people.**
Or **Alleluia.**

I will fulfill my vows before those who fear the LORD.
  The lowly shall eat their fill;
they who seek the LORD shall praise him:
  "May your hearts live forever!" ℟

All the ends of the earth
  shall remember and turn to the LORD;
all the families of the nations
  shall bow down before him. ℟

To him alone shall bow down
  all who sleep in the earth;
before him shall bend
  all who go down into the dust. ℟

And to him my soul shall live;
  my descendants shall serve him.
Let the coming generation be told of the LORD
  that they may proclaim to a people yet to be born
  the justice he has shown. ℟

SECOND READING *(1 John 3:18–24)*

Children, let us love not in word or speech but in deed and truth.

Now this is how we shall know that we belong to the truth and reassure our hearts before him in whatever our hearts condemn, for God is greater than our hearts and knows everything. Beloved, if our hearts do not condemn us, we have confidence in God and receive from him whatever we ask, because we keep his commandments and do what pleases him. And his commandment is this: we should believe in the name of his Son, Jesus Christ, and love one another just as he commanded us. Those who keep his commandments remain in him, and he in them, and the way we know that he remains in us is from the Spirit he gave us.

The word of the Lord. *Thanks be to God.*

ALLELUIA *(John 15:4a, 5b)*
Alleluia, alleluia. Remain in me as I remain in you, says the Lord. Whoever remains in me will bear much fruit. *Alleluia, alleluia.*

GOSPEL *(John 15:1-8)*
A reading from the holy Gospel according to John.
Glory to you, O Lord.

Jesus said to his disciples: "I am the true vine, and my Father is the vine grower. He takes away every branch in me that does not bear fruit, and every one that does he prunes so that it bears more fruit. You are already pruned because of the word that I spoke to you. Remain in me, as I remain in you. Just as a branch cannot bear fruit on its own unless it remains on the vine, so neither can you unless you remain in me. I am the vine, you are the branches. Whoever remains in me and I in him will bear much fruit, because without me you can do nothing. Anyone who does not remain in me will be thrown out like a branch and wither; people will gather them and throw them into a fire and they will be burned. If you remain in me and my words remain in you, ask for whatever you want and it will be done for you. By this is my Father glorified, that you bear much fruit and become my disciples."

The Gospel of the Lord. *Praise to you, Lord Jesus Christ.*

PROFESSION OF FAITH *(page 13)*

PRAYER OF THE FAITHFUL

PREPARATION OF GIFTS *(page 16)*

PRAYER OVER THE OFFERINGS

O God, who by the wonderful exchange effected in this sacrifice
have made us partakers of the one supreme Godhead,
grant, we pray,
that, as we have come to know your truth,
we may make it ours by a worthy way of life.
Through Christ our Lord. *Amen.*

PREFACE *(Easter 1–5, pages 24–26)*

• TAKING A CLOSER LOOK •

✝ **Hellenists** "Hellenists" (from *Hellas*, Greek for Greece) were those from other nations who spoke Greek and were more receptive to the influence of Greek culture. Though the Romans ruled the Mediterranean nations, Greek literature and ideas formed the basis for education, and the Greek language was used for international communication and business. To be educated often meant to be able to speak and read Greek (like St. Paul and the other New Testament authors who all wrote in Greek). For Jews, Hellenism posed a threat because its education was rooted in religious beliefs and social values that were not compatible with the Jewish monotheistic belief that Yahweh was the one and only God.

COMMUNION ANTIPHON *(Cf. John 15:1, 5)*

I am the true vine and you are the branches, says the Lord.
Whoever remains in me, and I in him, bears fruit in plenty,
alleluia.

PRAYER AFTER COMMUNION

Graciously be present to your people, we pray, O Lord,
and lead those you have imbued with heavenly mysteries
to pass from former ways to newness of life.
Through Christ our Lord. *Amen.*

SOLEMN BLESSING: EASTER TIME *(Optional, page 60)*

DISMISSAL *(page 57)* ✢

✤ RESPONDING TO THE WORD ✤

The disciples were afraid of Saul the persecutor and did not trust his "conversion."

➡ *What evidence do I trust to accept someone's religious sincerity?*

John tells us that genuine love is shown not just in words but in everyday deeds.

➡ *When have my Christian words not been matched by my Christian deeds?*

Jesus tells us that we can only survive if we join ourselves to his life.

➡ *What can I do this week to invite Jesus to "remain in me"?*

May 6

MAY
6

Jesus' love will transform us

In today's gospel, Jesus calls his disciples and us his friends. Friendship is a valuable gift. It requires generosity, honesty, and mutual love. A true friend understands us even when we remain silent and accepts us as we are. Jesus' self-giving love for us, his friends, forms the model for the love we are to have for one another.

Jesus has no secrets with his disciples. He opens his heart to them, revealing to them the knowledge the Father has given him and his love for each of them. He demonstrates his profound love and that of his Father by laying down his life for us, suffering and dying on the cross for our salvation. His love has no limits—embracing everyone and giving everything. Jesus invites us to enter into his love and to express this love in our daily lives. This challenging love consists in making sacrifices and reaching out to others freely. It involves loving to the end, with Jesus' same compassion and selflessness. Only if we love one another as he has loved us can we be his true friends.

Jesus offers us his love and friendship, a relationship that will transform our lives and give us true joy. Let us accept his offer today by having faith in him and sharing his merciful love with others.

■ Nada Mazzei

ENTRANCE ANTIPHON *(Cf. Isaiah 48:20)*
Proclaim a joyful sound and let it be heard; proclaim to the ends
of the earth: The Lord has freed his people, alleluia.

INTRODUCTORY RITES *(page 10)*

COLLECT
Grant, almighty God,
that we may celebrate with heartfelt devotion these days of joy,
which we keep in honor of the risen Lord,
and that what we relive in remembrance
we may always hold to in what we do.
Through our Lord Jesus Christ, your Son,
who lives and reigns with you in the unity of the Holy Spirit,
one God, for ever and ever. *Amen.*

FIRST READING *(Acts 10:25-26, 34-35, 44-48)*
When Peter entered, Cornelius met him and, falling at his
feet, paid him homage. Peter, however, raised him up, saying, "Get up. I myself am also a human being."

Then Peter proceeded to speak and said, "In truth, I see that
God shows **no partiality**.✝ Rather, in every nation whoever fears
him and acts uprightly is acceptable to him."

While Peter was still speaking these things, the Holy Spirit
fell upon all who were listening to the word. The circumcised believers who had accompanied Peter were astounded that the gift
of the Holy Spirit should have been poured out on the Gentiles
also, for they could hear them speaking in tongues and glorifying
God. Then Peter responded, "Can anyone withhold the water
for baptizing these people, who have received the Holy Spirit

even as we have?" He ordered them to be baptized in the name of Jesus Christ.

The word of the Lord. *Thanks be to God.*

RESPONSORIAL PSALM *(Psalm 98:1, 2-3, 3-4)*

℟ **The Lord has revealed to the nations his saving power.**
 Or **Alleluia.**

Sing to the LORD a new song,
 for he has done wondrous deeds;
his right hand has won victory for him,
 his holy arm. ℟
The LORD has made his salvation known:
 in the sight of the nations he has revealed his justice.
He has remembered his kindness and his faithfulness
 toward the house of Israel. ℟
All the ends of the earth have seen
 the salvation by our God.
Sing joyfully to the LORD, all you lands;
 break into song; sing praise. ℟

SECOND READING *(1 John 4:7-10)*

Beloved, let us love one another, because love is of God; everyone who loves is begotten by God and knows God. Whoever is without love does not know God, for God is love. In this way the love of God was revealed to us: God sent his only Son into the world so that we might have life through him. In this is love: not that we have loved God, but that he loved us and sent his Son as expiation for our sins.

The word of the Lord. *Thanks be to God.*

ALLELUIA *(John 14:23)*
Alleluia, alleluia. Whoever loves me will keep my word, says the Lord, and my Father will love him and we will come to him. *Alleluia, alleluia.*

GOSPEL *(John 15:9-17)*
A reading from the holy Gospel according to John.
Glory to you, O Lord.

Jesus said to his disciples: "As the Father loves me, so I also love you. Remain in my love. If you keep my commandments, you will remain in my love, just as I have kept my Father's commandments and remain in his love.

"I have told you this so that my joy may be in you and your joy might be complete. This is my commandment: love one another as I love you. No one has greater love than this, to lay down one's life for one's friends. You are my friends if you do what I command you. I no longer call you slaves, because a slave does not know what his master is doing. I have called you friends, because I have told you everything I have heard from my Father. It was not you who chose me, but I who chose you and appointed you to go and bear fruit that will remain, so that whatever you ask the Father in my name he may give you. This I command you: love one another."

The Gospel of the Lord. *Praise to you, Lord Jesus Christ.*

PROFESSION OF FAITH *(page 13)*

PRAYER OF THE FAITHFUL

PREPARATION OF GIFTS *(page 16)*

PRAYER OVER THE OFFERINGS

May our prayers rise up to you, O Lord,
together with the sacrificial offerings,
so that, purified by your graciousness,
we may be conformed to the mysteries of your mighty love.
Through Christ our Lord. *Amen.*

PREFACE *(Easter 1–5, pages 24–26)*

• TAKING A CLOSER LOOK •

✣ **No partiality** In the first century, personal relationships were most often strictly voluntary and so were based on the benefactor's favoritism or partiality. A wealthy or powerful person (the benefactor) could freely choose who among many potential candidates would receive his or her favor or gift. In religious terms, God's partiality was revealed in the free choice of Israel from among all the nations to be God's covenant partner. Peter realized that he had misunderstood God's partiality as limiting the covenant relationship only to Jews. God actually shows no partiality but invites all humanity—both Jews and Gentiles—into the new covenant.

COMMUNION ANTIPHON *(John 14:15–16)*

If you love me, keep my commandments, says the Lord, and I will ask the Father and he will send you another Paraclete, to abide with you for ever, alleluia.

PRAYER AFTER COMMUNION

Almighty ever-living God,
who restore us to eternal life in the Resurrection of Christ,
increase in us, we pray, the fruits of this paschal Sacrament
and pour into our hearts the strength of this saving food.
Through Christ our Lord. *Amen.*

SOLEMN BLESSING: EASTER TIME *(Optional, page 60)*

DISMISSAL *(page 57)* ✦

• RESPONDING TO THE WORD •

Peter's life is changed when he realizes that God shows no partiality.

⇨ *What might I do this week to notice and affirm God's love for those outside the Church?*

John summarizes God's whole existence as love—the power uniting us into a new community.

⇨ *How might I imitate God's love in some small way by relating more deeply to others?*

Jesus challenges us to love others as we love him.

⇨ *How might I respond to this challenge by my love for others at home, at work, or at school this week?*

May 10

All dioceses in the United States, except those within the ecclesiastical provinces of Boston, Hartford, New York, Newark, Philadelphia, and Omaha, transfer the celebration of the Ascension of the Lord from Thursday to this coming Sunday.

If the Ascension is celebrated on Thursday in your diocese, see the Mass for the Ascension on page 369. Then on Sunday use the Mass for the Seventh Sunday of Easter on page 375.

May 13

Share the good news!

On this feast of the Ascension of the Lord, the Church pays special attention to communication in our world, and encourages us to spread the good news of God's saving grace, revealed in Jesus and made present through the power of the Holy Spirit.

The accounts of the Ascension in both Acts and Mark entrust us, as Jesus himself entrusted the eleven, to share the good news. The sacraments equip us for the task of witnessing to the whole of creation. In baptism, we became light to the world. In confirmation, we received the gifts of the Holy Spirit that empower us to be the Christ-bearers of unity.

And through the celebration of the Eucharist, we are nourished and strengthened for our mission.

Communicating the good news is a work in progress. There has never been a time in history when people did not need the news of salvation. When much of the communication around us tears down rather than builds up, we have the opportunity to build bridges through our encounters with others.

Jesus is the benchmark for all of our communications. Following his example, may our lives communicate God's love and mercy and be a sign of hope to the world.

■ LOUISE MCEWAN

THE ASCENSION OF THE LORD
(MASS DURING THE DAY)

ENTRANCE ANTIPHON *(Acts 1:11)*

Men of Galilee, why gaze in wonder at the heavens?
This Jesus whom you saw ascending into heaven
will return as you saw him go, alleluia.

INTRODUCTORY RITES *(page 10)*

COLLECT

Gladden us with holy joys, almighty God,
and make us rejoice with devout thanksgiving,
for the Ascension of Christ your Son
is our exaltation,
and, where the Head has gone before in glory,
the Body is called to follow in hope.
Through our Lord Jesus Christ, your Son,
who lives and reigns with you in the unity of the Holy Spirit,
one God, for ever and ever. *Amen.*

Or

Grant, we pray, almighty God,
that we, who believe that your Only Begotten Son, our Redeemer,
ascended this day to the heavens,
may in spirit dwell already in heavenly realms.
Who lives and reigns with you in the unity of the Holy Spirit,
one God, for ever and ever. *Amen.*

FIRST READING *(Acts 1:1-11)*

In the first book, Theophilus, I dealt with all that Jesus did and
taught until the day he was taken up, after giving instructions

through the Holy Spirit to the apostles whom he had chosen. He presented himself alive to them by many proofs after he had suffered, appearing to them during forty days and speaking about the kingdom of God. While meeting with them, he enjoined them not to depart from Jerusalem, but to wait for "the promise of the Father about which you have heard me speak; for John baptized with water, but in a few days you will be baptized with the Holy Spirit."

When they had gathered together they asked him, "Lord, are you at this time going to restore the kingdom to Israel?" He answered them, "It is not for you to know the times or seasons that the Father has established by his own authority. But you will receive power when the Holy Spirit comes upon you, and you will be my witnesses in Jerusalem, throughout Judea and Samaria,* and to the ends of the earth." When he had said this, as they were looking on, he was lifted up, and a cloud took him from their sight. While they were looking intently at the sky as he was going, suddenly two men dressed in white garments stood beside them. They said, "Men of Galilee, why are you standing there looking at the sky? This Jesus who has been taken up from you into heaven will return in the same way you have seen him going into heaven."

The word of the Lord. *Thanks be to God.*

RESPONSORIAL PSALM *(Psalm 47:2-3, 6-7, 8-9)*

℟ **God mounts his throne to shouts of joy: a blare of trumpets for the Lord.** *Or* **Alleluia.**

All you peoples, clap your hands,
   shout to God with cries of gladness,
for the LORD, the Most High, the awesome,
   is the great king over all the earth. ℟
God mounts his throne amid shouts of joy;

the LORD, amid trumpet blasts.
Sing praise to God, sing praise;
    sing praise to our king, sing praise. ℟

For king of all the earth is God;
    sing hymns of praise.
God reigns over the nations,
    God sits upon his holy throne. ℟

An alternate reading follows.

SECOND READING *(Ephesians 1:17-23)*

Brothers and sisters: May the God of our Lord Jesus Christ, the Father of glory, give you a Spirit of wisdom and revelation resulting in knowledge of him. May the eyes of your hearts be enlightened, that you may know what is the hope that belongs to his call, what are the riches of glory in his inheritance among the holy ones, and what is the surpassing greatness of his power for us who believe, in accord with the exercise of his great might: which he worked in Christ, raising him from the dead and seating him at his right hand in the heavens, far above every principality, authority, power, and dominion, and every name that is named not only in this age but also in the one to come. And he put all things beneath his feet and gave him as head over all things to the church, which is his body, the fullness of the one who fills all things in every way.

The word of the Lord. *Thanks be to God.*

Or

SECOND READING *(Ephesians 4:1-13)*
For the shorter version, omit the indented parts in brackets.

Brothers and sisters, I, a prisoner for the Lord, urge you to live in a manner worthy of the call you have received, with all humility and gentleness, with patience, bearing with one another through love, striving to preserve the unity of the spirit through the bond of peace: one body and one Spirit, as you were also called to the one hope of your call; one Lord, one faith, one baptism; one God and Father of all, who is over all and through all and in all.

But grace was given to each of us according to the measure of Christ's gift.

[Therefore, it says:

He ascended on high and took prisoners captive;
he gave gifts to men.

What does "he ascended" mean except that he also descended into the lower regions of the earth? The one who descended is also the one who ascended far above all the heavens, that he might fill all things.]

And he gave some as apostles, others as prophets, others as evangelists, others as pastors and teachers, to equip the holy ones for the work of ministry, for building up the body of Christ, until we all attain to the unity of faith and knowledge of the Son of God, to mature to manhood, to the extent of the full stature of Christ.

The word of the Lord. *Thanks be to God.*

ALLELUIA *(Matthew 28:19a, 20b)*
Alleluia, alleluia. Go and teach all nations, says the Lord; I am with you always, until the end of the world. *Alleluia, alleluia.*

GOSPEL *(Mark 16:15-20)*
A reading from the holy Gospel according to Mark.
Glory to you, O Lord.

Jesus said to his disciples: "Go into the whole world and proclaim **the gospel**✝ to every creature. Whoever believes and is baptized will be saved; whoever does not believe will be condemned. These signs will accompany those who believe: in my name they will drive out demons, they will speak new languages. They will pick up serpents with their hands, and if they drink any deadly thing, it will not harm them. They will lay hands on the sick, and they will recover."

So then the Lord Jesus, after he spoke to them, was taken up into heaven and took his seat at the right hand of God. But they went forth and preached everywhere, while the Lord worked with them and confirmed the word through accompanying signs.

The Gospel of the Lord. ***Praise to you, Lord Jesus Christ.***

PROFESSION OF FAITH *(page 13)*

PRAYER OF THE FAITHFUL

PREPARATION OF GIFTS *(page 16)*

PRAYER OVER THE OFFERINGS
We offer sacrifice now in supplication, O Lord,
to honor the wondrous Ascension of your Son:
grant, we pray,

● TAKING A CLOSER LOOK ●

✝ **The gospel** In everyday usage the word "gospel" (Greek, *evangelion*; Anglo-Saxon, *godspell*), meant "good news," often about an important event, such as the birthday of the emperor or a national victory in war. The Christian good news of Jesus Christ includes both his message about a new kind of community for all and his victory over the forces of evil, sin, and death by his resurrection. In the hands of the gospel writers, "gospel" became a unique Christian format for proclaiming the good news through the retelling of Jesus' life story.

that through this most holy exchange
we, too, may rise up to the heavenly realms.
Through Christ our Lord. *Amen.*

PREFACE *(Ascension of the Lord 1–2, page 27)*

COMMUNION ANTIPHON *(Matthew 28:20)*
Behold, I am with you always, even to the end of the age, alleluia.

PRAYER AFTER COMMUNION
Almighty ever-living God,
who allow those on earth to celebrate divine mysteries,
grant, we pray,
that Christian hope may draw us onward
to where our nature is united with you.
Through Christ our Lord. *Amen.*

SOLEMN BLESSING: THE ASCENSION OF THE LORD *(Optional, page 61)*

DISMISSAL *(page 57)* ✣

• RESPONDING TO THE WORD •

Jesus' ascension ends his time on earth but not his presence for salvation.

➡ *How might I witness to the good news of Jesus' abiding presence with us still?*

Paul asks that we grow in the knowledge of Christ and the new relationship he made possible with God.

➡ *What new insight about Christ has been most meaningful for me this Easter season?*

After his ascension, Jesus continued to work through the disciples.

➡ *When have I most felt that God was working though me?*

SEVENTH SUNDAY OF EASTER

ENTRANCE ANTIPHON *(Cf. Psalm 27 [26]:7-9)*
O Lord, hear my voice, for I have called to you; of you my heart
has spoken: Seek his face; hide not your face from me, alleluia.

INTRODUCTORY RITES *(page 10)*

COLLECT
Graciously hear our supplications, O Lord,
so that we, who believe that the Savior of the human race
is with you in your glory,
may experience, as he promised,
until the end of the world,
his abiding presence among us.
Who lives and reigns with you in the unity of the Holy Spirit,
one God, for ever and ever. ***Amen.***

FIRST READING *(Acts 1:15-17, 20a, 20c-26)*

Peter stood up in the midst of the brothers—there was a
group of about one hundred and twenty persons in the one
place—. He said, "My brothers, the Scripture had to be fulfilled
which the Holy Spirit spoke beforehand through the mouth
of David, concerning Judas, who was the guide for those who
arrested Jesus. He was numbered among us and was allotted a
share in this ministry.

"For it is written in the Book of Psalms:
   May another take his office.

"Therefore, it is necessary that one of the men who accompanied us the whole time the Lord Jesus came and went
among us, beginning from the baptism of John until the day on
which he was taken up from us, become with us a witness to his

resurrection." So they proposed two, Judas called Barsabbas, who was also known as Justus, and Matthias. Then they prayed, "You, Lord, who know the hearts of all, show which one of these two you have chosen to take the place in this apostolic ministry from which Judas turned away to go to his own place." Then they gave lots to them, and the lot fell upon Matthias, and he was counted with the eleven apostles.

The word of the Lord. *Thanks be to God.*

RESPONSORIAL PSALM *(Psalm 103:1-2, 11-12, 19-20)*

℟ **The Lord has set his throne in heaven.** *Or* **Alleluia.**

Bless the LORD, O my soul;
    and all my being, bless his holy name.
Bless the LORD, O my soul,
    and forget not all his benefits. ℟

For as the heavens are high above the earth,
    so surpassing is his kindness toward those who fear him.
As far as the east is from the west,
    so far has he put our transgressions from us. ℟

The LORD has established his throne in heaven,
    and his kingdom rules over all.
Bless the LORD, all you his angels,
    you mighty in strength, who do his bidding. ℟

SECOND READING *(1 John 4:11-16)*

Beloved, if God so loved us, we also must love one another. No one has ever seen God. Yet, if we love one another, God remains in us, and his love is brought to perfection in us.

This is how we know that we remain in him and he in us, that he has given us of his Spirit. Moreover, we have seen and testify

that the Father sent his Son as **savior of the world.**✝ Whoever
acknowledges that Jesus is the Son of God, God remains in him
and he in God. We have come to know and to believe in the love
God has for us.

God is love, and whoever remains in love remains in God and
God in him.

The word of the Lord. *Thanks be to God.*

ALLELUIA *(See John 14:18)*
Alleluia, alleluia. I will not leave you orphans, says the Lord. I will
come back to you, and your hearts will rejoice. *Alleluia, alleluia.*

GOSPEL *(John 17:11b–19)*
A reading from the holy Gospel according to John.
Glory to you, O Lord.

Lifting up his eyes to heaven, Jesus prayed, saying: "Holy
Father, keep them in your name that you have given me, so
that they may be one just as we are one. When I was with them
I protected them in your name that you gave me, and I guarded
them, and none of them was lost except the son of destruction, in
order that the Scripture might be fulfilled. But now I am coming
to you. I speak this in the world so that they may share my joy
completely. I gave them your word, and the world hated them,
because they do not belong to the world any more than I belong
to the world. I do not ask that you take them out of the world but
that you keep them from the evil one. They do not belong to the
world any more than I belong to the world. Consecrate them in
the truth. Your word is truth. As you sent me into the world, so
I sent them into the world. And I consecrate myself for them, so
that they also may be consecrated in truth."

The Gospel of the Lord. *Praise to you, Lord Jesus Christ.*

PROFESSION OF FAITH *(page 13)*

PRAYER OF THE FAITHFUL

PREPARATION OF GIFTS *(page 16)*

PRAYER OVER THE OFFERINGS
Accept, O Lord, the prayers of your faithful
with the sacrificial offerings,
that through these acts of devotedness
we may pass over to the glory of heaven.
Through Christ our Lord. *Amen.*

PREFACE *(Easter 1–5, pages 24–26, or Ascension 1–2, page 27)*

• TAKING A CLOSER LOOK •

✢ **Savior of the world** Before it became a theological term, "savior" meant one who rescued someone from a difficult situation. Thus it was commonly attributed to the king, emperor, or general who saved the nation by winning a war. For the Jews, God was their primary savior because God rescued them from their oppression in Egypt. For Christians, Jesus is the savior because he rescued us from our broken relationship with God and offered us a new relationship under God's rule. In John's gospel, Jesus also overcomes the hostile forces resisting God's reordering of creation and community (which John calls "the world").

COMMUNION ANTIPHON *(John 17: 22)*
Father, I pray that they may be one as we also are one, alleluia.

PRAYER AFTER COMMUNION
Hear us, O God our Savior,
and grant us confidence,
that through these sacred mysteries
there will be accomplished in the body of the whole Church
what has already come to pass in Christ her Head.
Who lives and reigns for ever and ever. *Amen.*

SOLEMN BLESSING: EASTER TIME *(Optional, page 60)*

DISMISSAL *(page 57)* ❖

• RESPONDING TO THE WORD •

The eleven disciples chose to replace Judas so the group would be complete again.	God's love for us is the reason that God desires to be close to us.	Jesus prays that we continue his work and stay free of evil.
➥ *How would I have felt if the choice had been me?*	➥ *What might I do to encourage God to remain with me today and throughout this week?*	➥ *What can I do to be more attentive to the way that evil wants to change my relation to God and others?*

Witnesses of the good news

As the gospels show, every time the disciples experience the risen and ascended Christ, they are told to share this with others. Being a Christian can never be just a "me and Jesus" experience. We must continue the ministry and mission of Jesus in our world. Pentecost reminds us of this task and invites us to take the Easter message of Christ's resurrection and spread this good news to our world.

The remainder of the Church's year is called "ordinary time." This does not mean that this time is not important, but rather that it is "ordered" by our ever-deepening appreciation of how the mystery of our faith must be lived in our everyday lives.

During this time, Sunday by Sunday, we listen and respond to the Scripture readings and thus deepen our awareness of Jesus' life and teaching. As we better understand who he was, we also better understand who we are as his followers today.

Jesus' message was a new way to relate to God and to others, and this is what we share with our family, our friends, our fellow parishioners, and all those with whom we work and play. As individuals and communities, we begin to live right now as the kingdom community that Christ envisioned. We must dare to create communities based on justice and right relationships with one another, built on love and respect for each person as a beloved child of God.

Praying and living Pentecost all year

Find a time to pray quietly or gather the household. (You may wish to do this several times between Pentecost and the end of the liturgical year.) Pray this prayer to the Holy Spirit:

Come, Holy Spirit, fill the hearts of your faithful
and enkindle in them the fire of your love.
Send forth your Spirit and they shall be created,
and you shall renew the face of the earth.

The Holy Spirit has given each of us personal gifts to use for building the Christian community. Consider the following questions (if you are with others, reflect and share together):

• What are the Holy Spirit's gifts to me?
• What situation or event illustrates how that gift helps others?
• In what other ways might I use my gifts?

If you are with others, invite each person to proceed around the circle, laying a hand on each person's head, while saying:

May you use your gifts in the service of God and others.

When all have had a chance to bless and be blessed, pray:

O God, help us to use your gifts
to make the world a better place—
more filled with your presence,
more in keeping with your desires,
and more aligned with your will.
Send your Holy Spirit upon us now
so that we can recognize the gifts you have given,
more eagerly make them our own,
and more willingly share them with others.
Amen.

May 20

The Holy Spirit comes...

In the 1950s, we said "Holy Ghost." And in school, as exam time approached, we prayed to the Holy Ghost that we might study the right stuff; then, on the day of the exam, we prayed for help to remember what we had studied. As I grew up, this sometimes struck me as a trivialization of the mighty and treasured gifts of knowledge, wisdom, and understanding promised on the day of my confirmation.

Today, as we reflect on the today's readings, we see a richer picture of the One we now call "Holy Spirit." This Spirit has the power of wind and fire, but is conveyed on a breath. This Spirit comes bearing truth. This Spirit comes to turn societal values upside-down: self-centeredness and divisions give way to love and peace.

This Spirit first came to transform and energize Jesus' followers to bear Christ's presence in and to the world—to be his body. The Spirit's work continues in the Church to this day. We feel it most at work in and among us during our Sunday celebration, as we pray: "Grant that we, who are nourished by the Body and Blood of your Son and filled with his Holy Spirit, may become one body, one spirit in Christ" (Eucharistic Prayer 3).

■ **Margaret Bick**

MASS DURING THE DAY

ENTRANCE ANTIPHON *(Wisdom 1:7)*

The Spirit of the Lord has filled the whole world and
that which contains all things understands what is
said, alleluia.

Or *(Romans 5:5; cf. 8:11)*

The love of God has been poured into our hearts through the
Spirit of God dwelling within us, alleluia.

INTRODUCTORY RITES *(page 10)*

COLLECT

O God, who by the mystery of today's great feast
sanctify your whole Church in every people and nation,
pour out, we pray, the gifts of the Holy Spirit
across the face of the earth
and, with the divine grace that was at work
when the Gospel was first proclaimed,
fill now once more the hearts of believers.
Through our Lord Jesus Christ, your Son,
who lives and reigns with you in the unity of the Holy Spirit,
one God, for ever and ever. *Amen.*

FIRST READING *(Acts 2:1-11)*

When the time for **Pentecost**✝ was fulfilled, they were all
in one place together. And suddenly there came from
the sky a noise like a strong driving wind, and it filled the entire
house in which they were. Then there appeared to them tongues
as of fire, which parted and came to rest on each one of them.
And they were all filled with the Holy Spirit and began to speak

in different tongues, as the Spirit enabled them to proclaim.

Now there were devout Jews from every nation under heaven staying in Jerusalem. At this sound, they gathered in a large crowd, but they were confused because each one heard them speaking in his own language. They were astounded, and in amazement they asked, "Are not all these people who are speaking Galileans? Then how does each of us hear them in his native language? We are Parthians,* Medes,* and Elamites,* inhabitants of Mesopotamia,* Judea and Cappadocia,* Pontus and Asia, Phrygia* and Pamphylia,* Egypt and the districts of Libya near Cyrene, as well as travelers from Rome, both Jews and converts to Judaism, Cretans and Arabs, yet we hear them speaking in our own tongues of the mighty acts of God."

The word of the Lord. *Thanks be to God.*

RESPONSORIAL PSALM *(Psalm 104:1, 24, 29–30, 31, 34)*

℞ **Lord, send out your Spirit, and renew the face of the earth.**
  Or **Alleluia.**

Bless the LORD, O my soul!
  O LORD, my God, you are great indeed!
How manifold are your works, O LORD!
  The earth is full of your creatures. ℞
If you take away their breath, they perish
  and return to their dust.
When you send forth your spirit, they are created,
  and you renew the face of the earth. ℞
May the glory of the LORD endure forever;
  may the LORD be glad in his works!
Pleasing to him be my theme;
  I will be glad in the LORD. ℞

An alternate reading follows.

SECOND READING *(1 Corinthians 12:3b-7, 12-13)*

Brothers and sisters: No one can say, "Jesus is Lord," except by the Holy Spirit.

There are different kinds of spiritual gifts but the same Spirit; there are different forms of service but the same Lord; there are different workings but the same God who produces all of them in everyone. To each individual the manifestation of the Spirit is given for some benefit.

As a body is one though it has many parts, and all the parts of the body, though many, are one body, so also Christ. For in one Spirit we were all baptized into one body, whether Jews or Greeks, slaves or free persons, and we were all given to drink of one Spirit.

The word of the Lord. ***Thanks be to God.***

Or

SECOND READING *(Galatians 5:16-25)*

Brothers and sisters, live by the Spirit and you will certainly not gratify the desire of the flesh. For the flesh has desires against the Spirit, and the Spirit against the flesh; these are opposed to each other, so that you may not do what you want. But if you are guided by the Spirit, you are not under the law. Now the works of the flesh are obvious: immorality, impurity, lust, idolatry, sorcery, hatreds, rivalry, jealousy, outbursts of fury, acts of selfishness, dissensions, factions, occasions of envy, drinking bouts, orgies, and the like. I warn you, as I warned you before, that those who do such things will not inherit the kingdom of God. In contrast, the fruit of the Spirit is love, joy, peace, patience, kindness, generosity, faithfulness, gentleness, self-control.

Against such there is no law. Now those who belong to Christ Jesus have crucified their flesh with its passions and desires. If we live in the Spirit, let us also follow the Spirit.

The word of the Lord. *Thanks be to God.*

SEQUENCE *(Veni, Sancte Spiritus)*

Come, Holy Spirit, come!
And from your celestial home
   Shed a ray of light divine!
Come, Father of the poor!
Come, source of all our store!
   Come, within our bosoms shine.
You, of comforters the best;
You, the soul's most welcome guest;
   Sweet refreshment here below.
In our labor, rest most sweet;
Grateful coolness in the heat;
   Solace in the midst of woe.
O most blessed Light divine,
Shine within these hearts of yours,
   And our inmost being fill!
Where you are not, we have naught,
Nothing good in deed or thought,
   Nothing free from taint of ill.
Heal our wounds, our strength renew;
On our dryness pour your dew;
   Wash the stains of guilt away.
Bend the stubborn heart and will;
Melt the frozen, warm the chill;
   Guide the steps that go astray.

On the faithful, who adore
And confess you, evermore
   In your sevenfold gift descend.
Give them virtue's sure reward;
Give them your salvation, Lord;
   Give them joys that never end. Amen.
   Alleluia.

ALLELUIA

Alleluia, alleluia. Come, Holy Spirit, fill the hearts of your faithful and kindle in them the fire of your love. *Alleluia, alleluia.*

An alternate reading follows.

GOSPEL *(John 20:19-23)*

A reading from the holy Gospel according to John.
Glory to you, O Lord.

On the evening of that first day of the week, when the doors were locked, where the disciples were, for fear of the Jews, Jesus came and stood in their midst and said to them, "Peace be with you." When he had said this, he showed them his hands and his side. The disciples rejoiced when they saw the Lord. Jesus said to them again, "Peace be with you. As the Father has sent me, so I send you." And when he had said this, he breathed on them and said to them, "Receive the Holy Spirit. Whose sins you forgive are forgiven them, and whose sins you retain are retained."

   The Gospel of the Lord. *Praise to you, Lord Jesus Christ.*

Or

GOSPEL *(John 15:26–27; 16:12–15)*

A reading from the holy Gospel according to John.

Glory to you, O Lord.

Jesus said to his disciples: "When the Advocate comes whom I will send you from the Father, the Spirit of truth that proceeds from the Father, he will testify to me. And you also testify, because you have been with me from the beginning.

"I have much more to tell you, but you cannot bear it now. But when he comes, the Spirit of truth, he will guide you to all truth. He will not speak on his own, but he will speak what he hears, and will declare to you the things that are coming. He will glorify me, because he will take from what is mine and declare it to you. Everything that the Father has is mine; for this reason I told you that he will take from what is mine and declare it to you.'"

The Gospel of the Lord. *Praise to you, Lord Jesus Christ.*

PROFESSION OF FAITH *(page 13)*

PRAYER OF THE FAITHFUL

PREPARATION OF GIFTS *(page 16)*

PRAYER OVER THE OFFERINGS

Grant, we pray, O Lord,
that, as promised by your Son,
the Holy Spirit may reveal to us more abundantly
the hidden mystery of this sacrifice
and graciously lead us into all truth.
Through Christ our Lord. *Amen.*

PREFACE: THE MYSTERY OF PENTECOST

It is truly right and just, our duty and our salvation,
always and everywhere to give you thanks,
Lord, holy Father, almighty and eternal God.

For, bringing your Paschal Mystery to completion,
you bestowed the Holy Spirit today
on those you made your adopted children
by uniting them to your Only Begotten Son.
This same Spirit, as the Church came to birth,
opened to all peoples the knowledge of God
and brought together the many languages of the earth
in profession of the one faith.

Therefore, overcome with paschal joy,
every land, every people exults in your praise
and even the heavenly Powers, with the angelic hosts,
sing together the unending hymn of your glory,
as they acclaim:
Holy, Holy, Holy Lord God of hosts... (page 35)

⁜ TAKING A CLOSER LOOK ⁜

✙ **Pentecost** *Pentecost* (Greek, the "fiftieth day") was the Jewish feast that came fifty days after Passover. It celebrated the spring grain harvest and the offering to God of the firstfruits of the crop (Exodus 23:14-17). One of the three major Jewish feast days, over the centuries it became associated with the giving of the Law (or *Torah*) and focused more on covenant renewal. In the New Testament, this feast day echoes the Jewish themes with the descent of the Holy Spirit to form the Christian community and to harvest the firstfruits of its universal mission.

COMMUNION ANTIPHON *(Acts 2:4, 11)*

They were all filled with the Holy Spirit and spoke of the marvels of God, alleluia.

PRAYER AFTER COMMUNION

O God, who bestow heavenly gifts upon your Church,
safeguard, we pray, the grace you have given,
that the gift of the Holy Spirit poured out upon her
may retain all its force
and that this spiritual food
may gain her abundance of eternal redemption.
Through Christ our Lord. *Amen.*

SOLEMN BLESSING: THE HOLY SPIRIT *(Optional, page 62)*

DISMISSAL *(page 57)* ✦

• RESPONDING TO THE WORD •

The presence and power of God's Holy Spirit enabled the disciples to tell about Jesus.

➡ *When have I felt the Spirit's prompting to share my love for Jesus with others?*

Paul reminds us that we have each been given gifts by the Holy Spirit.

➡ *What gift do I claim and how am I using it to benefit others?*

Jesus reminds us that sharing God's Spirit enables the forgiveness of the sins that break down our relationships with God and others.

➡ *When have I felt the Spirit drawing me more deeply into relationships with others?*

May 27

Three in One

Trinity Sunday is a day to reflect upon and celebrate just who our God is. God is revealed to us first and foremost as a saving God. That is what today's first reading celebrates. The Jewish people knew their God's identity because of his saving acts.

Christian belief in the Trinity was not the result of philosophical reflection on the nature of God. Rather, it developed as Christians reflected on their experience of salvation in Jesus Christ and the presence of his spirit within their very souls.

Jesus and the Holy Spirit were experienced as doing what only God can do—saving us—and so they must be divine. But good Jews knew that God is One: this is the origin of the doctrine of the Trinity.

Only later did philosophical precision give us language like "three persons," "one nature," "hypostatic union," etc. These are important to keep Christian faith from being misunderstood, but they do not make up the core of our faith in the Trinity. The core is that the same God who saved the Jewish people from slavery in Egypt has also saved us from slavery to sin through his Son Jesus Christ, and that we can experience that salvation even today through the ministry of their Holy Spirit.

■ **BRETT SALKELD**

ENTRANCE ANTIPHON

Blest be God the Father, and the Only Begotten Son of God, and also the Holy Spirit, for he has shown us his merciful love.

INTRODUCTORY RITES *(page 10)*

COLLECT

God our Father, who by sending into the world
the Word of truth and the Spirit of sanctification
made known to the human race your wondrous mystery,
grant us, we pray, that in professing the true faith,
we may acknowledge the Trinity of eternal glory
and adore your Unity, powerful in majesty.
Through our Lord Jesus Christ, your Son,
who lives and reigns with you in the unity of the Holy Spirit,
one God, for ever and ever. *Amen.*

FIRST READING *(Deuteronomy 4:32-34, 39-40)*

Moses said to the people: "Ask now of the days of old, before your time, ever since God created man upon the earth; ask from one end of the sky to the other: Did anything so great ever happen before? Was it ever heard of? Did a people ever hear the voice of God speaking from the midst of fire, as you did, and live? Or did any god venture to go and take a nation for himself from the midst of another nation, by testings, by signs and wonders, by war, with strong hand and outstretched arm, and by great terrors, all of which the LORD, your God, did for you in Egypt before your very eyes? This is why you must now know, and fix in your heart, that the LORD is God in the heavens above and on earth below, and that there is no other. You must keep his statutes and commandments that I enjoin on you today, that you and your children after you may prosper, and that you may have long life on the land which the LORD, your God, is giving you forever."

The word of the Lord. *Thanks be to God.*

RESPONSORIAL PSALM *(Psalm 33:4-5, 6, 9, 18-19, 20, 22)*
℟· **Blessed the people the Lord has chosen to be his own.**
Or **Alleluia!**

Upright is the word of the LORD,
    and all his works are trustworthy.
He loves justice and right;
    of the kindness of the LORD the earth is full. ℟·
By the word of the LORD the heavens were made;
    by the breath of his mouth all their host.
For he spoke, and it was made;
    he commanded, and it stood forth. ℟·
See, the eyes of the LORD are upon those who fear him,
    upon those who hope for his kindness,
to deliver them from death
    and preserve them in spite of famine. ℟·
Our soul waits for the LORD,
    who is our help and our shield.
May your kindness, O LORD, be upon us
    who have put our hope in you. ℟·

SECOND READING *(Romans 8:14-17)*

Brothers and sisters: Those who are led by the Spirit of God are sons of God. For you did not receive a spirit of slavery to fall back into fear, but you received a Spirit of adoption, through whom we cry, "Abba, Father!" The Spirit himself bears witness with our spirit that we are children of God, and if children, then heirs, heirs of God and joint heirs with Christ, if only we suffer with him so that we may also be glorified with him.

The word of the Lord. ***Thanks be to God.***

ALLELUIA *(See Revelation 1:8)*
Alleluia, alleluia. Glory to the Father, the Son, and the Holy Spirit; to God who is, who was, and who is to come. *Alleluia, alleluia.*

GOSPEL *(Matthew 28:16-20)*
A reading from the holy Gospel according to Matthew.
Glory to you, O Lord.

The eleven disciples went to Galilee, to the mountain to which Jesus had ordered them. When they all saw him, they worshiped, but they doubted. Then Jesus approached and said to them, "All power in heaven and on earth has been given to me. Go, therefore, and make disciples of all nations, **baptizing**✝ them in the name of the Father, and of the Son, and of the Holy Spirit, teaching them to observe all that I have commanded you. And behold, I am with you always, until the end of the age."

The Gospel of the Lord. ***Praise to you, Lord Jesus Christ.***

PROFESSION OF FAITH *(page 13)*

PRAYER OF THE FAITHFUL

PREPARATION OF GIFTS *(page 16)*

PRAYER OVER THE OFFERINGS
Sanctify by the invocation of your name,
we pray, O Lord our God,
this oblation of our service,
and by it make of us an eternal offering to you.
Through Christ our Lord. ***Amen.***

PREFACE: THE MYSTERY OF THE MOST HOLY TRINITY

It is truly right and just, our duty and our salvation,
always and everywhere to give you thanks,
Lord, holy Father, almighty and eternal God.

For with your Only Begotten Son and the Holy Spirit
you are one God, one Lord:
not in the unity of a single person,
but in a Trinity of one substance.

For what you have revealed to us of your glory
we believe equally of your Son
and of the Holy Spirit,
so that, in the confessing of the true and eternal Godhead,
you might be adored in what is proper to each Person,
their unity in substance,
and their equality in majesty.

• TAKING A CLOSER LOOK •

✚ **Baptizing** Baptism means to immerse or wash in water and so becomes a natural sign for ritual purity or holiness. In Judaism, there were many ceremonial washings either in preparation for celebrating a ritual or as part of a cleansing right within a ritual. Thus John the Baptist uses a baptism of repentance (Mark 1:4) to symbolize one's desire to put off sinful ways and live as God wants. But for the Christian community, baptism replaced Jewish circumcision as the initiation ritual and sign of covenant belonging. This also meant that covenant membership was also open to women and not just for the men who were circumcised.

For this is praised by Angels and Archangels,
Cherubim, too, and Seraphim,
who never cease to cry out each day,
as with one voice they acclaim:
Holy, holy, holy, Lord God of hosts... (page 35)

COMMUNION ANTIPHON *(Galatians 4:6)*
Since you are children of God, God has sent into your hearts the
Spirit of his Son, the Spirit who cries out: Abba, Father.

PRAYER AFTER COMMUNION
May receiving this Sacrament, O Lord our God,
bring us health of body and soul,
as we confess your eternal holy Trinity and undivided Unity.
Through Christ our Lord. *Amen.*

BLESSING & DISMISSAL *(page 56)* ❖

• RESPONDING TO THE WORD •

Moses reviews the story of God's mighty deeds done for the covenant people.	We share the same path as Jesus—through suffering and death into new life with God.	Jesus promises to be with us always.
➡ *What mighty deeds of God's loving power have been at work in my life?*	➡ *How have the little deaths I have experienced opened me up to new life?*	➡ *Which experiences of Jesus' presence have been particularly important to me? Why?*

June 3

JUN
3

Be transformed!

Today we celebrate the great gift that Jesus left us before ascending to his Father: the gift of his real abiding presence and of his body and blood that we are invited to consume during the celebration of the Eucharist. What more could our God give to us? What more could we ask of our God?

Whenever we eat and drink, we are transformed. Most food is good for our body; it feeds our mind and enlivens our spirits. In fact, we feel better after we have eaten a good meal; we are full, satisfied, and energized.

Unexplainable food for life, the holy bread and wine fill us though we do not know how. Relying on our faith to believe that the true presence of our God makes his home in our body, heart, and soul, we come back again and again for more of this holy food. We have been invited to come, from here and from there, to eat and to drink as one in Christ.

On this great feast of the Most Holy Body and Blood of Christ, we gather not to explain how this mystery happens, but to fall on our knees in profound adoration, to celebrate with deep joy that God is truly present to each one of us.

■ Fr. Matthew Durham, CSB

ENTRANCE ANTIPHON *(Cf. Psalm 81 [80]:17)*
He fed them with the finest wheat and satisfied them with honey from the rock.

INTRODUCTORY RITES *(page 10)*

COLLECT
O God, who in this wonderful Sacrament
have left us a memorial of your Passion,
grant us, we pray,
so to revere the sacred mysteries of your Body and Blood
that we may always experience in ourselves
the fruits of your redemption.
Who live and reign with God the Father
in the unity of the Holy Spirit,
one God, for ever and ever. *Amen.*

FIRST READING *(Exodus 24:3-8)*

When Moses came to the people and related all the words and ordinances of the LORD, they all answered with one voice, "We will do everything that the LORD has told us." Moses then wrote down all the words of the LORD and, rising early the next day, he erected at the foot of the mountain an altar and twelve pillars for the twelve tribes of Israel. Then, having sent certain young men of the Israelites to offer holocausts and sacrifice young bulls as peace offerings to the LORD, Moses took half of the blood and put it in large bowls; the other half he splashed on the altar. Taking the book of the covenant, he read it aloud to the people, who answered, "All that the LORD has said, we will heed and do." Then he took the blood and sprinkled it on the people, saying, "This is the blood of the covenant that the LORD has made with you in accordance with all these words of his."

The word of the Lord. *Thanks be to God.*

RESPONSORIAL PSALM *(Psalm 116:12-13, 15-16, 17-18)*

R⫶ **I will take the cup of salvation, and call on the name of the Lord.** *Or* **Alleluia.**

How shall I make a return to the LORD
for all the good he has done for me?
The cup of salvation I will take up,
and I will call upon the name of the LORD. R⫶

Precious in the eyes of the LORD
is the death of his faithful ones.
I am your servant, the son of your handmaid;
you have loosed my bonds. R⫶

To you will I offer sacrifice of thanksgiving,
and I will call upon the name of the LORD.
My vows to the LORD I will pay
in the presence of all his people. R⫶

SECOND READING *(Hebrews 9:11-15)*

Brothers and sisters: When Christ came as high priest of the good things that have come to be, passing through the greater and more perfect tabernacle not made by hands, that is, not belonging to this creation, he entered once for all into the sanctuary, not with the blood of goats and calves but with his own blood, thus obtaining eternal redemption. For if the blood of goats and bulls and the sprinkling of a heifer's ashes can sanctify those who are defiled so that their flesh is cleansed, how much more will the blood of Christ, who through the eternal Spirit offered himself unblemished to God, cleanse our consciences from dead works to worship the living God.

For this reason he is **mediator of a new covenant:**✝ since a death has taken place for deliverance from transgressions under the first covenant, those who are called may receive the promised eternal inheritance.

The word of the Lord. *Thanks be to God.*

SEQUENCE

The shorter version begins at the asterisks.

Laud, O Zion, your salvation,
Laud with hymns of exultation,
    Christ, your king and shepherd true:

Bring him all the praise you know,
He is more than you bestow.
    Never can you reach his due.

Special theme for glad thanksgiving
Is the quick'ning and the living
    Bread today before you set:

From his hands of old partaken,
As we know, by faith unshaken,
    Where the Twelve at supper met.

Full and clear ring out your chanting,
Joy nor sweetest grace be wanting,
    From your heart let praises burst:

For today the feast is holden,
When the institution olden
    Of that supper was rehearsed.

Here the new law's new oblation,

By the new king's revelation,
    Ends the form of ancient rite:

Now the new the old effaces,
Truth away the shadow chases,
    Light dispels the gloom of night.

What he did at supper seated,
Christ ordained to be repeated,
    His memorial ne'er to cease:

And his rule for guidance taking,
Bread and wine we hallow, making
    Thus our sacrifice of peace.

This the truth each Christian learns,
Bread into his flesh he turns,
    To his precious blood the wine:

Sight has fail'd, nor thought conceives,
But a dauntless faith believes,
    Resting on a pow'r divine.

Here beneath these signs are hidden
Priceless things to sense forbidden;
    Sign, not things are all we see:

Blood is poured and flesh is broken,
Yet in either wondrous token
    Christ entire we know to be.

Whoso of this food partakes,
Does not rend the Lord nor breaks;
    Christ is whole to all that tastes:

Thousands are, as one, receivers,
One, as thousands of believers,
   Eats of him who cannot waste.

Bad and good the feast are sharing,
Of what divers dooms preparing,
   Endless death, or endless life.

Life to these, to those damnation,
See how like participation
   Is with unlike issues rife.

When the sacrament is broken,
Doubt not, but believe 'tis spoken,
   That each sever'd outward token
     doth the very whole contain.

Nought the precious gift divides,
Breaking but the sign betides
   Jesus still the same abides,
     still unbroken does remain.

* * *

The shorter form of the sequence begins here.

Lo! the angel's food is given
To the pilgrim who has striven;
     See the children's bread from heaven,
       which on dogs may not be spent.

Truth the ancient types fulfilling,
Isaac bound, a victim willing,

Paschal lamb, its lifeblood spilling,
    manna to the fathers sent.

Very bread, good shepherd, tend us,
Jesu, of your love befriend us,
    You refresh us, you defend us,
    Your eternal goodness send us
In the land of life to see.

You who all things can and know,
Who on earth such food bestow,
    Grant us with your saints, though lowest,
    Where the heav'nly feast you show,
Fellow heirs and guests to be. Amen. Alleluia.

ALLELUIA *(John 6:51)*
Alleluia, alleluia. I am the living bread that came down from
heaven, says the Lord; whoever eats this bread will live forever.
Alleluia, alleluia.

GOSPEL *(Mark 14:12-16, 22-26)*
A reading from the holy Gospel according to Mark.
Glory to you, O Lord.

On the first day of the Feast of Unleavened Bread, when they
sacrificed the Passover lamb, Jesus' disciples said to him,
"Where do you want us to go and prepare for you to eat the
Passover?" He sent two of his disciples and said to them, "Go
into the city and a man will meet you, carrying a jar of water.
Follow him. Wherever he enters, say to the master of the house,
'The Teacher says, "Where is my guest room where I may eat
the Passover with my disciples?" ' Then he will show you a large
upper room furnished and ready. Make the preparations for us

there." The disciples then went off, entered the city, and found it just as he had told them; and they prepared the Passover.

While they were eating, he took bread, said the blessing, broke it, gave it to them, and said, "Take it; this is my body." Then he took a cup, gave thanks, and gave it to them, and they all drank from it. He said to them, "This is my blood of the covenant, which will be shed for many. Amen, I say to you, I shall not drink again the fruit of the vine until the day when I drink it new in the kingdom of God." Then, after singing a hymn, they went out to the Mount of Olives.

The Gospel of the Lord. *Praise to you, Lord Jesus Christ.*

PROFESSION OF FAITH *(page 13)*

PRAYER OF THE FAITHFUL

PREPARATION OF GIFTS *(page 16)*

PRAYER OVER THE OFFERINGS
Grant your Church, O Lord, we pray,
the gifts of unity and peace,

• TAKING A CLOSER LOOK •

✚ **Mediator of a new covenant** In the biblical social world, many relationships were between unequals in honor and status. The patron/lord/benefactor controlled some essential good (food, water, protection, etc.) that the client/servant/petitioner needed. So there was a great need for brokers/mediators to put clients in touch with the right benefactors. In religion, the priest acted as this mediator, putting the people into relationship with God—the divine benefactor—who gives everything necessary for eternal life. For Christians, Christ is this "priest-broker," who through his death and resurrection mediates our new covenant relationship with God.

whose signs are to be seen in mystery
in the offerings we here present.
Through Christ our Lord. *Amen.*

PREFACE *(Most Holy Eucharist 1–2, pages 32–33)*

COMMUNION ANTIPHON *(John 6:57)*
Whoever eats my flesh and drinks my blood remains in me and I
in him, says the Lord.

PRAYER AFTER COMMUNION
Grant, O Lord, we pray,
that we may delight for all eternity
in that share in your divine life,
which is foreshadowed in the present age
by our reception of your precious Body and Blood.
Who live and reign for ever and ever. *Amen.*

BLESSING & DISMISSAL *(page 56)* ❖

• RESPONDING TO THE WORD •

The Israelites seal their covenant with blood and a promise to do all that God asks.	Jesus is the mediator between ourselves and God to deliver us from our sins.	Jesus promised to be present in the bread and cup of our Eucharist.
➡ *What covenant pledge might I make today to seal my relationship with God?*	➡ *What message would I wish Jesus to take to God for me today?*	➡ *How am I preparing each week to experience Jesus' eucharistic presence?*

June 10

Rooted in God

Today's readings are about faith and hope, virtues that are much needed in a world where people suffer the "demons" of poverty, racial inequality, fear of strangers, or fear of anyone who is different from what is accepted as "normal." When our safety and security are threatened, we try to hold on desperately to what we have and what we know.

Jesus gave freedom to those oppressed by demons because he was rooted in the love of God. The Pharisees, not being rooted in the love of God, were not able to bring freedom to those who were suffering. They sought safety in the law; it was familiar and tried. Jesus stepped outside those boundaries and turned to the indulgent love of God to free the suffering.

We, like the Pharisees, are sometimes trapped by our fears and, not being rooted in the love of God, we cannot think and act as Jesus did. In order to ask critical questions about why injustice exists, or to step outside of our comfort zone to try something different to alleviate suffering, we must be rooted in God.

In today's Eucharist, let us pray for grace to be rooted in God so that we, like Jesus, can confront evil and bring freedom to those who suffer.

■ **ANTHONY CHEZZI**

ENTRANCE ANTIPHON *(Cf. Psalm 27 [26]:1-2)*

The Lord is my light and my salvation; whom shall
I fear? The Lord is the stronghold of my life; whom
should I dread? When those who do evil draw near,
they stumble and fall.

INTRODUCTORY RITES *(page 10)*

COLLECT

O God, from whom all good things come,
grant that we, who call on you in our need,
may at your prompting discern what is right,
and by your guidance do it.
Through our Lord Jesus Christ, your Son,
who lives and reigns with you in the unity of the Holy Spirit,
one God, for ever and ever. *Amen.*

FIRST READING *(Genesis 3:9-15)*

After the man, Adam, had eaten of the tree, the LORD God called
to the man and asked him, "Where are you?" He answered, "I
heard you in the garden; but I was afraid, because I was naked, so
I hid myself." Then he asked, "Who told you that you were naked?
You have eaten, then, from the tree of which I had forbidden you
to eat!" The man replied, "The woman whom you put here with
me—she gave me fruit from the tree, and so I ate it." The LORD
God then asked the woman, "Why did you do such a thing?" The
woman answered, "The serpent tricked me into it, so I ate it."

Then the LORD God said to the serpent:

"Because you have done this, you shall be banned
 from all the animals
 and from all the wild creatures;
on your belly shall you crawl,

and dirt shall you eat
all the days of your life.
I will put enmity between you and the woman,
and between your offspring and hers;
he will strike at your head,
while you strike at his heel."

The word of the Lord. *Thanks be to God.*

RESPONSORIAL PSALM *(Psalm 130:1-2, 3-4, 5-6, 7-8)*

R. **With the Lord there is mercy, and fullness of redemption.**

Out of the depths I cry to you, O LORD;
LORD, hear my voice!
Let your ears be attentive
to my voice in supplication. R.
If you, O LORD, mark iniquities,
LORD, who can stand?
But with you is forgiveness,
that you may be revered. R.
I trust in the LORD;
my soul trusts in his word.
More than sentinels wait for the dawn,
let Israel wait for the LORD. R.
For with the LORD is kindness
and with him is plenteous redemption;
and he will redeem Israel
from all their iniquities. R.

SECOND READING *(2 Corinthians 4:13–5:1)*

Brothers and sisters: Since we have the same spirit of faith,
according to what is written, *I believed, therefore I spoke,* we
too believe and therefore we speak, knowing that the one who

raised the Lord Jesus will raise us also with Jesus and place us with you in his presence. Everything indeed is for you, so that the grace bestowed in abundance on more and more people may cause the thanksgiving to overflow for the glory of God. Therefore, we are not discouraged; rather, although our outer self is wasting away, our inner self is being renewed day by day. For this momentary light affliction is producing for us an eternal weight of glory beyond all comparison, as we look not to what is seen but to what is unseen; for what is seen is transitory, but what is unseen is eternal. For we know that if our earthly dwelling, a tent, should be destroyed, we have a building from God, a dwelling not made with hands, eternal in heaven.

The word of the Lord. ***Thanks be to God.***

ALLELUIA *(John 12:31b–32)*
Alleluia, alleluia. Now the ruler of this world will be driven out, says the Lord; and when I am lifted up from the earth, I will draw everyone to myself. *Alleluia, alleluia.*

GOSPEL *(Mark 3:20–35)*
A reading from the holy Gospel according to Mark.
Glory to you, O Lord.

Jesus came home with his disciples. Again the crowd gathered, making it impossible for them even to eat. When his relatives heard of this they set out to seize him, for they said, "He is out of his mind." The scribes who had come from Jerusalem said, "He is possessed by Beelzebul," and "By the prince of demons he drives out demons."

Summoning them, he began to speak to them in parables, "How can Satan drive out Satan? If a kingdom is divided against itself, that kingdom cannot stand. And if a house is divided against itself, that house will not be able to stand. And if Satan has risen up against himself and is divided, he cannot stand; that is the end of him. But no one can enter a strong man's house to plunder his property unless he first ties up the strong man. Then he can plunder the house. Amen, I say to you, all sins and all blasphemies that people utter will be forgiven them. But whoever blasphemes against the Holy Spirit will never have forgiveness, but is guilty of an everlasting sin." For they had said, "He has an unclean spirit."

His mother and his brothers arrived. Standing outside they sent word to him and called him. A crowd seated around him told him, "Your mother and your brothers and your sisters are outside asking for you." But he said to them in reply, "Who are my mother and my brothers?" And looking around at those seated in the circle he said, "Here are my mother and my brothers. For whoever does the will of God is my brother and sister and mother."

The Gospel of the Lord. *Praise to you, Lord Jesus Christ.*

PROFESSION OF FAITH *(page 13)*

PRAYER OF THE FAITHFUL

PREPARATION OF GIFTS *(page 16)*

• TAKING A CLOSER LOOK •

✝ **LORD** The New American Bible uses LORD in small capital letters to indicate the sacred name of God revealed to Moses and the Israelites: *Yahweh*. The word "Lord" has the same number of letters as God's sacred name: since the Hebrew language wrote only the consonants and not the vowels, God's name was written: YHWH (in English). God's name was so sacred that the Jews did not speak it aloud. Instead, they said *Adonai*, the Hebrew word for Lord.

PRAYER OVER THE OFFERINGS

Look kindly upon our service, O Lord, we pray,
that what we offer
may be an acceptable oblation to you
and lead us to grow in charity.
Through Christ our Lord. *Amen.*

PREFACE *(Sundays in Ordinary Time, pages 28–32)*

COMMUNION ANTIPHON *(Psalm 18 [17]:3)*

The Lord is my rock, my fortress, and my deliverer; my God is
my saving strength.

Or *(1 John 4:16)*

God is love, and whoever abides in love abides in God, and God
in him.

PRAYER AFTER COMMUNION

May your healing work, O Lord,
free us, we pray, from doing evil
and lead us to what is right.
Through Christ our Lord. *Amen.*

BLESSING & DISMISSAL *(page 56)* ✛

⏤ • RESPONDING TO THE WORD • ⏤

God confronts Adam and Eve after they have sinned.	**Paul reminds us that our true home is with God.**	**Jesus' struggle was against evil wherever it was hiding.**
⇨ *For what sins do I want to ask for God's forgiveness today?*	⇨ *How does hearing this passage change my perspective today?*	⇨ *What evil might be hidden in my words and actions?*

June 17

We give thanks!

"To his own disciples he explained everything in private." The closing words of today's gospel capture the essence of our need for a personal and private prayer life. Sometimes everything starts to make more sense when we are alone with our Lord.

Sitting quietly with Jesus, we consider the profound wisdom of his message: simply sow small seeds. Each word or action is a small seed. We have no idea when or where it will sprout and grow. We don't have to. The grain will eventually mature, ready for harvest. The tree will one day branch out, ready to support a nest.

With faith, we listen attentively as Jesus speaks to us. We ponder how and where to scatter the seeds given to us. We delight in all that is green and growing. We learn what is complete, what is now ready for harvest.

Jesus offers simple words and everyday images: trees, plants, birds. In the Eucharist, he offers bread and wine, gifts of the harvest, each offering once hidden in a very tiny seed.

Gathering in a community and receiving the gift of the word, our common faith is strengthened and supported. Privately, we receive the Lord into our very being; the harvest of grain and vine nourishing both body and soul. We come forward, with open hands, and we are blessed. We give thanks.

■ **BRENDA MERK HILDEBRAND**

ENTRANCE ANTIPHON *(Cf. Psalm 27 (26):7,9)*

O Lord, hear my voice, for I have called to you; be my help. Do not abandon or forsake me, O God, my Savior!

INTRODUCTORY RITES *(page 10)*

COLLECT

O God, strength of those who hope in you,
graciously hear our pleas,
and, since without you mortal frailty can do nothing,
grant us always the help of your grace,
that in following your commands
we may please you by our resolve and our deeds.
Through our Lord Jesus Christ, your Son,
who lives and reigns with you in the unity of the Holy Spirit,
one God, for ever and ever. ***Amen.***

FIRST READING *(Ezekiel 17:22-24)*

Thus says the Lord GOD:

I, too, will take from the crest of the cedar,
  from its topmost branches tear off a tender shoot,
and plant it on a high and lofty mountain;
  on the mountain heights of Israel I will plant it.
It shall put forth branches and bear fruit,
  and become a majestic cedar.
Birds of every kind shall dwell beneath it,
  every winged thing in the shade of its boughs.
And all the trees of the field shall know
  that I, the LORD,
bring low the high tree,
  lift high the lowly tree,

wither up the green tree,
  and make the withered tree bloom.
As I, the LORD, have spoken, so will I do.
The word of the Lord. *Thanks be to God.*

RESPONSORIAL PSALM *(Psalm 92:2-3, 13-14, 15-16)*
R. Lord, it is good to give thanks to you.

It is good to give thanks to the LORD,
  to sing praise to your name, Most High,
to proclaim your kindness at dawn
  and your faithfulness throughout the night. R.
The just one shall flourish like the palm tree,
  like a cedar of Lebanon shall he grow.
They that are planted in the house of the LORD
  shall flourish in the courts of our God. R.
They shall bear fruit even in old age;
  vigorous and sturdy shall they be,
declaring how just is the LORD,
  my rock, in whom there is no wrong. R.

SECOND READING *(2 Corinthians 5:6-10)*
Brothers and sisters: We are always courageous, although we
know that while we are at home in the body we are away
from the Lord, for we walk by faith, not by sight. Yet we are
courageous, and we would rather leave the body and go home to
the Lord. Therefore, we aspire to please him, whether we are at
home or away. For we must all appear before the judgment seat
of Christ, so that each may receive recompense, according to
what he did in the body, whether good or evil.
  The word of the Lord. *Thanks be to God.*

ALLELUIA

Alleluia, alleluia. The seed is the word of God, Christ is the sower. All who come to him will live for ever. *Alleluia, alleluia.*

GOSPEL *(Mark 4:26-34)*

A reading from the holy Gospel according to Mark.
Glory to you, O Lord.

Jesus said to the crowds: "This is how it is with the kingdom of God; it is as if a man were to scatter seed on the land and would sleep and rise night and day and through it all the seed would sprout and grow, he knows not how. Of its own accord the land yields fruit, first the blade, then the ear, then the full grain in the ear. And when the grain is ripe, he wields the sickle at once, for the harvest has come."

He said, "To what shall we compare the kingdom of God, or what **parable**✝ can we use for it? It is like a mustard seed that, when it is sown in the ground, is the smallest of all the seeds on the earth. But once it is sown, it springs up and becomes the largest of plants and puts forth large branches, so that the birds of the sky can dwell in its shade." With many such parables he spoke the word to them as they were able to understand it. Without parables he did not speak to them, but to his own disciples he explained everything in private.

The Gospel of the Lord. *Praise to you, Lord Jesus Christ.*

PROFESSION OF FAITH *(page 13)*

PRAYER OF THE FAITHFUL

PREPARATION OF GIFTS *(page 16)*

PRAYER OVER THE OFFERINGS

O God, who in the offerings presented here
provide for the twofold needs of human nature,
nourishing us with food
and renewing us with your Sacrament,
grant, we pray,
that the sustenance they provide
may not fail us in body or in spirit.
Through Christ our Lord. *Amen.*

PREFACE *(Sundays in Ordinary Time, pages 28–32)*

● TAKING A CLOSER LOOK ●

✝ **Parable** A parable (from the Greek word *parabole*, to "throw together" things for comparison or illustration) is a short realistic story intended to encourage reflection by connecting the parable to our own life. Since one can connect the parable to various aspects of one's life or that of one's family or community, parables are open-ended in their application.

Parables were a common teaching device of the Jewish rabbis and important to Jesus in his teaching, because the only way we have to talk about what is unfamiliar to us (God's ruling presence or "kingdom") is in terms that are familiar to us (our everyday life and world). Thus, parables challenge the audience to think about their meaning and change their lives because of what they discover.

COMMUNION ANTIPHON *(Psalm27 [26]:4)*

There is one thing I ask of the Lord, only this do I seek: to live in the house of the Lord all the days of my life.

Or *(John 17:11)*

Holy Father, keep in your name those you have
given me, that they may be one as we are one, says the Lord.

PRAYER AFTER COMMUNION

As this reception of your Holy Communion, O Lord,
foreshadows the union of the faithful in you,
so may it bring about unity in your Church.
Through Christ our Lord. *Amen.*

BLESSING & DISMISSAL *(page 56)* ⁑

⁙ RESPONDING TO THE WORD ⁙

All on earth is under the rule of God, who can "bring low the high tree, lift high the lowly tree."

➲ *What situations in life make me forget how truly powerful God is?*

Paul reminds us to look forward to an eternal life with God after we die.

➲ *How can this reminder change the way I live today?*

The mustard seed can't grow until it is planted in the ground.

➲ *What opportunities do I have to sow the seed of God's word so that it can grow in others?*

June 24

A way out of darkness

The Church celebrates John the Baptist's natural birth with a feast of his "nativity," assigned exactly six months before the nativity of Christ. The fact that Christ praised John the Baptist so highly encouraged a special veneration.

Today's first reading is the second of the four Servant Songs of the prophet Isaiah. John was the servant made ready and fit for the preaching of God's word. He was the sharp-edged sword who pointed out the true light to the nations, the one whose salvation would reach to the ends of the earth. St. Paul spoke of John, who heralded the Messiah's coming by proclaiming a baptism of repentance to all the people of Israel.

Because John represents the old, he is born of an elderly couple; because he represents the new, he is revealed as a prophet in his mother's womb. John's preceding Jesus was clearly fixed in the Christian tradition: in two of the three gospels that begin their story before the public ministry with Jesus' first appearance on earth, John the Baptist is brought forth to precede the appearance as well.

John always defined his humanity in terms of its limitations. He came to teach us that there is a way out of the darkness and sadness of both the world and the human condition. That way is Jesus himself.

■ FR. THOMAS ROSICA, CSB

ENTRANCE ANTIPHON *(John 1:6-7; Luke 1:17)*

A man was sent from God, whose name was John.
He came to testify to the light, to prepare a people
fit for the Lord.

INTRODUCTORY RITES *(page 10)*

COLLECT

O God, who raised up Saint John the Baptist
to make ready a nation fit for Christ the Lord,
give your people, we pray,
the grace of spiritual joys
and direct the hearts of all the faithful
into the way of salvation and peace.
Through our Lord Jesus Christ, your Son,
who lives and reigns with you in the unity of the Holy Spirit,
one God, for ever and ever. *Amen.*

FIRST READING *(Isaiah 49:1-6)*

Hear me, O coastlands,
    listen, O distant peoples.
The LORD called me from birth,
    from my mother's womb he gave me my name.
He made of me a sharp-edged sword
    and concealed me in the shadow of his arm.
He made me a polished arrow,
    in his quiver he hid me.
You are my servant, he said to me,
    Israel, through whom I show my glory.

Though I thought I had toiled in vain,
    and for nothing, uselessly, spent my strength,

yet my reward is with the LORD,
    my recompense is with my God.
For now the LORD has spoken
    who formed me as his servant from the womb,
that Jacob may be brought back to him
    and Israel gathered to him;
and I am made glorious in the sight of the LORD,
    and my God is now my strength!
It is too little, he says, for you to be my servant,
    to raise up the tribes of Jacob,
    and restore the survivors of Israel;
I will make you a light to the nations,
    that my salvation may reach to the ends of the earth.
The word of the Lord. ***Thanks be to God.***

RESPONSORIAL PSALM *(Psalm 139:1b–3, 13–14ab, 14c–15)*
R̶ **I praise you, for I am wonderfully made.**

O LORD, you have probed me, you know me:
    you know when I sit and when I stand;
    you understand my thoughts from afar.
My journeys and my rest you scrutinize,
    with all my ways you are familiar. R̶
Truly you have formed my inmost being;
    you knit me in my mother's womb.
I give you thanks that I am fearfully, wonderfully made;
    wonderful are your works. R̶
My soul also you knew full well;
    nor was my frame unknown to you
When I was made in secret,
    when I was fashioned in the depths of the earth. R̶

SECOND READING *(Acts 13:22-26)*

In those days, Paul said: "God raised up David as king; of him God testified, *I have found David, son of Jesse, a man after my own heart; he will carry out my every wish*. From this man's descendants God, according to his promise, has brought to Israel a savior, Jesus. John heralded his coming by proclaiming a baptism of **repentance**✛ to all the people of Israel; and as John was completing his course, he would say, 'What do you suppose that I am? I am not he. Behold, one is coming after me; I am not worthy to unfasten the sandals of his feet.'

"My brothers, sons of the family of Abraham, and those others among you who are God-fearing, to us this word of salvation has been sent."

The word of the Lord. *Thanks be to God.*

ALLELUIA *(See Luke 1:76)*

Alleluia, alleluia. You, child, will be called prophet of the Most High, for you will go before the Lord to prepare his way. *Alleluia, alleluia.*

GOSPEL *(Luke 1:57-66, 80)*

A reading from the holy Gospel according to Luke.
Glory to you, O Lord.

When the time arrived for Elizabeth to have her child she gave birth to a son. Her neighbors and relatives heard that the Lord had shown his great mercy toward her, and they rejoiced with her. When they came on the eighth day to circumcise the child, they were going to call him Zechariah after his father, but his mother said in reply, "No. He will be called John." But they answered her, "There is no one among your relatives who has this name." So they made signs, asking his father what he wished him to be called. He asked for a tablet and wrote, "John is his name," and all were amazed. Immediately his mouth was opened, his tongue freed, and he spoke blessing God. Then fear came upon all their neighbors, and all these matters were discussed throughout the hill country of Judea. All who heard these things took them to heart, saying, "What, then, will this child be?" For surely the hand of the Lord was with him.

The child grew and became strong in spirit, and he was in the desert until the day of his manifestation to Israel.

The Gospel of the Lord. *Praise to you, Lord Jesus Christ.*

PROFESSION OF FAITH *(page 13)*

PRAYER OF THE FAITHFUL

PREPARATION OF GIFTS *(page 16)*

PRAYER OVER THE OFFERINGS
We place these offerings on your altar, O Lord,
to celebrate with fitting honor the nativity of him
who both foretold the coming of the world's Savior
and pointed him out when he came.
Who lives and reigns for ever and ever. *Amen.*

PREFACE: THE MISSION OF THE PRECURSOR
It is truly right and just, our duty and our salvation,
always and everywhere to give you thanks,
Lord, holy Father, almighty and eternal God,
through Christ our Lord.

In his Precursor, Saint John the Baptist,
we praise your great glory,

for you consecrated him for a singular honor
among those born of women.

His birth brought great rejoicing;
even in the womb he leapt for joy
at the coming of human salvation.
He alone of all the prophets
pointed out the Lamb of redemption.

And to make holy the flowing waters,
he baptized the very author of Baptism
and was privileged to bear him supreme witness
by the shedding of his blood.

And so, with the Powers of heaven,
we worship you constantly on earth,
and before your majesty
without end we acclaim:
Holy, Holy, Holy Lord God of hosts... *(page 35)*

• TAKING A CLOSER LOOK •

✛ **Repentance**   Because we tend to limit the meaning of
repentance to being sorry for something, repentance is a somewhat inadequate translation of the Greek word *metanoia*, which
describes a change of mind and heart and attitude demanded by
personal conversion (which John the Baptist preached). It demands
a re-forming of our self and our life by turning toward God and away
from the evil forces that pervade our world. It is a lifelong challenge
to order ourselves and our world according to the vision and values
of Jesus and live out the obligations of belonging to his community
of disciples.

COMMUNION ANTIPHON *(Cf. Luke 1:78)*

Through the tender mercy of our God, the Dawn from on high will visit us.

PRAYER AFTER COMMUNION

Having feasted at the banquet of the heavenly Lamb,
we pray, O Lord,
that, finding joy in the nativity of Saint John the Baptist,
your Church may know as the author of her rebirth
the Christ whose coming John foretold.
Who lives and reigns for ever and ever. *Amen.*

BLESSING & DISMISSAL *(page 56)* ❖

• RESPONDING TO THE WORD •

We are called to share in the task of bringing everyone to God.	John the Baptist proclaimed a baptism of repentance.	John's task is to make Jesus known to others.
➨ *What can I do today to draw someone closer to God?*	➨ *For what sins do I want to ask for God's forgiveness today?*	➨ *How can I share my knowledge of Christ today?*

July 1

Are you up to the challenge?

As I began to study Scripture, I was often struck by the many paradoxes I read. It seemed as though Jesus says one thing but means the opposite. He said one would find his life when he loses it. This made my head spin. What did those words mean? What was Jesus trying to teach me?

In today's gospel, Jesus says, "Do not be afraid; just have faith." Here's another paradox: he is challenging me to walk by faith, not by sight, even when I do not understand. Jesus is calling me to believe him when I am searching for and trying to find answers to my questions. I am often a "doubting Thomas." I am beginning to realize that believing Jesus is not just hearing his words but absorbing them. My faith develops and grows as I gain insight from the words and example of Jesus. I begin to understand what's behind and beyond the words he proclaims. I realize there is much more than meets the eye beyond what Jesus is saying.

Today's gospel clearly shows us who Jesus truly is. He is the Son of God. He could sense that "power had gone out from him" when the hemorrhaging woman touched his garment. Yet, he was fully human—another paradox. Jesus is inviting and challenging us to walk in faith. May we begin to live not according to our limited view but by God's limitless possibilities.

◼ **GERRY SOBIE**

ENTRANCE ANTIPHON *(Psalm 47 [46]:2)*

All peoples, clap your hands. Cry to God with shouts of joy!

INTRODUCTORY RITES *(page 10)*

COLLECT

O God, who through the grace of adoption
chose us to be children of light,
grant, we pray,
that we may not be wrapped in the darkness of error
but always be seen to stand in the bright light of truth.
Through our Lord Jesus Christ, your Son,
who lives and reigns with you in the unity of the Holy Spirit,
one God, for ever and ever. *Amen.*

FIRST READING *(Wisdom 1:13-15; 2:23-24)*

God did not make death,
nor does he rejoice in the destruction of the living.
For he fashioned all things that they might have being;
and the creatures of the world are wholesome,
and there is not a destructive drug among them
nor any domain of the netherworld on earth,
for justice is undying.
For God formed man to be imperishable;
the image of his own nature he made him.
But by the envy of the devil, death entered the world,
and they who belong to his company experience it.
The word of the Lord. *Thanks be to God.*

RESPONSORIAL PSALM *(Psalm 30:2, 4, 5-6, 11, 12, 13)*

℟ **I will praise you, Lord, for you have rescued me.**

I will extol you, O LORD, for you drew me clear
  and did not let my enemies rejoice over me.
O LORD, you brought me up from the netherworld;
  you preserved me from among those going down
    into the pit. ℟

Sing praise to the LORD, you his faithful ones,
  and give thanks to his holy name.
For his anger lasts but a moment;
  a lifetime, his good will.
At nightfall, weeping enters in,
  but with the dawn, rejoicing. ℟

Hear, O LORD, and have pity on me;
  O LORD, be my helper.
You changed my mourning into dancing;
  O LORD, my God, forever will I give you thanks. ℟

SECOND READING *(2 Corinthians 8:7, 9, 13-15)*

Brothers and sisters: As you excel in every respect, in faith, discourse, knowledge, all earnestness, and in the love we have for you, may you excel in this gracious act also.

For you know the gracious act of our Lord Jesus Christ, that though he was rich, for your sake he became poor, so that by his poverty you might become rich. Not that others should have relief while you are burdened, but that as a matter of equality your abundance at the present time should supply their needs, so that their abundance may also supply your needs, that there may be equality. As it is written:

Whoever had much did not have more,

and whoever had little did not have less.
The word of the Lord. ***Thanks be to God.***

ALLELUIA *(See 2 Timothy 1:10)*
Alleluia, alleluia. Our Savior Jesus Christ destroyed death
and brought life to light through the Gospel. *Alleluia, alleluia.*

GOSPEL *(Mark 5:21–43)*
For the shorter version, omit the indented part in brackets.

A reading from the holy Gospel according to Mark.
Glory to you, O Lord.

When Jesus had crossed again in the boat to the other side,
a large crowd gathered around him, and he stayed close
to the sea. One of the synagogue officials, named Jairus,* came
forward. Seeing him he fell at his feet and pleaded earnestly with
him, saying, "My daughter is at the point of death. Please, come
lay your hands on her that she may get well and live." He went off
with him, and a large crowd followed him and pressed upon him.

[There was a woman afflicted with hemorrhages for twelve
years. She had suffered greatly at the hands of many doctors
and had spent all that she had. Yet she was not helped but
only grew worse. She had heard about Jesus and came up behind him in the crowd and touched his cloak. She said, "If I
but touch his clothes, I shall be cured." Immediately her flow
of blood dried up. She felt in her body that she was healed of
her affliction. Jesus, aware at once that power had gone out
from him, turned around in the crowd and asked, "Who has
touched my clothes?" But his disciples said to Jesus, "You see
how the crowd is pressing upon you, and yet you ask, 'Who
touched me?'" And he looked around to see who had done it.
The woman, realizing what had happened to her, approached

in fear and trembling. She fell down before Jesus and told him the whole truth. He said to her, "Daughter, **your faith has saved you.** ✝ Go in peace and be cured of your affliction."]

While he was still speaking, people from the synagogue official's house arrived and said, "Your daughter has died; why trouble the teacher any longer?" Disregarding the message that was reported, Jesus said to the synagogue official, "Do not be afraid; just have faith." He did not allow anyone to accompany him inside except Peter, James, and John, the brother of James. When they arrived at the house of the synagogue official, he caught sight of a commotion, people weeping and wailing loudly. So he went in and said to them, "Why this commotion and weeping? The child is not dead but asleep." And they ridiculed him. Then he put them all out. He took along the child's father and mother and those who were with him and entered the room where the child was. He took the child by the hand and said to her, "*Talitha koum*," which means, "Little girl, I say to you, arise!" The girl, a child of twelve, arose immediately and walked around. At that they were utterly astounded. He gave strict orders that no one should know this and said that she should be given something to eat.

The Gospel of the Lord. *Praise to you, Lord Jesus Christ.*

PROFESSION OF FAITH *(page 13)*

PRAYER OF THE FAITHFUL

PREPARATION OF GIFTS *(page 16)*

PRAYER OVER THE OFFERINGS

O God, who graciously accomplish
the effects of your mysteries,
grant, we pray,
that the deeds by which we serve you
may be worthy of these sacred gifts.
Through Christ our Lord. *Amen.*

PREFACE *(Sundays in Ordinary Time, pages 28–32)*

COMMUNION ANTIPHON *(Cf. Psalm 103 [102]:1)*

Bless the Lord, O my soul,
and all within me, his holy name.

Or *(John 17:20–21)*

O Father, I pray for them, that they may be one in us, that the
world may believe that you have sent me, says the Lord.

• TAKING A CLOSER LOOK •

✠ **Your faith has saved you** In Greek, the same word
(*sodzo*) means both heal and save. Thus the gospel writers can
use this word to join physical healing from illness or disease with
spiritual healing from sin (whatever breaks down our relationship
with God). Those who approach Jesus for bodily healing are also
cleansed from spiritual sin and restored to relationship with God
and the community. The outer healing alerts us to the inner reconciliation that happens when we commit ourselves in faith to a
relationship with Jesus.

PRAYER AFTER COMMUNION

May this divine sacrifice we have offered and received
fill us with life, O Lord, we pray,
so that, bound to you in lasting charity,
we may bear fruit that lasts for ever.
Through Christ our Lord. *Amen.*

BLESSING & DISMISSAL *(page 56)* ✢

• RESPONDING TO THE WORD •

God created us
for life and shared
divine life with us.

➡ *When have I most
felt God's life-giving
power at work in me?*

Paul urges us to im-
itate the way Christ
shared his riches
with us and share
our own riches with
those in need.

➡ *What might I do
this week to help meet
someone else's needs?*

Jesus shows great
concern for the sick
child and helps her.

➡ *What might I do
this week to help a
child be more healthy
or free?*

July 8

Suffering for Christ

In serving the Lord, we may find that we are rejected by those closest to us. We may suffer hardships for simply trying to do what is right. Jesus encourages us in these moments. He reminds us that our suffering is not meaningless. In experiencing hurt and isolation, we also come to realize our own limitations, our weaknesses, and our need for God's help. This is the beginning of true maturity in faith.

Like an attentive gardener, God prunes us of the need to seek the approval of others—God rids us of our pride. When we no longer are dependent on the approval of others we become freer to seek God's approval. When God's approval is what our heart seeks, we begin to see the world as God does and have a more accurate understanding of our role in it.

Dependency on the approval of others is a form of pride, which distorts reality, making us less resilient. To suffer for Christ also means to be healed from our pride. We must remember that in our sufferings we remain in good company. Many of the saints suffered slander and persecution by those closest to them. Intimacy with the Lord means we will share in his suffering; but we will also share in greater freedom and ultimately—joy.

■ CHERIDAN SANDERS

ENTRANCE ANTIPHON *(Cf. Psalm 48 [47]:10-11)*

Your merciful love, O God, we have received in the midst of your temple. Your praise, O God, like your name, reaches the ends of the earth; your right hand is filled with saving justice.

INTRODUCTORY RITES *(page 10)*

COLLECT

O God, who in the abasement of your Son
have raised up a fallen world,
fill your faithful with holy joy,
for on those you have rescued from slavery to sin
you bestow eternal gladness.
Through our Lord Jesus Christ, your Son,
who lives and reigns with you in the unity of the Holy Spirit,
one God, for ever and ever. *Amen.*

FIRST READING *(Ezekiel 2:2-5)*

As the Lord spoke to me, the spirit entered into me and set me on my feet, and I heard the one who was speaking say to me: Son of man, I am sending you to the Israelites, rebels who have rebelled against me; they and their ancestors have revolted against me to this very day. Hard of face and obstinate of heart are they to whom I am sending you. But you shall say to them: Thus says the Lord God! And whether they heed or resist—for they are a rebellious house—they shall know that a **prophet**✝ has been among them.

The word of the Lord. *Thanks be to God.*

RESPONSORIAL PSALM *(Psalm 123:1-2, 2, 3-4)*

℟ **Our eyes are fixed on the Lord, pleading for his mercy.**

To you I lift up my eyes
    who are enthroned in heaven—
as the eyes of servants
    are on the hands of their masters. ℟
As the eyes of a maid
    are on the hands of her mistress,
so are our eyes on the LORD, our God,
    till he have pity on us. ℟
Have pity on us, O LORD, have pity on us,
    for we are more than sated with contempt;
our souls are more than sated
    with the mockery of the arrogant,
    with the contempt of the proud. ℟

SECOND READING *(2 Corinthians 12:7-10)*

Brothers and sisters: That I, Paul, might not become too elated, because of the abundance of the revelations, a thorn in the flesh was given to me, an angel of Satan, to beat me, to keep me from being too elated. Three times I begged the Lord about this, that it might leave me, but he said to me, "My grace is sufficient for you, for power is made perfect in weakness." I will rather boast most gladly of my weaknesses, in order that the power of Christ may dwell with me. Therefore, I am content with weaknesses, insults, hardships, persecutions, and constraints, for the sake of Christ; for when I am weak, then I am strong.

The word of the Lord. *Thanks be to God.*

ALLELUIA *(See Luke 4:18)*
Alleluia, alleluia. The Spirit of the Lord is upon me, for he sent me to bring glad tidings to the poor. *Alleluia, alleluia.*

GOSPEL *(Mark 6:1-6)*
A reading from the holy Gospel according to Mark.
Glory to you, O Lord.

Jesus departed from there and came to his native place, accompanied by his disciples. When the sabbath came he began to teach in the synagogue, and many who heard him were astonished. They said, "Where did this man get all this? What kind of wisdom has been given him? What mighty deeds are wrought by his hands! Is he not the carpenter, the son of Mary, and the brother of James and Joses and Judas and Simon? And are not his sisters here with us?" And they took offense at him. Jesus said to them, "A **prophet**✝ is not without honor except in his native place and among his own kin and in his own house." So he was not able to perform any mighty deed there, apart from curing a few sick people by laying his hands on them. He was amazed at their lack of faith.

The Gospel of the Lord. *Praise to you, Lord Jesus Christ.*

PROFESSION OF FAITH *(page 13)*

PRAYER OF THE FAITHFUL

PREPARATION OF GIFTS *(page 16)*

PRAYER OVER THE OFFERINGS

May this oblation dedicated to your name
purify us, O Lord,
and day by day bring our conduct
closer to the life of heaven.
Through Christ our Lord. *Amen.*

PREFACE *(Sundays in Ordinary Time, pages 28–32)*

COMMUNION ANTIPHON

(Psalm 34 [33]:9) Taste and see that the Lord is good; blessed the man who seeks refuge in him.

Or *(Matthew 11:28)*

Come to me, all who labor and are burdened, and I will refresh you, says the Lord.

• TAKING A CLOSER LOOK •

✛ **Prophet** Prophets are those who speak for or on behalf of God to the community. Their major task was not to foretell the future but to forth-tell God's presence in the events affecting their nation. In a world that did not clearly separate issues of religion and politics, the prophets reminded the kings that God was present and active in the political and social crises of the community. Like lobbyists for the rule of God, they demanded that courses of action in times of crisis must follow what God desires and not simply what is most expedient according to human political wisdom.

PRAYER AFTER COMMUNION

Grant, we pray, O Lord,
that, having been replenished by such great gifts,
we may gain the prize of salvation
and never cease to praise you.
Through Christ our Lord. *Amen.*

BLESSING & DISMISSAL *(page 56)* ✣

• RESPONDING TO THE WORD •

Ezekiel is commanded to prophesy even though his audience will be unreceptive.

➡ *What gives me the courage to go on when others are unreceptive to my witness?*

Paul learns the hard way that his weakness is a showcase for God's strength.

➡ *When have my weaknesses been an unexpected source of blessing for me and others around me?*

Jesus' neighbors were unreceptive because they could not see beyond their rigid stereotypes.

➡ *How might I be missing what Jesus is calling me to discover?*

July 15

Share the message of salvation!

It is frustrating to believe that you are right while no one seems to listen.

Watching a friend make life-changing decisions that can lead to misery and ruin, you will find it impossible not to get involved and to offer advice. The warned friend will often stubbornly push ahead in the ruinous direction, showing only resentment for you and your cautionary message. "Don't listen to me, then. You deserve whatever you get," you mutter angrily under your breath.

That is not the message that Jesus imparts to the apostles or to us as he sends us on our mission to spread the good word. We may not be casting out their demons, anointing them, or curing them, but the task that Jesus assigns us is not that different than his direction to the apostles.

Live simply and share the message of salvation as best you can. When that message falls on deaf ears, do not become irate and further harden the hearts of those who refuse to listen. Shake the dust off your feet and leave the path open to try again.

■ FRANK CAMPBELL

ENTRANCE ANTIPHON *(Cf. Psalm 17 [16]:15)*

As for me, in justice I shall behold your face; I shall
be filled with the vision of your glory.

INTRODUCTORY RITES *(page 10)*

COLLECT

O God, who show the light of your truth
to those who go astray,
so that they may return to the right path,
give all who for the faith they profess
are accounted Christians
the grace to reject whatever is contrary to the name of Christ
and to strive after all that does it honor.
Through our Lord Jesus Christ, your Son,
who lives and reigns with you in the unity of the Holy Spirit,
one God, for ever and ever. *Amen.*

FIRST READING *(Amos 7:12-15)*

Amaziah,* priest of **Bethel**,† said to Amos, "Off with you,
visionary, flee to the land of Judah! There earn your bread
by prophesying, but never again prophesy in Bethel; for it is the
king's sanctuary and a royal temple." Amos answered Amaziah,
"I was no prophet, nor have I belonged to a company of prophets; I was a shepherd and a dresser of sycamores. The LORD took
me from following the flock, and said to me, Go, prophesy to my
people Israel."

The word of the Lord. *Thanks be to God.*

RESPONSORIAL PSALM *(Psalm 85:9-10, 11-12, 13-14)*
℟ Lord, let us see your kindness and grant us your salvation.

I will hear what God proclaims;
  the LORD—for he proclaims peace.
Near indeed is his salvation to those who fear him,
  glory dwelling in our land. ℟
Kindness and truth shall meet;
  justice and peace shall kiss.
Truth shall spring out of the earth,
  and justice shall look down from heaven. ℟
The LORD himself will give his benefits;
  our land shall yield its increase.
Justice shall walk before him,
  and prepare the way of his steps. ℟

SECOND READING *(Ephesians 1:3-14)*
The shorter version ends at the asterisks.

Blessed be the God and Father of our Lord Jesus Christ,
who has blessed us in Christ with every spiritual blessing
in the heavens, as he chose us in him, before the foundation of
the world, to be holy and without blemish before him. In love
he destined us for adoption to himself through Jesus Christ,
in accord with the favor of his will, for the praise of the glory
of his grace that he granted us in the beloved. In him we have
redemption by his blood, the forgiveness of transgressions, in
accord with the riches of his grace that he lavished upon us. In
all wisdom and insight, he has made known to us the mystery of
his will in accord with his favor that he set forth in him as a plan
for the fullness of times, to sum up all things in Christ, in heaven
and on earth.

* * *

In him we were also chosen, destined in accord with the purpose of the One who accomplishes all things according to the intention of his will, so that we might exist for the praise of his glory, we who first hoped in Christ. In him you also, who have heard the word of truth, the gospel of your salvation, and have believed in him, were sealed with the promised Holy Spirit, which is the first installment of our inheritance toward redemption as God's possession, to the praise of his glory.

The word of the Lord. *Thanks be to God.*

ALLELUIA *(See Ephesians 1:17–18)*
Alleluia, alleluia. May the Father of our Lord Jesus Christ enlighten the eyes of our hearts, that we may know what is the hope that belongs to our call. *Alleluia, alleluia.*

GOSPEL *(Mark 6:7–13)*
A reading from the holy Gospel according to Mark.
Glory to you, O Lord.

Jesus summoned the Twelve and began to send them out two by two and gave them authority over unclean spirits. He instructed them to take nothing for the journey but a walking stick—no food, no sack, no money in their belts. They were, however, to wear sandals but not a second tunic. He said to them, "Wherever you enter a house, stay there until you leave. Whatever place does not welcome you or listen to you, leave there and shake the dust off your feet in testimony against them." So they went off and preached repentance. The Twelve drove out many demons, and they anointed with oil many who were sick and cured them.

The Gospel of the Lord. *Praise to you, Lord Jesus Christ.*

PROFESSION OF FAITH *(page 13)*

PRAYER OF THE FAITHFUL

PREPARATION OF GIFTS *(page 16)*

PRAYER OVER THE OFFERINGS

Look upon the offerings of the Church, O Lord,
as she makes her prayer to you,
and grant that, when consumed by those who believe,
they may bring ever greater holiness.
Through Christ our Lord. *Amen.*

PREFACE *(Sundays in Ordinary Time, pages 28–32)*

❖ TAKING A CLOSER LOOK ❖

✚ **Bethel** Located about fourteen miles north of Jerusalem, Bethel (Hebrew, "house of God") was a sacred site dating back to the time of Abraham, who built an altar there (Genesis 12:8) and Jacob, who had his famous dream there of the ladder to heaven (Genesis 28:10-20). It was a place for worship, national assembly, and prophetic activity before these functions were taken over by Jerusalem and its temple under King David.

COMMUNION ANTIPHON *(Cf. Psalm 84 [83]:4-5)*

The sparrow finds a home, and the swallow a nest for her young:
by your altars, O Lord of hosts, my King and my God. Blessed
are they who dwell in your house, for ever singing your praise.

Or *(John 6:57)*

Whoever eats my flesh and drinks my blood remains in me and I
in him, says the Lord.

PRAYER AFTER COMMUNION

Having consumed these gifts, we pray, O Lord,
that, by our participation in this mystery,
its saving effects upon us may grow.
Through Christ our Lord. ***Amen.***

BLESSING & DISMISSAL *(page 56)* ❖

❖ RESPONDING TO THE WORD ❖

Amos recounts how God came to him amidst his regular job and commissioned him to witness.	Paul reminds us that God has chosen us, adopted us, and lavished many gifts on us.	Jesus commissions the disciples to begin sharing in Christ's work.
➡ *When has God's presence in my regular tasks prompted me to do something new?*	➡ *For which gifts am I especially thankful today?*	➡ *To whom is Christ sending me now to bring his healing power?*

July 22

The Lord is my Shepherd...

Today we hear the beloved twenty-third psalm, "The Lord is my Shepherd." On my desk, I have a memorial card with this psalm and a picture of my friend Melvin, a member of L'Arche for 33 years. In L'Arche, we normally conclude dinner by reciting the Lord's Prayer, but Melvin was Jewish and his housemates chose to stand with him in solidarity by reciting this psalm that Melvin loved.

Melvin had an intellectual disability. He also had the heart of a shepherd. He discovered his longing to help people who are poor when serving meals at the Good Shepherd refuge. He worked daily for many years at the food bank, traveling by bus and subway each way. People there loved him for his kindness and humor.

What does it mean to declare that the Lord is our Shepherd and we shall lack nothing? Is it really true, or are these just beautiful words? Of course we will lack at times, perhaps desperately. In today's gospel, Jesus and his followers badly needed a rest, but Jesus finds the compassion to teach the crowd. The answer is that even at such times, God feeds us and leads us by still waters in our innermost being, but it may take us some time to discover and trust in this. Let us give thanks for God's faithfulness.

■ BETH PORTER

ENTRANCE ANTIPHON *(Psalm 54 [53]:6, 8)*

See, I have God for my help. The Lord sustains my
soul. I will sacrifice to you with willing heart, and
praise your name, O Lord, for it is good.

INTRODUCTORY RITES *(page 10)*

COLLECT

Show favor, O Lord, to your servants
and mercifully increase the gifts of your grace,
that, made fervent in hope, faith and charity,
they may be ever watchful in keeping your commands.
Through our Lord Jesus Christ, your Son,
who lives and reigns with you in the unity of the Holy Spirit,
one God, for ever and ever. *Amen.*

FIRST READING *(Jeremiah 23:1-6)*

Woe to the shepherds who mislead and scatter the flock of
my pasture, says the LORD. Therefore, thus says the LORD,
the God of Israel, against the shepherds who shepherd my people:
You have scattered my sheep and driven them away. You have not
cared for them, but I will take care to punish your evil deeds.
I myself will gather the remnant of my flock from all the lands to
which I have driven them and bring them back to their meadow;
there they shall increase and multiply. I will appoint shepherds
for them who will shepherd them so that they need no longer fear
and tremble; and none shall be missing, says the LORD.

Behold, the days are coming, says the LORD,
    when I will raise up a righteous shoot to David;
as king he shall reign and govern wisely,
    he shall do what is just and right in the land.
In his days Judah shall be saved,

Israel shall dwell in security.
This is the name they give him:
"The LORD our justice."
The word of the Lord. *Thanks be to God.*

RESPONSORIAL PSALM *(Psalm 23:1-3, 3-4, 5, 6)*

R̸ The Lord is my shepherd; there is nothing I shall want.

The LORD is my shepherd; I shall not want.
In verdant pastures he gives me repose;
beside restful waters he leads me;
he refreshes my soul. R̸
He guides me in right paths
for his name's sake.
Even though I walk in the dark valley
I fear no evil; for you are at my side
with your rod and your staff
that give me courage. R̸
You spread the table before me
in the sight of my foes;
you anoint my head with oil;
my cup overflows. R̸
Only goodness and kindness follow me
all the days of my life;
and I shall dwell in the house of the LORD
for years to come. R̸

SECOND READING *(Ephesians 2:13-18)*

Brothers and sisters: In Christ Jesus you who once were far
off have become near by the blood of Christ.

For he is our peace, he who made both one and broke down
the dividing wall of enmity, through his flesh, abolishing the law

with its commandments and legal claims, that he might create in himself one new person in place of the two, thus establishing peace, and might reconcile both with God, in one body, through the cross, putting that enmity to death by it. He came and preached peace to you who were far off and peace to those who were near, for through him we both have access in one Spirit to the Father.

The word of the Lord. *Thanks be to God.*

ALLELUIA *(John 10:27)*
Alleluia, alleluia. My sheep hear my voice, says the Lord; I know them, and they follow me. *Alleluia, alleluia.*

GOSPEL *(Mark 6:30–34)*
A reading from the holy Gospel according to Mark.
Glory to you, O Lord.

The apostles gathered together with Jesus and reported all they had done and taught. He said to them, "Come away by yourselves to a deserted place and rest a while." People were coming and going in great numbers, and they had no opportunity even to eat. So they went off in the boat by themselves to a deserted place. People saw them leaving and many came to know about it. They hastened there on foot from all the towns and arrived at the place before them.

When he disembarked and saw the vast crowd, his heart was moved with **pity**[+] for them, for they were like sheep without a shepherd; and he began to teach them many things.

The Gospel of the Lord. *Praise to you, Lord Jesus Christ.*

PROFESSION OF FAITH *(page 13)*

PRAYER OF THE FAITHFUL

PREPARATION OF GIFTS *(page 16)*

PRAYER OVER THE OFFERINGS
O God, who in the one perfect sacrifice
brought to completion varied offerings of the law,
accept, we pray, this sacrifice from your faithful servants
and make it holy, as you blessed the gifts of Abel,
so that what each has offered to the honor of your majesty
may benefit the salvation of all.
Through Christ our Lord. *Amen.*

PREFACE *(Sundays in Ordinary Time, pages 28-32)*

✦ TAKING A CLOSER LOOK ✦

✚ **Pity** Pity, in its common modern sense of "to feel sorry for someone," is not a very good translation of what Jesus feels here. The Greek word is much closer to our sense of compassion, that is, a strong emotional reaction that is felt deep within in response to someone else's difficulty or suffering. This strong sense of compassion is the springboard that launches Jesus into action. Thus it echoes the divine compassion that prompted God to come down to deliver the people from their Egyptian oppressors (see Exodus 3:7).

COMMUNION ANTIPHON *(Psalm 111 [110]:4-5)*
The Lord, the gracious, the merciful,
has made a memorial of his wonders; he gives food to those
who fear him.

Or *(Revelation 3:20)*
Behold, I stand at the door and knock, says the Lord. If anyone
hears my voice and opens the door to me, I will enter his house
and dine with him, and he with me.

PRAYER AFTER COMMUNION
Graciously be present to your people, we pray, O Lord,
and lead those you have imbued with heavenly mysteries
to pass from former ways to newness of life.
Through Christ our Lord. *Amen.*

BLESSING & DISMISSAL *(page 56)* ❖

❖ RESPONDING TO THE WORD ❖

God's example instructs us that we must have both justice and compassion.

❖ What might I do today to be more just and compassionate toward others?

The Holy Spirit helps us to pray when we don't know how.

❖ For what help with my prayer do I ask the Holy Spirit today?

Jesus tells us that God's presence (kingdom) often starts out very small but can grow very large.

❖ How has my awareness of God grown recently?

July 29

Jesus knows what we need

In today's gospel, Jesus demonstrates his great compassion for us. Having created us to be both material and spiritual in nature, he knows intimately the needs of both our bodies and souls.

We hear that a great crowd was following Jesus. He fed their souls by giving them hope. As the most perfect parent, however, he also cared for their bodies, feeding them with miraculous, overflowing generosity.

Jesus proves that his love for us is not just a theory, but also something tangible. What did the people in the crowd do to receive Jesus' generosity? They followed him closely and gave him all they had: five loaves and two fishes. No doubt this humble offering seemed woefully inadequate, but they brought it nonetheless. Jesus transformed it beyond all expectations.

Let us then try to remember to stay close to him, to completely trust him, and to give him everything we have, even if it is very humble. He is the One who cares for us more than we can imagine. He takes five loaves and two fishes and turns them into a banquet. As did King David, let us pray the words of today's psalm: "Let all your works give you thanks, O Lord, and let your faithful ones bless you."

■ **NATALIA LJAHOVIC**

JUL 29

ENTRANCE ANTIPHON *(Cf. Psalm 68 [67]:6-7, 36)*

God is in his holy place, God who unites those
who dwell in his house; he himself gives might and
strength to his people.

INTRODUCTORY RITES *(page 10)*

COLLECT

O God, protector of those who hope in you,
without whom nothing has firm foundation, nothing is holy,
bestow in abundance your mercy upon us
and grant that, with you as our ruler and guide,
we may use the good things that pass
in such a way as to hold fast even now
to those that ever endure.
Through our Lord Jesus Christ, your Son,
who lives and reigns with you in the unity of the Holy Spirit,
one God, for ever and ever. *Amen.*

FIRST READING *(2 Kings 4:42-44)*

A man came from Baal-shalishah* bringing to Elisha, the man
of God, twenty **barley loaves**✝ made from the firstfruits,
and fresh grain in the ear. Elisha said, "Give it to the people
to eat." But his servant objected, "How can I set this before a
hundred people?" Elisha insisted, "Give it to the people to eat."
"For thus says the LORD, 'They shall eat and there shall be some
left over.'" And when they had eaten, there was some left over, as
the LORD had said.

The word of the Lord. *Thanks be to God.*

RESPONSORIAL PSALM *(Psalm 145:10-11, 15-16, 17-18)*
R̶ The hand of the Lord feeds us; he answers all our needs.

Let all your works give you thanks, O LORD,
    and let your faithful ones bless you.
Let them discourse of the glory of your kingdom
    and speak of your might. R̶
The eyes of all look hopefully to you,
    and you give them their food in due season;
you open your hand
    and satisfy the desire of every living thing. R̶
The LORD is just in all his ways
    and holy in all his works.
The LORD is near to all who call upon him,
    to all who call upon him in truth. R̶

SECOND READING *(Ephesians 4:1-6)*

B rothers and sisters: I, a prisoner for the Lord, urge you to
   live in a manner worthy of the call you have received, with
all humility and gentleness, with patience, bearing with one
another through love, striving to preserve the unity of the spirit
through the bond of peace: one body and one Spirit, as you were
also called to the one hope of your call; one Lord, one faith, one
baptism; one God and Father of all, who is over all and through
all and in all.

    The word of the Lord. *Thanks be to God.*

ALLELUIA *(Luke 7:16)*
Alleluia, alleluia. A great prophet has risen in our midst.
God has visited his people. *Alleluia, alleluia.*

GOSPEL *(John 6:1-15)*

A reading from the holy Gospel according to John.

Glory to you, O Lord.

Jesus went across the Sea of Galilee. A large crowd followed him, because they saw the signs he was performing on the sick. Jesus went up on the mountain, and there he sat down with his disciples. The Jewish feast of Passover was near. When Jesus raised his eyes and saw that a large crowd was coming to him, he said to Philip, "Where can we buy enough food for them to eat?" He said this to test him, because he himself knew what he was going to do. Philip answered him, "Two hundred days' wages worth of food would not be enough for each of them to have a little." One of his disciples, Andrew, the brother of Simon Peter, said to him, "There is a boy here who has five **barley loaves**✝ and two fish; but what good are these for so many?" Jesus said, "Have the people recline." Now there was a great deal of grass in that place. So the men reclined, about five thousand in number. Then Jesus took the loaves, gave thanks, and distributed them to those who were reclining, and also as much of the fish as they wanted. When they had had their fill, he said to his disciples, "Gather the fragments left over, so that nothing will be wasted." So they collected them, and filled twelve wicker baskets with fragments from the five barley loaves that had been more than they could eat. When the people saw the sign he had done, they said, "This is truly the Prophet, the one who is to come into the world." Since Jesus knew that they were going to come and carry him off to make him king, he withdrew again to the mountain alone.

The Gospel of the Lord. *Praise to you, Lord Jesus Christ.*

PROFESSION OF FAITH *(page 13)*

PRAYER OF THE FAITHFUL

PREPARATION OF GIFTS *(page 16)*

PRAYER OVER THE OFFERINGS
Accept, O Lord, we pray, the offerings
which we bring from the abundance of your gifts,
that through the powerful working of your grace
these most sacred mysteries may sanctify our present way of life
and lead us to eternal gladness.
Through Christ our Lord. *Amen.*

PREFACE *(Sundays in Ordinary Time, pages 28–32)*

• TAKING A CLOSER LOOK •

✝ **Barley loaves** Barley was one of the two main Palestinian grain crops, along with wheat. It was planted in the autumn and harvested in April, a month or so earlier than wheat. At the end of the harvest was the feast of Pentecost. The bread made from barley was coarser than wheat bread, and it was much more commonly used among the poorer people. Since barley was so important for the poor, any failure of the barley crop brought much hardship.

COMMUNION ANTIPHON *(Psalm 103 [102]: 2)*

Bless the Lord, O my soul, and never forget all his benefits.

Or *(Matthew 5:7–8)*

Blessed are the merciful, for they shall receive mercy. Blessed are the clean of heart, for they shall see God.

PRAYER AFTER COMMUNION

We have consumed, O Lord, this divine Sacrament,
the perpetual memorial of the Passion of your Son;
grant, we pray, that this gift,
which he himself gave us with love beyond all telling,
may profit us for salvation.
Through Christ our Lord. *Amen.*

BLESSING & DISMISSAL *(page 56)* ✤

❖ RESPONDING TO THE WORD ❖

Elisha is not worried that sharing will exhaust his resources.

➡ *When have I experienced someone else's gift of generosity after I have been generous with others?*

Paul notes many ways in which we are united.

➡ *Which sign of unity is most important to me? Why?*

Jesus' wondrous sharing of bread leaves everyone satisfied.

➡ *When has my sharing of the Eucharist left me feeling especially nourished?*

August 5

What are we hungry for?

I remember my difficult, three-day ski mountaineering trek with a friend where we encountered many challenges. We used up our food supply sooner than expected. On the third day, carrying a heavy pack and skiing our way back to our starting point, the only thing we had left to eat was a sweet pudding powder. I experienced a sugar rush, but half an hour later, I was just as famished as before.

What do we really feed on? Success? Being accepted by others? Perfectionism? Financial security? Status? These things may give us a "sugar rush," but they leave us just as hungry as before.

Today's gospel reading invites us to seek what nourishes us, to strive after "the bread of God...which comes down from heaven and gives life to the world."

This life-giving food is a free gift. But how do we access this gift? Jesus tells each one of us today, "whoever comes to me will never hunger." Every day, as we grow in our personal relationship with the Lord, the words of today's psalm can ring true for each one of us. The Lord wants to give us food "in abundance" so that we can proclaim the "glorious deeds of the LORD" in our daily lives.

◼ EMMANUEL MARTEL

ENTRANCE ANTIPHON *(Psalm 70 [69]:2, 6)*
O God, come to my assistance; O Lord, make haste
to help me! You are my rescuer, my help; O Lord,
do not delay.

INTRODUCTORY RITES *(page 10)*

COLLECT
Draw near to your servants, O Lord,
and answer their prayers with unceasing kindness,
that, for those who glory in you as their Creator and guide,
you may restore what you have created
and keep safe what you have restored.
Through our Lord Jesus Christ, your Son,
who lives and reigns with you in the unity of the Holy Spirit,
one God, for ever and ever. *Amen.*

FIRST READING *(Exodus 16:2-4, 12-15)*

The whole Israelite community grumbled against Moses and
Aaron. The Israelites said to them, "Would that we had
died at the LORD's hand in the land of Egypt, as we sat by our
fleshpots and ate our fill of bread! But you had to lead us into
this desert to make the whole community die of famine!"

Then the LORD said to Moses, "I will now rain down bread
from heaven for you. Each day the people are to go out and
gather their daily portion; thus will I test them, to see whether
they follow my instructions or not.

"I have heard the grumbling of the Israelites. Tell them: In the
evening twilight you shall eat flesh, and in the morning you shall
have your fill of bread, so that you may know that I, the LORD,
am your God."

In the evening quail came up and covered the camp. In the morning a dew lay all about the camp, and when the dew evaporated, there on the surface of the desert were fine flakes like hoarfrost on the ground. On seeing it, the Israelites asked one another, "What is this?" for they did not know what it was. But Moses told them, "This is the bread that the LORD has given you to eat."

The word of the Lord. *Thanks be to God.*

RESPONSORIAL PSALM *(Psalm 78:3-4, 23-24, 25, 54)*

℟ **The Lord gave them bread from heaven.**

What we have heard and know,
  and what our fathers have declared to us,
We will declare to the generation to come
  the glorious deeds of the LORD and his strength
  and the **wonders**✝ that he wrought. ℟

He commanded the skies above
  and opened the doors of heaven;
he rained manna upon them for food
  and gave them heavenly bread. ℟

Man ate the bread of angels,
  food he sent them in abundance.
And he brought them to his holy land,
  to the mountains his right hand had won. ℟

SECOND READING *(Ephesians 4:17, 20-24)*

Brothers and sisters: I declare and testify in the Lord that you must no longer live as the Gentiles do, in the futility of their minds; that is not how you learned Christ, assuming that you have heard of him and were taught in him, as truth is in Jesus, that you should put away the old self of your former way of life, corrupted through deceitful desires, and be renewed in the spirit of your minds, and put on the new self, created in God's way in righteousness and holiness of truth.

The word of the Lord. ***Thanks be to God.***

ALLELUIA *(Matthew 4:4b)*

Alleluia, alleluia. One does not live on bread alone, but on every word that comes forth from the mouth of God. *Alleluia, alleluia.*

GOSPEL *(John 6:24–35)*

A reading from the holy Gospel according to John.

Glory to you, O Lord.

When the crowd saw that neither Jesus nor his disciples were there, they themselves got into boats and came to Capernaum* looking for Jesus. And when they found him across the sea they said to him, "Rabbi, when did you get here?" Jesus answered them and said, "Amen, amen, I say to you, you are looking for me not because you saw **signs**✝ but because you ate the loaves and were filled. Do not work for food that perishes but for the food that endures for eternal life, which the Son of Man will give you. For on him the Father, God, has set his seal." So they said to him, "What can we do to accomplish the works of God?" Jesus answered and said to them, "This is the work of God, that you believe in the one he sent." So they said to him, "What sign can you do, that we may see and believe in you? What can you do? Our ancestors ate manna in the desert, as it is written: *He gave them bread from heaven to eat.*" So Jesus said to them, "Amen, amen, I say to you, it was not Moses who gave the bread from heaven; my Father gives you the true bread from heaven. For the bread of God is that which comes down from heaven and gives life to the world."

So they said to him, "Sir, give us this bread always." Jesus said to them, "I am the bread of life; whoever comes to me will never hunger, and whoever believes in me will never thirst."

The Gospel of the Lord. *Praise to you, Lord Jesus Christ.*

PROFESSION OF FAITH *(page 13)*

PRAYER OF THE FAITHFUL

PREPARATION OF GIFTS *(page 16)*

PRAYER OVER THE OFFERINGS

Graciously sanctify these gifts, O Lord, we pray,
and, accepting the oblation of this spiritual sacrifice,
make of us an eternal offering to you.
Through Christ our Lord. *Amen.*

PREFACE *(Sundays in Ordinary Time, pages 28–32)*

• TAKING A CLOSER LOOK •

✦ **Signs and wonders** Although we use the word 'miracle' to describe these events, the biblical writers used the terms "deeds of power," "signs," and "wonders." These are God's actions to re-order our world from the domination of Satan and evil powers that frustrate God's plan for a covenant community. Jesus' deeds of power are directly related to his kingdom message. They are the first signs (his resurrection to new life will be the final sign) that God is reordering our world. Like Jesus' parables and meals, Jesus' cures, exorcisms, and resuscitations are signs of God's presence breaking into our world to change it forever.

COMMUNION ANTIPHON *(Wisdom 16:20)*
You have given us, O Lord, bread from heaven, endowed with all
delights and sweetness in every taste.

Or *(John 6:35)*
I am the bread of life, says the Lord; whoever comes to me will
not hunger and whoever believes in me will not thirst.

PRAYER AFTER COMMUNION
Accompany with constant protection, O Lord,
those you renew with these heavenly gifts
and, in your never-failing care for them,
make them worthy of eternal redemption.
Through Christ our Lord. *Amen.*

BLESSING & DISMISSAL *(page 56)* ✢

• RESPONDING TO THE WORD •

God feeds the Israelites in the wilderness.	**Paul encourages us to adopt a new way of life modeled on Christ.**	**Jesus says he is the bread that gives us life.**
➡ *When has God provided for me in recent weeks?*	➡ *What might I do to be more like Christ today?*	➡ *How has Jesus nourished my life this week?*

August 12

True manna

We live in a world where suffering manifests itself in many ways, including the hunger for necessities like food, shelter, and work. Our suffering and hunger are not only material but also spiritual. Today's gospel recounts the doubts the Jews had upon hearing Jesus' testimony about being the bread of life for those who believe in him. While the physical and superficial define many aspects of our lives, this gospel inspires us to reflect on whether temporary fixes will truly satisfy our hunger and suffering. We need our faith in God, our refuge and redemption, to ultimately feed and sustain us on our journey to be with God in heaven.

Jesus highlights the power of faith that nourishes beyond the material sense of manna, the bread provided by God from heaven that sustained the Israelites in the wilderness. Jesus offers himself as the *true* manna—the Eucharist, the foundation of our spiritual life. He reveals that those who believe in him and take the Eucharist as the living bread will transcend the suffering in this world and live on with him in eternal life.

Even amidst our struggles and suffering, may we find the nourishment, faith, and hope in the true manna—Jesus and his promise of salvation.

■ CHRISTL DABU

ENTRANCE ANTIPHON *(Cf. Psalm 74 [73]:20, 19, 22, 23)*
Look to your covenant, O Lord, and forget not the
life of your poor ones for ever. Arise, O God, and
defend your cause, and forget not the cries of those
who seek you.

INTRODUCTORY RITES *(page 10)*

COLLECT
Almighty ever-living God,
whom, taught by the Holy Spirit,
we dare to call our Father,
bring, we pray, to perfection in our hearts
the spirit of adoption as your sons and daughters,
that we may merit to enter into the inheritance
which you have promised.
Through our Lord Jesus Christ, your Son,
who lives and reigns with you in the unity of the Holy Spirit,
one God, for ever and ever. *Amen.*

FIRST READING *(1 Kings 19:4-8)*
Elijah went a day's journey into the desert, until he came
to a broom tree and sat beneath it. He prayed for death
saying: "This is enough, O LORD! Take my life, for I am no
better than my fathers." He lay down and fell asleep under the
broom tree, but then an **angel**✝ touched him and ordered him
to get up and eat. Elijah looked and there at his head was a
hearth cake and a jug of water. After he ate and drank, he lay
down again, but the angel of the LORD came back a second
time, touched him, and ordered, "Get up and eat, else the
journey will be too long for you!" He got up, ate, and drank;

then strengthened by that food, he walked forty days and forty nights to the mountain of God, Horeb.

The word of the Lord. *Thanks be to God.*

RESPONSORIAL PSALM *(Psalm 34:2-3, 4-5, 6-7, 8-9)*

R. Taste and see the goodness of the Lord.

I will bless the LORD at all times;
    his praise shall be ever in my mouth.
Let my soul glory in the LORD;
    the lowly will hear me and be glad. R.
Glorify the LORD with me,
    let us together extol his name.
I sought the LORD, and he answered me
    and delivered me from all my fears. R.
Look to him that you may be radiant with joy,
    and your faces may not blush with shame.
When the afflicted man called out, the LORD heard,
    and from all his distress he saved him. R.
The **angel**✝ of the LORD encamps
    around those who fear him and delivers them.
Taste and see how good the LORD is;
    blessed the man who takes refuge in him. R.

SECOND READING *(Ephesians 4:30–5:2)*

Brothers and sisters: Do not grieve the Holy Spirit of God, with which you were sealed for the day of redemption. All bitterness, fury, anger, shouting, and reviling must be removed from you, along with all malice. And be kind to one another, compassionate, forgiving one another as God has forgiven you in Christ.

So be imitators of God, as beloved children, and live in love, as Christ loved us and handed himself over for us as a sacrificial offering to God for a fragrant aroma.

The word of the Lord. *Thanks be to God.*

ALLELUIA *(John 6:51)*
Alleluia, alleluia. I am the living bread that came down from heaven, says the Lord; whoever eats this bread will live forever. *Alleluia, alleluia.*

GOSPEL *(John 6:41-51)*
A reading from the holy Gospel according to John.
Glory to you, O Lord.

The Jews murmured about Jesus because he said, "I am the bread that came down from heaven," and they said, "Is this not Jesus, the son of Joseph? Do we not know his father and mother? Then how can he say, 'I have come down from heaven'?" Jesus answered and said to them, "Stop murmuring among yourselves. No one can come to me unless the Father who sent me draw him, and I will raise him on the last day. It is written in the prophets: *They shall all be taught by God.* Everyone who listens to my Father and learns from him comes to me. Not that anyone has seen the Father except the one who is from God; he has seen the Father. Amen, amen, I say to you, whoever believes has eternal life. I am the bread of life. Your ancestors ate the manna in the desert, but they died; this is the bread that comes down from heaven so that one may eat it and not die. I am the living bread that came down from heaven; whoever eats this bread will live forever; and the bread that I will give is my flesh for the life of the world."

The Gospel of the Lord. *Praise to you, Lord Jesus Christ.*

PROFESSION OF FAITH *(page 13)*

PRAYER OF THE FAITHFUL

PREPARATION OF GIFTS *(page 16)*

PRAYER OVER THE OFFERINGS
Be pleased, O Lord, to accept the offerings of your Church,
for in your mercy you have given them to be offered
and by your power you transform them
into the mystery of our salvation.
Through Christ our Lord. *Amen.*

PREFACE *(Sundays in Ordinary Time, pages 28-32)*

• TAKING A CLOSER LOOK •

✣ **Angel** An angel (Greek, *angelos*) was a spiritual messenger sent by God for a particular purpose. Sometimes angels conveyed information, while at other times they carried out God's judgment or punishment. Especially in the earlier books of the Old Testament, it is not always clear whether the angel of the Lord is the form that God takes to interact with humans or is actually a different being from God. By the New Testament time, angels were thought of as distinct spiritual beings whose task was to serve God by their heavenly worship and by sharing in God's struggle against evil.

COMMUNION ANTIPHON *(Psalm 147:12, 14)*

O Jerusalem, glorify the Lord, who gives you your fill of finest wheat.

Or *(Cf. John 6:51)*

The bread that I will give, says the Lord, is my flesh for the life of the world.

PRAYER AFTER COMMUNION

May the communion in your Sacrament
that we have consumed, save us, O Lord,
and confirm us in the light of your truth.
Through Christ our Lord. *Amen.*

BLESSING & DISMISSAL *(page 56)* ❖

• RESPONDING TO THE WORD •

Elijah was nourished by God when he thought his troubles were too great.	Paul urges us to eliminate bitterness and grow in compassion.	Jesus promises to nourish us with his life.
➡ How has God strengthened me in times of trouble?	➡ What bitterness keeps me from being more compassionate toward someone?	➡ When has my participation in the Eucharist been especially life-giving?

August 15

A promise of transformation

Both Mary and Elizabeth were in peculiar situations. Neither should be with child, according to the wisdom of this world. But they welcomed these unexpected events as gifts from God. Their greetings were exuberant. Mary, unwed and pregnant, came to assist her older cousin Elizabeth during the final months. From this young woman comes a hymn of praise for a God whose promises are great.

We read the Magnificat on the feast of the Assumption of Mary. The song reminds us that we do not wait for death to enter into God's presence.

We belong to God already. God is not distant, but moves through our lives in the most personal of ways. God also speaks to the world in words far from neutral or detached. The broken and forgotten are lifted up. Those secure in their own sufficiency are strangely empty. The power that seems ultimate collapses before God's truth.

Mary and Elizabeth—young and old—trusted you. God, help me to believe that this promise of transformation and justice includes me and our world today.

■ **JEANNE SCHULER**

MASS DURING THE DAY

ENTRANCE ANTIPHON *(Cf. Revelation 12:1)*

A great sign appeared in heaven: a woman clothed
with the sun, and the moon beneath her feet, and
on her head a crown of twelve stars.

Or

Let us all rejoice in the Lord, as we celebrate the feast day in
honor of the Virgin Mary, at whose Assumption the Angels
rejoice and praise the Son of God.

INTRODUCTORY RITES *(page 10)*

COLLECT

Almighty ever-living God,
who assumed the Immaculate Virgin Mary, the Mother of your Son,
body and soul into heavenly glory,
grant, we pray,
that, always attentive to the things that are above,
we may merit to be sharers of her glory.
Through our Lord Jesus Christ, your Son,
who lives and reigns with you in the unity of the Holy Spirit,
one God, for ever and ever. *Amen.*

FIRST READING *(Revelation 11:19a; 12:1-6a, 10ab)*

God's temple in heaven was opened, and the ark of his covenant could be seen in the temple.

A great sign appeared in the sky, a woman clothed with the sun,
with the moon under her feet, and on her head a crown of twelve
stars. She was with child and wailed aloud in pain as she labored
to give birth. Then another sign appeared in the sky; it was a huge

red dragon, with seven heads and ten horns, and on its heads were seven diadems. Its tail swept away a third of the stars in the sky and hurled them down to the earth. Then the dragon stood before the woman about to give birth, to devour her child when she gave birth. She gave birth to a son, a male child, destined to rule all the nations with an iron rod. Her child was caught up to God and his throne. The woman herself fled into the desert where she had a place prepared by God.

Then I heard a loud voice in heaven say:
"Now have salvation and power come,
    and the Kingdom of our God
    and the authority of his Anointed One."
The word of the Lord. *Thanks be to God.*

RESPONSORIAL PSALM *(Psalm 45:10, 11, 12, 16)*
℟ **The queen stands at your right hand, arrayed in gold.**

The queen takes her place at your right hand in gold of Ophir. ℟
Hear, O daughter, and see; turn your ear,
    forget your people and your father's house. ℟
So shall the king desire your beauty;
    for he is your lord. ℟
They are borne in with gladness and joy;
    they enter the palace of the king. ℟

SECOND READING *(1 Corinthians 15:20-27)*

Brothers and sisters: Christ has been raised from the dead, the firstfruits⁺ of those who have fallen asleep. For since death came through man, the resurrection of the dead came also through man. For just as in Adam all die, so too in Christ shall all be brought to life, but each one in proper order: Christ the firstfruits; then, at his coming, those who belong to Christ; then comes the end, when he hands over the Kingdom to his God and Father, when he has destroyed every sovereignty and every authority and power. For he must reign until he has put all his enemies under his feet. The last enemy to be destroyed is death, for "he subjected everything under his feet."

The word of the Lord. *Thanks be to God.*

ALLELUIA

Alleluia, alleluia. Mary is taken up to heaven; a chorus of angels exults. *Alleluia, alleluia.*

GOSPEL *(Luke 1:39-56)*

A reading from the holy Gospel according to Luke.
Glory to you, O Lord.

Mary set out and traveled to the hill country in haste to a town of Judah, where she entered the house of Zechariah* and greeted Elizabeth. When Elizabeth heard Mary's greeting, the infant leaped in her womb, and Elizabeth, filled with the Holy Spirit, cried out in a loud voice and said, "Blessed are you among women, and blessed is the fruit of your womb. And how does this happen to me, that the mother of my Lord should come to me? For at the moment the sound of your greeting reached my ears, the infant in my womb leaped for joy. Blessed are you who believed that what was spoken to you by the Lord would be fulfilled."

And Mary said:

"My soul proclaims the greatness of the Lord;
    my spirit rejoices in God my Savior
    for he has looked with favor on his lowly servant.
From this day all generations will call me blessed:
    the Almighty has done great things for me
    and holy is his Name.

He has mercy on those who fear him
in every generation.
He has shown the strength of his arm,
and has scattered the proud in their conceit.
He has cast down the mighty from their thrones,
and has lifted up the lowly.
He has filled the hungry with good things,
and the rich he has sent away empty.
He has come to the help of his servant Israel
for he has remembered his promise of mercy,
the promise he made to our fathers,
to Abraham and his children forever."

Mary remained with her about three months and then returned
to her home.

The Gospel of the Lord. *Praise to you, Lord Jesus Christ.*

PROFESSION OF FAITH *(page 13)*

PRAYER OF THE FAITHFUL

PREPARATION OF GIFTS *(page 16)*

PRAYER OVER THE OFFERINGS

May this oblation, our tribute of homage,
rise up to you, O Lord,
and, through the intercession of the most Blessed Virgin Mary,
whom you assumed into heaven,
may our hearts, aflame with the fire of love,
constantly long for you.
Through Christ our Lord. *Amen.*

PREFACE: THE GLORY OF MARY ASSUMED INTO HEAVEN

It is truly right and just, our duty and our salvation,
always and everywhere to give you thanks,
Lord, holy Father, almighty and eternal God,
through Christ our Lord.

For today the Virgin Mother of God
was assumed into heaven
as the beginning and image
of your Church's coming to perfection
and a sign of sure hope and comfort to your pilgrim people;
rightly you would not allow her
to see the corruption of the tomb
since from her own body she marvelously brought forth
your incarnate Son, the Author of all life.

And so, in company with the choirs of Angels,
we praise you, and with joy we proclaim:

Holy, Holy, Holy Lord God of hosts... (page 35)

• TAKING A CLOSER LOOK •

✣ **Firstfruits** The firstfruits are the initial agricultural products and so represent the rest of the harvest. Like the firstborn son and first offspring of animals, they were considered sacred to God, the source of all good. The reason for their sacred character is not clearly indicated, but perhaps it was associated with the idea that in them God continued the process of creating new life, or perhaps they were a token of the people's need to thank God for the continuation of life. So if Christ is the firstfruits of the resurrection, then the new life that first appears in him will also be found in all those who share his life.

COMMUNION ANTIPHON *(Luke 1:48–49)*

All generations will call me blessed, for he who is mighty has done great things for me.

PRAYER AFTER COMMUNION

Having received the Sacrament of salvation,
we ask you to grant, O Lord,
that, through the intercession of the Blessed Virgin Mary,
whom you assumed into heaven,
we may be brought to the glory of the resurrection.
Through Christ our Lord. *Amen.*

SOLEMN BLESSING: THE BLESSED VIRGIN MARY *(Optional, page 62)*

DISMISSAL *(page 57)* ❖

• RESPONDING TO THE WORD •

The woman and her child are a sign that God's power conquers evil.

➡ *How might I work to overcome evil in my life and be a sign of God's work?*

Christ's resurrection and then Mary's assumption show God's life-giving power.

➡ *How has my growing relationship with Christ been stirring God's new life in me?*

Mary's prayer reveals that she shares God's outlook and values.

➡ *To which word or phrase from Mary's prayer is my attention most drawn today?*

August 19

Drink, eat, and live!

Today's readings invite us to consider the parallel paradoxes and promises of our faith: wisdom and foolishness, eating and being satisfied, boasting and humility, fear and courage, dying and living forever, eating Jesus' flesh and blood for salvation.

We die in order to live. We surrender to suffering in order to lessen the hold our pain has on us. We give in to the common good to be free as individuals. We lay aside our childish desires so as to become adults who can revel in the joy and gift of mature insight into our own condition.

I remember when my first child was about eight months old and was "helping" me with the laundry. As soon as I folded a shirt or towel, Grace pulled it out and "folded" it again. I was beginning to get frustrated and wondered if I should leave it until she was asleep. I looked at her face shining with joy and purpose and at once I realized that the joy, the loving, and the wisdom was in the fun *and* the mess. This was surely the bread and wine, the flesh and blood, of mothering. And so, gradually, I learned to drink and eat of it and live. Today, I pray that we all open our eyes to see these moments of invitation and accept them.

■ **Maureen Wicken**

ENTRANCE ANTIPHON *(Psalm 84 [83]:10–11)*

Turn your eyes, O God, our shield; and look on the face of your anointed one; one day within your courts is better than a thousand elsewhere.

INTRODUCTORY RITES *(page 10)*

COLLECT

O God, who have prepared for those who love you
good things which no eye can see,
fill our hearts, we pray, with the warmth of your love,
so that, loving you in all things and above all things,
we may attain your promises,
which surpass every human desire.
Through our Lord Jesus Christ, your Son,
who lives and reigns with you in the unity of the Holy Spirit,
one God, for ever and ever. *Amen.*

FIRST READING *(Proverbs 9:1-6)*

Wisdom has built her house,
    she has set up her seven columns;
she has dressed her meat, mixed her wine,
    yes, she has spread her table.
She has sent out her maidens; she calls
    from the heights out over the city:
"Let whoever is simple turn in here."
    To the one who lacks understanding, she says,
"Come, eat of my food,
    and drink of the wine I have mixed!
Forsake foolishness that you may live;
    advance in the way of understanding."
The word of the Lord. *Thanks be to God.*

RESPONSORIAL PSALM *(Psalm 34:2-3, 4-5, 6-7)*
R. Taste and see the goodness of the Lord.

I will bless the LORD at all times;
  his praise shall be ever in my mouth.
Let my soul glory in the LORD;
  the lowly will hear me and be glad. R.
Glorify the LORD with me,
  let us together extol his name.
I sought the LORD, and he answered me
  and delivered me from all my fears. R.
Look to him that you may be radiant with joy,
  and your faces may not blush with shame.
When the poor one called out, the LORD heard,
  and from all his distress he saved him. R.

SECOND READING *(Ephesians 5:15-20)*
Brothers and sisters: Watch carefully how you live, not as
foolish persons but as wise, making the most of the opportunity, because the days are evil. Therefore, do not continue
in ignorance, but try to understand what is the will of the Lord.
And do not get drunk on wine, in which lies debauchery, but
be filled with the Spirit, addressing one another in psalms and
hymns and spiritual songs, singing and playing to the Lord in
your hearts, giving thanks always and for everything in the name
of our Lord Jesus Christ to God the Father.
  The word of the Lord. *Thanks be to God.*

ALLELUIA *(John 6:56)*
Alleluia, alleluia. Whoever eats my flesh and drinks my blood
remains in me and I in him, says the Lord. *Alleluia, alleluia.*

GOSPEL *(John 6:51–58)*

A reading from the holy Gospel according to John.

Glory to you, O Lord.

Jesus said to the crowds: "I am the living bread that came down from heaven; whoever eats this bread will live forever; and the bread that I will give is my flesh for the life of the world."

The Jews quarreled among themselves, saying, "How can this man give us his flesh to eat?" Jesus said to them, "Amen, amen, I say to you, unless you eat the flesh of the Son of Man and drink his blood, you do not have life within you. Whoever eats my flesh and drinks my blood has **eternal life,** ✝ and I will raise him on the last day. For my flesh is true food, and my blood is true drink. Whoever eats my flesh and drinks my blood remains in me and I in him. Just as the living Father sent me and I have life because of the Father, so also the one who feeds on me will have life because of me. This is the bread that came down from heaven. Unlike your ancestors who ate and still died, whoever eats this bread will live forever."

The Gospel of the Lord. *Praise to you, Lord Jesus Christ.*

PROFESSION OF FAITH *(page 13)*

PRAYER OF THE FAITHFUL

PREPARATION OF GIFTS *(page 16)*

PRAYER OVER THE OFFERINGS

Receive our oblation, O Lord,
by which is brought about a glorious exchange,
that, by offering what you have given,
we may merit to receive your very self.
Through Christ our Lord. *Amen.*

PREFACE *(Sundays in Ordinary Time, pages 28–32)*

COMMUNION ANTIPHON *(Psalm 130 [129]:7)*

With the Lord there is mercy; in him is plentiful redemption.

Or *(John 6:51-52)*

I am the living bread that came down from heaven, says the
Lord. Whoever eats of this bread will live for ever.

❖ TAKING A CLOSER LOOK ❖

✛ **Eternal life** John's gospel describes the destiny of believers
as eternal life, that is, a life that shares in the divine type of life that
has no visible beginning or ending. It is a permanent and undying
existence in the presence of God forever. Normally human life ends
with death, but though death ends our physical life, our relationship to God continues because God chooses to share the divine life
with us. Eternal life, then, is qualitatively different from natural life,
for it is a life that death cannot destroy. Eternal life is our future
destiny, but it begins here and now in us by our association with
Jesus and our participation in God's Holy Spirit.

PRAYER AFTER COMMUNION

Made partakers of Christ through these Sacraments,
we humbly implore your mercy, Lord,
that, conformed to his image on earth,
we may merit also to be his coheirs in heaven.
Who lives and reigns for ever and ever. *Amen.*

BLESSING & DISMISSAL *(page 56)* ✦

• RESPONDING TO THE WORD •

Wisdom invites us to share in her banquet.	Paul encourages us to live with a spirit of thankfulness.	Jesus gives himself so that we might live more fully with God.
➡ *What steps might I take to learn more about God?*	➡ *What thanks might I give God today for the blessings I have been given recently?*	➡ *What might I do to prepare myself to receive the Eucharist more reverently this week?*

August 26

"This saying is hard..."

To do or not to do? That is the question. Every day, we have countless choices and decisions to make. As Christians headed toward eternal life, we are called to align our lives and choices to the example and teachings that Jesus provided.

It's not easy. Jesus' disciples experienced the difficulty of keeping faith, and some left. We too have left him many times; but after wandering aimlessly, we realize once again that he was right.

There is something truly heart-warming about someone saying "I'm sorry" in all sincerity. When my four-year-old looks at me and says, "Mama, I'm sorry," my heart melts and my only possible response is to scoop him up in a big hug.

I imagine it is similar with our heavenly Father. God's only response to our failure and regret is pure compassion and unconditional love. If we allow ourselves to receive God's love, we in turn become more compassionate and more loving ourselves. God wastes no opportunities for our good.

The beauty of the Eucharist is that as we continue, day-by-day, on our earthly pilgrimage, amidst all its challenges, God gives us the nourishment we need to continue, to grow stronger, and to eventually reach our eternal destination.

▮ NATALIA KONONENKO

ENTRANCE ANTIPHON *(Cf. Psalm 86 [85]:1-3)*

Turn your ear, O Lord, and answer me; save the servant who
trusts in you, my God. Have mercy on me, O Lord, for I cry to
you all the day long.

INTRODUCTORY RITES *(page 10)*

COLLECT

O God, who cause the minds of the faithful
to unite in a single purpose,
grant your people to love what you command
and to desire what you promise,
that, amid the uncertainties of this world,
our hearts may be fixed on that place
where true gladness is found.
Through our Lord Jesus Christ, your Son,
who lives and reigns with you in the unity of the Holy Spirit,
one God, for ever and ever. *Amen.*

FIRST READING *(Joshua 24:1-2a, 15-17, 18b)*

Joshua gathered together all the tribes of Israel at Shechem,*
summoning their elders, their leaders, their judges, and their officers. When they stood in ranks before God, Joshua addressed all
the people: "If it does not please you to serve the LORD, decide today whom you will serve, the gods your fathers served beyond the
River or the gods of the Amorites in whose country you are now
dwelling. As for me and my household, we will serve the LORD."

But the people answered, "Far be it from us to forsake the
LORD for the service of other gods. For it was the LORD,
our God, who brought us and our fathers up out of the land
of Egypt, out of a state of slavery. He performed those great
miracles before our very eyes and protected us along our entire

journey and among the peoples through whom we passed. Therefore we also will serve the LORD, for he is our God."

The word of the Lord. ***Thanks be to God.***

RESPONSORIAL PSALM *(Psalm 34:2–3, 16–17, 18–19, 20–21)*
R⁘ **Taste and see the goodness of the Lord.**

I will bless the LORD at all times;
   his praise shall be ever in my mouth.
Let my soul glory in the LORD;
   the lowly will hear me and be glad. R⁘

The LORD has eyes for the just,
   and ears for their cry.
The LORD confronts the evildoers,
   to destroy remembrance of them from the earth. R⁘

When the just cry out, the LORD hears them,
   and from all their distress he rescues them.
The LORD is close to the brokenhearted;
   and those who are crushed in spirit he saves. R⁘

Many are the troubles of the just one,
   but out of them all the LORD delivers him;
he watches over all his bones;
   not one of them shall be broken. R⁘

SECOND READING *(Ephesians 5:21-32)*
*The shorter version begins at the asterisks. The passage in brackets
is only read in the short form.*

Brothers and sisters: Be subordinate to one another out of reverence for Christ. **Wives should be subordinate to their husbands**✝ as to the Lord. For the husband is head of his wife just as Christ is head of the church, he himself the savior of the body. As the church is subordinate to Christ, so wives should be subordinate to their husbands in everything.

✳ ✳ ✳

[Brothers and sisters: Live in love, as Christ loved us.]

Husbands, love your wives,✛ even as Christ loved the church and handed himself over for her to sanctify her, cleansing her by the bath of water with the word, that he might present to himself the church in splendor, without spot or wrinkle or any such thing, that she might be holy and without blemish. So also husbands should love their wives as their own bodies. He who loves his wife loves himself. For no one hates his own flesh but rather nourishes and cherishes it, even as Christ does the church, because we are members of his body.

> For this reason a man shall leave his father and his mother
>   and be joined to his wife,
> and the two shall become one flesh.

This is a great mystery, but I speak in reference to Christ and the church. The word of the Lord. *Thanks be to God.*

ALLELUIA *(John 6:63, 68)*
Alleluia, alleluia. Your words, Lord, are Spirit and life; you have the words of everlasting life. *Alleluia, alleluia.*

GOSPEL *(John 6:60–69)*
A reading from the holy Gospel according to John.
Glory to you, O Lord.

Many of Jesus' disciples who were listening said, "This saying is hard; who can accept it?" Since Jesus knew that his disciples were murmuring about this, he said to them, "Does this shock you? What if you were to see the Son of Man ascending to where he was before? It is the spirit that gives life, while the flesh is of no avail. The words I have spoken to you are Spirit and life. But there are some of you who do not believe." Jesus knew from the beginning the ones who would not believe and the one who would betray him. And he said, "For this reason I have told you that no one can come to me unless it is granted him by my Father."

As a result of this, many of his disciples returned to their former way of life and no longer accompanied him. Jesus then said to the Twelve, "Do you also want to leave?" Simon Peter answered him, "Master, to whom shall we go? You have the words of eternal life. We have come to believe and are convinced that you are the Holy One of God."

The Gospel of the Lord. *Praise to you, Lord Jesus Christ.*

PROFESSION OF FAITH *(page 13)*

PRAYER OF THE FAITHFUL

PREPARATION OF GIFTS *(page 16)*

PRAYER OVER THE OFFERINGS
O Lord, who gained for yourself a people by adoption

❖ TAKING A CLOSER LOOK ❖

✝ **Wives should be subordinate to their husbands/ Husbands, love your wives.** In Paul's time, marriages were arranged by families, and their purpose was to increase the family's status or wealth and to continue the family through children. People did not marry necessarily for love, as is common today. Paul's advice for women repeats what was already known about rightly ordered relationships in the household: women were expected to obey (be subordinate). For the men, however, Paul's advice is shocking and challenging. He requires them to love their wives (not necessarily part of the family marriage agreement!) with the self-sacrificing love that Christ had for the Church.

through the one sacrifice offered once for all,
bestow graciously on us, we pray,
the gifts of unity and peace in your Church.
Through Christ our Lord. *Amen.*

PREFACE *(Sundays in Ordinary Time, pages 28–32)*

COMMUNION ANTIPHON *(Cf. Psalm 104 [103]:13-15)*
The earth is replete with the fruits of your work, O Lord; you
bring forth bread from the earth and wine to cheer the heart.

Or *(Cf. John 6:54)*
Whoever eats my flesh and drinks my blood has eternal life, says
the Lord, and I will raise him up on the last day.

PRAYER AFTER COMMUNION
Complete within us, O Lord, we pray,
the healing work of your mercy
and graciously perfect and sustain us,
so that in all things we may please you.
Through Christ our Lord. *Amen.*

BLESSING & DISMISSAL *(page 56)* ✦

• RESPONDING TO THE WORD •

Joshua and the people renewed their commitment to God.	Paul encourages us to live in love, creating the kind of community that God wants.	Many people left Jesus because his message and lifestyle were too hard.
➡ *What can I do today to renew my commitment to God?*	➡ *What loving thing can I do to help build God's community?*	➡ *What parts of Jesus' message are hard for me to follow?*

September 2

SEP
2

Listen with your mind and your heart

Jesus said, "Hear me, all of you, and understand." He means: *listen with all your mind and with all your heart.*

Being in the pew on Sunday does not mean we have listened or understood the Scripture readings of the day. To help us focus and internalize the Word of God that we hear on Sunday, we may need to invest a bit more time and preparation throughout the week prior.

For example, on Wednesday we can pray for openness of heart, to be able to receive the good news more generously. Then, over the next few days, we can read and re-read the coming Sunday's readings so

they become more and more familiar in our mind and have an opportunity to touch our heart. For additional help, we can invest in a Scripture commentary or read one online.

Our exercise of internalizing the word of God will require some patience, persistence, reflection, and prayer. But if we are willing to invest more of ourselves by spending more time with the word of God, we may find that it starts to change how we think, how we see the world around us, how we act, and how we live. We will start to become the very person God wishes us to be.

■ HARRY MCAVOY

ENTRANCE ANTIPHON *(Cf. Psalm 86 [85]:3, 5)*
Have mercy on me, O Lord, for I cry to you all the day long.
O Lord, you are good and forgiving, full of mercy to all who call
to you.

INTRODUCTORY RITES *(page 10)*

COLLECT
God of might, giver of every good gift,
put into our hearts the love of your name,
so that, by deepening our sense of reverence,
you may nurture in us what is good
and, by your watchful care,
keep safe what you have nurtured.
Through our Lord Jesus Christ, your Son,
who lives and reigns with you in the unity of the Holy Spirit,
one God, for ever and ever. *Amen.*

FIRST READING *(Deuteronomy 4:1-2, 6-8)*

Moses said to the people: "Now, Israel, hear the statutes
and decrees which I am teaching you to observe, that
you may live, and may enter in and take possession of the land
which the LORD, the God of your fathers, is giving you. In your
observance of the commandments of the LORD, your God,
which I enjoin upon you, you shall not add to what I command
you nor subtract from it. Observe them carefully, for thus
will you give evidence of your wisdom and intelligence to the
nations, who will hear of all these statutes and say, 'This great
nation is truly a wise and intelligent people.' For what great nation is there that has gods so close to it as the LORD, our God,
is to us whenever we call upon him? Or what great nation has
statutes and decrees that are as just as this whole law which I

am setting before you today?"

The word of the Lord. *Thanks be to God.*

RESPONSORIAL PSALM *(Psalm 15:2-3, 3-4, 4-5)*

R⏾ **One who does justice will live in the presence of the Lord.**

Whoever walks blamelessly and does justice;
    who thinks the truth in his heart
    and slanders not with his tongue. R⏾
Who harms not his fellow man,
    nor takes up a reproach against his neighbor;
by whom the reprobate is despised,
    while he honors those who fear the LORD. R⏾
Who lends not his money at usury
    and accepts no bribe against the innocent.
Whoever does these things
    shall never be disturbed. R⏾

SECOND READING *(James 1:17-18, 21b-22, 27)*

Dearest brothers and sisters: All good giving and every
perfect gift is from above, coming down from the Father
of lights, with whom there is no alteration or shadow caused by
change. He willed to give us birth by the word of truth that we
may be a kind of firstfruits of his creatures.

Humbly welcome the word that has been planted in you and
is able to save your souls.

Be doers of the word and not hearers only, deluding yourselves.

Religion that is pure and undefiled before God and the Father
is this: to **care for orphans and widows**✝ in their affliction and to
keep oneself unstained by the world.

The word of the Lord. *Thanks be to God.*

ALLELUIA *(James 1:18)*

Alleluia, alleluia. The Father willed to give us birth by the word of truth that we may be a kind of firstfruits of his creatures. *Alleluia, alleluia.*

GOSPEL *(Mark 7:1-8, 14-15, 21-23)*

A reading from the holy Gospel according to Mark.

Glory to you, O Lord.

When the Pharisees with some scribes who had come from Jerusalem gathered around Jesus, they observed that some of his disciples ate their meals with unclean, that is, unwashed, hands.—For the Pharisees and, in fact, all Jews, do not eat without carefully washing their hands, keeping the tradition of the elders. And on coming from the marketplace they do not eat without purifying themselves. And there are many other things that they have traditionally observed, the purification of cups and jugs and kettles and beds.—So the Pharisees and scribes questioned him, "Why do your disciples not follow the tradition of the elders but instead eat a meal with unclean hands?" He responded, "Well did Isaiah prophesy about you hypocrites, as it is written:

This people honors me with their lips,
but their hearts are far from me;
in vain do they worship me,
teaching as doctrines human precepts.

You disregard God's commandment but cling to human tradition."

He summoned the crowd again and said to them, "Hear me, all of you, and understand. Nothing that enters one from outside can defile that person; but the things that come out from within are what defile.

"From within people, from their hearts, come evil thoughts, unchastity, theft, murder, adultery, greed, malice, deceit, licentiousness, envy, blasphemy, arrogance, folly. All these evils come from within and they defile."

The Gospel of the Lord. *Praise to you, Lord Jesus Christ.*

PROFESSION OF FAITH *(page 13)*

PRAYER OF THE FAITHFUL

PREPARATION OF GIFTS *(page 16)*

PRAYER OVER THE OFFERINGS
May this sacred offering, O Lord,
confer on us always the blessing of salvation,
that what it celebrates in mystery
it may accomplish in power.
Through Christ our Lord. *Amen.*

PREFACE *(Sundays in Ordinary Time, pages 28–32)*

✤ Taking a Closer Look ✤

✤ **Care for orphans and widows** In the tightly structured society of biblical times, families had to rely on themselves and their relatives for protection and sustenance rather than on the legal system. Women and children were socially "located" in relation to their household, in particular to the head of the household (the father, husband, or master). Widows, orphans, and foreigners residing in the land who were not connected to a household were thus "dislocated" and vulnerable because they lacked a protective male. In Israel, God assumed the role of protector of widows and orphans and promised to take vengeance on those who would seek to exploit these vulnerable ones.

COMMUNION ANTIPHON *(Psalm 31 [30]:20)*

How great is the goodness, Lord, that you keep for those who fear you.

Or *(Matthew 5:9–10)*

Blessed are the peacemakers, for they shall be called children of God. Blessed are they who are persecuted for the sake of righteousness, for theirs is the Kingdom of Heaven.

PRAYER AFTER COMMUNION

Renewed by this bread from the heavenly table,
we beseech you, Lord,
that, being the food of charity,
it may confirm our hearts
and stir us to serve you in our neighbor.
Through Christ our Lord. *Amen.*

BLESSING & DISMISSAL *(page 56)* ❖

❖ RESPONDING TO THE WORD ❖

God's guidelines for the covenant people's behavior were not always easy to keep.

➡ Which of God's commandments is particularly troublesome for me now?

James tells us to be doers of the word and not hearers only.

➡ When and for what reasons have I been an eager hearer but a reluctant doer?

Jesus warns that the real roots of sin are our inner attitudes.

➡ What attitude is giving me trouble lately and pushing me toward wrong actions?

September 9

SEP
9

Reaching beyond barriers

Isaiah calls forth courage in each of us. "Be strong, fear not!" For God will save, giving sight to the blind and hearing to the deaf. During the exile in Babylon, the Israelites must have felt abandoned and alone. Isaiah's news of God's everlasting love was a glimmer of light in the darkness.

In today's gospel, Jesus shares God's love as he overcomes social barriers and heals through touch. In a time of stringent purity laws, this was a bold act of mercy. Illness and disability were seen as a sign of the presence of sin. Jesus reaches beyond this boundary, healing the broken and demonstrating his love for the marginalized.

St. James calls each of us to follow in Jesus' footsteps; may we participate in the kingdom by reaching beyond barriers in order to show kindness and love to others. The sign of God's miraculous love is present to us every day through words and deeds that, inspired by grace, bring healing and comfort. These small miracles bring God's light to the places of darkness in our world. If we open our hearts to this visceral love, won't we also want to zealously share the good news?

■ VANESSA AND MICHAEL
NICHOLAS-SCHMIDT

ENTRANCE ANTIPHON *(Psalm 119 [118]:137, 124)*

You are just, O Lord, and your judgment is right; treat your servant in accord with your merciful love.

INTRODUCTORY RITES *(page 10)*

COLLECT

O God, by whom we are redeemed and receive adoption,
look graciously upon your beloved sons and daughters,
that those who believe in Christ
may receive true freedom
and an everlasting inheritance.
Through our Lord Jesus Christ, your Son,
who lives and reigns with you in the unity of the Holy Spirit,
one God, for ever and ever. *Amen.*

FIRST READING *(Isaiah 35:4–7a)*

Thus says the LORD:
    Say to those whose hearts are frightened:
    Be strong, fear not!
Here is your God,
    he comes with vindication;
with divine recompense
    he comes to save you.
Then will the eyes of the blind be opened,
    the ears of the deaf be cleared;
then will the lame leap like a stag,
    then the tongue of the mute will sing.
Streams will burst forth in the desert,
    and rivers in the steppe.
The burning sands will become pools,

and the thirsty ground, springs of water.
The word of the Lord. *Thanks be to God.*

RESPONSORIAL PSALM *(Psalm 146:6-7, 8-9, 9-10)*
R⁄ **Praise the Lord, my soul! Or Alleluia!**

The God of Jacob keeps faith forever,
    secures justice for the oppressed,
    gives food to the hungry.
The LORD sets captives free. R⁄
The LORD gives sight to the blind;
    the LORD raises up those who were bowed down.
The LORD loves the just;
    the LORD protects strangers. R⁄
The fatherless and the widow the Lord sustains,
    but the way of the wicked he thwarts.
The LORD shall reign forever;
    your God, O Zion,* through all generations. Alleluia. R⁄

SECOND READING *(James 2:1-5)*

My brothers and sisters, show no partiality as you adhere to the faith in our glorious Lord Jesus Christ. For if a man with gold rings and fine clothes comes into your assembly, and a poor person in shabby clothes also comes in, and you pay attention to the one wearing the fine clothes and say, "Sit here, please," while you say to the poor one, "Stand there," or "Sit at my feet," have you not made distinctions among yourselves and become judges with evil designs?

Listen, my beloved brothers and sisters. Did not God choose those who are poor in the world to be rich in faith and heirs of the kingdom that he promised to those who love him?

The word of the Lord. *Thanks be to God.*

ALLELUIA *(See Matthew 4:23)*
Alleluia, alleluia. Jesus proclaimed the Gospel of the kingdom and cured every disease among the people. *Alleluia, alleluia.*

GOSPEL *(Mark 7:31–37)*
A reading from the holy Gospel according to Mark.
Glory to you, O Lord.

Again Jesus left the district of Tyre* and went by way of Sidon* to the Sea of Galilee, into the district of the Decapolis.* And people brought to him a deaf man who had a speech impediment and begged him to **lay his hand on him**.✝ He took him off by himself away from the crowd. He put his finger into the man's ears and, spitting, touched his tongue; then he looked up to heaven and groaned, and said to him, "*Ephphatha!**"—that is, "Be opened!"—And immediately the man's ears were opened, his speech impediment was removed, and he spoke plainly. He ordered them not to tell anyone. But the more he ordered them not to, the more they proclaimed it. They were exceedingly astonished and they said, "He has done all things well. He makes the deaf hear and the mute speak."

The Gospel of the Lord. *Praise to you, Lord Jesus Christ.*

PROFESSION OF FAITH *(page 13)*

PRAYER OF THE FAITHFUL

PREPARATION OF GIFTS *(page 16)*

PRAYER OVER THE OFFERINGS

O God, who give us the gift of true prayer and of peace,
graciously grant that, through this offering,
we may do fitting homage to your divine majesty
and, by partaking of the sacred mystery,
we may be faithfully united in mind and heart.
Through Christ our Lord. *Amen.*

PREFACE *(Sundays in Ordinary Time, pages 28–32)*

COMMUNION ANTIPHON *(Cf. Psalm 42 [41]:2-3)*

Like the deer that yearns for running streams, so my soul is
yearning for you, my God; my soul is
thirsting for God, the living God.

Or *(John 8:12)*

I am the light of the world, says the Lord; whoever follows me
will not walk in darkness, but will have the light of life.

❖ TAKING A CLOSER LOOK ❖

✝ **Lay his hand on him** The hand (especially the right hand) was a natural symbol for power and strength. Thus the laying on of hands signified the transfer of power or strength or holiness. It was part of the rituals for sacrifice, for the consecration of priests, and for conferring blessings. It also served as the medium for the transfer of spiritual and physical healing power from the healer to the one being healed. Although Jesus sometimes heals from a distance or merely by the power of his word, most often he transmits his healing power through his loving touch.

PRAYER AFTER COMMUNION
Grant that your faithful, O Lord,
whom you nourish and endow with life
through the food of your Word and heavenly Sacrament,
may so benefit from your beloved Son's great gifts
that we may merit an eternal share in his life.
Who lives and reigns for ever and ever. *Amen.*

BLESSING & DISMISSAL *(page 56)* ✣

• RESPONDING TO THE WORD •

Isaiah encourages us to "Be strong, fear not!" because God is with us.

➡ *When has God's presence helped to calm my fears?*

James warns us not to be misled by outer appearances and misjudge the worth of others.

➡ *What leads me to overlook the hidden riches of the poor?*

Jesus opens the ears of a man who is deaf.

➡ *What might Jesus be doing to open my ears so I can pay more attention to what God is trying to say to me?*

September 16

**SEP
16**

Walking with Christ

Jesus and his disciples set out for the villages of Caesarea in Philippi. These journeys would not have been easy by our modern standards. Dusty, uneven terrain, hot and all on foot. Yet that is when he asked his disciples: "Who do people say that I am?"

Walking with Christ is a spiritual journey fed by prayer, Scripture reading and the Eucharist. However, it is revealed by works. Jesus does not ask us to arrive at our destination before we begin doing acts of mercy. The Christian journey is always about imperfect people bringing Christ to an imperfect world, now, through him.

When your acts of mercy defend the unborn, the sick, the dying, marriage, the cost of this discipleship can be high. It can be lonely and overwhelming. God's plan is not that we do this in our own strength. He is able to do within us whatever he has called us to do, whether to serve, to speak the truth or to stand and defend.

Let the Mass today be your prayerful next step. Then give God glory and praise as you boldly proclaim the Messiah to our broken world.

■ **JOHANNE BROWNRIGG**

ENTRANCE ANTIPHON *(Cf. Sirach 36:18)*

Give peace, O Lord, to those who wait for you, that your prophets be found true. Hear the prayers of your servant, and of your people Israel.

INTRODUCTORY RITES *(page 10)*

COLLECT

Look upon us, O God,
Creator and ruler of all things,
and, that we may feel the working of your mercy,
grant that we may serve you with all our heart.
Through our Lord Jesus Christ, your Son,
who lives and reigns with you in the unity of the Holy Spirit,
one God, for ever and ever. *Amen.*

FIRST READING *(Isaiah 50:5-9a)*

The Lord GOD opens my ear that I may hear;
    and I have not rebelled,
      have not turned back.
I gave my back to those who beat me,
    my cheeks to those who plucked my beard;
my face I did not shield
    from buffets and spitting.

The Lord GOD is my help,
    therefore I am not disgraced;
I have set my face like flint,
    knowing that I shall not be put to shame.
He is near who upholds my right;
    if anyone wishes to oppose me,
      let us appear together.

Who disputes my right?
> Let that man confront me.
See, the Lord GOD is my help;
> who will prove me wrong?
The word of the Lord. *Thanks be to God.*

RESPONSORIAL PSALM *(Psalm 116:1-2, 3-4, 5-6, 8-9)*

℟ **I will walk before the Lord, in the land of the living.**
> *Or* **Alleluia.**

I love the LORD because he has heard
> my voice in supplication,
Because he has inclined his ear to me
> the day I called. ℟

The cords of death encompassed me;
> the snares of the netherworld seized upon me;
> I fell into distress and sorrow,
and I called upon the name of the LORD,
> "O LORD, save my life!" ℟

Gracious is the LORD and just;
> yes, our God is merciful.
The Lord keeps the little ones;
> I was brought low, and he saved me. ℟

For he has freed my soul from death,
> my eyes from tears, my feet from stumbling.
I shall walk before the LORD
> in the land of the living. ℟

SECOND READING *(James 2:14-18)*

What good is it, my brothers and sisters, if someone says he has faith but does not have works? Can that faith save him? If a brother or sister has nothing to wear and has no food

for the day, and one of you says to them, "Go in peace, keep
warm, and eat well," but you do not give them the necessities
of the body, what good is it? So also faith of itself, if it does not
have works, is dead.

Indeed someone might say, "You have faith and I have works."
Demonstrate your faith to me without works, and I will demonstrate my faith to you from my works.

The word of the Lord. *Thanks be to God.*

ALLELUIA *(Galatians 6:14)*
Alleluia, alleluia. May I never boast except in the cross of our
Lord through which the world has been crucified to me and I to
the world. *Alleluia, alleluia.*

GOSPEL *(Mark 8:27–35)*
A reading from the holy Gospel according to Mark.
Glory to you, O Lord.

Jesus and his disciples set out for the villages of Caesarea*
Philippi. Along the way he asked his disciples, "Who do people
say that I am?" They said in reply, "John the Baptist, others Elijah,
still others one of the prophets." And he asked them, "But who do
you say that I am?" Peter said to him in reply, "You are the Christ."
Then he warned them not to tell anyone about him.

He began to teach them that the Son of Man must suffer
greatly and be rejected by the elders, the chief priests, and the
scribes, and be killed, and rise after three days. He spoke this
openly. Then Peter took him aside and began to rebuke him.
At this he turned around and, looking at his disciples, rebuked
Peter and said, "Get behind me, **Satan.**✝ You are thinking not as
God does, but as human beings do."

He summoned the crowd with his disciples and said to them,

"Whoever wishes to come after me must deny himself, take up his cross, and follow me. For whoever wishes to save his life will lose it, but whoever loses his life for my sake and that of the gospel will save it."

The Gospel of the Lord. *Praise to you, Lord Jesus Christ.*

PROFESSION OF FAITH *(page 13)*

PRAYER OF THE FAITHFUL

PREPARATION OF GIFTS *(page 16)*

PRAYER OVER THE OFFERINGS
Look with favor on our supplications, O Lord,
and in your kindness accept these, your servants' offerings,
that what each has offered to the honor of your name
may serve the salvation of all.
Through Christ our Lord. *Amen.*

PREFACE *(Sundays in Ordinary Time, pages 28–32)*

● TAKING A CLOSER LOOK ●

✝ **Satan** In the earlier books of the Bible (especially Job), the "satan" or accuser is a kind of legal prosecutor in the divine assembly who questions the sincerity of human faith. After the exile, as the Jews began to stress God as transcendent and supremely good, they found it difficult to account for evil in the world. Gradually, they developed the figure of Satan as an evil spirit who is subordinate but hostile to God, struggling with God for domination of the earth and tempting humans from following God's ways. Jesus' triumph over Satan encourages us to resist temptations that lead us away from being sons and daughters of God.

COMMUNION ANTIPHON *(Cf. Psalm 36 [35]:8)*

How precious is your mercy, O God! The children of men seek shelter in the shadow of your wings.

Or *(Cf. 1 Corinthians 10:16)*

The chalice of blessing that we bless is a communion in the Blood of Christ; and the bread that we break is a sharing in the Body of the Lord.

PRAYER AFTER COMMUNION

May the working of this heavenly gift, O Lord, we pray,
take possession of our minds and bodies,
so that its effects, and not our own desires,
may always prevail in us.
Through Christ our Lord. *Amen.*

BLESSING & DISMISSAL *(page 56)* ✣

• RESPONDING TO THE WORD •

God's servant must put up with hardship to do what God asks.	James knows that works are necessary to make faith relevant.	Jesus asks the disciples to tell him who they think he is.
➡ How do I respond to hardship and difficulties in living as God requires?	➡ What works am I doing that show my desire to follow Christ more closely?	➡ How would I answer Jesus' question today?

September 23

**SEP
23**

A very different story

Christianity is often castigated for teaching that our God is an angry God whose wrath at human sin required a perfect human sacrifice to appease God's bad temper. And we can even admit that some Christians do misrepresent the gospel in this way. But today's readings tell a very different story.

It is not God who demands the death of the innocent, but us. The reading from Wisdom lays bare the human response to innocence. It makes us uncomfortable. And so, when God comes to us as an innocent man, we cannot bear his presence and crucify him.

In the letter of James, and in today's gospel, we see the human dynamics that underlie our propensity to sacrifice the innocent. But we also see Christ's answer to those dynamics. If we are not to be people who sacrifice the innocent, we must be, as James says, "peaceable, gentle, compliant, full of mercy and good fruits, without inconstancy or insincerity." Or, as Jesus says, "If anyone wishes to be first, he shall be the last of all and the servant of all."

The sacrifice we offer at Mass today, then, is not an innocent victim presented to an angry God, but a loving victim who offered himself to God precisely by offering himself to us.

🔲 **Brett Salkeld**

ENTRANCE ANTIPHON

I am the salvation of the people, says the Lord. Should they cry to
me in any distress, I will hear them, and I will be their Lord
for ever.

INTRODUCTORY RITES *(page 10)*

COLLECT

O God, who founded all the commands of your sacred Law
upon love of you and of our neighbor,
grant that, by keeping your precepts,
we may merit to attain eternal life.
Through our Lord Jesus Christ, your Son,
who lives and reigns with you in the unity of the Holy Spirit,
one God, for ever and ever. *Amen.*

FIRST READING *(Wisdom 2:12, 17-20)*

The wicked say:
   Let us beset the just one, because he is obnoxious to us;
      he sets himself against our doings,
   reproaches us for transgressions of the law
      and charges us with violations of our training.
   Let us see whether his words be true;
      let us find out what will happen to him.
   For if the just one be the son of God, God will defend him
      and deliver him from the hand of his foes.
   With revilement and torture let us put the just one to the test
      that we may have proof of his gentleness
      and try his patience.
   Let us condemn him to a shameful death;
      for according to his own words, God will take care of him.
The word of the Lord. *Thanks be to God.*

RESPONSORIAL PSALM *(Psalm 54:3–4, 5, 6–8)*

R⎩ **The Lord upholds my life.**

O God, by your name save me,
   and by your might defend my cause.
O God, hear my prayer;
   hearken to the words of my mouth. R⎩
For the haughty men have risen up against me,
   the ruthless seek my life;
   they set not God before their eyes. R⎩
Behold, God is my helper;
   the Lord sustains my life.
Freely will I offer you sacrifice;
   I will praise your name, O LORD, for its goodness. R⎩

SECOND READING *(James 3:16–4:3)*

Beloved: Where jealousy and selfish ambition exist, there is disorder and every foul practice. But the wisdom from above is first of all pure, then peaceable, gentle, compliant, full of mercy and good fruits, without inconstancy or insincerity. And the fruit of righteousness is sown in peace for those who cultivate peace.

Where do the wars and where do the conflicts among you come from? Is it not from your passions that make war within your members? You covet but do not possess. You kill and envy but you cannot obtain; you fight and wage war. You do not possess because you do not ask. You ask but do not receive, because you ask wrongly, to spend it on your passions.

The word of the Lord. ***Thanks be to God.***

ALLELUIA *(See 2 Thessalonians 2:14)*
Alleluia, alleluia. God has called us through the Gospel to possess the glory of our Lord Jesus Christ. *Alleluia, alleluia.*

GOSPEL *(Mark 9:30-37)*
A reading from the holy Gospel according to Mark.
Glory to you, O Lord.

Jesus and his disciples left from there and began a journey through Galilee, but he did not wish anyone to know about it. He was teaching his disciples and telling them, "The Son of Man is to be handed over to men and they will kill him, and three days after his death the Son of Man will rise." But they did not understand the saying, and they were afraid to question him.

They came to Capernaum* and, once inside the house, he began to ask them, "What were you arguing about on the way?" But they remained silent. They had been discussing among themselves on the way who was the greatest. Then he sat down, called the Twelve, and said to them, "If anyone wishes to be first, he shall be the last of all and the servant of all." Taking a **child**,✝ he placed it in the their midst, and putting his arms around it, he said to them, "Whoever receives one child such as this in my name, receives me; and whoever receives me, receives not me but the One who sent me."

The Gospel of the Lord. *Praise to you, Lord Jesus Christ.*

PROFESSION OF FAITH *(page 13)*

PRAYER OF THE FAITHFUL

PREPARATION OF GIFTS *(page 16)*

PRAYER OVER THE OFFERINGS
Receive with favor, O Lord, we pray,
the offerings of your people,
that what they profess with devotion and faith
may be theirs through these heavenly mysteries.
Through Christ our Lord. *Amen.*

PREFACE *(Sundays in Ordinary Time, pages 28–32)*

⸭ TAKING A CLOSER LOOK ⸭

✚ **Child** A child had very little social status, yet required much attention from the parents to survive to maturity. Thus the child was a perfect illustration of Jesus' point that the disciples are to seek their greatness or high status in service to those who have the least status. We might note the curious translation that expresses the Greek term here for child as neuter gender, that is, it does not identify the child as a boy or girl but as an "it." To make his case even clearer, we might imagine Jesus bringing forth a young girl, whose social status was even lower than that of a boy.

COMMUNION ANTIPHON *(Psalm 119 [118]:4-5)*

You have laid down your precepts to be carefully kept; may my ways be firm in keeping your statutes.

Or *(John 10:14)*

I am the Good Shepherd, says the Lord; I know my sheep, and mine know me.

PRAYER AFTER COMMUNION

Graciously raise up, O Lord,
those you renew with this Sacrament,
that we may come to possess your redemption
both in mystery and in the manner of our life.
Through Christ our Lord. *Amen.*

BLESSING & DISMISSAL *(page 56)* ✧

• RESPONDING TO THE WORD •

The innocent person often suffers at the hands of the wicked.

➡ *When did my innocence not protect me from suffering?*

James reminds us that our desires can often lead us away from God.

➡ *What desires are prominent in me now, and where are they leading me?*

Jesus tells the disciples that their greatness will come only from service.

➡ *What service am I doing that would make Jesus happy?*

September 30

SEP 30

Eternal treasures

Today's readings make a clear distinction between our desires for worldly riches and the riches that we receive as a result of just living by following God's law. The riches of the world seem more appealing at first glance—status, power, wealth, material things. They seem to bring with them freedom, opportunities, and comfort. Wealth in and of itself is not a bad thing: what matters is how one acquires it and what one does with it.

Pope John Paul I once said, "It is not wrong to want to live better; what is wrong is a style of life which is presumed to be better when it is directed towards 'having' rather than 'being,' and which wants to have more, not in order to be more but in order to spend life in enjoyment as an end in itself." Today's reading from James sends a warning specifically to the rich who oppress others for their own benefit.

If we can re-direct our worldly riches and possessions (we all have some!) to serve us in a way that helps us gather eternal treasures, we can be rewarded with eternal life in the kingdom of God—which begins already here on earth through the good fruits that result from spiritually-healthy choices and just actions: peace, joy, kindness, charity, and well-being. May God bless all of our good efforts!

■ NATALIA KONONENKO

ENTRANCE ANTIPHON *(Deuteronomy 3:31, 29, 30, 43, 42)*

All that you have done to us, O Lord, you have done with true judgment, for we have sinned against you and not obeyed your commandments. But give glory to your name and deal with us according to the bounty of your mercy.

INTRODUCTORY RITES *(page 10)*

COLLECT

O God, who manifest your almighty power
above all by pardoning and showing mercy,
bestow, we pray, your grace abundantly upon us
and make those hastening to attain your promises
heirs to the treasures of heaven.
Through our Lord Jesus Christ, your Son,
who lives and reigns with you in the unity of the Holy Spirit,
one God, for ever and ever. *Amen.*

FIRST READING *(Numbers 11:25-29)*

The Lord came down in the cloud and spoke to Moses. Taking some of the spirit that was on Moses, the Lord bestowed it on the seventy elders; and as the spirit came to rest on them, they prophesied.

Now two men, one named Eldad and the other Medad, were not in the gathering but had been left in the camp. They too had been on the list, but had not gone out to the tent; yet the spirit came to rest on them also, and they prophesied in the camp. So, when a young man quickly told Moses, "Eldad and Medad are prophesying in the camp," Joshua, son of Nun, who from his youth had been Moses' aide, said, "Moses, my lord, stop them." But Moses answered him, "Are you jealous for my sake? Would that all the people of the Lord were prophets! Would that the

Lᴏʀᴅ might bestow his spirit on them all!"
The word of the Lord. ***Thanks be to God.***

RESPONSORIAL PSALM *(Psalm 19:8, 10, 12-13, 14)*
℞ **The precepts of the Lord give joy to the heart.**

The law of the Lᴏʀᴅ is perfect,
  refreshing the soul;
the decree of the Lord is trustworthy,
  giving wisdom to the simple. ℞
The fear of the Lᴏʀᴅ is pure,
  enduring forever;
the ordinances of the Lᴏʀᴅ are true,
  all of them just. ℞
Though your servant is careful of them,
  very diligent in keeping them,
Yet who can detect failings?
  Cleanse me from my unknown faults! ℞
From wanton sin especially, restrain your servant;
  let it not rule over me.
Then shall I be blameless and innocent
  of serious sin. ℞

SECOND READING *(James 5:1-6)*
Come now, you rich, weep and wail over your impending miseries. Your wealth has rotted away, your clothes have become moth-eaten, your gold and silver have corroded, and that corrosion will be a testimony against you; it will devour your flesh like a fire. You have stored up treasure for the last days. Behold, the wages you withheld from the workers who harvested your fields are crying aloud; and the cries of the harvesters have reached the ears of the Lord of hosts. You have lived on earth in

luxury and pleasure; you have fattened your hearts for the day of slaughter. You have condemned; you have murdered the righteous one; he offers you no resistance.

The word of the Lord. *Thanks be to God.*

ALLELUIA *(See John 17:17b, 17a)*
Alleluia, alleluia. Your word, O Lord, is truth; consecrate us in the truth. *Alleluia, alleluia.*

GOSPEL *(Mark 9:38–43, 45, 47–48)*
A reading from the holy Gospel according to Mark.
Glory to you, O Lord.

At that time, John said to Jesus, "Teacher, we saw someone driving out demons in your name, and we tried to prevent him because he does not follow us." Jesus replied, "Do not prevent him. There is no one who performs a mighty deed in my name who can at the same time speak ill of me. For whoever is not against us is for us. Anyone who gives you a cup of water to drink because you belong to Christ, amen, I say to you, will surely not lose his reward.

"Whoever causes one of these little ones who believe in me to sin, it would be better for him if a great millstone were put around his neck and he were thrown into the sea. If your hand causes you to sin, cut it off. It is better for you to enter into life maimed than with two hands to go into **Gehenna**,*⸸ into the unquenchable fire. And if your foot causes you to sin, cut if off. It is better for you to enter into life crippled than with two feet to be thrown into Gehenna. And if your eye causes you to sin, pluck it out. Better for you to enter into the kingdom of God with one eye than with two eyes to be thrown into Gehenna, where 'their worm does not die, and the fire is not quenched.' "

The Gospel of the Lord. *Praise to you, Lord Jesus Christ.*

PROFESSION OF FAITH *(page 13)*

PRAYER OF THE FAITHFUL

PREPARATION OF GIFTS *(page 16)*

PRAYER OVER THE OFFERINGS
Grant us, O merciful God,
that this our offering may find acceptance with you
and that through it the wellspring of all blessing
may be laid open before us.
Through Christ our Lord. *Amen.*

PREFACE *(Sundays in Ordinary Time, pages 28–32)*

• TAKING A CLOSER LOOK •

✠ **Gehenna** Located west and south of Jerusalem, Gehenna (Hebrew, valley of Hinnom) divided the tribes of Judah and Benjamin. Some of the kings of Judah used its heights for idolatrous human sacrifices and so incurred God's wrath. Jeremiah cursed it and called it a place of fire and destruction. This association soon made it a synonym for the place of God's punishment of the wicked after death—hell. It was distinguished both from heaven or paradise, where the just received their reward, and from Hades, which was either the abode of all the dead or where the wicked wait until God's final judgment.

COMMUNION ANTIPHON *(Cf. Psalm 119 [118]:49-50)*

Remember your word to your servant, O Lord, by which you have given me hope. This is my comfort when I am brought low.

Or *(1 John 3:16)*

By this we came to know the love of God: that Christ laid down his life for us; so we ought to lay down our lives for one another.

PRAYER AFTER COMMUNION

May this heavenly mystery, O Lord,
restore us in mind and body,
that we may be coheirs in glory with Christ,
to whose suffering we are united
whenever we proclaim his Death.
Who lives and reigns for ever and ever. ***Amen.***

BLESSING & DISMISSAL *(page 56)* ❖

❖ RESPONDING TO THE WORD ❖

God's Spirit can empower the most unlikely people.	James reminds us that the pursuit of riches will ultimately not satisfy us.	Jesus reminds us that even small kindnesses done in his spirit will bring great rewards.
➡ *What unlikely "prophet" surprised me by being someone from whom I learned much about God?*	➡ *When has my desire for riches drawn me away from a proper relationship with God or others?*	➡ *What small acts of kindness done to me do I recall and still appreciate very much?*

OCT
7

October 7

Trusting in God's love

In today's gospel reading, Jesus' disciples rebuke those trying to bring children to Jesus. But Jesus tells them: "The kingdom of God belongs to such as these. Amen, I say to you, whoever does not accept the kingdom of God like a child will not enter it."

This passage reminds me of once, long ago, when life was getting to me. I tossed my toddler daughter in the car, and we took off for the beach. I didn't even make clear to her where we were going. We just went.

We arrived, and she played, delighted as I sat and pondered. All this time, she had never questioned where we were going, never fought it. She had just come along for the ride, accepting and happy.

I could have seen naïveté in her acceptance, and perhaps that is one way to look at it. But at the time, I simply saw trust: trust in where I was taking her, because she trusted that I loved her and would only want the best for her.

Like God's love for me, can I accept where God takes me? May we trust in God, and welcome God's reign of love in our lives.

■ **AMY WELBORN**

ENTRANCE ANTIPHON *(Cf. Esther 4:17)*

Within your will, O Lord, all things are established, and there is none that can resist your will. For you have made all things, the heaven and the earth, and all that is held within the circle of heaven; you are the Lord of all.

INTRODUCTORY RITES *(page 10)*

COLLECT

Almighty ever-living God,
who in the abundance of your kindness
surpass the merits and the desires of those who entreat you,
pour out your mercy upon us
to pardon what conscience dreads
and to give what prayer does not dare to ask.
Through our Lord Jesus Christ, your Son,
who lives and reigns with you in the unity of the Holy Spirit,
one God, for ever and ever. *Amen.*

FIRST READING *(Genesis 2:18-24)*

The Lord God said: "It is not good for the man to be alone. I will make a suitable partner for him." So the Lord God formed out of the ground various wild animals and various birds of the air, and he brought them to the man to see what he would call them; whatever the man called each of them would be its name. The man gave names to all the cattle, all the birds of the air, and all wild animals; but none proved to be the suitable partner for the man.

So the Lord God cast a deep sleep on the man, and while he was asleep, he took out one of his ribs and closed up its place with flesh. The Lord God then built up into a woman the rib that he had taken from the man. When he brought her to the man, the man said:

"This one, at last, is bone of my bones
     and flesh of my flesh;
this one shall be called 'woman,'
     for out of 'her man' this one has been taken."
That is why a man leaves his father and mother and clings to his
wife, and the two of them become one flesh.

The word of the Lord. ***Thanks be to God.***

RESPONSORIAL PSALM *(Psalm 128:1-2, 3, 4-5, 6)*
℟. May the Lord bless us all the days of our lives.

Blessed are you who fear the LORD,
     who walk in his ways!
For you shall eat the fruit of your handiwork;
     blessed shall you be, and favored. ℟.
Your wife shall be like a fruitful vine
     in the recesses of your home;
your children like olive plants
     around your table. ℟.
Behold, thus is the man blessed
     who fears the Lord.
The LORD bless you from Zion:*
     may you see the prosperity of Jerusalem
     all the days of your life. ℟.
May you see your children's children.
     Peace be upon Israel! ℟.

SECOND READING *(Hebrews 2:9-11)*

Brothers and sisters: He "for a little while" was made "lower
than the angels," that by the grace of God he might taste
death for everyone.

For it was fitting that he, for whom and through whom all

things exist, in bringing many children to glory, should make the leader to their salvation perfect through suffering. He who consecrates and those who are being consecrated all have one origin. Therefore, he is not ashamed to call them "brothers."

The word of the Lord. *Thanks be to God.*

ALLELUIA *(1 John 4:12)*
Alleluia, alleluia. If we love one another, God remains in us and his love is brought to perfection in us. *Alleluia, alleluia.*

GOSPEL *(Mark 10:2-16)*
The short form ends at the asterisks.

A reading from the holy Gospel according to Mark.
Glory to you, O Lord.

The Pharisees approached Jesus and asked, "Is it lawful for a husband to **divorce**✝ his wife?" They were testing him. He said to them in reply, "What did Moses command you?" They replied, "Moses permitted a husband to write a bill of divorce and dismiss her." But Jesus told them, "Because of the hardness of your hearts he wrote you this commandment. But from the beginning of creation, *God made them male and female. For this reason a man shall leave his father and mother and be joined to his wife, and the two shall become one flesh.* So they are no longer two but one flesh. Therefore what God has joined together, no human being must separate." In the house the disciples again questioned Jesus about this. He said to them, "Whoever divorces his wife and marries another commits adultery against her; and if she divorces her husband and marries another, she commits adultery."

* * *

And people were bringing children to him that he might

touch them, but the disciples rebuked them. When Jesus saw this he became indignant and said to them, "Let the children come to me; do not prevent them, for the kingdom of God belongs to such as these. Amen, I say to you, whoever does not accept the kingdom of God like a child will not enter it." Then he embraced them and blessed them, placing his hands on them.

The Gospel of the Lord. *Praise to you, Lord Jesus Christ.*

PROFESSION OF FAITH *(page 13)*

PRAYER OF THE FAITHFUL

PREPARATION OF GIFTS *(page 16)*

PRAYER OVER THE OFFERINGS
Accept, O Lord, we pray,
the sacrifices instituted by your commands
and, through the sacred mysteries,
which we celebrate with dutiful service,

• TAKING A CLOSER LOOK •

✠ **Divorce** The particular meaning of divorce is directly related to the cultural customs of marriage. For ancient people, marriage was primarily an arrangement between families, without much emotional attachment between husband and wife. Dissolving a marriage did not mean the untangling of years of emotional commitment but rather the untangling of family alliances. In Judaism, only a husband could initiate divorce, which entailed sending the wife back to her family with her personal wealth (dowry) and forfeiting whatever compensation (bride price) he might have made to her family at the time of marriage.

graciously complete the sanctifying work
by which you are pleased to redeem us.
Through Christ our Lord. *Amen.*

PREFACE *(Sundays in Ordinary Time, pages 28–32)*

COMMUNION ANTIPHON *(Lamentations 3:25)*
The Lord is good to those who hope in him, to the soul that
seeks him.

Or *(Cf. 1 Corinthians 10:17)*
Though many, we are one bread, one body, for we all partake of
the one Bread and one Chalice.

PRAYER AFTER COMMUNION
Grant us, almighty God,
that we may be refreshed and nourished
by the Sacrament which we have received,
so as to be transformed into what we consume.
Through Christ our Lord. *Amen.*

BLESSING & DISMISSAL *(page 56)* ✤

• Responding to the Word •

God saw that being alone is not good for humans.	Jesus became "perfect" (or "complete") through suffering.	God's desire is that marriage partners share a life-long commitment to one another.
➡ *What might I do this week to make sure that someone does not feel so alone?*	➡ *When did my suffering make me feel more complete or increase my compassion for others?*	➡ *What has made my commitments difficult to fulfill?*

October 14

OCT 14

Put Jesus first!

"What must I do?" asked the rich man. Jesus' answer is a challenge. It is not just one more thing the man must add to his "to-do" list, but *the* essential thing. Jesus asks him to give up everything and follow him. It is not a simple question or a simple answer. The rich man had accomplished much and was ready to do more. But Jesus' reply knocks the wind out of his sails. Jesus is calling the man, and us, to trust more deeply—to sacrifice and be transformed.

It is easy to get caught up in depending upon ourselves, but our relationship with Jesus calls us to a radical trust. Give up our plans, our back-up plans, our safety nets, and our stockpiles. Put Jesus first and let everything else go. Until we lay down our lives, we are still serving only in part.

Jesus' answer, said with love, convicts the man of holding back. His words shock the man out of his illusion that he was on his way to eternal life. He must accept the challenge to go deeper. It is no easy thing—he must sacrifice everything to follow Jesus. But it seemed impossible to him. What happened to the man? Did he later accept the challenge? Will we? Remember, we are not alone: as Jesus reminds us in today's gospel, "All things are possible for God."

■ **KELLY BOURKE**

ENTRANCE ANTIPHON *(Psalm 130 [129]:3–4)*
If you, O Lord, should mark iniquities, Lord, who could stand?
But with you is found forgiveness, O God of Israel.

INTRODUCTORY RITES *(page 10)*

COLLECT
May your grace, O Lord, we pray,
at all times go before us and follow after
and make us always determined
to carry out good works.
Through our Lord Jesus Christ, your Son,
who lives and reigns with you in the unity of the Holy Spirit,
one God, for ever and ever. *Amen.*

FIRST READING *(Wisdom 7:7–11)*

I prayed, and prudence was given me;
  I pleaded, and the spirit of **wisdom**✝ came to me.
I preferred her to scepter and throne,
and deemed riches nothing in comparison with her,
  nor did I liken any priceless gem to her;
because all gold, in view of her, is a little sand,
  and before her, silver is to be accounted mire.
Beyond health and comeliness I loved her,
and I chose to have her rather than the light,
  because the splendor of her never yields to sleep.
Yet all good things together came to me in her company,
  and countless riches at her hands.
The word of the Lord. *Thanks be to God.*

RESPONSORIAL PSALM *(Psalm 90:12–13, 14–15, 16–17)*

℟ **Fill us with your love, O Lord, and we will sing for joy!**

Teach us to number our days aright,
　that we may gain wisdom of heart.
Return, O LORD! How long?
　Have pity on your servants! ℟
Fill us at daybreak with your kindness,
　that we may shout for joy and gladness all our days.
Make us glad, for the days when you afflicted us,
　for the years when we saw evil. ℟
Let your work be seen by your servants
　and your glory by their children;
and may the gracious care of the Lord our God be ours;
　prosper the work of our hands for us!
　Prosper the work of our hands! ℟

SECOND READING *(Hebrews 4:12–13)*

Brothers and sisters: Indeed the word of God is living and effective, sharper than any two-edged sword, penetrating even between soul and spirit, joints and marrow, and able to discern reflections and thoughts of the heart. No creature is concealed from him, but everything is naked and exposed to the eyes of him to whom we must render an account.

The word of the Lord. *Thanks be to God.*

ALLELUIA *(Matthew 5:3)*

Alleluia, alleluia. Blessed are the poor in spirit, for theirs is the kingdom of heaven. *Alleluia, alleluia.*

GOSPEL *(Mark 10:17–30)*
The shorter version ends at the asterisks.

A reading from the holy Gospel according to Mark.
Glory to you, O Lord.

As Jesus was setting out on a journey, a man ran up, knelt down before him, and asked him, "Good teacher, what must I do to inherit eternal life?" Jesus answered him, "Why do you call me good? No one is good but God alone. You know the commandments: *You shall not kill; you shall not commit adultery; you shall not steal; you shall not bear false witness; you shall not defraud; honor your father and your mother.*" He replied and said to him, "Teacher, all of these I have observed from my youth." Jesus, looking at him, loved him and said to him, "You are lacking in one thing. Go, sell what you have, and give to the poor and you will have treasure in heaven; then come, follow me." At that statement his face fell, and he went away sad, for he had many possessions.

Jesus looked around and said to his disciples, "How hard it is for those who have wealth to enter the kingdom of God!" The disciples were amazed at his words. So Jesus again said to them in reply, "Children, how hard it is to enter the kingdom of God! It is easier for a camel to pass through the eye of a needle than for one who is rich to enter the kingdom of God." They were exceedingly astonished and said among themselves, "Then who can be saved?" Jesus looked at them and said, "For human beings it is impossible, but not for God. All things are possible for God."

* * *

Peter began to say to him, "We have given up everything and followed you." Jesus said, "Amen, I say to you, there is no one who has given up house or brothers or sisters or mother or father or children or lands for my sake and for the sake of the gospel who will not receive a hundred times more now in this present age: houses and brothers and sisters and mothers and children and lands, with persecutions, and eternal life in the age to come."

The Gospel of the Lord. *Praise to you, Lord Jesus Christ.*

PROFESSION OF FAITH *(page 13)*

PRAYER OF THE FAITHFUL

PREPARATION OF GIFTS *(page 16)*

PRAYER OVER THE OFFERINGS
Accept, O Lord, the prayers of your faithful
with the sacrificial offerings,
that, through these acts of devotedness,
we may pass over to the glory of heaven.
Through Christ our Lord. *Amen.*

❖ TAKING A CLOSER LOOK ❖

✢ **Wisdom** For the Jews, wisdom was the practical understanding of how the world and society worked, and so it helped people cope with the complexities of everyday life, especially sickness and suffering, death and disaster. Since wisdom did not rely on divine revelation but rather on practical human experience and observation of nature, it summarized the most helpful advice for responsible living, which the Jews shared with many ancient Near Eastern peoples. The Jews, though, sought to merge this secular tradition with the religious guidelines of their covenant instruction (Torah). Thus wisdom joined the pursuit of knowledge to the ordering of life in relation to God.

PREFACE *(Sundays in Ordinary Time, pages 28–32)*

COMMUNION ANTIPHON *(Cf. Psalm 34 [33]:11)*
The rich suffer want and go hungry, but those who seek the Lord lack no blessing.

Or *(1 John 3:2)*
When the Lord appears, we shall be like him, for we shall see him as he is.

PRAYER AFTER COMMUNION
We entreat your majesty most humbly, O Lord,
that, as you feed us with the nourishment
which comes from the most holy Body and Blood of your Son,
so you may make us sharers of his divine nature.
Who lives and reigns for ever and ever. *Amen.*

BLESSING & DISMISSAL *(page 56)* ✣

• RESPONDING TO THE WORD •

True wisdom can be more valuable to us than many material things.	God's word can penetrate deep into our inner self and reveal things we might not want to see.	Jesus challenges the rich man to give up his riches and follow.
➡ *What wisdom have I found most valuable for my daily guidance?*	➡ *When has God's word in Scripture revealed surprising depths about myself and about God?*	➡ *What riches of mine is Jesus asking me to give up in order to follow him more closely today?*

October 21

OCT
21

God knows exactly what we need

"The Son of Man did not come to be served but to serve and to give his life as a ransom for many." We can often identify with both James and John from this gospel passage when we directly ask God for what we want. Or perhaps we do it indirectly? We attend Mass regularly, act more obediently, and secretly hope God is noticing and will make our requests come to fruition.

I think of how often I have treated Jesus like that one friend whom people call only when they need something. Imagine if your phone rang only when people needed something from you. It would become pretty tiresome. However, Jesus does not scold his disciples or us for these requests.

Jesus makes reference to his ultimate sacrifice. He tries to tell them that he has come to die on the cross, to pay for the sins of the world, so that we may have a loving relationship with God.

God hears all of our requests. God knows exactly what we need and when we need it. I, myself, have made some pretty steep requests, and while God does not answer when I want, God answers when I need it. God gives me so much more than what I asked for: God gave the ultimate sacrifice of Jesus.

■ JACKI LAVIGNE

ENTRANCE ANTIPHON *(Cf. Psalm 17 [16]:6, 8)*

To you I call; for you will surely heed me, O God; turn your ear to me; hear my words. Guard me as the apple of your eye; in the shadow of your wings protect me.

INTRODUCTORY RITES *(page 10)*

COLLECT

Almighty ever-living God,
grant that we may always conform our will to yours
and serve your majesty in sincerity of heart.
Through our Lord Jesus Christ, your Son,
who lives and reigns with you in the unity of the Holy Spirit,
one God, for ever and ever. *Amen.*

FIRST READING *(Isaiah 53:10-11)*

The LORD was pleased
to crush him in infirmity.

If he gives his life as an offering for sin,
he shall see his descendants in a long life,
and the will of the LORD shall be accomplished through him.

Because of his affliction
he shall see the light in fullness of days;
through his suffering, my servant shall justify many,
and their guilt he shall bear.
The word of the Lord. *Thanks be to God.*

RESPONSORIAL PSALM *(Psalm 33:4-5, 18-19, 20, 22)*

℟ **Lord, let your mercy be on us, as we place our trust in you.**

Upright is the word of the LORD,
and all his works are trustworthy.

He loves justice and right;
  of the kindness of the LORD the earth is full. ℟
See, the eyes of the LORD are upon those who fear him,
  upon those who hope for his kindness,
To deliver them from death
  and preserve them in spite of famine. ℟
Our soul waits for the LORD,
  who is our help and our shield.
May your kindness, O LORD, be upon us
  who have put our hope in you. ℟

SECOND READING *(Hebrews 4:14–16)*

Brothers and sisters: Since we have a great high priest who has passed through the heavens, Jesus, the Son of God, let us hold fast to our confession. For we do not have a high priest who is unable to sympathize with our weaknesses, but one who has similarly been tested in every way, yet without sin. So let us confidently approach the **throne of grace**✝ to receive mercy and to find grace for timely help.

The word of the Lord. *Thanks be to God.*

ALLELUIA *(Mark 10:45)*
Alleluia, alleluia. The Son of Man came to serve and to give his life as a ransom for many. *Alleluia, alleluia.*

GOSPEL *(Mark 10:35–45)*
The shorter version begins at the asterisks.

A reading from the holy Gospel according to Mark.
Glory to you, O Lord.

James and John, the sons of Zebedee, came to Jesus and said to him, "Teacher, we want you to do for us whatever we ask of you." He replied, "What do you wish me to do for you?" They answered him, "Grant that in your glory we may sit one at your right and the other at your left." Jesus said to them, "You do not know what you are asking. Can you drink the cup that I drink or be baptized with the baptism with which I am baptized?" They said to him, "We can." Jesus said to them, "The cup that I drink, you will drink, and with the baptism with which I am baptized, you will be baptized; but to sit at my right or at my left is not mine to give but is for those for whom it has been prepared." When the ten heard this, they became indignant at James and John.

✳ ✳ ✳

Jesus summoned them [the Twelve] and said to them, "You know that those who are recognized as rulers over the Gentiles lord it over them, and their great ones make their authority over them felt. But it shall not be so among you. Rather, whoever wishes to be great among you will be your servant; whoever wishes to be first among you will be the slave of all. For the Son of Man did not come to be served but to serve and to give his life as a ransom for many."

The Gospel of the Lord. ***Praise to you, Lord Jesus Christ.***

PROFESSION OF FAITH *(page 13)*

PRAYER OF THE FAITHFUL

PREPARATION OF GIFTS *(page 16)*

PRAYER OVER THE OFFERINGS

Grant us, Lord, we pray,
a sincere respect for your gifts,
that, through the purifying action of your grace,
we may be cleansed by the very mysteries we serve.
Through Christ our Lord. *Amen.*

PREFACE *(Sundays in Ordinary Time, pages 28–32)*

COMMUNION ANTIPHON *(Cf. Psalm 33 [32]:18-19)*

Behold, the eyes of the Lord are on those who fear him, who
hope in his merciful love, to rescue their souls from death, to
keep them alive in famine.

Or *(Mark 10:45)*

The Son of Man has come to give his life as a ransom for many.

• TAKING A CLOSER LOOK •

✠ **Throne of grace** The throne of grace is the chair on
which a wealthy patron or head of a household receives the petitioners seeking help. In the biblical world, everyone in one way
or another depended on the resources held by the king or these
wealthy patrons. So each morning these patrons would receive
those who sought "favors" or "gifts" (Greek, *charis*). In the reading, the author pictures God in heaven, seated on a throne like a
powerful king who is receiving petitioners. Like those who need
help, we approach God as our merciful benefactor or gift-giver
who will supply us with what we ask.

PRAYER AFTER COMMUNION

Grant, O Lord, we pray,
that, benefiting from participation in heavenly things,
we may be helped by what you give in this present age
and prepared for the gifts that are eternal.
Through Christ our Lord. *Amen.*

BLESSING & DISMISSAL *(page 56)* ✣

• RESPONDING TO THE WORD •

Through suffering, God's servant helps many others.	Jesus knows our human weaknesses.	Jesus encourages us to become great through serving others.
➲ How has my suffering made me more ready to help others who suffer?	➲ Which weakness do I want Jesus to help me with today?	➲ What hidden service can I do for someone this week?

October 28

The key to the cure

Do you know what you want? *Really want?* Sometimes we want things that we do not need, which might even be harmful to us. Or are we blind because we have not thought it through, are being impulsive, or have not dug deep enough into our heart and soul to see what we want.

Try keeping it simple—an act that requires confidence and humility. Bartimaeus follows this principle. He knows what he wants: his sight. Furthermore, he has faith that he will get his sight even before he asks for the miracle from Jesus. Jesus cures Bartimaeus and reveals the key to the cure.

How many of us cling to things that interfere with getting closer to God? Often, we wear them like a cloak—envy, gluttony, greed or avarice, lust, pride, sloth and wrath. These sins are often confused with what we need and want, and we sometimes try to justify hanging onto them. But in the end, we find that they distance us from God.

The miraculous key that Jesus identified is faith. Do we have the courage to fling off our cloak? It is that simple—faith can help us find the way when we are blinded by confusion over what is important. Faith will save us.

■ PATRICK M. DOYLE

ENTRANCE ANTIPHON *(Cf. Psalm 105 [104]:3-4)*

Let the hearts that seek the Lord rejoice; turn to the Lord and his strength; constantly seek his face.

INTRODUCTORY RITES *(page 10)*

COLLECT

Almighty ever-living God,
increase our faith, hope and charity,
and make us love what you command,
so that we may merit what you promise.
Through our Lord Jesus Christ, your Son,
who lives and reigns with you in the unity of the Holy Spirit,
one God, for ever and ever. *Amen.*

FIRST READING *(Jeremiah 31:7-9)*

Thus says the LORD:
　Shout with joy for Jacob,
　　exult at the head of the nations;
　　proclaim your praise and say:
　The LORD has delivered his people,
　　the remnant of Israel.
Behold, I will bring them back
　　from the land of the north;
I will gather them from the ends of the world,
　　with the blind and the lame in their midst,
the mothers and those with child;
　　they shall return as an immense throng.
They departed in tears,
　　but I will console them and guide them;
I will lead them to brooks of water,
　　on a level road, so that none shall stumble.

For I am a father to Israel,
  Ephraim* is my first-born.
The word of the Lord. *Thanks be to God.*

RESPONSORIAL PSALM *(Psalm 126:1-2, 2-3, 4-5, 6)*
℟ **The Lord has done great things for us; we are filled with joy.**

When the LORD brought back the captives of Zion,*
  we were like men dreaming.
Then our mouth was filled with laughter,
  and our tongue with rejoicing. ℟
Then they said among the nations,
  "The LORD has done great things for them."
The LORD has done great things for us;
  we are glad indeed. ℟
Restore our fortunes, O LORD,
  like the torrents in the southern desert.
Those that sow in tears
  shall reap rejoicing. ℟
Although they go forth weeping,
  carrying the seed to be sown,
They shall come back rejoicing,
  carrying their sheaves. ℟

SECOND READING *(Hebrews 5:1-6)*

Brothers and sisters: Every high priest is taken from among men and made their representative before God, to offer gifts and sacrifices for sins. He is able to deal patiently with the ignorant and erring, for he himself is beset by weakness and so, for this reason, must make sin offerings for himself as well as for the people. No one takes this honor upon himself but only when called by God, just as Aaron was. In the same way, it was not

Christ who glorified himself in becoming high priest, but rather the one who said to him:

You are my son:
    this day I have begotten you;
just as he says in another place:
You are a priest forever
    according to the order of Melchizedek.
The word of the Lord. ***Thanks be to God.***

ALLELUIA *(See 2 Timothy 1:10)*
Alleluia, alleluia. Our Savior Jesus Christ destroyed death and brought life to light through the Gospel. *Alleluia, alleluia.*

GOSPEL *(Mark 10:46–52)*
A reading from the holy Gospel according to Mark.
Glory to you, O Lord.

As Jesus was leaving Jericho* with his disciples and a sizable crowd, Bartimaeus,* a blind man, the son of Timaeus,* sat by the roadside begging. On hearing that it was Jesus of Nazareth, he began to cry out and say, "Jesus, **son of David**,✝ have pity on me." And many rebuked him, telling him to be silent. But he kept calling out all the more, "Son of David, have pity on me." Jesus stopped and said, "Call him." So they called the blind man, saying to him, "Take courage; get up, Jesus is calling you." He threw aside his cloak, sprang up, and came to Jesus. Jesus said to him in reply, "What do you want me to do for you?" The blind man replied to him, "Master, I want to see." Jesus told him, "Go your way; your faith has saved you." Immediately he received his sight and followed him on the way.

The Gospel of the Lord. ***Praise to you, Lord Jesus Christ.***

PROFESSION OF FAITH *(page 13)*

PRAYER OF THE FAITHFUL

PREPARATION OF GIFTS *(page 16)*

PRAYER OVER THE OFFERINGS
Look, we pray, O Lord,
on the offerings we make to your majesty,
that whatever is done by us in your service
may be directed above all to your glory.
Through Christ our Lord. *Amen.*

PREFACE *(Sundays in Ordinary Time, pages 28–32)*

● TAKING A CLOSER LOOK ●

✠ **Son of David** "Son of David" is a title indicating that the crowds recognize Jesus not only as an Israelite of the tribe of Judah (from which we get the word "Jew") but also of the royal bloodline of King David, who unified the twelve tribal peoples into a single kingdom around 1000 BC. The title reveals the crowd's hope that Jesus is indeed David's long-awaited successor, the one chosen and anointed (Hebrew, *messiah;* Greek, *christos*) by God to restore the Jewish nation into a kingdom dedicated to life with God.

COMMUNION ANTIPHON *(Cf. Psalm 20 [19]:6)*

We will ring out our joy at your saving help and exult in the name of our God.

Or *(Ephesians 5:2)*

Christ loved us and gave himself up for us, as a fragrant offering to God.

PRAYER AFTER COMMUNION

May your Sacraments, O Lord, we pray,
perfect in us what lies within them,
that what we now celebrate in signs
we may one day possess in truth.
Through Christ our Lord. *Amen.*

BLESSING & DISMISSAL *(page 56)* ✦

⸻

• RESPONDING TO THE WORD •

God promises to gather the people and end their suffering.	**Jesus is our representative before God.**	**Jesus helps a blind man to see.**
➡ *What signs of God's activity do I detect in the Church today?*	➡ *What problem or need do I want Jesus to take before God today?*	➡ *For what do I need Jesus' help to "see" more clearly about my life today?*

November 1

Our models of holiness

When people are asked, "Who have been the models of holiness and the greatest examples for your life?" the first response is often the popular saints—Francis of Assisi, Thérèse of Lisieux, and so forth. The likes of such great men and women grace the Church calendar throughout the year.

But when we start to think of the people whose lives and faith have inspired and nourished us, our thoughts might then turn to less well-known "saints": parents, grandparents, neighbors, community leaders, religious, and parish priests. Many of these have been wonderful examples for us and a strong influence on our lives. Some have already gone on to live with God.

Today is their day. On this solemn feast, we rejoice in all the saints who are now living with God, yet who may not be so well-known and celebrated as to have their own feast day. Today we particularly remember the saints of our own lives. We give thanks to God, and to these saints, for the grace they have been for us. And we hope to join their company one day.

■ MSGR. STEPHEN J. ROSSETTI

ENTRANCE ANTIPHON

Let us all rejoice in the Lord, as we celebrate the feast day in
honor of all the Saints, at whose festival the Angels rejoice
and praise the Son of God.

INTRODUCTORY RITES *(page 10)*

COLLECT

Almighty ever-living God,
by whose gift we venerate in one celebration
the merits of all the Saints,
bestow on us, we pray,
through the prayers of so many intercessors,
an abundance of the reconciliation with you
for which we earnestly long.
Through our Lord Jesus Christ, your Son,
who lives and reigns with you in the unity of the Holy Spirit,
one God, for ever and ever. *Amen.*

FIRST READING *(Revelation 7:2–4, 9–14)*

I, John, saw another angel come up from the East, holding the
seal of the living God. He cried out in a loud voice to the
four angels who were given power to damage the land and the
sea, "Do not damage the land or the sea or the trees until we put
the seal on the foreheads of the servants of our God." I heard
the number of those who had been marked with the seal, **one
hundred and forty-four thousand**✝ marked from every tribe of
the children of Israel.

After this I had a vision of a great multitude, which no one
could count, from every nation, race, people, and tongue. They
stood before the throne and before the Lamb, wearing white
robes and holding palm branches in their hands. They cried out

in a loud voice:
> "Salvation comes from our God, who is seated on the throne,
> and from the Lamb."

All the angels stood around the throne and around the elders
and the four living creatures. They prostrated themselves before
the throne, worshiped God, and exclaimed:
> "Amen. Blessing and glory, wisdom and thanksgiving,
> honor, power, and might
> be to our God forever and ever. Amen."

Then one of the elders spoke up and said to me, "Who are these
wearing white robes, and where did they come from?" I said to
him, "My lord, you are the one who knows." He said to me, "These
are the ones who have survived the time of great distress; they have
washed their robes and made them white in the Blood of the Lamb."

The word of the Lord. ***Thanks be to God.***

RESPONSORIAL PSALM *(Psalm 24:1bc–2, 3–4ab, 5–6)*
℟ **Lord, this is the people that longs to see your face.**

The LORD's are the earth and its fullness;
  the world and those who dwell in it.
For he founded it upon the seas
  and established it upon the rivers. ℟

Who can ascend the mountain of the LORD?
  or who may stand in his holy place?
One whose hands are sinless, whose heart is clean,
  who desires not what is vain. ℟

He shall receive a blessing from the LORD,
  a reward from God his savior.
Such is the race that seeks him,
  that seeks the face of the God of Jacob. ℟

SECOND READING *(1 John 3:1-3)*

Beloved: See what love the Father has bestowed on us that we may be called the children of God. Yet so we are. The reason the world does not know us is that it did not know him. Beloved, we are God's children now; what we shall be has not yet been revealed. We do know that when it is revealed we shall be like him, for we shall see him as he is. Everyone who has this hope based on him makes himself pure, as he is pure.

The word of the Lord. ***Thanks be to God.***

ALLELUIA *(Matthew 11:28)*

Alleluia, alleluia. Come to me, all you who labor and are burdened, and I will give you rest, says the Lord. *Alleluia, alleluia.*

GOSPEL *(Matthew 5:1-12a)*

A reading from the holy Gospel according to Matthew.
Glory to you, O Lord.

When Jesus saw the crowds, he went up the mountain, and after he had sat down, his disciples came to him. He began to teach them, saying:
"Blessed are the poor in spirit,
for theirs is the Kingdom of heaven.
Blessed are they who mourn,
for they will be comforted.
Blessed are the meek,
for they will inherit the land.
Blessed are they who hunger and thirst for righteousness,
for they will be satisfied.
Blessed are the merciful,
for they will be shown mercy.

Blessed are the clean of heart,
    for they will see God.
Blessed are the peacemakers,
    for they will be called children of God.
Blessed are they who are persecuted for the sake of righteousness,
    for theirs is the Kingdom of heaven.
Blessed are you when they insult you and persecute you and
utter every kind of evil against you falsely because of me. Rejoice
and be glad, for your reward will be great in heaven."
    The Gospel of the Lord. *Praise to you, Lord Jesus Christ.*

PROFESSION OF FAITH *(page 13)*

PRAYER OF THE FAITHFUL

PREPARATION OF GIFTS *(page 16)*

PRAYER OVER THE OFFERINGS
May these offerings we bring in honor of all the Saints
be pleasing to you, O Lord,
and grant that, just as we believe the Saints
to be already assured of immortality,
so we may experience their concern for our salvation.
Through Christ our Lord. *Amen.*

PREFACE: THE GLORY OF JERUSALEM, OUR MOTHER
It is truly right and just, our duty and our salvation,
always and everywhere to give you thanks,
Lord, holy Father, almighty and eternal God.

For today by your gift we celebrate the festival of your city,
the heavenly Jerusalem, our mother,
where the great array of our brothers and sisters

already gives you eternal praise.

Towards her, we eagerly hasten as pilgrims advancing by faith,
rejoicing in the glory bestowed upon those exalted members
   of the Church
through whom you give us, in our frailty, both strength
   and good example.

And so, we glorify you with the multitude of Saints and Angels,
as with one voice of praise we acclaim:
Holy, Holy, Holy Lord God of hosts... *(page 35)*

COMMUNION ANTIPHON *(Matthew 5:8–10)*
Blessed are the clean of heart, for they shall see God. Blessed
are the peacemakers, for they shall be called children of God.
Blessed are they who are persecuted for the sake of righteousness,
for theirs is the Kingdom of Heaven.

❖ TAKING A CLOSER LOOK ❖

✟ **One hundred and forty-four thousand**

Although some Christian groups have taken this number as the actual
count of those saved, it is evident both from the general way large numbers are used in the Bible and from what follows that this is a symbolic
number. For people without sophisticated mathematics, large numbers
are almost always symbolic, the way we say "million" or "zillion" for
emphasis. In everyday life, counting to 144,000 of anything would be
a major chore. The number means that an incredibly large number of
Jews are saved. But this is not all the saved because there is an additional "great multitude" of non-Jews. This is John's way of saying that
the number of those saved is innumerable.

PRAYER AFTER COMMUNION

As we adore you, O God, who alone are holy
and wonderful in all your Saints,
we implore your grace,
so that, coming to perfect holiness in the fullness of your love,
we may pass from this pilgrim table
to the banquet of our heavenly homeland.
Through Christ our Lord. *Amen.*

SOLEMN BLESSING: ALL SAINTS *(Optional, page 63)*

DISMISSAL *(page 57)* ✢

● RESPONDING TO THE WORD ●

John has a heavenly vision of all the saints.

➡ *Which saints have been particularly helpful as examples for my Christian life?*

As God's children, we will be changed because we imitate God.

➡ *Which of God's characteristics can I try harder to imitate this week?*

Jesus' beatitudes describe the kind of behaviors that should characterize us as Christians.

➡ *Which beatitude is easiest (or hardest) for me to live by right now?*

November 4

Fall in love with God!

The Great Commandment is at the heart of today's readings. We hear it in Deuteronomy and then it is said by Jesus in Mark's gospel. This declaration of God's unity and call to love God with all our being and to love our neighbor as ourself is still central in Jewish worship today. It is called the "Shema"—Hebrew for "Hear!"—because God has a message for us that will make the difference between life and death.

The scribe who queried Jesus about the greatest commandment agrees with Jesus: to love God and our neighbor whole-heartedly is the path to life in God's kingdom. But how can we love this way? Most of us are so busy, so distracted, with so much coming at us. How do we even choose our priorities?

Many holy women and men have recommended "falling in love with God." "Nothing is more practical," said Fr. Pedro Arrupe, the late Superior General of the Jesuits. Why practical? Because when we are in love, we know our priorities—we know each day how we will devote our time and talents. And when we are in love, we find time to nourish our relationship. Fr. Pedro said, "Fall in love, stay in love, and it will decide everything." Let us sincerely seek the quiet we need to hear God's love for us, opening ourselves to love God passionately. All else will follow.

■ BETH PORTER

ENTRANCE ANTIPHON *(Cf. Psalm 38 [37]:22-23)*

Forsake me not, O Lord, my God; be not far from me! Make haste and come to my help, O Lord, my strong salvation!

INTRODUCTORY RITES *(page 10)*

COLLECT

Almighty and merciful God,
by whose gift your faithful offer you
right and praiseworthy service,
grant, we pray,
that we may hasten without stumbling
to receive the things you have promised.
Through our Lord Jesus Christ, your Son,
who lives and reigns with you in the unity of the Holy Spirit,
one God, for ever and ever. *Amen.*

FIRST READING *(Deuteronomy 6:2-6)*

Moses spoke to the people, saying: "Fear the LORD,✝ your God, and keep, throughout the days of your lives, all his statutes and commandments which I enjoin on you, and thus have long life. Hear then, Israel, and be careful to observe them, that you may grow and prosper the more, in keeping with the promise of the LORD, the God of your fathers, to give you a land flowing with milk and honey.

"Hear, O Israel! The LORD is our God, the LORD alone! Therefore, you shall love the LORD, your God, with all your heart, and with all your soul, and with all your strength. Take to heart these words which I enjoin on you today."

The word of the Lord. *Thanks be to God.*

RESPONSORIAL PSALM *(Psalm 18:2-3, 3-4, 47, 51)*

R̷ **I love you, Lord, my strength.**

I love you, O Lord, my strength,
　　O Lord, my rock, my fortress, my deliverer. R̷
My God, my rock of refuge,
　　my shield, the horn of my salvation, my stronghold!
Praised be the Lord, I exclaim,
　　and I am safe from my enemies. R̷
The Lord lives! And blessed be my rock!
　　Extolled be God my savior.
You who gave great victories to your king
　　and showed kindness to your anointed. R̷

SECOND READING *(Hebrews 7:23-28)*

Brothers and sisters: The levitical priests were many because
they were prevented by death from remaining in office, but
Jesus, because he remains forever, has a priesthood that does not
pass away. Therefore, he is always able to save those who approach God through him, since he lives forever to make intercession for them.

It was fitting that we should have such a high priest: holy,
innocent, undefiled, separated from sinners, higher than the
heavens. He has no need, as did the high priests, to offer sacrifice day after day, first for his own sins and then for those of the
people; he did that once for all when he offered himself. For the
law appoints men subject to weakness to be high priests, but the
word of the oath, which was taken after the law, appoints a son,
who has been made perfect forever.

The word of the Lord. ***Thanks be to God.***

ALLELUIA *(John 14:23)*
Alleluia, alleluia. Whoever loves me will keep my word, says
the Lord; and my Father will love him and we will come to him.
Alleluia, alleluia.

GOSPEL *(Mark 12:28b–34)*
A reading from the holy Gospel according to Luke.
Glory to you, O Lord.

One of the scribes came to Jesus and asked him, "Which is
the first of all the commandments?" Jesus replied, "The
first is this: *Hear, O Israel! The Lord our God is Lord alone! You
shall love the Lord your God with all your heart, with all your
soul, with all your mind, and with all your strength.* The second
is this: *You shall love your neighbor as yourself.* There is no other
commandment greater than these." The scribe said to him, "Well
said, teacher. You are right in saying, 'He is One and there is no
other than he.' And 'to love him with all your heart, with all your
understanding, with all your strength, and to love your neighbor
as yourself' is worth more than all burnt offerings and sacrifices."
And when Jesus saw that he answered with understanding, he
said to him, "You are not far from the kingdom of God." And no
one dared to ask him any more questions.

The Gospel of the Lord. *Praise to you, Lord Jesus Christ.*

PROFESSION OF FAITH *(page 13)*

PRAYER OF THE FAITHFUL

PREPARATION OF GIFTS *(page 16)*

PRAYER OVER THE OFFERINGS

May these sacrificial offerings, O Lord,
become for you a pure oblation,
and for us a holy outpouring of your mercy.
Through Christ our Lord. *Amen.*

PREFACE *(Sundays in Ordinary Time, pages 28–32)*

COMMUNION ANTIPHON *(Cf. Psalm 16 [15]:11)*

You will show me the path of life, the fullness of joy in your presence, O Lord.

Or *(John 6:58)*

Just as the living Father sent me and I have life because of the Father, so whoever feeds on me shall have life because of me, says the Lord.

❖ TAKING A CLOSER LOOK ❖

✛ **Fear the Lord** Fear of the Lord describes the reverent respect or awe that a person must have before God. Since God is so utterly different from anything created—awesome in power (almighty) and holiness—coming into God's presence always creates an apprehension about what might happen. Thus God often counsels the person, "Don't be afraid." Fear in God's presence thus changes to adoration. But it almost always carries an overtone of judgment because, when confronted by God's holiness, humans cannot help but recognize their distance from God (sinfulness). Fear of the Lord is also the beginning of wisdom for it is the experience of one's humble place in relation to God.

PRAYER AFTER COMMUNION

May the working of your power, O Lord,
increase in us, we pray,
so that, renewed by these heavenly Sacraments,
we may be prepared by your gift
for receiving what they promise.
Through Christ our Lord. *Amen.*

BLESSING & DISMISSAL *(page 56)* ✢

• RESPONDING TO THE WORD •

Moses encourages us to love God as completely as we can.	**Jesus is always able to save those who approach God through him.**	**Jesus summarizes our task as loving God and our neighbor.**
➡ *What can I do this week to strengthen my love for God?*	➡ *What difficulty would I like Jesus to help me with today?*	➡ *Which of these loves needs more attention in my life now?*

November 11

Make room for peace!

The gospel today cautions us: hypocrisy and inauthenticity are worse than useless. In fact, they are condemnable. Putting on a show of righteousness will fool no one, and it certainly does not do the deceiver any good.

Instead, we should cultivate authentic giving, like the poor widow who gave her last coins. Our gifts and our lives should be offered with humility and abandonment. If we grip tightly onto our last coin, we block God, grace, and the potential of being transformed for our greatest good. The tale of the poor widow is meant to spark a conversion of the heart. It calls us to great openness, to trust God as we surrender everything of value to our merciful God.

Our gospel reading underlines the necessity of each person accepting and relying on God's grace and goodness. Peace comes in every moment of conversion, of turning away from the darkness in our hearts and in the world. When we turn toward the Lord, and offer God everything, we make room for peace to break in.

■ KATE McGEE

ENTRANCE ANTIPHON *(Cf. Psalm 88 [87]:3)*

Let my prayer come into your presence. Incline your
ear to my cry for help, O Lord.

INTRODUCTORY RITES *(page 10)*

COLLECT

Almighty and merciful God,
graciously keep from us all adversity,
so that, unhindered in mind and body alike,
we may pursue in freedom of heart
the things that are yours.
Through our Lord Jesus Christ, your Son,
who lives and reigns with you in the unity of the Holy Spirit,
one God, for ever and ever. *Amen.*

FIRST READING *(1 Kings 17:10–16)*

In those days, Elijah the prophet went to Zarephath.* As
he arrived at the entrance of the city, a widow was gathering sticks there; he called out to her, "Please bring me a small
cupful of water to drink." She left to get it, and he called out
after her, "Please bring along a bit of bread." She answered,
"As the Lord, your God, lives, I have nothing baked; there is
only a handful of flour in my jar and a little oil in my jug. Just
now I was collecting a couple of sticks, to go in and prepare
something for myself and my son; when we have eaten it, we
shall die." Elijah said to her, "Do not be afraid. Go and do as
you propose. But first make me a little cake and bring it to me.
Then you can prepare something for yourself and your son. For
the Lord, the God of Israel, says, 'The jar of flour shall not go
empty, nor the jug of oil run dry, until the day when the Lord
sends rain upon the earth.'" She left and did as Elijah had said.

She was able to eat for a year, and he and her son as well; the jar of flour did not go empty, nor the jug of oil run dry, as the LORD had foretold through Elijah.

The word of the Lord. *Thanks be to God.*

RESPONSORIAL PSALM *(Psalm 146:7, 8-9, 9-10)*
℟ **Praise the Lord, my soul!** *Or* **Alleluia!**

The LORD keeps faith forever,
   secures justice for the oppressed,
   gives food to the hungry.
The LORD sets captives free. ℟
The LORD gives sight to the blind;
   the LORD raises up those who were bowed down.
The LORD loves the just;
   the LORD protects strangers. ℟
The fatherless and the widow he sustains,
   but the way of the wicked he thwarts.
The LORD shall reign forever;
   your God, O Zion,* through all generations. Alleluia. ℟

SECOND READING *(Hebrews 9:24-28)*

Christ did not enter into a sanctuary made by hands, a copy of the true one, but heaven itself, that he might now appear before God on our behalf. Not that he might offer himself repeatedly, as the high priest enters each year into the sanctuary with blood that is not his own; if that were so, he would have had to suffer repeatedly from the foundation of the world. But now once for all he has appeared at the end of the ages to take away sin by his sacrifice. Just as it is appointed that human beings die once, and after this the judgment, so also Christ, offered once to take away the sins of many, will appear a second time, not to take away sin but to bring salvation to those who eagerly await him.

The word of the Lord. ***Thanks be to God.***

ALLELUIA *(Matthew 5:3)*
Alleluia, alleluia. Blessed are the poor in spirit, for theirs is the kingdom of heaven. ***Alleluia, alleluia.***

GOSPEL *(Mark 12:38–44)*
The shorter version begins at the asterisks.

A reading from the holy Gospel according to Mark.
Glory to you, O Lord.

I n the course of his teaching Jesus said to the crowds, "Beware of the scribes, who like to go around in long robes and accept greetings in the marketplaces, seats of honor in synagogues, and places of honor at banquets. They devour the houses of widows and, as a pretext recite lengthy prayers. They will receive a very severe condemnation."

* * *

He [Jesus] sat down opposite **the treasury**✝ and observed how the crowd put money into the treasury. Many rich people put in large sums. A poor widow also came and put in two small coins worth a few cents. Calling his disciples to himself, he said to them, "Amen, I say to you, this poor widow put in more than all the other contributors to the treasury. For they have all contributed from their surplus wealth, but she, from her poverty, has contributed all she had, her whole livelihood."

The Gospel of the Lord. ***Praise to you, Lord Jesus Christ.***

PROFESSION OF FAITH *(page 13)*

PRAYER OF THE FAITHFUL

PREPARATION OF GIFTS *(page 16)*

PRAYER OVER THE OFFERINGS
Look with favor, we pray, O Lord,
upon the sacrificial gifts offered here,
that, celebrating in mystery the Passion of your Son,
we may honor it with loving devotion.
Through Christ our Lord. *Amen.*

PREFACE *(Sundays in Ordinary Time, pages 28–32)*

• Taking a Closer Look •

✦ **The treasury** In the ancient world, the temple building and its surrounding area (sanctuary) were considered God's house. So the temple often included storerooms inaccessible to the public in which were kept not only the things needed for worship but also the money gathered for its upkeep. Each year, Jews throughout the world were required to contribute one half *shekel* (equivalent to about two days' wages) for the upkeep of the temple. In the Jerusalem temple sanctuary, there were thirteen different trumpet-shaped chests into which people put their specific types of contributions such as yearly taxes or bird offerings. It is likely into one of these chests that the widow put her contribution.

COMMUNION ANTIPHON *(Cf. Psalm 23 [22]:1–2)*
The Lord is my shepherd; there is nothing I shall want. Fresh and green are the pastures where he gives me
repose, near restful waters he leads me.

Or *(Cf. Luke 24:35)*
The disciples recognized the Lord Jesus in the breaking of bread.

PRAYER AFTER COMMUNION
Nourished by this sacred gift, O Lord,
we give you thanks and beseech your mercy,
that, by the pouring forth of your Spirit,
the grace of integrity may endure
in those your heavenly power has entered.
Through Christ our Lord. *Amen.*

BLESSING & DISMISSAL *(page 56)* ✣

• RESPONDING TO THE WORD •

Small gifts sometimes reap unexpected rewards.

➡ *When has some small service of mine had unexpectedly good results?*

Christ's self-sacrifice helped others come closer to God.

➡ *What sacrifice might I make this week to help someone else discover God's healing love?*

Though the widow's gift was small, Jesus recognized that it was actually very generous.

➡ *What might I do this week to give more generously of my time, my treasure, and my talents?*

November 18

Death is followed by life

In today's gospel, Jesus reminds his disciples to learn the lesson of the fig tree, that summer will follow new leaves. He asks us to also be attentive to the end of things. As we near the close of the Church year, we practice being attentive to the ends of things: suffering, darkness, things falling apart.

Jesus promised that when we see darkness and destruction, suffering and pain, "he is near, at the gates." Ironically, in the most difficult times of our lives, many of us are more likely to feel alone and distanced from God. It is easy to see summer coming after the spring and harder to recognize the winter as the birthplace of spring. Jesus is inviting his disciples, and us, to remember that he draws near now, in the chaos of our world.

The central mystery of our faith is that death is followed by life. No matter how messy life has become, God invites us to be the people who pay attention, who wait for and expect new life.

May our hearts turn with gratitude toward God in the midst of struggle, hoping to see what gifts God will bring out of the difficulty.

■ **LEAH PERRAULT**

ENTRANCE ANTIPHON *(Jeremiah 29:11, 12, 14)*

The Lord said: I think thoughts of peace and not of affliction. You will call upon me, and I will answer you, and I will lead back your captives from every place.

INTRODUCTORY RITES *(page 10)*

COLLECT

Grant us, we pray, O Lord our God,
the constant gladness of being devoted to you,
for it is full and lasting happiness
to serve with constancy
the author of all that is good.
Through our Lord Jesus Christ, your Son,
who lives and reigns with you in the unity of the Holy Spirit,
one God, for ever and ever. *Amen.*

FIRST READING *(Daniel 12:1-3)*

In those days, I Daniel, heard this word of the LORD:
"At that time there shall arise
  Michael,✝ the great prince,
  guardian of your people;
it shall be a time unsurpassed in distress
  since nations began until that time.
At that time your people shall escape,
  everyone who is found written in the book.

"Many of those who sleep in the dust of the earth shall awake;
  some shall live forever,
  others shall be an everlasting horror and disgrace.

"But the wise shall shine brightly
   like the splendor of the firmament,
and those who lead the many to justice
   shall be like the stars forever."
The word of the Lord. *Thanks be to God.*

RESPONSORIAL PSALM *(Psalm 16:5, 8, 9-10, 11)*
R. You are my inheritance, O Lord!

O LORD, my allotted portion and my cup,
   you it is who hold fast my lot.
I set the LORD ever before me;
   with him at my right hand I shall not be disturbed. R.
Therefore my heart is glad and my soul rejoices,
   my body, too, abides in confidence;
because you will not abandon my soul to the netherworld,
   nor will you suffer your faithful one to undergo corruption. R.
You will show me the path to life,
   fullness of joys in your presence,
   the delights at your right hand forever. R.

SECOND READING *(Hebrews 10:11-14, 18)*
Brothers and sisters: Every priest stands daily at his ministry, offering frequently those same sacrifices that can never take away sins. But this one offered one sacrifice for sins, and took his seat forever at the right hand of God; now he waits until his enemies are made his footstool. For by one offering he has made perfect forever those who are being consecrated.

   Where there is forgiveness of these, there is no longer offering for sin.

The word of the Lord. *Thanks be to God.*

ALLELUIA *(Luke 21:36)*
Alleluia, alleluia. Be vigilant at all times and pray that you have the strength to stand before the Son of Man. *Alleluia, alleluia.*

GOSPEL *(Mark 13:24–32)*
A reading from the holy Gospel according to Mark.
Glory to you, O Lord.

J esus said to his disciples: "In those days after that tribulation
　　the sun will be darkened,
　　　　and the moon will not give its light,
　　and the stars will be falling from the sky,
　　　　and the powers in the heavens will be shaken.

"And then they will see 'the Son of Man coming in the clouds' with great power and glory, and then he will send out the angels and gather his elect from the four winds, from the end of the earth to the end of the sky.

"Learn a lesson from the fig tree. When its branch becomes tender and sprouts leaves, you know that summer is near. In the same way, when you see these things happening, know that he is near, at the gates. Amen, I say to you, this generation will not pass away until all these things have taken place. Heaven and earth will pass away, but my words will not pass away.

"But of that day or hour, no one knows, neither the angels in heaven, nor the Son, but only the Father."

The Gospel of the Lord. *Praise to you, Lord Jesus Christ.*

PROFESSION OF FAITH *(page 13)*

PRAYER OF THE FAITHFUL

PREPARATION OF GIFTS *(page 16)*

PRAYER OVER THE OFFERINGS
Grant, O Lord, we pray,
that what we offer in the sight of your majesty
may obtain for us the grace of being devoted to you
and gain us the prize of everlasting happiness.
Through Christ our Lord. *Amen.*

PREFACE *(Sundays in Ordinary Time, pages 28–32)*

● Taking a Closer Look ●

✢ **Michael** The ancient worldview considered heaven and earth as two separate and distinct realms (see Luke 16:26). Thus intermediaries (angels) were needed to bridge these two worlds. In the Bible there are three named angels who represent the primary roles of angels. Michael ("Who is like the Lord?") is a warrior against evil, "captain of the heavenly host" (Revelation 12:7-9), and special protector of Israel (Daniel 12:1) and of the Church. Gabriel ("God is mighty") is a messenger who announces the Messiah's coming (Daniel 9) and the births of John the Baptist and Jesus (Luke 1). Raphael ("God heals") serves as a guardian angel protecting Tobiah on his journey (Tobit 5-12).

COMMUNION ANTIPHON *(Psalm 73 [72]:28)*
To be near God is my happiness, to place my hope in God the
Lord.

Or *(Mark 11:23–24)*
Amen, I say to you: Whatever you ask in prayer, believe that you
will receive, and it shall be given to you, says the Lord.

PRAYER AFTER COMMUNION
We have partaken of the gifts of this sacred mystery,
humbly imploring, O Lord,
that what your Son commanded us to do
in memory of him
may bring us growth in charity.
Through Christ our Lord. *Amen.*

BLESSING & DISMISSAL *(page 56)* ✣

◆ RESPONDING TO THE WORD ◆

God will reward
those who "lead
many to justice."

➡ *What might I do
this week to help
bring justice to some
oppressive situation?*

Jesus' self-sacrifice
took away our sins,
that is, it put us into
the right relation-
ship with God and
others.

➡ *What in my rela-
tionships with God
and others needs my
attention most today?*

Jesus prepares us
for meeting God
and the judgment
that will happen.

➡ *What might I be
most worried about
if I faced God's judg-
ment today? Why?*

November 25

Which king will you choose?

In today's gospel, the kingdom of heaven and the kingdom of earth clash. Although Pilate is not a king, he is the representative of the most powerful ruler in the world: Caesar. It is the day that the "king of earth" finally meets Christ the King face to face. We must all decide for ourselves to which of these kings we will pledge our allegiance.

What does the king of earth promise us? Just think of everything with which Satan tempted Jesus in the desert. Power, fame, worldly glory, material riches, pleasure, and so on. We are tempted by these temporary gratifications all the time. Meanwhile, Christ the King makes it clear that following him will be difficult. His subjects are certain to face trials and persecutions and suffer for their loyalty to him.

Yet which king will lead us to joy? The short-term gratifications of the king of earth are illusions. They do not lead to lasting joy or peace, but rather to loneliness, emptiness, and misery. We are the children of God, made in God's image. Only in God will the deepest longings of our soul be satisfied. Only in God will we find rest. The whole Bible boils down to a choice: to which king will you pledge allegiance? Give your life to Christ the King, who lives and reigns now and forever.

■ CONNOR BROWNRIGG

ENTRANCE ANTIPHON *(Revelation 5:12; 1:6)*

How worthy is the Lamb who was slain, to receive
power and divinity, and wisdom and strength and
honor. To him belong glory and power for ever
and ever.

INTRODUCTORY RITES *(page 10)*

COLLECT

Almighty ever-living God,
whose will is to restore all things
in your beloved Son, the King of the universe,
grant, we pray,
that the whole creation, set free from slavery,
may render your majesty service
and ceaselessly proclaim your praise.
Through our Lord Jesus Christ, your Son,
who lives and reigns with you in the unity of the Holy Spirit,
one God, for ever and ever. *Amen.*

FIRST READING *(Daniel 7:13–14)*

A s the visions during the night continued, I saw
one like a Son of man coming,
   on the clouds of heaven;
when he reached the Ancient One
   and was presented before him,
the one like a Son of man received dominion, glory, and kingship;
   all peoples, nations, and languages serve him.
His dominion is an everlasting dominion
   that shall not be taken away,
   his kingship shall not be destroyed.
   The word of the Lord. *Thanks be to God.*

RESPONSORIAL PSALM *(Psalm 93:1, 1-2, 5)*
℞ The Lord is king; he is robed in majesty.

The LORD is king, in splendor robed;
  robed is the LORD and girt about with strength. ℞
And he has made the world firm,
  not to be moved.
Your throne stands firm from of old;
  from everlasting you are, O LORD. ℞
Your decrees are worthy of trust indeed;
  holiness befits your house,
  O LORD, for length of days. ℞

SECOND READING *(Revelation 1:5-8)*
Jesus Christ is the faithful witness, the firstborn of the dead and ruler of the kings of the earth. To him who loves us and has freed us from our sins by his blood, who has made us into a kingdom, priests for his God and Father, to him be glory and power forever and ever. Amen.

  Behold, he is coming amid the clouds,
    and every eye will see him,
    even those who pierced him.
  All the peoples of the earth will lament him.
    Yes. Amen.

"I am **the Alpha and the Omega**,"✠ says the Lord God, "the one who is and who was and who is to come, the almighty."
  The word of the Lord. *Thanks be to God.*

ALLELUIA *(Mark 11:9, 10)*
Alleluia, alleluia. Blessed is he who comes in the name of the Lord! Blessed is the kingdom of our father David that is to come! *Alleluia, alleluia.*

GOSPEL *(John 18:33b–37)*

A reading from the holy Gospel according to John.
Glory to you, O Lord.

Pilate said to Jesus, "Are you the King of the Jews?" Jesus answered, "Do you say this on your own or have others told you about me?" Pilate answered, "I am not a Jew, am I? Your own nation and the chief priests handed you over to me. What have you done?" Jesus answered, "My kingdom does not belong to this world. If my kingdom did belong to this world, my attendants would be fighting to keep me from being handed over to the Jews. But as it is, my kingdom is not here." So Pilate said to him, "Then you are a king?" Jesus answered, "You say I am a king. For this I was born and for this I came into the world, to testify to the truth. Everyone who belongs to the truth listens to my voice."

The Gospel of the Lord. *Praise to you, Lord Jesus Christ.*

PROFESSION OF FAITH *(page 13)*

PRAYER OF THE FAITHFUL

PREPARATION OF GIFTS *(page 16)*

PRAYER OVER THE OFFERINGS

As we offer you, O Lord, the sacrifice
by which the human race is reconciled to you,
we humbly pray
that your Son himself may bestow on all nations
the gifts of unity and peace.
Through Christ our Lord. *Amen.*

PREFACE: CHRIST, KING OF THE UNIVERSE

It is truly right and just, our duty and our salvation,
always and everywhere to give you thanks,
Lord, holy Father, almighty and eternal God.

For you anointed your Only Begotten Son,
our Lord Jesus Christ, with the oil of gladness
as eternal Priest and King of all creation,
so that, by offering himself on the altar of the Cross
as a spotless sacrifice to bring us peace,
he might accomplish the mysteries of human redemption
and, making all created things subject to his rule,
he might present to the immensity of your majesty
an eternal and universal kingdom,
a kingdom of truth and life,
a kingdom of holiness and grace,
a kingdom of justice, love and peace.

● TAKING A CLOSER LOOK ●

✚ **The Alpha and the Omega** Alpha (A) and omega (Ω) are
the first and last letters of the Greek alphabet, the equivalent of our
English A and Z, representing the beginning and ending ("from A to
Z"). When applied to God they indicate that God's eternal existence
spans the lesser extent of creation and human history. We decorate
the Easter candle with these letters and bless it with the words,
"Christ yesterday and today; the Beginning and the End; the Alpha;
and the Omega. All time belongs to him; and all the ages. To him be
glory and power; through every age and for ever. Amen."

And so, with Angels and Archangels,
with Thrones and Dominions,
and with all the hosts and Powers of heaven,
we sing the hymn of your glory,
as without end we acclaim:
Holy, Holy, Holy Lord God of hosts... (page 35)

COMMUNION ANTIPHON (Psalm 29 [28]:10–11)
The Lord sits as King for ever. The Lord will bless his people
with peace.

PRAYER AFTER COMMUNION
Having received the food of immortality,
we ask, O Lord,
that, glorying in obedience
to the commands of Christ, the King of the universe,
we may live with him eternally in his heavenly Kingdom.
Who lives and reigns for ever and ever. *Amen.*

BLESSING & DISMISSAL (page 56) ✛

• RESPONDING TO THE WORD •

Jesus has received rule over me and my life.	Jesus' love binds us into his kingdom community.	Jesus says that those who belong to his kingdom listen to his voice.
➡ *What do I most reluctantly give Jesus control over?*	➡ *How has being part of the kingdom made a difference in my life?*	➡ *What might I do to be more attentive to what Jesus is calling me to be and do?*

Praying and Living the Eucharist

Praying with the Scriptures

The Bible's message is that God desires to be with us in our world for a relationship. God invites us into a relationship that will not end with death but will go on forever. Building and nurturing this relationship is what living with Christ is all about.

Each week our Sunday Scripture readings help us to deepen our relationship with Jesus. Through Scripture, we learn who God is and who we are. We also discover ways to grow in our relationship with God and with others. By reading, reflecting, and discussing the meaning of these readings, we find keys to imitating Jesus' example, making his vision and values our own and discovering what a relationship with God demands.

A EUCHARISTIC FORMAT: PATTERN FOR OUR SPIRITUALITY

In our Eucharist and also in our preparation for the Eucharist, we imitate Jesus' actions at the Last Supper—*take, bless, break, share.* Jesus' command to *do this in his memory* characterizes not just our worship but our very lives and mission as Christians.

Participating in the eucharistic liturgy and living eucharistic lives is our way of thanking Jesus and of celebrating and nurturing his continual presence with us, not only in church but in all the moments and situations of our daily lives. Through our deepening experience of Christ in word and sacrament, we announce and celebrate the good news of God's presence among us.

The elements of the simple eucharistic format—*take, bless, break, share*—provide a pattern that can assist us in our goal of praying and living the Eucharist.

⟫ TAKE To "take" is to accept the reality of the moment, to open ourselves to God's presence and God's gifts as they present themselves to us. We take a few moments of quiet to become centered, prayerful, and attentive to God's presence.

⟫ BLESS To "bless" is to acknowledge God's role in something—as in the biblical acclamation, *Bless the Lord, O my soul!* When we think of God's creation, how can we not give thanks and praise? The word "eucharist" actually comes from the Greek *eucharistia* ("thanksgiving").

⟫ BREAK To "break" the bread of our lives is to be willing to break through to the deeper meaning of our experience. To do that, we explore Sacred Scripture, we think about the ways that God is speaking to us in the events of our lives, we reflect on the words of Jesus, we listen to the wisdom of the Church's teachings—we open ourselves to the voice of God as it whispers to us in our daily experiences. And we discover God's love and forgiveness in the midst of our own brokenness.

⟫ SHARE Christian spirituality is not a narrowly focused "God and me" affair. Christians discover that "I" is never alone; "I" is always an "I *in Christ*." And as one realizes his or her identity as a member of Christ's body, one discovers that the true "I" is really a "we."

We have been called into communion with God and with one another. Our own experience of Jesus leads us to ministry, to share the gifts that God has given us, and to bring the fruits of our prayer to others and to our world.

SAMPLE FORMAT FOR PERSONAL REFLECTION

» **TAKE** Find a quiet spot where you can read, reflect, and pray. If you wish to record your thoughts and experiences, have your prayer journal handy. Take a few moments of quiet to become prayerful and centered.

» **BLESS** Begin your reflection time with a prayer. You may wish to use a spontaneous prayer, the Collect for the coming Sunday, or one from the *Treasury of Prayers* (page 592).

» **BREAK**

- *Read:* Read the Scripture readings from the coming Sunday. Pause in silence to be attentive to God's message for you today.
- *Reflect:* Read the Sunday reflection found at the start of the coming Sunday.
- *Respond:* To explore the meaning of the readings, consider first the questions in the *Responding to the Word* at the end of each Sunday. If you wish to explore the readings further, choose one or more of the *Basic Questions for Exploring Scripture* (page 578).

After reflecting on the questions and writing down your answers in your prayer journal, if you wish, take some time to be quiet and attentive to Christ's presence with you—where he wants to dwell right now.

» **SHARE** Close with a spontaneous prayer, one chosen from the Mass for the coming Sunday, or one from the *Treasury of Prayers* (page 592).

Now you are better prepared to share the good news with others in the coming week!

Basic Questions for Exploring Scripture

There are several basic questions and some follow-up questions that we can use to explore any biblical reading. *(Note that not all of these questions are equally answered in every passage.)*

What does this text tell me about God? about Jesus? about the Holy Spirit?

● Does this confirm what I already know? ● Is there something new here that I had not noticed before? ● What does God want me to know or do?

What does God/Jesus/the Holy Spirit do in relation to us and our world?

● How is the divine presence and power revealed? ● Why does God come to us? ● What is required of us to do or not do?

What does this text tell me about myself?

● How am I like the person(s) in Scripture? ● How would I respond if this happened to me? ● How would I be changed if I did what the text says? ● What challenged me to live out my faith more fully? ● What surprised me the most about this passage? ● What puzzled me the most? ● What made me most comfortable? Why? ● What made me most uncomfortable? Why?

What do I learn about the community that God desires?

● What does this text tell me about how to love God? ● What does this text tell me about how to love others? ● What guidelines for better community living does the passage offer?

The Practice of Lectio Divina

Lectio divina ("sacred reading") is a contemplative way of reading Sacred Scripture that has been part of the Christian tradition since the third century.

We may find it helpful to think of it as involving three "moments" or stages: reading, meditating, and praying.

READING

This *first moment* consists in our reading a short Scripture passage slowly, attentively, repeatedly—and aloud whenever possible. We may wish to choose the gospel reading for the coming Sunday and read it from the previous Monday all through the week.

Paying close attention to the story, and especially to the words themselves, we let ourselves *enjoy* the story and even grow to *love* the story and the very words in which it is told. When a word or phrase catches our attention, we may jot it down or simply stay with it for awhile to savor its message, allowing its fullness to penetrate our being.

MEDITATION

Reading leads us naturally to the *second moment*: meditation. Having settled on one section, phrase, or even a single word, we let its meaning unfold in our hearts.

Our meditation can take place as we sit in quiet prayer or as we perform the simple activities of our day. It may last an hour, a day, or over the course of a week.

During meditation, we may find ourselves focusing on the present: what does this text have to say about what is happening in my life or in the world around me now? Something in the text may jog a memory of an experience from our own lives. Or we may find that, when we return to our daily activities, some event or situation will unexpectedly bring us back to the text. In either case, the Holy Spirit may be trying to open up a dialogue with us!

PRAYER

Prayer, the *third moment*, also occurs naturally. This is not an intellectual exercise, but a dialogue with God. We respond authentically and spontaneously—as we would in a conversation with a close friend.

Our prayer may take four different forms:

- *Thanksgiving:* When the text reminds us of blessings and good things we have known, we praise and thank God.
- *Repentance:* When we become aware of wrong we have done or good we have failed to do, we humbly ask for forgiveness.
- *Petition:* When the text reminds us of our own needs or of the needs of others, we ask God for guidance and assistance.
- *Contemplation:* By grace, we may be led to a deeper moment of prayer in which we are no longer thanking or repenting or asking, but simply joyfully resting in God's presence, trustfully leaving ourselves in God's hands. This is called contemplative prayer.

I would like to recall and recommend the ancient tradition of ***lectio divina***: *the diligent reading of Sacred Scripture accompanied by prayer brings about that intimate dialogue in which the person reading hears God who is speaking, and in praying, responds to God with trusting openness of heart. If it is effectively promoted, this practice will bring to the Church— I am convinced of it—a new spiritual springtime."*

← POPE BENEDICT XVI

The Liturgical Calendar:
UNFOLDING THE MYSTERY OF CHRIST

One way the Church tells the story of God's saving activity is by its calendar. "Within the cycle of a year, she unfolds the whole mystery of Christ. Recalling thus the mysteries of redemption, the Church opens to the faithful the riches of her Lord's powers and mercies, so that they are in some way made present at all times, and the faithful are enabled to lay hold of them and become filled with saving grace" (Vatican II, *Constitution on the Sacred Liturgy*, #102). During this yearly cycle, we remember our story and deepen our understanding of its meaning for us.

The Church year is anchored by two segments: **Advent–Christmas–Epiphany** and **Lent–Holy Week–Easter**. **Pentecost** and the **Sundays in Ordinary Time** fill out the rest of the year. The overall pattern highlights the transitions from darkness to light to manifestation, and from promise to fulfillment to proclamation.

ADVENT, CHRISTMAS, AND EPIPHANY

Advent, the time of preparation for Christmas, begins on the fourth Sunday before Christmas. As December's darkness and short days permeate our lives, the Church proclaims that Christ comes as the light of the world. Christmas celebrates the mystery of God's incarnation—God-with-us as one of us in human flesh.

Christmas is followed by the Epiphany, celebrating the visit of the magi who traveled from afar to worship the babe in Bethlehem. They represent all the nations of the world searching for their savior. The revelation of God's light and the fulfillment of God's promise in Jesus lead to the proclamation of this good news. In the season after Epiphany, we share the news that God's love is available for every person, for all of creation!

LENT, HOLY WEEK, AND EASTER

The Church's greatest feast and most important rites were celebrated on Easter—the time of initiation, when new members would be baptized and emerge into a new life of fellowship. Today, the seasons of Lent and Easter retain this baptismal focus. Vatican II has renewed the ancient practice of initiation in its Rite of Christian Initiation for Adults (RCIA).

The forty days (excluding Sundays) of Lent recall Jesus' forty days in the wilderness prior to his public ministry. Lent is a time of inwardness, of spiritual discipline, and of growth. During Lent we seek out the shadows in our souls, inviting Christ's light to illumine them.

Lent concludes with Holy Week when we recall the last events of Jesus' life, beginning with his entry into Jerusalem (Passion or Palm Sunday). Then the most sacred Three Days (the Triduum) recall Jesus' Last Supper (Holy Thursday), his crucifixion and death (Good Friday), and his resurrection (Easter Vigil and Easter Day). Then, for fifty days, we bask in the joy of the resurrection and the promise of new life with God forever.

PENTECOST AND ORDINARY TIME

Witnesses are needed to guide others to discover the transforming presence of God. At Pentecost, the Holy Spirit descends on the disciples, uniting them as a community and giving them new tongues to proclaim the good news of God's triumph over death to the ends of the earth.

After Pentecost, we continue with Ordinary Time. It is "ordinary" not because it is common but because the Sundays are counted (they are "in order"). Each Sunday we follow Jesus and have the opportunity to move ever more deeply into sharing in his life, death, and resurrection.

As we attune ourselves to the rhythms of the Church's liturgical year, the mysteries of the Lord's life are made present, and our lives are sanctified by our participation.

Understanding the Lectionary

Since its beginning, the Church has gathered faithfully every Sunday to listen carefully to God's word. The Lectionary for Mass is the selection of the most important Bible readings for use at Mass. Through them the Church remembers and renews its relationship with God.

THE LECTIONARY'S ARRANGEMENT

The lectionary is not a chronological approach to reading the Bible, nor is it a book-by-book approach. Each week the gospel readings are closely linked to the seasons of the Church's life cycle, its liturgical calendar. In the first half of the Church year, we follow the major events of the life of Jesus, including his birth, death, resurrection, and the birth of the Church, and in the second half we study Jesus' actions and teachings.

In addition, the lectionary provides an opportunity to remember great persons in Church history on saints' days and to celebrate special events in the life of a parish, such as confirmation. Throughout the year, Scriptures have been chosen for their appropriateness for the occasions on which they are read.

THE EVOLUTION OF THE CURRENT LECTIONARY

From the time of the Council of Trent (1545-63), when the liturgy was fixed in the form that was familiar to all Catholics before Vatican II, the selection of lectionary readings consisted simply of a one-year cycle that included two Sunday readings, one from a New Testament letter or epistle and another from one of the gospels. The gospel readings were taken mostly from Matthew and Luke, with very few from Mark or John. The Old Testament was read only on Epiphany and during Holy Week.

The liturgical renewal of Vatican Council II (1962-65) directed that the "treasures of Scripture" be made more available so that the faithful would be fed on this richer fare. This momentous change reversed the previous limitation of Scripture by adding an additional reading that, for the first time in centuries, opened the riches of the Old Testament to the weekly Christian gathering (and the Acts of the Apostles during the Easter Season).

The new lectionary includes the following features:

- *Three-year Cycle of Readings:* The Sunday lectionary covers the most significant parts of the Old and New Testaments every three years. The three years, designated A, B, and C, always begin on the First Sunday of Advent. Each of the cycles focuses on one of the synoptic gospels. In Year A, Matthew is read; Year B, Mark; Year C, Luke. The Gospel of John is used during all three years on certain feast days, during Holy Week, and during the Easter season. Since the Gospel of Mark is so brief, the sixth chapter of John's gospel (on the Bread of Life) is read for five weeks of Year B.

- *Four Readings Every Sunday:* Each Sunday, four Scripture passages are assigned to be read: the first reading from the Old Testament (except during the Easter season), chosen to coincide thematically with the gospel; a responsorial psalm relating to the first reading or to the liturgical season; the second reading from the letters or other New Testament writings; and finally the gospel reading.

- *The selected readings are about:*
  - **Christ,** so as to unfold the mystery of Christ's person and teachings over the cycle of the year (see Vatican II, *Constitution on the Sacred Liturgy* [CSL], #102)
  - **Salvation history,** in order to show the place of Christ in God's plan of salvation, thus connecting God's work with Israel (Old Testament) to God's work in Christ (New Testament) (CSL, #5)
  - **"The guiding principles of the Christian life"** (CSL, #52), to help people understand the Christian message and live it more fully in their everyday lives.

This Year's Scriptures:
THE GOSPEL OF MARK

In the three-year lectionary cycle, the Sunday gospel readings for Year B are drawn primarily from Mark's gospel, which is the shortest of the four gospels and the earliest to be written. Mark invented what we call a gospel, that is, a consecutive narrative account of Jesus' ministry, death, and resurrection.

MARK'S GOSPEL LIFE OF JESUS

Mark's great achievement was to shape the many things that Jesus said and did into a gospel life of Jesus. Mark gives Jesus' life a narrative shape beginning with his baptism or empowerment for ministry, his Galilean ministry of announcing and starting God's kingdom community with his chosen followers, and finally his journey from Galilee to Jerusalem where he is crucified and rises to new life. Mark also anchors Jesus' many sayings that were remembered by the Christian community into particular events and situations in his life story.

But the key to Mark's shaping of the gospel life of Jesus is discovered in its structure. He took the life of Jesus and shaped it into a proclamation of the good news of our salvation. In order to make the life of Jesus into a gospel life, nothing is more important than the ending.

THE GOOD NEWS OF NEW LIFE

Mark's gospel ends with the resurrection of Jesus, not with his death. Had the gospel ended with his death, there would have been no "good news" to proclaim but only a rehash of the old news that everybody dies.

But Mark's gospel proclaims that death only ends the earthly life of Jesus, not his relationship with God. The resurrection demonstrates that God's creative power to give life triumphs over evil's destructive desire to deal death. The good news is that what happens to Jesus in the middle of history will also happen to his followers (including us!) who dare to follow his way of relationship to God through death to new life.

As we hear, read, reflect, and pray about Mark's gospel this year, we will also discover how he shapes his gospel to proclaim who Christ is and to meet the special needs of his community.

A SUFFERING COMMUNITY

Mark's gospel was most likely written between 65 and 70 AD. During this period, for the first time in its history, the Christian community experienced government persecution. In Rome, Nero had blamed Christians for the terrible fire in the summer of the year 64. In Palestine, the Jews were carrying out a full scale rebellion against the Roman occupying forces, and Christians feared that they would be included in any punishments since the Romans did not differentiate between Jews and Christians at this time.

This time of suffering and persecution was thus a time of challenge. Would Christians give up their faith or keep it despite persecution or the threat of death? Mark's gospel is written to help answer these questions.

A SUFFERING CHRIST

Mark stresses that to understand the kind of Christ or Messiah that Jesus is, we must grasp the significance of his suffering, which occurs not only at the end of his life but accompanies him even during his ministry. Every attempt to understand Jesus apart from his suffering ends in misunderstanding. Jesus is misunderstood by his own family, rejected by the religious leaders and the people, and even abandoned by his own disciples. Feeling abandoned even by God his Father, Jesus dies alone on the cross.

The main thrust of Mark's gospel is to identify Jesus, "the Christ, the son of God" (1:1) as the Suffering Servant described by the prophet Isaiah (52:13–53:12). Throughout the first half of the gospel, Mark confirms the conventional Jewish expectations about the Messiah. Jesus appears as a prophetic teacher and lawgiver like Moses, a miracle worker like Elijah and a kingdom builder like David (although his kingdom is spiritual rather than political).

Mark then turns all of these tidy expectations on their head. Jesus is indeed the Messiah, but he "must suffer greatly and be rejected by the elders, the chief priests, and the scribes, and be killed, and rise after three days" (8:31). The rest of the gospel shows how the suffering Messiah fulfills God's plan for salvation.

Mark presents Jesus' passion as the great reversal of the common expectation that the Messiah would be a glorious king like David who would free the Jewish people from their oppressive Roman overlords. Jesus is indeed a king, but one who is crowned with thorns, mocked and beaten, and enthroned on a cross in humiliation with a sign indicating that he is "the King of the Jews." Mark's final picture of an abandoned Jesus dying alone outside the holy city challenges all the usual expectations about Jesus as a glorious and triumphant Messiah.

FOLLOWING CHRIST'S WAY TO GOD

Mark emphasizes that a Christian disciple is one who can take up his or her cross and follow Jesus on this way of suffering. He shows that any other claim to discipleship—for example, family ties, being one of the twelve apostles, personal knowledge of Jesus, or religious tradition—will always end in failure.

Although Mark offers Jesus as the model for Christians who are suffering and feel themselves abandoned by God, Mark offers no easy comfort. Jesus will not return miraculously to save us from our suffering. The only solution is to take up one's cross as Jesus did. For only by living through the suffering and death does resurrection follow. Suffering is not the end but the door to a new existence with God, who never abandons us.

Mark's invention of this new gospel form was immediately recognized as exactly what the Christian community needed. He gave Christians a new identity by showing both who Jesus was—the Christ who had to suffer—and who they were as his disciples—people who were called to take up their own cross and follow Jesus.

They were on the way, going up to Jerusalem, and Jesus went ahead of them. They were amazed, and those who followed were afraid. Taking the Twelve aside again, he began to tell them what was going to happen to him. "Behold, we are going up to Jerusalem, and the Son of Man will be handed over to the chief priests and the scribes, and they will condemn him to death and hand him over to the Gentiles who will mock him, spit upon him, scourge him, and put him to death, but after three days he will rise."

✦ MARK 10:32-34

Liturgical and Devotional Prayer:
WHAT'S THE DIFFERENCE?

There are real differences between liturgical and devotional prayer, but they are linked; we need both, and both have the same goal: to help us grow in our life as Catholic disciples of our Lord. But just what are the major differences between these types of prayer? Here are a few central elements:

Liturgical prayer—officially, the celebration of the seven sacraments and the Liturgy of the Hours—is always primary. These celebrations are primary because these are the privileged ways we enter into Christ's paschal mystery (his life, death, and resurrection that bring life to the world) and learn to live this mystery in our own lives. While we are meant to pray these prayers in a deeply personal way, they are also always intended to link us to the whole Church at prayer. They belong to everybody, which is why the Church insists that individuals may not change them. Liturgical prayer *shapes us* into being ever more perfect members of the Body of Christ.

Devotional prayers, in the words of Vatican II's *Constitution on the Sacred Liturgy*, "should be so drawn up that they harmonize with the liturgical seasons, accord with the sacred liturgy, are in some fashion derived from it, and lead people to it, since the liturgy by its very nature far surpasses any of them" (#13). Devotions are meant to be prayed in a deeply personal way, and may or may not have a communal dimension. *We shape* these prayers to meet our personal prayer needs and encounter God in our daily lives, which in turn helps make us ready for full, conscious, and active participation in the liturgy. There are no required forms of devotional prayer—individuals are free to create or adopt and pray them as meets their needs, within the guidelines set by the Church.

What kind of guidelines? Along with the quote from the *Constitution on the Sacred Liturgy* given above, the Church advises, for example, that these devotions not be overly sentimental. They should not lead one into superstition or be based solely on legendary tales. They should not be added to the liturgy or preferred to liturgical prayer. People are free to pray them or not. They should help us relate emotionally—with the heart and not just the intellect—to the central mysteries of our faith. They should increase our yearning for liturgical prayer and help us pray the Mass deeply and reverently. And their ultimate aim should be the same as that of the liturgy: to say with St. Paul, "I live now, not I, but Christ lives in me" (Galatians 2:20).

Mass and Eucharistic Adoration provide an example of the difference between liturgical and devotional prayer. The Mass is the weekly or daily way we join ourselves to the dying and rising of the Lord. We gather through, with, and in Christ to offer thanks and praise to the Father and to be transformed by the Holy Spirit into the body and blood of Christ in our world—and to eat and drink of Christ's body and blood that we are, and are becoming.

Eucharistic Adoration (in the form of prayer before the tabernacle), on the other hand, is a wonderful way to pause in our busy lives, to step into the presence of God, and to marvel at the great mystery of love celebrated in the Eucharist, to thank God for it, and to pray about what it means to share in Christ's Body and Blood and be his disciples in the world around us.

Of the two, the Mass is always primary, because it is the action of our entering into the paschal mystery. Adoration is meant to strengthen our desire to participate in the Mass and to pray it more deeply, with our heart, mind, and soul. Because Adoration is derived from the eucharistic liturgy and meant to lead us back to the eucharistic liturgy, it has the same goal as the liturgy: to praise and thank God and to help us lead more Christ-like lives in all that we do.

Prayer is the source and origin of every upward journey toward God. Let us each, then, turn to prayer and say to our Lord God: "Lead me, O Lord, on your path, that I may walk in your truth."

🗢 St. Bonaventure

A Treasury
of Prayers

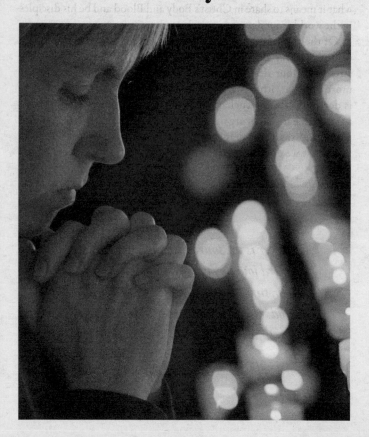

PRAYERS FROM THE BIBLE

The Lord's Prayer: found in Matthew 6:9-13 and in Luke 11:2-4, it is also used in our eucharistic liturgy (page 53)

Song of Moses: from Exodus 15 (page 299)

Paul's Prayers: from 1 Corinthians 1 (page 70), Ephesians 1 (page 371) and 1 Thessalonians 5 (page 90)

Canticle of Zechariah (Benedictus): *Luke 1:68-79*
Blessed be the Lord, the God of Israel;
  he has come to his people and set them free.
He has raised up for us a mighty savior,
  born of the house of his servant David.
Through his prophets he promised of old
  that he would save us from our enemies,
  from the hands of all who hate us.
He promised to show mercy to our fathers
  and to remember his holy covenant.
This was the oath he swore
  to our father Abraham: to set us free from the hands of our enemies,
  free to worship him without fear,
  holy and righteous in his sight all the days of our life.
You, my child, shall be called the prophet of the Most High,
  for you will go before the Lord to prepare his way,
  to give his people knowledge of salvation
  by the forgiveness of their sins.
In the tender compassion of our God
  the dawn from on high shall break upon us,

to shine on those who dwell in darkness and the shadow of death,
and to guide our feet into the way of peace.

Canticle of Mary (Magnificat): *Luke 1:46-55*

My soul proclaims the greatness of the Lord,
   my spirit rejoices in God my Savior
   for he has looked with favor upon his lowly servant.
From this day all generations will call me blessed:
   the Almighty has done great things for me,
   and holy is his Name.
He has mercy on those who fear him in every generation.
He has shown the strength of his arm,
   and has scattered the proud in their conceit.
He has cast down the mighty from their thrones,
   and has lifted up the lowly.
He has filled the hungry with good things,
   and the rich he has sent away empty.
He has come to the help of his servant Israel
   for he has remembered his promise of mercy,
   the promise he made to our fathers,
   to Abraham and his children for ever.

The Song of Simeon: *Luke 2:29-32*

Lord, now let your servant go in peace;
   your word has been fulfilled:
my own eyes have seen the salvation
   which you have prepared in the sight of every people:
a light to reveal you to the nations
   and the glory of your people Israel.

Paul's Blessing: *Ephesians 3:16-21*
May you be strengthened with power
through God's Spirit in your inner self.
May Christ dwell in your hearts through faith;
so that you, rooted and grounded in love, may have
strength to comprehend with all the holy ones
what is the breadth and length and height and depth,
and to know the love of Christ
that surpasses knowledge, so that you may be filled
with all the fullness of God.
Now to God, who by the power at work within us is able
to accomplish far more than all we ask or imagine,
be glory in the church and in Christ Jesus
to all generations, forever and ever. Amen.

TRADITIONAL PRAYERS FOR EUCHARISTIC ADORATION

The Divine Praises
Blessed be God.
Blessed be his holy name.
Blessed be Jesus Christ, true God and true man.
Blessed be the name of Jesus.
Blessed be his most Sacred Heart.
Blessed be his most Precious Blood.
Blessed be Jesus in the most holy sacrament of the altar.
Blessed be the Holy Spirit, the Paraclete.
Blessed be the great Mother of God, Mary most holy.
Blessed be her holy and immaculate conception.

Blessed be her glorious assumption.
Blessed be the name of Mary, Virgin and Mother.
Blessed be St. Joseph, her most chaste spouse.
Blessed be God in his angels and in his saints.

O Saving Host (O Salutaris Hostia) *By St. Thomas Aquinas*

O saving Victim, opening wide
The gate of Heaven to us below;
Our foes press hard on every side;
Your aid supply; Your strength bestow.
To your great name be endless praise,
Immortal Godhead, One in Three.
O grant us endless length of days,
In our true native land with thee.
Amen.

Latin Text:
O salutaris Hostia,
Quae cæli pandis ostium:
Bella premunt hostilia,
Da robur, fer auxilium.
Uni trinoque Domino
Sit sempiterna gloria,
Qui vitam sine termino
Nobis donet in patria.
Amen.

Sing My Tongue (Pange Lingua Gloriosi) *By St. Thomas Aquinas*

Sing, my tongue, the Savior's glory,
of his flesh the mystery sing;
of the blood, all price exceeding,
shed by our immortal King,
destined, for the world's redemption,
from a noble womb to spring.

Of a pure and spotless Virgin
born for us on earth below,
He, as Man, with us conversing,
stayed, the seeds of truth to sow;
then he closed in solemn order
wond'rously his Life of woe.

On the night of that Last Supper,
seated with his chosen band,
He, the Paschal Victim eating,
first fulfills the Law's command;
then as Food to his Apostles
gives himself with his own hand.

Word-made-Flesh, the bread of nature
by his Word to Flesh he turns;
wine into his Blood he changes;
what though sense no change discerns?
Only be the heart in earnest,
faith her lesson quickly learns.

Down in adoration falling,
This great Sacrament we hail,
O'er ancient forms of worship
Newer rites of grace prevail;
Faith will tell us Christ is present,
When our human senses fail.

To the Everlasting Father,
And the Son who made us free
And the Spirit, God proceeding
From them each eternally,
Be salvation, honor, blessing,
Might and endless majesty.
Amen. Alleluia.

Latin Text:
Pange, lingua, gloriosi
Corporis mysterium,
Sanguinisque pretiosi,
quem in mundi pretium
fructus ventris generosi
Rex effudit Gentium.

Nobis datus, nobis natus
ex intacta Virgine,
et in mundo conversatus,
sparso verbi semine,
sui moras incolatus
miro clausit ordine.

In supremae nocte coenae
recumbens cum fratribus
observata lege plene
cibis in legalibus,
cibum turbae duodenae
se dat suis manibus.

Verbum caro, panem verum
verbo carnem efficit:
fitque sanguis Christi merum,
et si sensus deficit,
ad firmandum cor sincerum
sola fides sufficit.

Tantum ergo Sacramentum
veneremur cernui:
et antiquum documentum
novo cedat ritui:
praestet fides supplementum
sensuum defectui.

Genitori, Genitoque
laus et jubilatio,
salus, honor, virtus quoque
sit et benedictio:
Procedenti ab utroque
compar sit laudatio.
Amen. Alleluja.

PRAYERS FROM THE CHRISTIAN TRADITION

Glory be to the Father

Glory be to the Father,
    and to the Son,
    and to the Holy Spirit.
As it was in the beginning, is now,
    and ever shall be, world without end. Amen.

Hail, Holy Queen (Salve Regina)

Hail, holy Queen, mother of mercy,
our life, our sweetness and our hope.
To you do we cry, poor banished children of Eve;
to you do we send up our sighs,
mourning and weeping in this valley of tears.
Turn then, most gracious advocate,
your eyes of mercy toward us,
and after this, our exile, show unto us
the blessed fruit of your womb, Jesus.
O clement, O loving, O sweet Virgin Mary.

The Hail Mary

Hail Mary, full of grace, the Lord is with thee.
Blessed art thou among women
and blessed is the fruit of thy womb, Jesus.
Holy Mary, Mother of God, pray for us sinners,
now and at the hour of our death. Amen.

The Memorare

Remember, most gracious Virgin Mary,
that never was it known that anyone
who fled to your protection, implored your help,
and sought your intercession, was left unaided.
Inspired with this confidence, I fly to you,
O Virgin of virgins, my mother.
To you do I come; before you I stand,
sinful and sorrowful.
Mother of the Word Incarnate,
despise not my petitions
but in your mercy hear and answer me. Amen.

Anima Christi

Soul of Christ, be my sanctification;
Body of Christ, be my salvation;
Blood of Christ, fill all my veins;
Water of Christ's side, wash out my stains;
Passion of Christ, my comfort be;
O good Jesu, listen to me;
In Thy wounds I fain would hide;
Ne'er to be parted from Thy side;
Guard me, should the foe assail me;
Call me when my life shall fail me;
Bid me come to Thee above,
With Thy saints to sing Thy love,
World without end. Amen.
(Translation by Bl. John Henry Cardinal Newman)

Act of Contrition

My God, I am sorry for my sins with all my heart.
In choosing to do wrong and failing to do good,
I have sinned against you
whom I should love above all things.
I firmly intend, with your help,
to do penance,
to sin no more,
and to avoid whatever leads me to sin.
Our Savior Jesus Christ suffered and died for us.
In his name, my God, have mercy. Amen.

Regina Caeli (Queen of Heaven)

O Queen of heaven, rejoice, alleluia!
    For he whom you chose to bear, alleluia!
Is risen as he said, alleluia!
    Pray for us to God, alleluia!
Rejoice and be glad, O Virgin Mary, alleluia!
    For the Lord is truly risen, alleluia!

O God, by the resurrection of your Son, our Lord,
You were pleased to make glad the whole world;
grant, we beseech you, that through
the intercession of the Virgin Mary, his mother,
we may attain the joys of everlasting life,
through the same Christ our Lord. Amen.

The Angelus

The angel of the Lord declared unto Mary,
    and she conceived of the Holy Spirit. *Hail Mary...*
Behold, the handmaid of the Lord;
    be it done to me according to your word. *Hail Mary...*
And the word was made flesh,
    and dwelt among us. *Hail Mary...*

Pray for us, O holy Mother of God;
    that we may be made worthy of the promises of Christ.

Pour forth, we beseech you, O Lord,
your grace into our hearts
that we, to whom the incarnation of your Son
was made known by the message of an angel,
may by his passion and cross
be brought to the glory of his resurrection.
We ask this through the same Christ, our Lord. Amen.

THE ROSARY

Like the prayer beads that are used in many religious traditions, the rosary keeps our hands moving while our minds and hearts are meditating on the mysteries of Jesus' life, death, and resurrection. While using the rosary, we focus on twenty events or mysteries in the life and death of Jesus and reflect on how we share with Mary in the saving work of Christ today. Reading a related passage from the Bible helps to deepen meditation on a particular mystery. The Scripture citations given here are not exhaustive. Many other biblical texts are also be suitable for your prayerful reflection.

To pray the rosary:

- Begin the rosary at the crucifix, making the Sign of the Cross and praying the **Apostles' Creed**
- At the first large bead say the **Our Father**, then for the three beads pray the **Hail Mary** for each of the gifts of faith, hope, and love, then **Glory be to the Father.**
- For each mystery, begin with the **Our Father** (the single bead), then recite the **Hail Mary** ten times, and end with **Glory be to the Father**

The Five Joyful Mysteries
The Annunciation (Luke 1:26-38)
The Visitation (Luke 1:39-56)
The Nativity (Luke 2:1-20)
The Presentation (Luke 2:22-38)
The Finding in the Temple (Luke 2:41-52)

The Five Mysteries of Light
The Baptism in the Jordan (Matthew 3:13-17)
The Wedding at Cana (John 2:1-12)
The Proclamation of the Kingdom (Mark 1:14-15)
The Transfiguration (Luke 9:28-36)
The First Eucharist (Matthew 26:26-29)

The Five Sorrowful Mysteries
The Agony in the Garden (Matthew 26:36-56)
The Scourging at the Pillar (Matthew 27:20-26)
The Crowning with Thorns (Matthew 27:27-30)
The Carrying of the Cross (Matthew 27:31-33)
The Crucifixion (Matthew 27:34-60)

The Five Glorious Mysteries
The Resurrection (John 20:1-18)
The Ascension (Acts 1:9-11)
The Descent of the Holy Spirit (John 20:19-23)
The Assumption of Mary (John 11:26)
The Crowning of Mary (Philippians 2:1-11)

PRAYERS FROM THE SAINTS

Teach and strengthen us

Christ Jesus, we ask not that you would spare us affliction,
but that you will not abandon us in it.
When we encounter affliction,
teach us to see you in it as our sole comforter.
Let affliction strengthen our faith,
fortify our hope, and purify our love.
Grant us the grace to see how we can use
our affliction to your glory,
and to desire no other comforter but you,
our Savior, Strengthener, and Friend. Amen.

• ST. BERNADETTE SOUBIROUS (1884-1879)

Lord, make me an instrument of your peace

Lord, make me an instrument of your peace.
Where there is hatred, let me sow love;
where there is injury, pardon;
where there is doubt, faith;
where there is despair, hope;
where there is darkness, light;
and where there is sadness, joy.
Divine Master, grant that I may not so much seek
to be consoled as to console,
to be understood as to understand,
to be loved as to love.
For it is in giving that we receive,
in pardoning that we are pardoned,
and in dying that we are born to eternal life. Amen.

• INSPIRED BY ST. FRANCIS OF ASSISI (1181/82-1226)

To be like Jesus

O God, make us more like Jesus.
Help us to bear difficulty, pain, disappointment, sorrow,
knowing that in your perfect working and design
you can use such bitter experiences
to shape our characters
and make us more like our Lord.
We look with hope for that day
when we shall be wholly like Christ,
because we shall see him as he is. Amen.

- ST. IGNATIUS OF ANTIOCH (D. 107)

Help me to seek you

Grant me, O Lord my God,
a mind to know you, a heart to seek you,
wisdom to find you, conduct pleasing to you,
faithful perseverance in waiting for you,
and a hope of finally embracing you. Amen.

- ST. THOMAS AQUINAS (1225-1274)

May the angel of peace watch over us

May God the Father, who made us, bless us.
May God the Son send his healing among us.
May God the Holy Spirit move within us
and give us eyes to see with, ears to hear with,
and hands that your work might be done.
May we walk and preach the word of God to all.
May the angel of peace watch over us
and lead us at last by God's grace to the kingdom. Amen.

- ST. DOMINIC (1170-1221)

May we serve others
Make us worthy, Lord,
to serve others throughout the world
who live and die in poverty and hunger.
Give them, through our hands,
this day their daily bread.
And by our understanding love,
give peace and joy. Amen.
● St. Mother Teresa of Calcutta (1920-1997)

For generous service
Lord Jesus, teach me to be generous;
teach me to serve you as you deserve,
to give and not to count the cost,
to fight and not to heed the wounds,
to toil and not to seek for rest,
to labor and not to seek reward,
except that of knowing that I do your will. Amen.
● St. Ignatius Loyola (1491-1556)

Jesus, our Lover
Jesus Christ, the love that gives love.
You are higher than the highest star;
you are deeper than the deepest sea;
you cherish us as your own family;
you embrace us as your own spouse;
you rule over us as your own subjects;
you welcome us as your dearest friends.
Let all the world worship you! Amen.
● St. Hildegard of Bingen (1098-1179)

MORNING PRAYERS

Perfect and strengthen us

Almighty God, reveal to us what we do not know;
perfect in us what is lacking;
strengthen in us what we know;
and keep us faultless in your service,
through Jesus Christ our Lord. Amen.

● POPE ST. CLEMENT I OF ROME (FIRST CENTURY)

Open and enlighten us

Jesus, open the eyes of my heart,
that I may hear your word and understand and do your will.
Open the eyes of my mind
to the understanding of your gospel teachings.
Speak to me the hidden and secret things of your wisdom.
Enlighten my mind and understanding
with the light of your knowledge,
not only to cherish those things that are written,
but to do them. Amen.

● ST. JOHN CHRYSOSTOM (347-407)

Help us to follow your will

O Lord, whose way is perfect,
help us, we pray, always to trust in your goodness;
that, walking with you in faith
and following you in all simplicity,
we may possess quiet and contented minds,
and cast all our care on you, because you care for us;
for the sake of Jesus Christ our Lord. Amen.

● CHRISTINA ROSSETTI (1830-1894)

EVENING PRAYERS

You are the One

Spirit of truth, you are the reward to the saints,
the comforter of souls, light in the darkness,
riches to the poor, treasure to lovers,
food for the hungry, comfort to the wanderer.
To sum up, you are the one in whom all treasures are contained. Amen.

● St. Mary Magdalene de'pazzi (1566-1607)

Be with me

Alone with none but you, my God,
I journey on my way.
What need I fear, when you are near,
O King of night and day?
More safe am I within your hand
than if a host did round me stand.
Be a bright flame before me, a guiding star above me,
a smooth path beneath me, a kindly shepherd behind me,
today—tonight—and forever. Amen.

● St. Columba (521-597)

Be with us

Watch, dear Lord,
with those who wake, or watch, or weep tonight,
and give your angels charge over those who sleep.
Tend your sick ones, O Lord Jesus Christ.
Rest your weary ones. Bless your dying ones.
Soothe your suffering ones. Pity your afflicted ones.
Shield your joyous ones. And all for your love's sake. Amen.

● St. Augustine of Hippo (354-430)

RECEIVING COMMUNION OUTSIDE MASS

In the celebration of the Eucharist we recognize the presence of Christ in the priest, in the word proclaimed, in the prayer and song of the assembly, and above all in the consecrated elements. Our eucharistic communion with Christ and one another is the living sign of our belonging to Jesus' kingdom community. So from its beginning, the Christian community has always made provision for those who are unable to be present to celebrate this eucharistic communion with Christ. The communion ritual outside of Mass mirrors the same four parts that give the Mass its structure: an introductory rite, a liturgy of the word, a liturgy of the Eucharist, and a concluding rite. You may wish to begin with the following prayers of preparation:

For the extraordinary minister of Holy Communion

O loving God, may your healing and nurturing presence be clearly evident in my whole being today: in my speaking and listening, in my attitude of compassion and understanding. Help me to communicate to those who are homebound the love and care of Christ and of our Christian community from whom I am sent. Let all that is in my mind, all that comes from my lips and from within my heart, reflect the greatness of your love. Amen.

For the communicant

This prayer may be said by the communicant, a family or household member, or the minister.

O loving and faithful God, you invite us to share in the eucharistic food, a sign of your commitment to be with us each day of our life's journey. Despite our personal limitations, you love us completely and nourish us with your divine life. Give us the strength we need to meet whatever challenges that we are now experiencing. Amen.

INTRODUCTORY RITE

May the blessing of God, the love of Christ,
the power of the Holy Spirit,
and the good wishes of our parish community be with you.
And with your spirit.

Use the Collect from any Sunday or from Holy Thursday (page 254).

LITURGY OF THE WORD

Jesus' words offer comfort in our time of need
and invite us to continue to be like Jesus
even in the difficult times of our lives.

Read aloud one of the Sunday Scripture readings from this missal or a reading from the suggestions below. After some time for quiet reflection, pray the Responsorial Psalm together and/or share one or two thoughts about the reading.

The following readings from this missal are also especially appropriate for a communion service.

> Holy Thursday: Mass of the Lord's Supper, page 254
> Feast of the Most Holy Body and Blood of Christ, page 398
> Jesus, the bread of life (John 6:41-51), page 467
> A spirit of wisdom (Ephesians 1:17-23), page 371
> Come to me (Isaiah 55:1-11), page 302
> The Holy Spirit is given to us (Romans 5:1-2, 5-8), page 197
> God so loved the world (John 3:14-21), page 206
> The loaves and fishes (John 6:1-15), page 455

RECEPTION OF THE EUCHARIST

The Lord's Prayer
Hearing God's word has drawn us together, and now we deepen our communion by sharing the body of Christ. To prepare ourselves for his coming, let us pray as he taught us: ***Our Father...***

Invitation to communion
This bread that we share is the body of Christ,
the sign of his endless love and the gift of himself
so that we may live with God now and forever.
Take and eat this bread with confidence that Jesus' presence in it
will nourish you, heal and strengthen you, and transform you from within.

As the bread is given, the minister says:
The Body of Christ. ***Amen.***

CONCLUDING RITE

After communion, allow time for quiet reflection to attend to Jesus' presence. You may wish to say a prayer such as the Anima Christi (page 601) or Psalm 23 (page 210).

Prayer after communion
Pray this prayer after communion or one from a Sunday:
Gracious God, you have nourished us with the bread that makes us one in Christ. Fill us with your Spirit, make us one in peace and love, and help us to bring your salvation and joy to those we meet today. We ask this through Christ our Lord. ***Amen.***

Conclude by sharing a sign of peace with one another.

Pronunciation Guide for Biblical Words

*Many biblical personal and place names are familiar to us and so offer little problem with their pronunciation. The following lists only unfamiliar names that might be difficult to pronounce. Words marked with an asterisk (*) in the readings are found in this pronunciation guide. The **bold syllable** indicates the accent for the word.*

Amaziah (am-uh-**zai**-uh)

Arimathea (ehr-uh-muh-**thee**-uh)

Baal-shalishah
   (bay-uhl-**shuh**-lai-shuh)

Babylon (**bab**-i-lon)

Barabbas (bar-**ab**-ass)

Bartimaeus (bar-ti-**may**-us)

Bethany (**beth**-a-nee)

Bethphage (beth-**fa**-gay)

Bethsaida (beth-**sigh**-da)

Caesar (**see**-sar)

Caesarea (say-sa-**ree**-a)

Caiaphas (**keye**-a-fas)

Capernaum (ka-**per**-nah-um)

Cappadocia (kappa-**doe**-sha)

Cephas (**see**-fas)

Chaldeans (kal-**dee**-ans)

cherubim (**chair**-u-bim)

Cyrenian (sigh-**reen**-ee-an)

Decapolis (day-**cap**-o-lis)

Didymus (**did**-ee-mus)

Elamites (**ee**-la-mights)

Ephah (**ef**-ah)

Ephphatha (ef-**faf**-tha)

Ephraim (**ef**-ra-eem)

Gabbatha (**gab**-ba-tha)

Gehenna (ge-**hen**-na)

Gethsemane (geth-**sem**-an-ee)

Golgotha (**gol**-gaw-tha)

Horeb (**hoe**-reb)

hyssop (**hiss**-awp)

Jairus (**jeye**-rus)

Jericho (**jer**-i-ko)

Judean (jew-**dee**-an)

Kidron (**kid**-ron)

lema sabachthani
   (**lay**-ma sa-back-**than**-ee)

Levites (**Leev**-eyets)

Malchus (**mal**-kus)

Massah (**mass**-ah)

Medes (**meeds**)

Meribah (**mer**-i-bah)

Mesopotamia
   (messo-po-**tay**-mee-ah)

Midian (**mid**-ee-uhn)

Moriah (more-**eye**-ah)

Nazorean (naz-o-**ree**-an)

Nineveh (**nin**-e-va)

Pamphylia (pam-**fill**-ee-a)

Parthians (**par**-thee-ans)

Phrygia (**frige**-ee-a)

praetorium (pray-**tor**-ee-um)

Quirinius (kwe-**rin**-ee-us)

Salome (sa-**lo**-may)

Samaria (sa-**mare**-ee-a)

Sanhedrin (san-**heed**-ren)

Seba (**see**-bah)

Sheba (**shee**-ba)

Shechem (**shek**-em)

Sidon (**sigh**-don)

Siloam (**sill**-o-ahm)

Sychar (si-**kar**)

Tarshish (**tar**-sheesh)

Timaeus (ti-**may**-us)

Tyre (**tire**)

Yahweh-yireh
   (**yah**-way-yi-reh)

Zarephath (**zar**-eh-fafth)

Zechariah (zek-uh-**rahy**-uh)

Zion (**zeye**-on)